THE SYNTAX OF DESIRE
LANGUAGE AND LOVE IN AUGUSTINE,
THE MODISTAE, DANTE

ELENA LOMBARDI

The Syntax of Desire

Language and Love in Augustine, the Modistae, Dante

UNIVERSITY OF TORONTO PRESS
Toronto Buffalo London

© University of Toronto Press Incorporated 2007
Toronto Buffalo London
Printed in Canada

ISBN 978-0-8020-9070-6

Printed on acid-free paper

Library and Archives Canada Cataloguing in Publication

Lombardi, Elena, 1969–
　　The syntax of desire : language and love in Augustine, the Modistae,
Dante / Elena Lombardi.

　　Includes bibliographical references and index.
　　ISBN 978-0-8020-9070-6 (bound)

　　1. Augustine, Saint, Bishop of Hippo – Language.　2. Dante Alighieri,
1265–1321 – Language.　3. Speculative grammar.　4. Dante Alighieri,
1265–1321. Paradiso.　5. Dante Alighieri, 1265–1321. Inferno.　6. Desire
in literature.　7. Love in literature.　I. Title.

P156.L64 2007　　　415　　　C2007-902065-8

University of Toronto Press acknowledges the financial assistance to its
publishing program of the Canada Council for the Arts and the Ontario
Arts Council.

University of Toronto Press acknowledges the financial support for its
publishing activities of the Government of Canada through the Book
Publishing Industry Development Progam (BPIDP).

For my father
'If winter comes ...'

Contents

Acknowledgments

This book was born in the wonderful cultural environment created at New York University by my graduate teachers: John Freccero, Maria Luisa Ardizzone, Barbara Spackman, and Francesco Erspamer. In different ways and disciplines they have shaped and developed my thinking. John Freccero has inspired this book with his extraordinary teaching and writing on Dante and Augustine.

At McGill, I was blessed by the friendship of Maggie Kilgour and Amilcare Iannucci, 'la cara e buona imagine paterna,' and by the brightness of my students. A very special thanks goes to John Zucchi, who trusted my work with great patience and understanding.

This book has benefited of the invaluable help of three readers: Manuele Gragnolati, Cristoph Holzhey, and Eric Ormsby. Zyg Barański has been a very precious advisor and source of inspiration over the years.

For sharing their lives with mine I thank Stefano Albertini and Julio Anguita, Giovanna Bertazzoni, Carla Bino, Annamaria Digirolamo, Francesca Cadel, Ilaria Fusina, Nicola Gardini, Mici Gragnolati, Alexander Ignatiev, Hana Levy, Giulio Tonellotto, Laura Toppan, and Maria Ludovica Vertova.

This book wouldn't have been written without the support and the love of my mother Lucia, my sister Alessandra, my partner Sergey, and our son Alessandro, and with the incorporeal but providential help of my father Erminio, my aunt Dina, and my grandmother Felicita.

THE SYNTAX OF DESIRE
LANGUAGE AND LOVE IN AUGUSTINE,
THE MODISTAE, DANTE

Introduction

In principio erat Sermo. 'Discourse,' not 'the Word,' is one of the oldest Latin translations of the complex polysemy involving the second person of the Trinity. Dangerously evocative of temporality, it was soon replaced by *Verbum.* When Erasmus, with crystalline humanistic intuition, tried to reinstate it, he encountered stern opposition.[1] Tertullian's and Lactantius's *sermo* – from *serere*, 'to weave' (words together) – represents the inaugural ghostly trace of a metaphysics of syntax, of which this book brings some chapters to the fore.

The unfolding of the eternal *Sermo/Verbum* into articulated discourse (time, Creation, creature) establishes the temporality, difference, mortality, and transience that is mirrored in human language and life – the necessity to 'sound and pass' so that another sign can be born and die, and the meaning of the sentence be captured as a whole. The principal clause is opened by the Fall, which initiates the chaotic dispersion of signs and things, and is 'terminated' by the Incarnation, the paradoxical embodiment of the Word that allows for the reconstruction of meaning. An act of intellectual lust, and one of embodied charity, they both signal the central role played by desire in the metaphysics of language. Time, history, mortal language, and body are all imbued (perfumed, coloured) with desire: it creeps into the interstices between unrelated signs, which evoke the horror of an abyss, and traces the junctures through which articulated discourse can be followed back to 'the beginning.'

When the twelfth-century grammarian Magister Guido described syntax as the web of relations that guides the wandering traveller on the good road,[2] he was playing with a commonplace medieval theme: that a journey is a meaningful *nostos*, which implies the finding of a direction midway, making the road both old and new, and defying the endlessness of both linearity and circularity. A labour of language, but mostly a labour of desire, mortal life is a pilgrimage away from and toward God.

At its simplest, syntax in language is the abstract pattern that accounts for the binding and government of the sentence, thus allowing for a full stop and a moment of silence from which the reproduction of meaning takes place. In the Middle Ages, however, no theory of language could be supported without its metaphysical counterpart. Besides the various developments of medieval 'linguistics,' it is actually difficult to locate a medieval theory of language within one discipline, since it evolves in the encounter, and often in the clash, between the lowest and the highest points of the ladder of education, between grammar and theology, between the doctrine of the Word and the science of words, which constantly illuminate and interact with each other.

At the very beginning of Christian thought, it was Augustine who first drew an analogy between two sets of 'words.' In the last book of the *De Trinitate*, he explains that the human being is endowed with two words: the word of the mouth (the 'word that sounds without' – *quod foris sonat* – utterance, speech) and the word of the heart ('the word that shines within' – *quod intus lucet* – a unified core of meaning that belongs to no language). The two words of humankind mirror the two Words of God: the Word 'in the Beginning' (a timeless core of meaning) and the Word made flesh (the utterance, the speech of God's Word in history, Christ, who becomes in turn the interior teacher of human beings, the one who signals the true meaning of signs inside them). The two sets of words are kept discrete by systems of likeness (in itself twofold, according to the Pauline *per speculum in aenigmate*) and unlikeness (the most profound and inescapable aspect of unlikeness being the eternity of the Word and the mortality of human words). These dividers between God and creature firmly mark medieval epistemology, until a vision 'face to face' is granted.

However, a partial reconciliation between the two poles is provided by syntax, as a form of collaboration between words and the Word, reality and transcendence, time and eternity. By descending on time and applying order, meaning, and beauty upon it, syntax scans and organizes time into meaningful sentences; it can be envisioned as a fabric woven from time and eternity. In human speech, only when all the words, one after the other, are uttered in time is the sentence completed and meaningful. In the life of an individual, death affords retrospective meaning to one's existence, allowing the story to be told, and in a Christian context providing a new opening toward salvation or damnation. In Christian history, the Christ event represents a full stop that allows for a rereading and an understanding of prior history.[3] 'In hac Verbi copula stupet omnis regula':[4] in the body performatively created by the Word, the rules of grammar are bewildered – both subverted and enhanced: the transience and mortality of words and things are redeemed through the syntax imparted by eternity turning into a sign.

In this book, I examine the workings of syntax in relation to those of another articulating element – desire, which, like syntax, is one of the qualifying features of the self and at the same time the means to trespass and overcome one's own boundaries and limitations. 'I desire, therefore I exist': Jacques Lacan's reformulation of the Cartesian *cogito* establishes with incontrovertible rhetoric the centrality of desire to the human experience. A part of the (biological, one is tempted to say) endowment of the person, desire is also the only truly connective force, bridging the gulf between the self and the mysterious 'other' or the unknown 'Other.' A body- and time-related factor, desire nevertheless opens vertiginous windows on the unknown.

Like syntax, desire is a movement marked by very clear boundaries: it begins with the desired thing and ends with the achieved thing. Desire progresses toward its own completion, moving from maximum desire and minimum achievement to maximum achievement and minimum desire. By marching in the direction of its satisfaction, desire scans time: the plenitude of desire marks time as a full stop and closes a meaningful sentence. Like syntax, desire, by unfolding in time, provides an active operation of knowledge. Just as in language the pattern of syntax necessarily passes through a tangible sign, the word, so too does the pattern of desire work in close cooperation with the body. Moreover, desire, just as language, has a twofold status in the Middle Ages. A prerogative of the soul, desire is nonetheless located in the body – not necessarily a sexual body, but definitely a sensual one. Just as meaning is embodied and enclosed by words and thereby marches toward its own beginning (toward itself as expressed meaning) on the vehicle of syntax, so does the embodied soul return to its own Maker by tracing and mapping out a discourse of desire.

This book examines the way in which syntax and desire shape three medieval 'grammars' – theological, linguistic, and poetic grammar. In the theories and practice of language as presented by Augustine, the

Modistae, and Dante, syntax and desire dovetail seamlessly: whenever language is observed in its aspects of unfolding, combination, and binding, an event of desire is at stake. Desire is the thread that weaves the unfolding of the Word and words, the glue that binds the single units of the sentence, the power of attraction that underlies the orderly drive toward expression in speech and universe. Nested in the very core of language – the Augustinian interior word and Modistic syntax – desire branches simultaneously toward the exterior discourse of signs and things and its metaphysical presuppositions. By journeying on the surface of language and, in the manner of syntax, bridging time (body, sign) and eternity (God, meaning), desire constructs an active operation of knowledge. The balance between language and desire is given by the fact that the absolute signified of language and the supreme object of desire coincide in God. The most extreme encounter between syntax and desire takes place in the poetic word, which is a product of desire and holds a very special position in the dialectic between words and the Word. Poetry, by factorizing language into its components of sound and meaning, and by privileging the former over the latter, binds the fallen human word with yet another syntax, the system of rhyme and rhythm, and projects it (rather than mirroring it) onto its metaphysical counterpart.

The three grammars examined in this book are located at the beginning and at the end of the complex and nonlinear history of medieval linguistic thought. Grammar, a very peculiar kind of metalanguage, a 'language about language,'[5] falls historically within the domain of three categories of scholars – philosophers, rhetoricians, and (later) grammarians – and reveals the continuous interplay between innovative and conservative eras.[6] Antiquity developed a complete philosophical and grammatical thought on language through the positions of Plato, Aristotle, and the Stoics, the adaptations of the rhetoricians (mainly in Roman context), and the description and systematization of the School of Alexandria in Greece and of Donatus and Priscian in Rome. The basis of the medieval grammatical system was, in turn, produced by Donatus and Priscian. This is the grammatical framework Augustine relied upon, and it was solidly maintained throughout the Middle Ages.

Grammar occupies a very stable place in the foundation of the medieval system of knowledge. It is the first discipline of *trivium*, the osmotic grouping of the sciences of language, which ranges from the most elementary to the most sophisticated outlook on linguistic events (letters, literature, expressions, thought) and in turn articulates language to the 'reality' of the sciences of the *quadrivium*. Throughout the whole Middle Ages grammar encompassed the study of two subjects, Latin language and literature – in Quintilian's words it is 'recte loquendi scientia et poetarum enarratio' (the science of speaking correctly and the exposition of the poets).[7] For the scholars of late antiquity and the Middle Ages, literature (< *littera*) is nothing more than the Latin translation of the Greek *grammatica* (< γράμμα).[8] The standard study of language covered, in order of difficulty, Donatus's *Ars grammatica* (divided into *Ars minor* and *Ars maior*) and Priscian's *Institutiones grammaticae* (also divided into *Priscianus maior*, Books 1–16 and *Priscianus minor*, Books 17–28), while the *auctores* consisted of a variable set of texts, comprising both classical and Christian prose and poetry writers.[9]

At first sight, then, the medieval grammatical system does not seem to diverge substantially from that of antiquity. But three variables make it profoundly new. First, the role and position of grammar are quite paradoxical. As Vivien Law perceptively observes, 'scholars in the ancient world had thought about language predominantly from the point of view of the native speaker; now, because of the language policy of the Church of Rome, they were compelled to adopt the view-point of the foreign learner.'[10] Not only does this reflect on the quality of the medieval treatises on grammar, most of which read like textbooks for language learning, but it also makes of grammar itself a 'self-estranged' discipline, as it represents the study of the 'only' language (since vernaculars were not recognized as such), which becomes over time more and more artificial – an inconsistency that Dante grappled with and tried to reconcile with mixed success. This estranged quality of medieval language emerged with quite a force at the end of the Middle Ages, with the contemporaneous blooming of the vernacular languages and of Modistic grammar, which retreated into Latin in search of a universal grammar. This is not, however, the only paradox involving Medieval Latin, which bore the uneasy weight of both secular tradition and religious universality. As Christianity progressively lost touch with Hebrew and Greek (the sacred language and the ancient language of the sacred texts respectively), Latin became the 'Ur-sprache,' the sacred language of the Middle Ages. But, as grammar testifies, Latin in the Middle Ages was also, and foremost, the language of the literature and poetry of the Roman *auctores*.[11] The cultural and linguistic revolution brought about by early Christianity – inaugurated by Augustine's famously contemptuous challenge to ancient linguistic prestige ('melius est reprehendant nos grammatici, quam non intellegant populi')[12] – therefore evolved into a tortuous, centuries-long process of rejection and assimilation of classical language and literature.

Moreover, medieval grammatical thought, since its beginning, was inextricably entwined, often controversially, with fundamental tenets of Christianity. This entanglement raises problems ranging from the connections between words and the Word, to the role of the sciences of language in biblical interpretation, to a number of thorny logico-theological problems in the later Middle Ages.

A third aspect of the medieval concept of grammar that distinguishes it from classical grammatical theories is the view that medieval language is post-lapsarian and post-Babelic: medieval scholars were engaged in an adamant yet desperate quest for a lost homology between *res* and *verba*. From Isidore's etymologies to the late medieval correspondence between the modes of being and the modes of signifying, medieval linguistics strove to reconstruct or interpret a divine and universal core of language that was lost through sin. There was, on the one hand, an unquestioning belief in the existence and possibility of a straightforward, true, and chaste 'meaning.' On the other hand, the acknowledgement of the actual obscurity in language, which constitutes both a problematic obstacle and a form of pleasure in interpretation. Framed and shaped according to the Pauline dictum for Christian life – *per speculum in aenigmate* – medieval culture, trusting and catching a glimpse of the existence of the mirror, took a guilty pleasure in the enigma.

The history of grammar in the Middle Ages is traditionally divided very roughly into two parts, basically corresponding to the standard division between the early and late Middle Ages. In the first period (seventh to eleventh century), grammar was perceived as holding a quiet instrumental position, a legacy of the systematization of Donatus and Priscian, and it was used mainly in the study of the *auctores*. In the second period (eleventh to fourteenth century), the onset of dialectic and logic forced grammar to step away from literature and establish a closer dialogue with philosophy. The late thirteenth century witnessed a strong and renewed interest in grammar, which involved not only grammarians but also philosophers and theologians. The onset of logic established grammar as a science, allowing it to interact more independently with the other disciplines and with the 'new' sciences of nature that emerged after the arrival of the 'new' Aristotle. It is also traditionally accepted that, in very general terms, early medieval grammar is mostly descriptive and related to word-forms, whereas later medieval grammar is more normative and concerned with syntax. The reality is of course much more complex, and recent studies are on the one hand bringing to light substantial (and as yet unknown or disregarded) philosophical and theoretical aspects of early grammatical thought, especially with respect to syntax and to the timeless question of the relationship between thought and speech,[13] and on the other hand elucidating the conservative traits in late medieval grammar. Nonetheless, the transition from a philology-oriented grammar to a philosophy-oriented one was remarkable, was not completely peaceful, and certainly had a strong impact on the intellectual community.

Logic's influence on grammar meant that the role of syntax in language was emphasized and instilled the notion that words cannot be considered in isolation – as it was more typical of early medieval linguistic thought, dominated by etymologies – but rather must be examined as 'happening' in context. Syntax for a medieval author is the *order* that presides over the sentence, the regular succession of words through which the sentence unfolds. It is the *combination* of words, often viewed as the rather violent relationship of *exigentia* and/or *regimen*, an association in which one term requires, attracts, and governs another by forcing it into construction. Syntax is *consignification*, the necessity for words to function and to be considered in context and the acknowledgement that many words are powerless (because meaningless) in isolation and must join, interlace, 'give and expect' – lose their oneness and self-sufficiency – in order to participate in the unfolding of meaning.

Unfolding, joining, sharing: these three events are always ambivalent for the medieval mind. On the one hand, they signal mortality, the loss of a primal unity-as-eternity, even sin; on the other hand, when mastered and performed correctly, they are the only way to undo the very sin that created them, and to reconstruct the shattered unity. They are the enigma: whether dangerous or pleasurable, it is the only viable path. Consignification, for instance, was often viewed with suspicion by medieval thinkers, who perceived it as a form of dispersion, if not corruption, of some primal connection between words and meaning. One telling example is Bernard of Chartres' explanation of the relation between words such as *albedo*, *albet*, and *albus*, as reported by John of Salisbury. The transition from the purity of substantive to the progressive and degenerative syntactical sharing of verb and adjective is compared to the deflowering of a virgin. *Albedo* can be compared to the undefiled virgin ('significat virginem incorruptam') because it signifies whiteness absolutely, without any syntactic intervention ('sine omni participatione

subiecti'). *Albet* is the same virgin, but as she is entering the bedchamber, because it allows the participation of a subject ('Albet autem eandem principaliter, et si participationem personae admittat'). Finally,
albus represents the despoiled virgin ('eandem sed corruptam') because
it allows and requires even closer syntactic participation, causing mixing
and corruption ('eandem significant qualitatem, sed infusam commixtamque substantiae, et iam quodam modo magis corruptam').[14] The
substantive, which can be considered in isolation, suggests a pure relation between words and meaning, whereas the more 'accidental' expressions – those that involve the participation of other parts of speech –
cause the corruption of the 'virginity' of meaning.[15]

Importantly, however, the almost sinful entrance into context is also a
step toward and into life and desire. Although reprehensible, the devo-
lution from the terseness of the mirror to the murkiness of the enigma
is profoundly interesting to medieval religious culture, as testified by the
medieval fascination with a text such as the Song of Songs.[16] This text is
about a moment of suspension: no longer mirror, not yet enigma, but
somehow both – a moment of infinite possibilities (and limitless interpretation), an expectation that is already fulfilment and that therefore
momentarily annihilates time and mortality in the very act of affirming
it. This moment is called desire.

'I desire, therefore It exists.' This is the medieval reformulation of the
'law of desire' – a crucial but understudied chapter in the history of
desire, one that matches and occasionally even supersedes our contemporary obsession with desire.[17] Desire is the privileged channel through
which the (mortal, corruptible, sinful) human being experiences the
absolute perfection of God. Although always tending toward the infinite, medieval desire is far from being desperate or unfulfiled. It is, indeed, a paradoxical force: not yearning and not fulfilment, but both,
excluding both the detachment of satiety and the anxiety of longing.

Desire, like language, represents a form of knowledge in the Middle
Ages, one that substantiates a theory of desire (with philosophers and
theologians) and a practice of desire (with poets and mystics). Like the
focus on language, the centrality of desire in medieval culture is theologically based. Paul's establishment of the essence of the Christian God
as Love provided the starting point for a long and nuanced narrative of
theological desire that explores the modalities of the bridge or leap that
leads the Christian self to God. As a consequence, several fields of medieval culture are pervaded by the theme of desire. Cosmology and phys-

ics, for instance, are both based on desire: the circular movement of the heavens, stars, and planets is impressed by the desire that they experience for the Empyrean, the seat of God and the blessed. On earth, movement and life result from the mutual desire that joins matter and form. The Christian concept of history, founded on an allegorical reading of the Bible (Old Testament as the promise, New Testament as its fulfilment), appears as a long stretch of desire: the chaotic spin impressed by the Fall finds order and reference in Christ, not surprisingly called *Desideratus* in the Vulgate and by many Christian writers. The Christ event allows previous history to organize itself in a meaningful way and to direct the impetus of historical desire towards the end of time. Desire is indeed the foundation of medieval spirituality: the life of the Christian is described as a 'holy desire,' the soul's eager journey in time (and as such, in corruption, mortality, decay) toward its own beginning. The mortal body is a crucial locus for spiritual desire: through prayer and privation, the Christian learns how to direct his or her desire upward. Finally, desire structures the economy of salvation and the Christian other-world: the underlying punishment of hell is a 'desire without hope' (as Dante beautifully translates the theologians' *poena damni*, 'the punishment of loss'); purgatory is defined by a state of longing; and heaven is characterized by a paradoxical form of satisfaction, an 'actualized' version of desire. At the same time, secular versions of desire interact in intricate ways with Christian desire in medieval culture, and their mutual exchange radically alters the course of the Western history and culture of desire.

While today desire is almost exclusively synonymous with lack, medieval desire is interpreted by three notions: loss, lack, and fulfilment – a geometry that establishes desire as both human and transcendental. This status is inscribed into its etymology and subsequent transformations of its meaning. In classical (Latin) antiquity, *desiderium* (< *de sideribus*, 'from the stars') refers to dead people. Its first meaning is pain and regret for something or somebody that no longer exists and is forever lost.[18] The etymology *de sideribus* implies that the origin of this regret is located in the 'other' world, in a transcendental space, as opposed to the terrestrial space of human existence. However, the remote cause of the regret 'coming from the stars' is located in the very terrestrial and bodily space that it seems to bypass: it has to do with the disappearance of a tangible sign, namely a body. In antiquity the communication between the two worlds is severed: desire indicates an irreplaceable *loss*. *Desiderium* conveys a 'passive' notion of desire, as opposed to the 'active' *studium* and *appetitus*. It collapses within itself an intellectual and a physical notion: on the one hand, it is related to the body (it is indeed a *desire for a body*); on the other hand, since that body is lost, unattainable, concealed forever, desire is forced to become a pure intellectual notion.

As historians of language readily point out, the meanings of many words were subject to change in the transfer from pagan antiquity to Christianity, and *desiderium* is definitely one such term. With Christianity, *desiderium* began mainly to mean 'lack.' The switch from 'loss' to 'lack' revolves around the notion of death. The relationship between the individual and the (dead) body – which was irrevocably severed in antiquity – became crucial to Christians: resurrection is precisely about the re-clothing of the soul with a body – a 'perfected,' more splendid version of the body for those who are saved. Death itself confirms the hope in resurrection. The full stop of history, Christ, the *Desideratus*, is the event that closes the sentence of desire-as-loss, which was opened by the Fall, and initiates the sentence of desire-as-longing. This sentence is punctuated by performative signs (the sacraments and, in particular, the body of Christ in the Eucharist) that recall the promise of resurrection. The desiring wait for Christ and, after Christ, for resurrection represents therefore the syntax of Christian history: the drive that pushes time and history toward its unfolding and completion. Resurrection represents the second and ultimate full stop, that of the fullness of meaning and of the fulfilment of desire.

In the economy of salvation the notion of desire-as-lack that pervades human time and history can be turned into a loss (by sin and the subsequent damnation) or into *fulfilment*. This notion of fulfilment is very easy to explain and very difficult to grasp: it is an 'actualized' version of desire rather than the cessation and absence of it. Fulfilment at once contains both desire and its satisfaction. Desire as fulfilment is not pacified, but rather stimulated and satisfied at the same time. The medieval notion of fulfilment is best described by the mystical experience on earth, and by the blessedness of heaven: in fulfilment desire is 'now.'[19]

Comparing the three versions of desire with respect to time, we can say that desire-as-loss secludes itself in the past (the desired object is unattainable, thus excluding the possibility of satisfaction); desire-as-lack defers its happening to the future (the desired object stands as a promise/sign of satisfaction); desire-as-fulfilment actualizes itself in the present, whereby the past (the longed for object of desire) and the future (the achieved object of desire) coalesce. Fulfilment works, somehow, as Augustine's memory of the present, which includes simultaneously past, present, and future, and thus both supports and defies temporality. Comparing the three versions of desire with respect to movement, we could say that desire-as-loss traces a linear trajectory toward its own foreclosure; desire-as-fulfilment creates a circular motion around itself; and, as a combination of the linear and the circular, desire-as-lack spirals towards its own satisfaction.

The medieval formulation of desire takes as its point of departure the ideas of the classical world, as filtered through the Latin world. In the ancients' vision, desire is an ineluctable cosmic drive and, at the same time, a potentially destructive force for the self. In particular, erotic desire was viewed as a malady – a great opportunity for chaos, which poets welcome and philosophers fight.[20] Positing divinity as Love, Christianity established desire as the very nature of human experience. Desire, however, needed to be tamed and ordained in the pursuit of an end, a task to which Augustine was devoted. In his *Commentary on the Gospel of John*, Augustine glosses the Virgilian 'trahit sua quemque voluptas' as the desire for God that Christ inspires in every human being, thereby appropriating and amending the cosmic, all-driving force of ancient desire and, at the same time, emptying it of its chaotic impact.[21] A key to the Augustinian strategy is the distinction between the 'transitive' *uti* (the love of the creature referred to the creator) and the 'intransitive' *frui* (love per se). Human life is a long journey in the dimension of use, a 'holy desire' ('desiderium sanctum'), until the creature is joined and fulfiled in the fruition of God.

Another crucial chapter in the formulation of Christian desire is Gregory the Great (sixth and seventh century), who developed the idea of 'desiderium supernum,' through which the Christian experience is turned into a truly paradoxical dialectic. Christian life is portrayed as a pilgrimage of desire, one that feeds itself through the interplay of presence and absence, belonging and alienation. Although excluded from the plenitude of desire that the angels experience (which does not signal the end of desire, but rather its peak), the pilgrim does not merely yearn for the supernal homeland; s/he attains it in the very process of desiring. Here another extraordinary trait of medieval desire emerges: neither on earth nor in heaven is there a trace of 'fastidium,' that unhappy satiety that follows attainment.

Bernard of Clairvaux (twelfth century), who devoted eighteen years of his life to commenting on the Song of Songs, the biblical *locus* of desire, brought supernal desire to yet another level, by levering on the paradox of presence and absence and substantially deepening the vocabulary of desire to include the modalities of earthly love. Moreover, Bernard articulated the astonishing notion of a 'desiring' God. Bernard and the Cistercian tradition also constitute a link to the mystical tradition, which appropriated the language and modalities of erotic desire and applied them to the elaboration of the leap that leads to God. In particular, female mystics (such as Marguerite of Oingt, Mechtild of Hackeborn, and Mechtild of Magdeburg) visibly turned the mystical experience into a truly embodied one: in the body and through the body, the desire for God is actualized in the 'now.'

The twelfth century can be described as 'the golden age of desire.' Bernard, his opponent Abelard, his correspondent Hildegard of Bingen, the mystics, Andreas Cappellanus (who challenged Ovid in writing a medieval *Ars amandi*), the Provençal troubadours, and the French poets of the so-called tradition of courtly love, all operated in a relatively small geographical area during this era. The exchanges and negotiations between secular and religious literature produced milestones of Western love poetry as well as seminal themes in the Western culture of desire such as the notions of 'frustrated love' and 'amor de lohn.'

Desire also permeates the scientific tradition of medieval Aristotelianism, especially the 'high scholastics' of the thirteenth century. Medieval cosmology and physics are in fact founded upon desire: the even, circular movement of the heavens is driven by the desire they experience for the ever-quiet Empyrean, while on earth matter and form combine because they are spurred by a linear desire. However, a potential heterodoxy emerges here, since matter – established by Aristotle and his medieval commentators as the most desiring principle (and, one should add, a feminine principle) – is for the Middle Ages an indication of chaos and endless mortality, as entailed, for instance, by the Averroistic theory of the eternity of matter.

Finally, a particularly intriguing picture of desire is presented in the early Italian love poetry of the thirteenth and fourteenth centuries. As soon as the troubadours/courtly love tradition was imported to Italy, it underwent a radical change. Beginning with the Sicilian School and culminating with the Stilonovo, love and desire (and woman) were sublimated into a midway point between the poet and knowledge and/or God. Guido Cavalcanti, in particular, shaped his theory of love and desire in connection with medieval heterodox Aristotelianism along with medical science, providing a scientific and very pessimistic understanding of desire. Dante in contrast departed from the negative theorization of his 'first friend' and re-established desire as a form of connection with God in his early work. Later, his *Divine Comedy*, the 'poem of desire,' creates an eschatology ruled by desire, while integrating the cosmological desire of science, the courtly desire for women, as well as the mystical desire for God. With Francesco Petrarca's *Canzoniere*, we witness the elaboration of a 'newly old' notion of desire, one akin to both the ancients' love malady and to the modern sense of desire as a lack of an (objectified) body.

The medieval authors of theological, mystical, and secular literature developed an extremely original vocabulary and imagery of desire, and their terminology is extensive and nuanced. A variety of terms were employed (*cupiditas, libido, appetitus, desiderium, voluntas, affectus*, just to name the more relevant), and each author reworked and bent them to his or her specific objectives. Likewise, the imagery of desire weaves a complex and rich canvas, often surprising for the contemporary scholar, as it engages typically medieval practices (pilgrimage, exile) and 'forgotten' sensualities (thirst, hunger, touch), which show that the soul's desire is located in displaced loci of the mortal and resurrection body.

This book examines three episodes in which the discourses of language and desire intersect through the notion of syntax. Chapter 1 ('Augustine: The Syntax of the Word') explores Augustine's theory of words and the Word in connection with his theory of love and desire. Although celebrated as the founder of Western semiotics, Augustine outlines a very pessimistic theory of signs in the *De magistro* and the *De doctrina christiana*. Signs (words) are mere sound when not connected to signification and are therefore not bearers of knowledge. They belong to the transitive dimension of use, and historically they follow and mark the parable of descent that separates humans from God. The limitations and inadequacy of signs call for Christ's redemption in two ways: in a presence of Christ in the individual (*De magistro*) and in the Christ event in history (*De doctrina christiana*). In Augustine's treatise on Christian doctrine, the distinction between *res* and *signa* is conflated: both things and signs are transitory and must be pursued through the notion of use (*uti*), as opposed to enjoyment (*frui*), according to the rules of an order of love, which will bring the Christian back to the Word, in which the meaning of both signs and things resides. This conflation of signs and things is fostered by the fact that, according to Augustine, things are indeed signs produced in the performative universe of God, which is explored through three 'speech acts' of God's Word: Creation (in the beginning ...), the Word made flesh (in history), and conversion (in the individual). Christ – a Word that is not a sign and a man who is only a sign (*Confessions* 10.43) – constitutes the link between the two sets of W/words as described in *De Trinitate* 15. In the likeness between speech (exterior words) and universe, God's ruling of creation impresses a syntax, directed and interpreted by love through order/binding (*ordo amoris*) and hierarchy/government (*pondus amoris*). Temporality, the negative mark of the human word as an isolated sign, is partially redeemed when it assumes the form of an orderly unfolding of words one after the other, which thereby share the beauty of the created universe and, more importantly, participate in the reproduction of meaning. Human language in its syntactic disposition is thus redeemed from its semiotic dispersion: by mirroring the syntactic order that God imparts to the universe and through Christ's direction in history and in the individual, language becomes the vehicle for the recapitulation of 'true meaning.'

The end of the first chapter involves a discussion of the syntactic quality – as combination – of the Word 'in the beginning' and of the interior word of humankind. I focus on the birth of the interior word in the context of the trinitarian analogy and on the role played in it by *caritas* (as opposed to *cupiditas*), which acts as a glue (*gluten*) and sustains the Christian in the desiring search for the lost *imago Dei* by supervising the orderly generation of interior knowledge.

Chapter 2 ('Modistae: The Syntax of Nature') explores the primacy of syntax within the linguistic theory of the Modistae, a group of grammarians operating in Paris at the end of the thirteenth century, who systematized and concluded a long stream of linguistic thought known as speculative grammar. The system of the *modi significandi*, from which the Modistae derive their name, encases language within a series of syntactic connections: through the *modi* the grammarians bypass the word in isolation and consider the interactions between words.

Grammar's crucial position as the first discipline of the *trivium* is enhanced in the late Middle Ages, when it is posited as a speculative science and enjoys lively relations with other branches of the system of knowledge, especially logic and physics. The abstract target of the science of language was the notion of universal grammar/universal language, of which individual languages are mere accidents. The Modistae's grammar is based on the homology among reality, mind, and language, which they describe as occurring on three tracks (elements, properties, faculties) and according to a twofold status (active and passive). I focus in particular on the complexity of the triad *esse: intelligere:*

significare and on the notions of permanence and becoming, distinctive of noun and verb respectively. Hylomorphism is not just a terminological device for the grammarians, but indeed the founding pattern of a syntax that is deeply rooted in reality. The focus on the minimal and fundamental relationship of construction (that between *dependens* and *terminans*) leads me to highlight two features of Modistic language: the possibility of a heterodox reading of construction (i.e., a material principle governing a formal one) and the function of desire in language (the Aristotelian drive that spurs matter and form to unite). All three steps of the sentence formation (*constructio, congruitas, perfectio*) are indeed imbued with desire: from the first articulation to the final full stop, the sentence appears as a yearning movement that aims at stillness and peace.

Chapter 3 ('Dante: The Syntax of Poetry') begins with an assessment of some key aspects of the 'problem of language' in Dante. An analysis of two pairs of 'Heavenly refutations' – *Paradiso* 2 / *Convivio* 2.13 (Grammar in the Heaven of the Moon and the theory of rarity and density) and *Paradiso* 26 / *De vulgari eloquentia* 1.4 (Adam's language) – shows that Dante, from the vantage point of the fiction *sub specie aeternitatis*, heightened the contrast between the irremediably fallen human language and the seemingly unreachable language of God. A cross-comparison of *De vulgari eloquentia* and *Convivio* on the issue of Babel suggests that poetry enters the picture as a strong binding force, a syntax made up of rhyme and rhythm, which sustains the vernacular on its path to redemption.

Turning to the *Divine Comedy*, I first plumb the depths of the poetic inscription of Dante's contradictory theory of language through a cross-comparison of two 'puzzles' of language in *Inferno* 26–7 (Ulysses and Guido da Montefeltro) and *Paradiso* 15–17 (Cacciaguida). I then trace a map of language within the poem, which unfolds between two extremes: from distortion to brightness, from physical/material act to intellectual act, and from mere sound (*Inferno*) through sign (*Purgatorio*) to pure meaning (*Paradiso*). The extremes of this map present a specular image of aphasia, the dissolution of language. The map of desire highlights its twofold function as the mover of the production of language throughout the three canticles and as a structural definition as loss in *Inferno*, lack in *Purgatorio*, and fulfilment in *Paradiso*. The last canticle – itself a production of desire through language – provides a case in point for exploring the interplay among language, desire, and the body and to describe Dante's entire text as a 'syntax of poetry.'

The three core chapters explore different areas of the medieval cultural system but are linked by some common hypotheses on the role of syntax and desire. With very different presuppositions and outcomes, they examine the idea that the microcosm of the linguistic sentence is the mirror of the universe, and that the desire inscribed in it mirrors the universe's relation to God. The three chapters hold to the idea that syntax and desire construct eternity into intelligibility through difference. Syntax traces a pattern of recapitulation; it unfolds the meaning that is hidden yet apparent 'in the beginning' and integrates the beginning into the end. Balanced on a tightrope stretched between deferment and fulfilment, desire is a movement that begins in this world and vanishes into the o/Other, and at the same time unravels the discourse/movement of the o/Other toward the self.

The epilogue of this book looks briefly at syntax and desire in contemporary linguistics, philosophy, and psychoanalysis. The possibility of a dialogue between the pre-modern and the postmodern, acknowledged in various academic fields, in this case centres on the fact that the two ends of the spectrum are articulated around one crucial hinge: the profound emphasis on the signified in the Middle Ages is the specular opposite of the contemporary emphasis on the signifier. This fact shapes accordingly several aspects of the respective epistemologies, so that the two ages at times appear as the two sides of the same anatomy.

By engaging a dialogue between the pre-modern and the postmodern, I by no means intend to claim a medieval root for contemporary reflection, nor simply to apply a contemporary interpretive framework to the Middle Ages. Syntax and desire, as important themes in these two periods, are intensely and notably resonant. While the medieval linguistic quest looked at the possibility of a universal correspondence between words and things, the contemporary quest – equally adamant and perhaps equally desperate – searches for a universal mapping of the self through language. While meaning and fulfilment are the end point of the systems of language and desire in the Middle Ages, contemporary thought is characterized by an understanding of language as an endless interplay of signifiers and by systems of desire marked by loss or, at best, by lack. The richness of the medieval model, opportunely secularized, can therefore be helpful in rethinking certain aspects of the contemporary formulation of 'meaning-at-loss' and desire-as-lack. Syntax and desire are here interpreted as systems flexible enough to address the irremediable split that characterizes both the medieval and the contemporary subject. By simultaneously asserting and defying the divides specific to each age (such as time vs. eternity or self vs. other), syntax and desire appear as means of reconciliation rather than fracture, and emerge as a mark of intelligibility for both.

The disciplines I examine in the three main chapters of the book in a medieval context – philosophy, grammar, and poetry – are still very active in the twentieth century, and have a complex relationship with one another. So striking and at times so specular is the opposition resulting from the leap between the predominance of the signified to the 'imperialism of the signifier'[22] that it is no wonder that syntax still plays a crucial role in the reflection on language.

In the twentieth century, language has been the central prism through which the achievements of various disciplines are refracted and the hinge around which science and the humanities articulate. Encased in a sanctioned split between signified and signifier, contemporary reflections on language are suspended between a sense of loss and one of empowerment and conflate a wide range of other (often perceived as oppositive) couplets: mind and the body, order and creativity, power and subversion, etc. The sense of a split, fragmented, inevitably second-ary quality to human language pervades both contemporary philosophy of language and contemporary linguistic theory. From Saussure's dichotomies to generative grammar's deep and surface structures, lan-guage is characterized by an internal split and a sense of arbitrariness. This inherent extraneity extends beyond language, marking a fracture between language and the world and sanctioning the subject's estrange-ment from itself.[23] At the same time, however, the notion of the frag-mented quality of language ultimately still points to a primal unity and plenitude that is required and supposed as a 'before' and 'beyond' lan-guage. The force of language, it seems, is located, as in the Middle Ages, in its very weakness. Arbitrariness and estrangement mean creativity. Linguistics and related philosophical reflections are thus fascinated with the power of language to create, to act, to perform – that is to violate, deny, or absolve its very limitations.

The epilogue looks in particular at two eccentric theories in which the idea of syntax is not strictly confined to grammar: Wittgenstein's log-ical form as the unrepresentable syntax of the world and Saussure's combination of syntagmatic and associative relations. I then focus on the significance of grammatical syntax in the second half of the twenti-eth century through Chomsky's theory of language – which, although claiming as its eponymous hero a Cartesian predecessor, does not hide its liaison to logic and structural linguistics. Syntax plays an important role in the formulation of language as the interface between the world and the human being – whether it is located in the world (Wittgenstein) or in the individual (Chomksy). It also appears as the inherent order that regulates the constitutive fracture and dispersion of language (as the sum of the syntagmatic and associative relations in Saussure). I then move to two critiques of syntax, one coming from a psychoanalytic and feminist perspective (Kristeva) and the other from cognitive science (Lakoff), which together bring into focus two related elements: the body – the 'erased factor' of Cartesian metaphysics – and poetry. As an extreme state of language, almost its 'disease,' poetry appears as the locus for the solution of many shortcomings of language and for the redemption of the notion of meaning.

The notion of desire is one of the keys to contemporary culture and epistemology, yet it is a truly unstable concept. Lacan's famous definition of desire as an interval, a marginal and contorted space ('en-deçà' of demand and 'au-delà' of need), testifies to the difficulties of framing desire within any linear conceptual geometry. The subtlety and refinement of the contemporary theorization of desire offers a wide spectrum of perspectives and models for desire: from the more stable notion of 'triangular desire' (Girard); to Lacan's virtuosic acrobatics on the tightrope of the signifier; Deleuze's and Guattari's 'schizophrenic' and 'revolutionary' interpretations, which highlight the connections between desire and power/politics, much like Foucault's lifelong reflection on desire and pleasure; and the rich and fruitful formulation of desire in gender theory.

In contemporary models desire appears as the mark of an (irreparably) split postmodern subject and plays a central and controversial role in the dynamic between self and other (Other, others). Desire is located both at the centre and at the margins of this dynamic, and it is perceived at certain times as a connective force and at others as disruptive. Much of twentieth-century reflection on desire is grounded in psychoanalysis, which describes the subject's birth into society (Freud) and into articulated language (Lacan) as a constriction of conflicting desires, thus endorsing the idea of desire-as-loss. Endlessly, 'electrically' travelling along the signifying chain, the Lacanian desire is a paradoxical, eccentric, and irreducible force. Subsequent developments and critiques of this psychoanalytic/structuralist vision have striven to formulate desire as a more constructive force. Nested in the vertiginous margins of the cage that entraps the subject, desire appears as a truly revolutionary element, potentially subversive of the paternal (social, linguistic) order and signalling the presence of 'other' identities. Contemporary desire is so firmly tied to language that it is, indeed, a language: in its connective, syntagmatic, metonymic, performative, discursive, and novelistic aspects, it represents the trace of submerged, unfathomable, yet articulated language/s.

Is life language? This may be the metaphor of metaphors, haunting both scientific and humanistic thought since modern advancements in molecular biology brought to light the fact that DNA indeed retains (and at the same time escapes) a language-like structure,[24] made of letters, words, and especially 'enchained' sentences. This is a discourse in which meaning seems to reside in the whole rather than in single elements. The *intimior intimo* is revealing its secret, but whether it is a Wittgensteinian limit or an Augustinian 'god' is still an answer consigned to silence.

1 Augustine: The Syntax of the Word

At the end of his *Christian Philosophy of Saint Augustine*, Étienne Gilson describes the nature of Augustine's discourse as a chain doctrine, where 'everything stands together and holds together, so much so that Augustine cannot lay hold of one link in the chain without drawing the whole chain, and the historian who tries to examine it link by link is in constant danger of putting too much strain upon it and breaking it wherever he sets a provisional limit.'[1] With this warning in mind, in the following chapter I will take hold of a particularly crucial link of that chain, 'the doctrine of the W/word,' and follow its intricate connections with the other aspects of Augustine's thought. This link has a peculiar complexity: the doctrine of the W/word is not a unified theory and is scattered throughout different works; it serves different purposes in Augustine's theological construction; and it lies both at the heart of the system (when the bishop talked about the Word) and at its margins (when the ex-rhetorician used linguistic digressions to illustrate his points). In particular, I will establish a connection between his theories of language and love, showing how these two systems serve to bridge time and eternity: rooted in the inscrutable abyss of the Trinity, on earth language and love are among the first steps of the path that leads human beings back to God. Both systems, I will argue, work as syntaxes: through binding and government, by gluing scattered pieces and unfolding them in order, they direct the Christian's path toward God. Articulating likeness and unlikeness, oneness and difference, they re-address the deformed image that still links the Maker to the creature.

Augustine's placement of God with respect to the human being is famously hyperbolic: God stands at the same time at the minimal core ('intimior intimo meo') and at the maximal vertex ('superior summo meo') of the creature (*Confessions* 3.6.11).[2] The meeting of love and language takes place at both levels: in the 'chemistry' that gives birth to the interior word in the most secret and most sacred recess of the human, its internal trinitarian structure; and in the unfolding of cosmic and historical order (where order is love) in the form of a well-constructed speech. The meeting point between the two is Christ – at the same time the utterance of the Word and the meaning of the interior word of humankind.

The fundamental role played by Augustine in the birth of the Western theory of language and signs is well established.[3] Often called 'the founder of Western semiotics,' Augustine relied heavily on classical linguistic theories. However, his synthesis of classical reflection – one that slightly privileges the Stoic system among those provided by antiquity and grafts upon it the Platonic and Christian understandings of the sign[4] – meets, according to Tzvetan Todorov, for the first time two fundamental conditions: 'the fact that, with semiotics, we are dealing with a discourse whose object is knowledge (not poetic beauty or pure speculation), and the fact that its object is constituted by signs of various types (not by words alone).'[5] At the same time, the theory of signs and the theory of language also become tightly connected, indeed almost indistinguishable, since verbal signs are always singled out according to the statement 'all words are signs / most signs are words.' Augustine thereby inaugurates the intimate fusion of semiotics and the philosophy of language that is typical of Western culture.[6]

Augustine's work exhibits a continual reflection on sign and language that spanned his entire career. The main *loci* of the development of his thought are featured in such key texts as the *De magistro*, the *De doctrina christiana*, the *Confessions*, and the *De Trinitate*. Excerpts from these works – as well as from the *De ordine, De musica, De catechizandis rudibus*, and the commentaries on Genesis and on the Gospel of John – constitute a set of circumscribed and standard references for outlining Augustine's theory of language. However, a list of all the bits and pieces of his remarks on language would be nearly endless, offering monumental proof of the paramount presence of linguistic thought in the work of Augustine, and a pervasive memento of the strength and capillarity of his training as a rhetorician.

The constant and often shady interactions between the grammarian and the theologian were noted by Marrou, who distrusted the depth and relevance of Augustine's philosophy of language, claiming that the bishop remained 'toute sa vie un grammarien.'[7] Subsequent scholarship has inverted Marrou's argument, highlighting the impact of Augustine's grammatical training upon his thought and applauding the conflicts and intricacies of the development of a philosophy of language that is one with his theology – a 'theolinguistics' as it has been called.[8] The very act of trespassing, eluding and superseding the strictures of linguistic thought, makes Augustine a crucial figure in the Western philosophy of language: an 'impure' linguist, as Sebastiano Vecchio calls him and, as such, an innovator.[9] Suspended between linguistics and theology, Augustine's doctrine of the W/word lightens the (redeemed) human sign by disenfranchising it from unlikeness through order and 'stains' the Word with a dash of semiotic impurity – a subtle vein of difference where the lever of intelligibility may rest.

Augustine's theory of language is by no means a peaceful one. The torment of his quest rises from a fundamental split. On the one hand, signs/words are for Augustine an indication of imperfection. While constituting the basis for human experience, they carry the weight of limitation and inadequacy. They are the negative mark impressed on the human world as a consequence of the Fall and do not apply to the realm of God. On the other hand, Augustine's doctrine of the Word is from the beginning dangerously contiguous to his theory of language. In his article 'Verbum in early Augustine,' D.W. Johnson convincingly argues that 'this term does not take the cosmos noetos of the Greeks as its models, but is modeled, rather, on the expression of thought, and therefore more akin to speech than to Sapientia.'[10] Johnson examines the recurrence of Verbum in Augustine's work during the period 389–97 and notices how the newly converted rhetorician at the same time employed and mistrusted a linguistic framework in building his doctrine of the Word. The danger at this early stage of the development of the doctrine of the Word was not the linguistic dimension per se, but rather the temporality implied by it (words sound and pass, while the Word is eternal). Augustine's theory of language evolved under the pressure of his theology. As early as the De magistro, Augustine retreated to the inner recess of the human being and there placed Christ as the referent for true meaning. Later on, he consolidated his theory in a fourfold structure, refining his notion of the interior (non-linguistic) human word, which provides the missing piece in the analogy between language and the Word (De Trinitate 15).

Augustine devoted much of his energy to the problem of temporality, that is, to the reconciliation of the volatility of human words with the eternity of the Word. This challenging task is accomplished through the simple yet flexible notion of syntax. Taking his lead from conventional linguistic thought of late antiquity, Augustine 'the grammarian' has quite a basic and even repetitive understanding of linguistic construction as the parallel progression of phonological, morphological, and syntactical units: letters form syllables, syllables form words that form sentences – a pattern that is also easily traced in the grammarians who are his contemporaries. Within this parallel progression, the sentence unfolds in time according to some kind of inner, 'natural' order whose rules Augustine never systematized or described. Although basic, the structure of the sentence enters into a relation with many crucial aspects of Augustine's philosophy, such as the doctrine of Creation, the theory of time and memory, and the doctrine of the Trinity. In its simplicity and adaptability the pattern of syntax forces its grammatical confinement open and is found operating from the interior to the exterior of the human being, around the axis of time, and within the itinerary that leads from mankind to God. Another feature of linguistic construction that emerges within Augustine's 'theology of language' is the notion of binding – particularly crucial when his theolinguistics withdraws into the inner mysteries such as the self-recapitulating strategy of the Trinity and of the human interior word of man.

The notion of construction also drags together and conflates love and language.[11] Through the collapsing of a distinction between signs and things (*De doctrina christiana*), Augustine transforms the created universe into a semiotic chart, or a discourse that the believer must navigate and reconstruct by means of an order of love. Love in turns binds the interior discourse of the human being and makes it adhere to perfect knowledge.

As with his doctrine of the W/word, Augustine's theory of love appears at the same time all-pervasive and fundamental. Nested in eternity and in the mystery of the Trinity – which first makes itself understandable as the threefold interaction of the lover, the loved one, and love ('amans, quod amatur, amor'; *De Trinitate* 8.10.14) – the system of love works on earth according to a very simple economy, the distinction between use (*uti*) and enjoyment (*frui*) and the consequent articulation between *caritas*, the right understanding of that distinction that leads to order, and *cupiditas*, the misunderstanding of it that leads to disorder. The contrast between the selfless love directed to God and the selfish love directed to oneself pervades Augustine's work: in the *City of God*, for instance, it originates (and marks the border between) the two cities on which Augustine's vision of history is based.[12]

Love and language on earth share a crucial feature: they are fundamentally transitive. In the *De Trinitate*, while describing love within the first trinitarian analogy, Augustine compares it to the word, in order to dissipate the (very unchristian) doubt that love might love itself. Love and language are connective and inclusive, and they always point to both themselves and their object:

> Sicut enim verbum indicat aliquid, indicat etiam se ipsum, sed non se verbum indicat, nisi se aliquid indicare indicet; sic et caritas diligit quidem se, sed nisi se aliquid diligentem diligat, non caritate se diligit. Quid ergo diligit caritas nisi quod caritate diligimus? (8.8.12)

> [For, just as a word both indicates something and also indicates itself, but it does not indicate itself as a word, unless it indicates that it is indicating something, so, too, does love indeed love itself; but unless it loves itself as loving something, then it does not love itself as love. What, therefore, does love love, except that which we love with love?][13]

Augustine's vocabulary of love and desire is dynamic.[14] Only *caritas* (Christian love proper) and *libido* (unrestricted desire, passion) have fixed meanings and define the two opposite sides of the spectrum, which is filled with fluid terms such as *amor* ('neutral' love, love bound by will, but also desire), *appetitus* (the positive side of desire, mostly desire for knowledge), *desiderium* (mostly lack), *cupiditas* and *concupiscientia* (strong desire, often negative), *dilectio* (spiritual love, also fulfilment of desire), *delectatio* (pleasure-desire), and even *voluntas* (the Augustinian split will, which can 'swerve' for good or for bad).[15]

Three images of love and desire well represent the declensions of the discourse on words and the Word into the theme of love and the operation of love and desire within the universe and within the creature: *pondus* (weight), *ordo* (order), and *gluten* (glue). Love as *pondus* describes a drive with a momentum, which points universe and creature from chaos to order – a transition that entails a switch from desire to fulfilment. While the image of weight describes love/desire's operation in the universe as a movement toward order, love as *ordo* represents the map of that movement, the way in which the creature establishes a relation to the universe, according to a set of rules (*ordo amoris, ordinata dilectio*) that allow the human to reconstruct the universal order and hierarchy that points to God. Finally, love/desire works as a glue in the inner recess of the individual, and as such supervises the orderly generation of interior knowledge. As a form of memory, it glues together past and future into the present search for order and direction.[16] *Pondus, ordo,* and *gluten* are three aspects of a same syntax, which works in terms of direction (*pondus*), hierarchy (*ordo*), and binding (*gluten*), just as the construction of the w/Word does.

The Semiotic Universe of Mankind: Augustine's 'Theory of Things'

Augustine's theory of language is rooted in the linguistic thought of antiquity and in the liberal arts tradition. The first, and in many ways complete, description of it is found in the *De dialectica,* part of the series that the newly converted, awaiting baptism in Milano in 387, intended to dedicate to the seven liberal arts but never fully completed.[17] Soon, however, Augustine's theory of language joined his theology: the *De magistro* and the *De doctrina christiana* discuss the inherent limitation of the realm of signs while simultaneously postulating the necessary intervention of (God through) Christ, in order to reconnect signs to 'true' meaning.

The early dialogue *De magistro* (389) focuses on the relationship between verbal signs and knowledge, the fundamental question being 'What do we want to accomplish when speaking?' (1.1: 'Quid tibi videmur efficere velle, cum loquimur?'). The dialogue itself demonstrates the paradigm (and paradox) of learning, thus stated by Augustine's son Adeodatus: 'I have learned from the prompting of your words that words do nothing but prompt man to learn' (14.46).[18] Signs are indeed merely sound when unconnected through *significatio* to the thing they signify, but neither sound nor signification is learned through signs themselves.[19] The only purpose of signs is to point to things: 'Hactenus verba valerent, quibus ut plurimum tribuam, admonent tantum, ut quaeramus res, non exhibent, ut norimus' (10.36: words have force only to the extent that they remind us to look for things; they don't display them for us to know). Knowledge and learning are rooted in things: 'Ita magis signum re cognita quam signo dato ipsa re discitur' (10.33: Therefore, a sign is learned when the thing is known, rather than the thing being learned when the sign is given). Things, in turn, must not be compared to signs, but to an inner referent: Christ, the inner teacher.

De universis autem quae intellegimus, non loquentem qui personat foris, sed intus ipsi menti praesidentem consulimus veritatem, verbis fortasse ut consulamus admoniti. Ille autem, qui consulitur, docet, qui in interiore homine habitare dictus est Christus, *id est incommutabilis Dei Virtus atque sempiterna Sapientia:* quam quidem omnis rationalis anima consulit; sed tantum cuique panditur, quantum capere propter propriam sive malam sive bonam voluntatem potest. (11.38)

[Regarding each of the things we understand, however, we don't consult a speaker who makes sounds outside us, but the Truth that presides within over the mind itself, though perhaps words prompt us to consult Him. What is more, He Who is consulted, He Who is said to *dwell in the inner man*, does teach: Christ – that is, *the unchangeable power and everlasting wisdom of God*, which every rational soul does consult, but is disclosed to anyone, to the extent that he can apprehend it, according to his good or evil will.][20]

Learning, therefore, does not proceed from the outside teacher, who can merely supply a set of signs (words) that prompt the listener to consult the inside teacher, the guarantor of knowledge and ultimately of truth.[21] Ambiguity is never the fault of the inner teacher, but lies instead with defective signs (a slip of the tongue, etc.), in the weakness of the discernment of the hearer (12.40), or with the constitutional polyvalence and polysemy of signs. This last fault of the sign points to the importance of interpretation – an issue that is not explored in detail in the *De magistro* but becomes central to the *De doctrina christiana*.[22]

The system of learning and knowledge as sketched in the *De magistro* can be summed up as follows:

outside teacher → signs (words) ⇢ things ← knowledge and truth ← inside teacher

Things, as a result of their contiguity to inner truth, seem to represent the stable link in the system, whereas signs are granted only the transitive quality of pointing to and reminding things.

The same connections among signs, things, and knowledge are inscribed – in an abridged and apparently more sign-friendly version – at the beginning of the *De doctrina christiana*, a text that Augustine started writing soon after his consecration as bishop:[23] 'Omnis doctrina vel rerum est vel signorum, sed res per signa discuntur' (1.2.2: All teaching is teaching of either things or signs, but things are learnt through signs).[24] Things belong to the order of being, while signs, especially verbal signs, belong to the order of signifying. This distinction, which also sets the general framework for the *De doctrina christiana* itself (Book 1 deals with things, Book 2 with signs), is, however, immediately blurred by Augustine when he points out that a sign is itself a thing (because it cannot be no-thing), and things, in turn, can be signs when they point to other things.[25] Signs are then defined as things that are used to signify something else ('quid appellem signa, res eas videlicet, quae ad significandum aliquid adhibentur').

Augustine's discussion of signs in Book 2 begins with a distinction between natural signs, such as smoke signifying fire ('sicuti est fumus significans ignem,' 2.1.2), and conventional signs, which living beings exchange in order to communicate emotions, sensations, and knowledge ('data vero signa sunt, quae sibi quaeque viventia invicem dant ad demonstrandos quantum possunt, motus animi sui vel sensa aut intellecta quaelibet,' 1.2.3). Conventional signs are mainly verbal (words and letters), and within them a further distinction is made between *signa propria*, signs that directly describe their object, and *signa translata*, in which transposition takes place and which pertain to the realms of both rhetoric and biblical interpretation.

The history of signs is characterized by a progression toward obscurity. Although he does not discuss Eden and the Fall in the *De doctrina christiana*, references from other works suggest that Augustine believed that communication in Eden happened 'face to face,' the 'angelic way,' and that direct communication with God has been interrupted since the Fall. The 'slavery of signs' is hence one with original sin. Witness a passage from the *De Genesi contra Manichaeos* (2.4), where the fields and rain of Genesis 2:5 are interpreted respectively as the human soul and the truth coming directly from God. Before the Fall, there was no need for the clouds (the allegory, the obscurities) of the language of the scriptures, since the creature was 'watered' by truth from inside:

Post peccatum autem homo laborare coepit in terra, et necessarias habere illas nubes. Ante peccatum vero, cum viride agri et pabulum fecisset Deus, quo nomine invisibilem creaturam significari diximus, irrigabat eam fonte interiore, loquens in intellectum eius: ut non extrinsecus verba exciperet, tamquam ex supradictis nubibus pluviam, sed fonte suo, hoc est de intimis suis manante veritate, satiaretur.

[After sin man began to labor on earth and to have need of those clouds. But before sin God had made the green of the field and food, and we said that this expression signified the invisible creature. God watered it by an interior spring, speaking to its intellect, so that it did not receive words from the outside, as rain from the aforementioned clouds. Rather it was satisfied from its own spring, that is, by the truth flowing from its interior.][26]

The downfall of signs is a product of human discord and desire for supremacy, the tower of Babel being itself the sign of human pride ('superbiae signum') and a signal of the deceptive nature of signs.[27] The dispersion of Babel is only partially remedied by the availability of the scriptures in different languages (*De doctrina christiana* 2.5.6) and the willingness of the Christian to learn about languages and language in order to approach the difficulties of biblical interpretation – a way to wisdom that is initially powered by the fear of God, piety, and desire for knowledge (2.7.10). Babel represents then only the deepening of language's obscurity, which is constitutional and hides both peril and reward, the death of the letter and the life of the spirit. This inevitable obscurity forces Christians to embrace the hardships of interpretation and walk its dangerous paths through a strategic deployment of knowledge (the topic of Book 3). Two major perils are hidden in the incomplete, or incorrect, or impatient interpretation of signs: the error of the pagans, who referred signs to gods (Neptune = the sea),[28] and the slavery of the Jews, an enslavement to the letter, of the flesh, that made them mistake signs for things.[29] The distinction between slavery and freedom stands in the distinction between sign and its referent, with the conclusion that only meaning should be worshipped, and not the sign that bears it:

> Sub signo enim servit qui operatur aut veneratur aliquam rem significantem, nesciens quid significet. Qui vero aut operatur aut veneratur utile signum divinitus institutum, cuius vim significationemque intellegit, non hoc veneratur quod videtur et transit, sed illud potius quo talia cuncta referenda sunt. (3.9.13)

> [Someone who attends to and worships a thing which is meaningful but remains unaware of its meaning is a slave to a sign. But the person who attends to or worships a useful sign, one divinely instituted, and does realize its force and significance, does not worship a thing which is only apparent and transitory but rather the thing to which all such things are to be related.]

In history, Christ is figured as the redeemer of signs.[30] He set their confusion in order, providing a set of few ('pauca pro multis'), easy ('factu facillima'), elevated ('intellectu augustissima'), and chaste ('observatione castissima') signs – among which Augustine mentions baptism and Eucharist. These signs are not worshipped 'for bodily slavery' but rather for 'spiritual freedom.'[31] What Christ and the apostolic tradition teach, though, is not so much a clear and direct understanding of all signs, as much as the fact that 'signs are signs' and, as such, they point to something else. The referent might remain obscure, but the knowledge of its existence shields the Christian from the slavery of sin and sign, and of both sinful and literal interpretation:

> Qui autem non intellegit quid significet signum, et tamen signum esse intellegit, nec ipse premitur servitute. Melius est autem vel premi incognitis, sed utilibus signis, quam inutiliter ea interpretando, a iugo servitutis eductam cervicem laqueis erroris inserere. (3.9.13)

> [The person who does not understand what a sign means, but at least understands that it is a sign, is not in fact subjected to slavery. It is better to be dominated by unknown but useful signs than to interpret them in a useless way and so thrust one's neck, rescued from the yoke of slavery, into the toils of error.]

Signs might be complex, obscure, polysemous, but they do not enslave the Christian who is able to evaluate them as signs and is thereby spurred on to look for their meaning. Rowan Williams has written that 'a language which indefinitely postpones fulfilment or enjoyment is appropriate to the Christian discipline of spiritual homelessness, to the character of the believing life as a pilgrimage.'[32] But where to stop, then? In searching the intricacies of (scriptural) language, where can the Christian find an end point? The answer is that the order of love provides both the map and the landing for the journey of interpretation: it must end at the borders of the realm of charity. The difficulty of the letter is often a way of inducing the reader to recognize and combat cupidity, but charity is sown throughout the scriptures as an interpretative clue. When charity is reached in full, no transposition takes place; meaning is stable and understandable.

> Sic eversa tyrannide cupiditatis caritas regnat iustissimis legibus dilectionis Dei propter Deum, sui et proximi propter Deum. Servabitur ergo in locutionibus figuratis regula huiusmodi, ut tam diu versetur diligenti consideratione quod legitur, donec ad regnum caritatis interpretatio perducatur. Si autem hoc iam proprie sonat, nulla putetur figurata locutio. (3.15.23)

[So when the tyranny of lust has been overthrown love rules with laws that are utterly just: to love God on his own account, and to love oneself and one's neighbour on God's account. Therefore in dealing with figurative expressions we will observe a rule of this kind: the passage being read should be studied with careful consideration until its interpretation can be connected with the realm of love. If this point is made literally, then no kind of figurative expression need be considered.]

With the addition of an emphasis on the vital and/or dangerous ambiguity of signs, the *De doctrina christiana*, as the *De magistro*, underscores both the limitation of human signs and their potential for redemption through Christ. In the handbook of Christian rhetoric, however, the perspective on the inherent transience and imperfection of signs is enlarged and extended to things as well. In the first book of the treatise the bishop both sets and blurs the distinction between signs and things, by recalling that signs themselves are things ('omne signum etiam res aliqua est') and acknowledging that certain things, indeed, function as signs:

Proprie autem nunc res appellavi, quae non ad significandum aliquid adhibentur, sicuti est lignum, lapis, pecus atque huiusmodi cetera, sed non illud lignum quod in aquas amaras Moysen misisse legimus, ut amaritudine carerent neque ille lapis quem Iacob sibi ad caput posuerat, neque illud pecus quod pro filio immolavit Abraham. Hae namque ita res sunt, ut aliarum etiam signa sint rerum. (1.2.2)

[What I now call things in the strict sense are things such as logs, stones, sheep and so on, which are not employed to signify something; but I do not include the log which we read that Moses threw into the bitter waters to make them lose their bitter taste, or the stone which Jacob placed under his head, or the sheep which Abraham sacrificed in place of his son. These are things, but they are at the same time signs of other things.]

The *signa translata* discussed by Augustine in Books 2 and 3 are indeed nothing more than the sign of these things that function as signs:

Sunt autem signa vel propria vel translata. Propria dicuntur, cum his rebus significandis adhibentur, propter quas sunt istituta, sicut dicimus bovem, cum intellegimus pecus, quod omnes nobiscum latinae linguae homines hoc nomine vocant. Translata sunt, cum et ipsae res, quas propriis verbis significamus, ad aliquid aliud significandum usurpantur, sicut dicimus bovem, et per has duas syllabas intellegimus pecus, quod isto nomine appellari solet, sed rursus per illud pecus intellegimus evangelistam, quem significavit Scriptura interpretante Apostolo dicens: *Bovem triturantem non infrenabis.* (2.10.15)

[Signs are either proper or transposed.[33] They are called proper when used to signify the things for which they were invented, as for example, when we say *bovem* (ox) meaning the animal which we and all speakers of Latin call by that name. They are transposed when the actual things which we signify by the particular words are used to signify something else: when, for example, we say *bovem* and not only interpret these two syllables to mean the animal normally referred to by that name but also understand, by that animal, 'worker in the gospel,' which is what Scripture, as interpreted by the apostle, means when it says, 'You shall not muzzle the ox that treads out the grain.']

It is clear that the transposition of meaning does not happen in the sign itself but in the thing: a *signum translatum* then is merely a sign of what could be called a '*res translata.*' In Todorov's words, 'a sign is transposed when its signified becomes, in turn, a signifier; in other words, the proper sign is based on a single relation, the transposed sign on two successive operations.'[34] As examples of transposed things, Augustine singles out scriptural *loci*, so that the Christian allegorical reading becomes a matter of things as opposed to signs.

The semiotic implication of things, however, does not end with transposed signs. In Book 1 of the *De doctrina christiana* it is indeed extended to the whole world of things, so much so that one is tempted to talk about Augustine's 'theory of things' as opposed to his 'theory of signs' – a specular opposite to a postmodern understanding of a semiotic universe dominated by the endless interplay of signifiers. There is, in fact, a perspective according to which *all* things are simply transitive, exactly as signs: in the grander scheme – indeed the discourse – through which God governs fallen time and history.

Book 1 of the *De doctrina christiana* is devoted to the discussion of things and how the Christian should relate to them. The bishop's advice on the topic is clear and incontrovertible: things should be sorted out according to the distinction between use (the love for the creature as referred to the Creator) and enjoyment (the direct love for the Creator). That is, according to the order of love.[35] The inscription of the *uti/frui* distinction at the beginning of this treatise conflates, with a stunning move, the systems of *res* and *signa*. As Williams remarks, 'The distinction between *frui* and *uti* (1.3) is thus superimposed on the *res-signum* distinction … It is the means whereby Augustine links what he has to say about language with what he has to say about beings who "mean" and about the fundamentally desirous nature of those beings – a link which is undoubtedly the most original and interesting feature of the treatise' (139). I would add that this inscription also generates, for both systems, the need for order, signalling the centrality of the notion of syntax.

Love and order are brought together in the very first formulation of the *uti/frui* distinction in *De diversis quaestionibus* (question 30: 'utrum omnia in utilitate hominis creata sint' [whether all things are created for the use of man]). Here the notion of *frui* is connected to pleasure ('Frui ergo dicimur ea re de qua capimus voluptatem'), whereas *uti* relates to the transitive act of referring to the pleasurable thing ('utimur eam quam referimus ad id unde capienda voluptas est'). This simple rule stands between order and perversion.[36] In the same passage, use is defined as a form of decoding and interpretation: it is impossible to use something unless one knows its referent ('Nec uti quisque potest ea re quae quo referenda sit nescit'). Just as the sign is useless when it is not referred to the thing that it signifies, so too unrelated things are powerless or, worse, misdirecting.

In the first book of the *De doctrina christiana*, Augustine rephrases and elaborates the *uti/frui* distinction, stating that nothing but God should be approached in terms of enjoyment. Augustine explains the two terms through the beautiful image of the pilgrimage of desire, one of the most powerful Christian metaphors for the soul's search for God. Things to be used are, he says, like the vessels that transport the exile home, the only thing to be enjoyed, the place that the desire of the pilgrim indicates.

> Res ergo aliae sunt quibus fruendum est, aliae quibus utendum, aliae quae fruuntur et utuntur. Illae quibus fruendum est, nos beatos faciunt; istis quibus utendum est tendentes ad beatitudinem adiuvamur et quasi adminiculamur, ut ad illas quae nos beatos faciunt, pervenire atque his inhaerere possimus … Frui est enim amore inhaerere alicui rei propter seipsam. Uti autem, quod in usum venerit, ad id quod amas obtinendum referre, si tamen amandum est. Nam usus inlicitus abusus potius vel abusio nominandus est. Quomodo ergo, si essemus peregrini, qui beate vivere nisi in patria non possemus, eaque peregrinatione utique miseri et miseriam

finire cupientes, in patriam redire vellemus, opus esse vel terrestribus vel
marinis vehiculis quibus utendum esset ut ad patriam, qua fruendum erat,
pervenire valeremus; quod si amoenitates itineris et ipsa gestatio vehicu-
lorum nos delectaret, conversi ad fruendum his, quibus uti debuimus,
nollemus cito via finire et perversa suavitate implicati alienaremur a patria,
cuius suavitas faceret beatos, sic in huius mortalitatis vita peregrinantes a
Domino, si redire in patria volumus, ubi beati esse possimus, utendum est
hoc mundo, non fruendum, ut invisibilia Dei per ea, quae facta sunt, intellecta conspiciantur, hoc est, ut de corporalibus temporalibusque rebus
aeterna et spiritalia capiamus. (1.3–4)

[There are some things which are to be enjoyed, some which are to be
used and some whose function is both to enjoy and to use. Those which are
to be enjoyed make us happy; those which are to be used assist us and give
us a boost, so to speak, as we press on towards our happiness, so that we
may reach and hold fast to the things which make us happy ... To enjoy
something is to hold fast to it in love for its own sake. To use something is
to apply whatever it may be to the purpose of obtaining what you love – if
indeed it is something that ought to be loved. The improper use of something should be termed abuse. Suppose we were travelers who could live
happily only in our homeland, and because our absence made us unhappy,
we wished to put an end to our misery and return there: we would need
transport by land or sea which we could use to travel to our homeland, the
object of our enjoyment. But if we were fascinated by the delights of the
journey and the actual traveling, we would be perversely enjoying things
that we should be using; and we would be reluctant to finish our journey
quickly, being ensnared in the wrong kind of pleasure and estranged from
the homeland whose pleasures could make us happy. So in this mortal life
we are like travelers away from our Lord: if we wish to return to the homeland where we can be happy we must use this world, not enjoy it, in order
to discern the invisible attributes of God, which are understood through
what has been made or, in other words, to derive eternal and spiritual value
from corporeal and temporal things.]

In the subsequent part of the book, Augustine meticulously discusses
the rules of the order of love (*ordinata dilectio*) that should govern the
life of the Christian based upon an honest estimate of things.[37] He con-
cludes that God alone is to be enjoyed, while He in turn does not enjoy,
but uses mankind – yet to the human being's benefit rather than His
own.[38] The order of love becomes indeed the backbone of Augustine's

thought, spanning all branches of his doctrine, and resurfacing in all his works.

The process of navigating through things according to the rules of love in order to reach the longed-for homeland results in an orderly interpretation of a map of signs (indeed, as we shall see shortly, an articulated discourse) with the aim of approaching the absolute signified. Things, like signs, are transitive; they are vehicles that help with the tracing and following of a meaningful itinerary. The dimension of *uti* is constitutively transitive, like signification ('Uti autem, quod in usum venerit, ad id quod amas obtinendum referre, si tamen amandum est'):[39] by relegating things to the order of *uti*, Augustine equates them with signs and postulates for both the necessity of an order. The consequences of this move are significant for both Augustine's theory of language and his theology. As Todorov remarks, 'It follows that the only thing that is absolutely not a sign (because it is the object of enjoyment *par excellence*) is God. This fact, in our culture, imparts a reciprocal coloration of divinity to every ultimate signified' (41).

The map for the journey of life and that of the journey of language coincide: both guide the Christian pilgrim to reach the shores of charity through a well-organized journey of desire. A direct, appeased relation between sign and meaning – the one portrayed, for instance, by the simplicity of the *signum proprium* – can be found only in the absolute signified. Only then can the Christian enjoy the fulfilment (*frui*) of charity. Desire runs instead on the modulation of the *translata*. It must be both embraced and disciplined through the order of *uti*, in order not to turn an assiduous and incessant search into an endless one.

In conclusion: signs (words) are mere sound when disconnected from signification and are not bearers of knowledge. They belong to the transitive dimension of use, and in history they follow and mark the descending parable that separated humankind from God. Their limitation and inadequacy calls for Christ's redemption in two ways: in a presence of Christ in the individual (*De magistro*), and in the Christ event in history (*De doctrina christiana*). Importantly, in the grander scheme of history, things too are signs that have to be used and arranged according to an order of love. Signs point to things, whose meanings are verified in the inner man with the help of the interior teacher (Christ). Once learned and ordered among themselves, things in turn work as signs pointing to the ultimate and only signified – God. The fundamental imperfection of signs and things is therefore paradoxically vital: they provide the Christian with a map that allows him or her to reconstruct the absolute signified's ways of unfolding.

The Performative Universe of God

'Performative,' according to Austin's famous definition, 'indicates that the issuing of the utterance is the performing of an action – it is not normally thought as just saying something.'[40] A performative utterance doesn't fall under the (logical) domain of 'true or false'; its felicity or infelicity is dictated by the circumstances in which the sentence is uttered. Making use of Augustine's categories, one might add that performatives belong simultaneously to the order of signifying and to the order of being: they are words that *are* what they *mean*. Signs do not apply to the performative universe of God, who points to things with things. Creation, Incarnation, and the imperative of conversion represent three examples of the linguistic nature of Augustine's theology.

Ipse dixit et facta sunt

Creation, as described in the three commentaries on Genesis is a laborious and lengthy process.[41] My concern here is with the beginning of the process, the verbal act that initiates Creation and gives rise to what Eugene Vance calls suggestively a 'phonic metaphysics.'[42] The word of Creation is figured by Augustine as a speech act (albeit one that is very different from human speech), as plainly stated in Book 11 of the *Confessions*: 'ergo dixisti, et facta sunt atque in verbo tuo fecisti ea' (11.5: Therefore you spoke and they were made, and in your Word you made them).[43] And the Word is indeed a word, as Augustine explains in his commentary on Psalm 148:7.

> Qomodo hic ostendit quia per Verbum facta sunt? *Ipse dixit, et facta sunt; ipse mandavit, et creata sunt.* Nemo dicit, nemo mandat, nisi verbo.

> [How does he here show that they were made through the Word? He spoke, and they were made, he ordered, and they were created. No one speaks, no one orders except by a word.][44]

Whenever Augustine deals with the word of Creation, he shifts focus from Genesis to the Gospel of John – from 'in principio' to 'in principio erat Verbum.'[45] As Gilson explains, 'to obviate the difficulties which arise from the use of the word *principium*, Augustine prefers to interpret it symbolically. According to him, the phrase does not signify the beginning of time, but the principle of all things, i.e. the Word' (92). Perhaps the clearest formulation of this can be found in the following passage from the *de Genesi contra Manichaeos* (389):

> His respondemus Deum in principio fecisse coelum et terram, non in principio temporis, sed in Christo, cum Verbum esset apud Patrem, per quod facta et in quo facta sunt omnia. Dominus enim noster Iesus Christus, cum eum Iudaei interrogassent quis esset, respondit: *Principium quia et loquor vobis*. (1.2.3)[46]

> [We answer them that God made heaven and earth in the beginning, not in the beginning of time, but in Christ. For He was the word with the father, through whom and in whom all things were made. For, when the Jews asked him who he was, our Lord Jesus Christ answered, 'The beginning: that is why I am speaking to you.']

Augustine's main concern in dealing with the word of Creation is to avoid any semiotic (temporal and corporeal) involvement. 'Quomodo dixisti?' 'Quo verbo a te dictum est?' (How did you speak? What kind of word would you have used?) are the opening and closing questions of Book 11, chapter 6 of the *Confessions*. These are pressing issues, for if the word of Creation had been a sign that sounded and passed like all other signs ('verbis sonantibus et praetereuntibus'), the notion of Creation itself would be severely undermined, setting off a chain reaction that would endanger the very existence of God. Augustine promptly addresses these issues:

> Vocas itaque nos ad intellegendum *Verbum*, Deum *apud* te *Deum*, quod sempiterne dicitur et eo sempiterne dicuntur omnia. Neque enim finitur, quod dicebatur, et dicitur aliud, ut possint dici omnia, sed simul ac sempiterne omnia; alioquin iam tempus et mutatio et non vera aeternitas nec vera immortalitas ... Et ideo verbo tibi coaeterno simul et sempiterne dicis omnia, quae dicis, et fit, quidquid dicis ut fiat; nec aliter quam dicendo facis; nec tamen simul et sempiterna fiunt omnia quae dicendo facis. (11.7.9)

> [You call us, therefore, to understand the Word, God who is with you God. That word is spoken eternally, and by it all things are uttered eternally. It is

not the case that what was being said comes to an end, and something else is then said, so that everything is uttered in a succession with a conclusion, but everything is said in the simultaneity of eternity. Otherwise time and change would already exist, and there would not be a true eternity and true immortality ... And so by the Word coeternal with yourself, you say all that you say in simultaneity and eternity, and whatever you say will come about does come about. You do not cause it to exist other than by speaking. Yet not all that you cause to exist by speaking is made in simultaneity and eternity.]

At stake, then, is not signification, but temporality; not lexicon, but syntax. In the Word of God with God – absolute meaning – a whole discourse is contained simultaneously and eternally, a discourse that has no need for succession in order to mean ('nec finitur, quod dicebatur et dicitur aliud, ut possint dici omnia'). In the created universe, that discourse unfolds word by word, thing by thing. Within the discourse of history, which holds to the same laws as human speech, one very special sign/word is uttered: Christ. The Word made flesh is another (and in a way more complicated) aspect of the performative universe of God, where the semiotic threat, being closer, triggers its own solution.

In quantum enim homo, in tantum mediator

Augustine's account of Christ is complex and nuanced.[47] A passage such as the following from the Enarrationes in Psalmos reveals the arpeggio-like solution to which Augustine is forced by the double nature of Christ as God and man via the Word: 'totus homo cum Verbo, et Verbum cum homine, et homo et Verbum unus homo, et Verbum et homo unus Deus' (90.5).[48] The core of this complexity rests in the possibility of a cross-reading of Christ as a referent in the semiotic universe of humankind, because he is a sign produced in the performative universe of God. The function of Christ with respect to language is paradoxical: in utter subversion of the rules and roles of signification, he is at the same time a Word that is absolutely not a sign, and a thing that – precisely by being a thing – is only a sign. Or as Augustine describes it, Christ is a word that is not a mediator, and a man that is only a mediator: 'in quantum enim homo, in tantum mediator, in quantum autem Verbum, non medius, quia equalis Deo, et Deus apud Deum et simul unus Deus' (Confessions 10.43.68).

The simultaneous and eternal Word in the beginning is made available to the creature as a voice. Precisely by becoming a sign, a word that sounds and passes, Christ later points out for humans his own existence inside of them, as the Word that teaches inwardly, and to which all signs must be compared. The interior teacher is explicitly called the Word in the passage of the *Confessions* that immediately follows the one quoted above about the word of Creation (11.7.9). Thus, closure is provided to the suspended ending of the *De magistro*, where the teacher was referred to only as the Wisdom of God:

> Ipsum est Verbum tuum, quod et principium est, quia et loquitur nobis. Sic in Evangelio per carnem ait, et hoc insonuit foris auribus hominum, ut crederetur et intus quaereretur et inveniretur in aeterna veritate, ubi omnes discipulos bonus et solus magister docet. (11.8.10)

> [This reason is your Word, which is also the Beginning in that it also speaks to us. Thus in the gospel the Word speaks through the flesh, and this sounded externally in human ears, so that it should be believed and sought inwardly, found in the eternal truth where the Master who alone is good teaches all his disciples.]

The analogy between the sound of human exterior words and the Word made flesh is a crucial aspect of Augustine's 'theolinguistics,' which I will discuss in greater length later. For the moment, let us consider that God's 'utterance,' the Word made flesh, can be viewed – like Creation – as a performative act, where a word (albeit the Word) 'produces' a thing, the difference being that in this instance the Word is 'trapped,' so to speak, in the thing.

The conceptual difficulty and the fundamental impenetrability of Incarnation is always present to Augustine,[49] especially with respect to the danger of understanding the Incarnation of the Word as a conversion or mutation of Word into flesh.[50] As opposed to Creation, where the Word releases its utterance, Incarnation is a speech act that includes the word *and* the thing. Yet Incarnation is a speech act with a twist: God produces a man who is *only* a sign ('in quantum enim homo, in tantum mediator'). This, in turn, adds another layer of complexity and hides another twist in the speech act analogy I have drawn thus far. Jesus, God's sign to humans, operates on earth as a reverse of the performative: instead of his speech being an act, *his acts are words* – they are signs that point to something: 'Numquid forte et hic aliquid significat nobis Iesus, cuius facta verba sunt?' (*In Evangelium Ioannis* 25.2: Can it perhaps be that Jesus, whose deeds are words, here too signifies something to us?)[51]

While Augustine is very prudent, almost reticent in defining the modalities of Incarnation, always appealing to the inscrutability of its mystery, he is voluble when describing the workings of Christ as a sign. First, Christ is a very special sign, a distinguished sign, a 'signed sign,' one that bears a further mark, the seal of his father, as Augustine notes in his *Commentary on the Gospel of John*:

Ergo enim filius hominis illo modo, cum *Verbum caro factum est, et habitavit in nobis*. Ideo enim *hunc Deus Pater signavit*. Signare quid est, nisi proprium aliquid ponere? Hoc est enim signare, imponere aliquid quod non confundatur cum caeteris. Signare, est signum rei ponere. Cuicumque rei ponis signum, ideo ponis signum, ne confusa cum aliis, a te non possit agnosci. *Pater* ergo *eum signavit*. Quid est *signavit*? Proprium quiddam illi dedit, ne caeteris comparetur hominibus. (*In Evangelium Ioannis* 25.11)

[Therefore he was the Son of man in that way when 'the Word was made flesh, and dwelt among us.' For thus 'upon him God the father has set his seal.' What is to set the seal except to put some (mark) exclusively one's own? For to set the seal is this, to apply some (mark) which would not be confounded with others. To set the seal is to put a sign on a thing. You put your sign on something or other; you put the sign precisely so that it may not be confused with other things and can be recognized by you. Therefore, 'upon him the Father has set his seal.' What does 'has set his seal' mean? He has given him something exclusively his own that he might not be compared to other men.]

The fact that Christ is a sign makes it imperative for humans to transcend his happening in history. After all, as learned in the *De magistro* and the *De doctrina christiana*, the value of a sign lies only in its pointing to something else, and once this is achieved, the sign has to be disregarded. Christ as a sign, therefore, invites the Christian to transcend his own Incarnation, which belongs to the order of *uti* and not of *frui*:

Ex quo intelligitur quam nulla res in via tenere nos debeat, quando nec ipse Dominus, in quantum via nostra esse dignatus est, tenere nos voluerit, sed transire, ne rebus temporalibus, quamvis ab illo pro salute nostra susceptis et gestis, haereamus infirmiter, sed per eas potius curramus alacriter, ut ad eum ipsum, qui nostram naturam a temporalibus liberavit et collocavit ad dexteram Patris, provehi atque pervehi mereamur. (*De doctrina christiana* 1.34.38)

[From this it is to be inferred that nothing must detain us on our way, since not even the Lord, at least in his graciously chosen role of being our way, wanted to detain us; rather he wanted us to pass on, not sticking feebly to temporal things – even though they were accepted and endured by him for our salvation – but hastening eagerly through them so that we may achieve progress and success in our journey to the one who has freed our nature from temporal things and set it at the Father's right hand.]

The Christ event, his word-like actions, impresses on history – otherwise constituted of a series of unrelated signs and things – a crucial sense of order and direction. Christ's life might then be called the principal clause of a discourse that leads from the Word back to the Word. His death and resurrection mark time as a full stop, closing the up-till-then unfinished (and therefore non-meaningful) sentence and allowing recapitulation.

Another feature of Christ as a sign is the fact that his way of pointing is not unilateral. First, his own utterances require a double standard of interpretation, depending on whether they are uttered as God ('secundum formam Dei') or as man ('secundum formam servi,' *De Trinitate* 1.2). The entire Book 1 of the *De Trinitate* is dedicated to the examination of Christ's words in the gospel according to this distinction. Second, Christ's double nature makes him a double sign, which simultaneously points to and makes explicit the immense greatness of God's love for humankind (and to his greatness *tout court*) and the immense unlikeness that separates creature from Creator, thus setting – and pointing to – the superior and inferior limits of human experience. In the *Confessions* Augustine is both horrified and inflamed by the magnitude of both likeness and unlikeness: 'et inhorresco et inardesco: inhorresco in quantum dissimilis ei sum, inardesco in quantum similis ei sum' (11.9.11: It fills me with terror and burning love: with terror, inasmuch as I am utterly other than it, with burning love in that I am akin to it). Christ can therefore be understood as a 'dual sign,' one that works in two texts at the same time and recalls one to the other.[52] In a passage from his *Commentary on the Gospel of John*, Augustine stresses the concurrent existence of Christ in two texts:

Verbum, anima et caro unus Christus: Filius Dei et filius hominis unus Christus. Filius Dei semper, filius hominis ex tempore, tamen unus Christus secundum unitatem personae. In coelo erat, quando in terra loquebatur. Sic erat filius hominis in caelo, quomodo Filius Dei erat in terra; Filius

Dei in terra in suscepta carne, filius hominis in coelo in unitate personae.
(27.4)

[Therefore Christ is one, the Word, soul and flesh, one Christ; the Son of
God and the Son of man, one Christ. The Son of God always, the son of
man in time, nevertheless, one Christ according to the unity of the person.
He was in heaven when he was speaking on earth. So the Son of man was in
heaven as the Son of God was on earth; the Son of God was on earth in the
flesh he had taken, the Son of man was in heaven in the unity of person.]

Christ recalls at the same time two texts, one of likeness and eternity, the
other of difference and time, both beautifully described at the end of
the *Confessions*: the text of God, in which a simultaneous reading face to
face is granted, and the temporal text of man, which has to be read
through signs.[53] Christ radically – ontologically – changes both texts,
making the text of humankind meaningful and the text of God intelligible. He introduces likeness in the text of mankind by readjusting the
deformities that sin brought about to the image of God that the creature bears within and by redirecting signs toward the recapitulation of
meaning. At the same time he introduces difference in the text of God.
The very sign produced by Incarnation – Christ's (resurrected) body – is
raised to heaven there to become an *exemplum*, which explains and
points to the future life in God.[54]

Christ's body, a sign in heaven after his resurrection, continues to
serve the believer on earth by providing the sacraments, a set of concise,
simple, clear, performative signs that redeem and readdress signs for
human beings.[55] The most meaningful and difficult among them is the
Eucharist. In his *Commentary on the Gospel of John*, Augustine describes
the shock of the apostles at Christ's statement 'Eat my flesh,' as if it
meant that Jesus was about to cut himself in pieces and share his body
with the believers.[56] Or, even more graphically, 'carnem quippe sic
intellexerunt, quomodo in cadavere dilaniatur, aut in macello venditur,
non quomodo spiritu vegetatur' (27.5: they understood flesh as something that is torn to pieces in a carcass or sold in a meat market, not as
something that is enlivened by a spirit). What Christ offers to the believers, however, is a resurrected flesh that has again joined the Word and
therefore allows immortality: 'inter Verbum suscipiens et carnem resur-
gentem, mors media consumpta est' (26.10: between the Word taking
on flesh and the flesh rising, death, in the middle, was annihilated). In
obeying Christ's command to the apostles, the Christian, through the

Eucharist, is pointed both to sign in heaven and to meaning on earth: in heaven, to that bit of difference that has been implanted in perfect likeness (the body of Christ that signals the future blessedness of soul and body reunited), and on earth, to the presence of Christ as the inner referent for truth.

Tolle! Lege!

While Creation is a pure performative act, and Christ in history and the sacraments are performative signs that make of the Word of God both a sign and a referent for the Christian, conversion is a suspended performative moment that redirects signs toward significance. The conversion scene is a speech act that stands as a divide between the two parts of the *Confessions* – an anatomical cut that reveals a cross section of two texts: the temporal narrative of the conversion (the autobiography of the subject) and what can be termed, using Remo Bodei's suggestive expression, 'the autobiography of God.'[57] It is commonplace in Augustine's scholarship to interpret the 'region of unlikeness,' the narrative of the exterior man contained in Books 1–7, as a realm of loose signs that is not yet referred and compared to the inner truth, as well as a realm of unreferred desire. The famous passage on language learning – which could be summarized as 'I want (lack), therefore I speak'[58] – sets the stage for a process of education that consists of a constitutional misuse of the orders of language and desire. The persistence of the *imago dei* within the individual, although vanishing, much veiled and weighted down by sin, makes of the *perversio* in the first chapters the specular opposite of *conversio* – a 'disorderly order' of signs and things.

Signs and things cannot be transcended in the first section because the order of love is misused (things that should only be used are instead enjoyed), and there unfolds a map of desire as *cupiditas* that extends chronologically from language (and within language from grammar to rhetoric via poetry), to private life, to public life. In the second section (Books 10–13), the narrative of the inner man is detached from time, whose dissolution into silence oozes through Book 9. Here the gaze of the mind, turned inward, begins sorting out signs by consulting the interior teacher. The oft-noted disparity between the two sections of the text is the result of the recapitulation of two different but interrelated discourses: once 'my own beginning' (Book 1) has reached a full stop in conversion, its meaning is diffused 'in the Beginning' (Book 11). The trajectory of conversion orders and articulates the events of a life but also recalls the overarching Christian history, in which the Christ event parallels the moment of conversion.

The conversion scene (Book 8) is prepared and followed by a *balletto* of micro-narratives, organized as an interplay between orality and the written text.[59] In chapter 2, Simplicianus tells the story of Victorinus's conversion, which moves from being a private one to a public one, from a silent profession to a resounding proclamation. In chapter 6, Ponticianus not only relates the story of Antonius but also explains how the written account of Antonius's life was found 'by chance' in a hut and converted two of Ponticianus's colleagues. Augustine's own conversion in turn functions as the blueprint for the conversion of his alter ego, Alypius. Making use of terminology from the *De doctrina christiana*, these narratives function as *res/signa translatae/a*.

Augustine's own conversion is ignited by an uncanny connection between an oral, 'naked' sign and the written text of God (in which signs are things):

> Et ecce audio vocem de vicina domo cum canto dicentis et crebro repetentis quasi pueri an puellae, nescio: 'Tolle lege, Tolle lege.' Statimque mutato vultu intentissimus cogitare coepi, utrumnam solerent pueri in aliquo genere ludendi cantitare tale aliquid, nec occurrebat omnino audisse me uspiam repressoque impetu lacrimarum surrexi nihil aliud interpretans divinitus mihi iuberi, nisi ut aperirem codicem et legerem quod primum caput invenissem. (8.12.29)

> [Suddenly I heard a voice from the nearby house chanting as if it might be a boy or a girl (I do not know which), saying and repeating over and over again 'Pick up and read, pick up and read.' At once my countenance changed, and I began to think intently whether there might be some sort of children's game in which such a chant is used. But I could not remember having heard of one. I checked the flood of tears and stood up. I interpreted it solely as a divine command to me to open the book and read the first chapter I might find.]

In the first sentence, a disjuncture occurs in the relationship between sign and referent. Unable to attach the sound – interestingly androgynous ('pueri an puellae') – to a children's song, Augustine ends up interpreting it as an imperative from God. A short moment, fraught with expectation, stands between the two sides (between the 'cogitare coepi' and the 'repressoque impetu lacrimarum surrexi'). The relation of signification is stripped from the sign, and for a moment the soon-to-be converted character and the reader witness the suspension of the naked sign.

'Tolle! Lege!' as an imperative from God finds its first reference in the story of Anthony, a *signum translatum* that points to Augustine's own story, and matches it even on a textual level through the use of the imperatives (vade, vende, da, veni, sequere, which parallel Augustine's 'tolle! lege!') and in the instantaneousness of conversion:

> Audieram enim de Antonio quod ex evangelica lectione, cui forte super-venerat, admonitus fuerit, tamquam sibi diceretur quod legebatur: '*Vade vende omnia quae habes, da pauperibus et habebis thesaurum in caelis; et veni, sequere me*' et tali oraculo confestim ad te esse conversum. (Ibid.)

> [For I had heard how Anthony happened to be present at the gospel read-ing, and took it as an admonition addressed to himself when the words were read: 'Go, sell all you have, give to the poor, and you shall have trea-sure in heaven; and come, follow me.' By such an inspired utterance he was immediately 'converted to you.']

The detour in Anthony's story is reassuring and instructive: imperatives become actions. Accordingly, 'tolle! lege!' becomes 'arripui, aperui et legi in silentio' ('I grabbed, I read').

> Itaque concitus redii in eum locum, ubi sedebat Alypius; ibi enim posu-eram codicem Apostoli, cum inde surrexeram. Arripui, aperui et legi in silentio capitulum, quo primum coniecti sunt oculi mei: '*Non in comessatio-nibus et ebrietatibus, non in cubilibus et inpudicitiis, non in contentione et aemula-tione, sed induite Dominum Iesum Christum et carnis providentiam ne feceritis in concupiscientiis.*' (Ibid.)

> [So I hurried back to the place where Alypius was sitting. There I had put down the book of the apostle when I got up. I seized it, opened it and in silence read the first passage on which my eyes lit: 'Not in riots and drunken parties, not in eroticism and indecencies, not in strife and rivalry, but put on the Lord Jesus Christ and make no provisions for the flesh in its lusts.']

What Augustine reads is a summary of his previous life and yet another imperative for his future. In the last section of the scene, a sign is inserted in the codex. As with the androgynous voice of the children, it is once again an ambiguous sign ('digito aut nescio quo alio signo').

Nec ultra volui legere nec opus erat. Statim quippe cum fine hiusce sententiae quasi luce securitatis infusa cordi meo omnes dubitationis tenebrae diffugierunt. Tum interiecto aut digito aut nescio quo alio signo codicem clausi et tranquillo iam vultu indicavi[60] Alypio. Ille quid in se agetur (quod ego nesciebam) sic indicavit. Petit videre quid legissem: ostendi et attendit etiam ultra quam ego legeram. Et ignorabam quid sequeretur. Sequebatur vero: '*Infirmum autem in fide recipite.*' Quod ille ad se rettulit mihique aperuit. (8.12.29–30)

[I neither wished nor needed to read further. At once, with the last words of this sentence, it was as if a light of relief from all anxiety flooded into my heart. All the shadows of doubt were dispelled. Then I inserted my finger or some other mark in the book and closed it. With a face now at peace I told everything to Alypius. What had been going on his mind, which I did not know, he disclosed in this way. He asked to see the text I had been reading. I showed him, and he noticed a passage following that which I had read. I did not know how the text went on; but the continuation was 'Receive the person who is weak in faith.' Alypius applied this to himself, and he made that known to me.]

The bookmark can be interpreted as an indication that signs have a new referent (the scriptures and Christ, the inner teacher) and/or of the fact that Augustine himself, when he directs Alypius to the book ('indicavi') is ready to act as a sign in his friend's conversion. Alypius, in turn signals ('indicavit') his thought not by words but by following the 'tolle! lege!' injunction, picking up the book and reading from where Augustine left off. His actions further demonstrate the potentially endless transposition of the model.

Time and the Syllable

The analysis of the semiotic word of humankind and the performative word of God reveals a parallel functioning of speech and universe. The created universe appears as an immense discourse of things. Clouded by original sin, humans are left to interpret it through a rather weak and faulty system of signs. Both things and signs function in a disorganized and insufficient fashion; they remain meaningless and enslaving until

Christ – a complex sign performed in eternity and unfolding in time – provides a sense of direction, establishing an order of things (by marking their syntax as the principal clause) and redirecting signs toward a correct understanding of things.

The main features of speech and universe – time, succession, and order – recall and imply the problem of syntax. Universe and speech are both bound by time, which is in turn an Ur-sign, the sign of all signs, indeed the first of all signs – a trace of eternity, as Augustine describes it in his unfinished book on Genesis: 'ut signum, id est quasi vestigium aeternitatis tempus appareat.'[61] Like every other sign, time is transitive: it cannot but pass and thereby establishes an Ur-syntax in which all other signs are contained and articulated.

Augustine's theory of time, as expressed in Book 11 of the *Confessions*, is recognized as one of the most original and neatest aspects of his philosophy.[62] Framed within a discussion of eternity – Book 11 begins and ends with a reflection on the meaning of Genesis' 'In principio' (11.3 and 30–1) – time is defined in opposition to the stability of eternity ('non autem praeterire quicquam in aeterno, sed totum esse praesens' [11.11.13: 'in the eternal, nothing is transient, but the whole is present']). Time is what cannot be immediately present: 'nullum vero tempus totus esse praesens' (ibid.).[63] As the eternity of the Word of God is described as a simultaneous and eternal discourse (11.7–8), so too time is a speech that needs to unfold and be consumed in order to express meaning. That language is a model for time is well established in Augustinian scholarship. Taking this further, one could say that time *is* language,[64] and its intelligibility is lodged in language's minimal, yet most flexible, unit: the syllable.

In order to exist, the present tense must become past; it must paradoxically tend toward non-existence.[65] However, the present is the only tense that can be said to exist and span in a tri-dimensional way as 'present of the past' (*memoria*), 'present of the present' (*contuitus*), and 'present of the future' (*expectatio*) (11.20.26). Obeying a spatial metaphor that leads from (*ex*) the future, through (*per*) the present, and into (*in*) the past,[66] expectation transfers into memory, so that time becomes a dynamic dimension of the interior man (*distentio animi*)[67] and is measured inwardly: 'in te, anime meus, tempora metior' (11.27.36). The measurement of time is located in a linguistic entity: the syllable – a minimal unit of sound that is not yet a unit of meaning.

In chapter 27 (34–6), where the language model for time is proposed, Augustine focuses on three aspects of language: the sound (*vox corporis*);

the meeting of sound and sign, that is, the first, evanescent instance in which the sound reveals itself as organized into units aiming at meaning (*syllaba*); and finally, the interior aspect of language, that is, the moment in which thought is interiorly clothed by sound (*silentium*). The focus on sound serves to establish a negative paradigm: it is impossible to measure a voice before it sounds and after it has sounded, because in both cases it doesn't exist ('Futura erat, antequam sonaret, et non poterat metiri, quia nondum erat, et nunc non potest, quia iam non est'). Sound might then be measured in the present, but the voice doesn't 'stay' in the present: it moves between future and past ('Sed et tunc non stabat; ibat enim et praeteribat'). It is also impossible to fix and freeze the beginning and ending limits of the sound, because they interact dynamically. This leads to a paradox: time is measured, but not in the future, not in the past, or even in the present.[68]

This impasse is partially resolved by focusing on the syllable, in particular by bringing into play the relation between long and short syllables and, with it, the acknowledgment of difference. While a sound is uniform and undivided ('continuato tenore sine ulla distinctione'), in a verse such as 'Deus creator omnium' one can begin to appreciate the alternance of syllables: the first, third, fifth, and seventh syllables are half the length of the second, fourth, sixth, and eighth. The contrast between two syllables of different length establishes a sense of time, albeit evanescent, that is impressed in memory, where the elusive flowing of time is finally captured and stays 'infixed' ('infixum').[69] This small bit of stability that is achieved by the syllable allows Augustine to anchor much bigger units to memory, such as the impressions of passing things ('Affectionem, quam res praetereuntes in te faciunt et, cum illae praeterierint, manet'). Through the syllable, the material sound that initiated the discussion on time is transcended, and silence falls. In the recess of the interior creature, poems and entire discourses unfold and are measured, so that when Augustine returns to the initial, irreducible sound, it is safely lodged and stabilized in the soul.[70]

The minimal unit of language provides a way out from the isolation and irreducible uniformity of sound toward succession, composition, and difference. Syllables are then framed within a sequence that leads from letters to sentence. The famous example of the recitation of the psalm illustrates the syntax of time, the necessity to pass in order to achieve meaning. Syllables, words, things, lives, all rush to consume their future in order to be meaningful.

Dicturus sum canticum, quod novi: antequam incipiam, in totum exspectatio mea tenditur, cum autem coepero, quantum ex illa in praeteritum decerpsero, tenditur et memoria mea, atque distenditur vita huius actionis meae in memoriam propter quod dixi et in exspectationem propter quod dicturus sum; praesens tamen adest attentio mea, per quam traicitur quod erat futurum, ut fiat praeteritum. Quod quanto magis agitur et agitur, tanto breviata exspectatione prolongatur memoria, donec tota exspectatio consumatur, cum tota illa actio finita transierit in memoriam. Et quod in toto cantico, hoc in singulis particulis eius fit atque in singulis syllabis eius, hoc in actione longiore, cuius forte particula est illud canticum, hoc in tota vita hominis, cuius partes sunt omnes actiones hominis, hoc in toto saeculo *filiorum hominum,* cuius partes sunt omnes vitae hominum. (11.28.38)

[Suppose I am about to recite a psalm which I know. Before I begin, my expectation is directed towards the whole. But when I have begun, the verses from it which I take into the past become the object of my memory. The life of this act of mine is stretched in two ways, into my memory because of the words I have already said and into my expectation because of those which I am about to say. But my attention is on what is present: by that the future is transferred to become the past. As the action advances further and further, the shorter the expectation and the longer the memory, until all expectation is consumed, the entire action is finished, and it has passed into the memory. What occurs in the psalm as a whole occurs in its particular pieces and its individual syllables. The same is true of a longer action in which perhaps that psalm is a part. It is also valid of the entire life of an individual person, where all actions are parts of a whole, and of the total history of 'the sons of men' where all human lives are but parts.]

There is no sense in lingering in the present: it would be tantamount to contentment with one syllable rather than with a beautiful poem in its entirety.

Itaque, ut nonnulli perversi magis amant versum, quam artem ipsam qua conficitur versus, quia plus se auribus quam intellegentiae dediderunt: ita multi temporalia diligunt, conditricem vero ac moderatricem temporum divinam providentiam non requirunt; atque in ipsa dilectione temporalium nolunt transire quod amant, et tam sunt absurdi, quam si quisquam in recitatione praeclari carminis unam aliquam syllabam solam perpetuo vellet audire. Sed tales auditores carminum non inveniuntur; talibus autem rerum aestimatoribus plena sunt omnia; propterea quia nemo est, qui non facile non modo totum versum, sed etiam totum carmen possit audire; totum autem ordinem saeculorum sentire nullus hominum potest. (*De vera religione* 22.43)[71]

[Some perverse persons prefer a verse to the art of versifying, because they set more store by their ears than by their intelligence. So many love temporal things and do not look for divine providence which is the maker and governor of time. Loving temporal things, they do not want the things they love to pass away. They are just as absurd as anyone would be who, when a famous poem was being recited, wanted to hear one single syllable at the time. There are not such hearers of poems, but there are multitudes of people who think in this way about historical events. There is no one who cannot easily hear a whole verse or even a whole poem, but there is no one who can grasp the whole order of ages.]

In emphasizing an inherent need for the succession of (letters into) syllables into words and into discourse, Augustine relies upon the standard grammatical model of antiquity, as received and organized, for instance, by Donatus and Priscian. This fourfold structure of language implies a successive and parallel construction of the elements (letter, syllable, word, discourse).[72] In Priscian the consequence is clear: 'quemadmodum literae apte coeuntes faciunt syllabas et syllabae dictiones, sic et dictiones orationem.'[73]

Augustine draws on this understanding of grammar in the *De ordine*.[74] Later, in adapting the grammatical model to his theology, Augustine privileges the two middle terms, the hinges of sound and meaning, of the interior and exterior aspects of language: syllables and words. Letters, the minimal and numerically fixed unit of language, are too far from meaning: if considered by themselves, they signal indeed the 'death' of meaning.[75] In contrast, syllables are the real centre of Augustine's 'theogrammatical' model. Although still disconnected from meaning, they initiate the process of its construction: they are the limbs of a body (word) that enters a discourse (life). Indeed, some syllables, like the twitching segments of a worm, contain a fragment of signification.[76] As the bearers of inflection and length syllables are, as previously discussed, the prime and pristine example of time, language's constitutional trait. Moreover, in antiquity, syllables were considered the distinctive trait of poetry, the place where grammar and *litteratura* meet. As such, syllables also constitute the connection between language and music.

Augustine's *De musica* (391) – which bridges the project on the liberal arts and later theological implications – reads indeed as a treatise on metrics.[77] In it, the distinction between grammar and music is slight: music is a rational grammar, one that holds to the superior authority of numbers, as opposed to that of the texts of antiquity.[78] The technical reflection on the musical quality of syllables (Books 1–5) blooms in Book 6 into a wide fresco on time, memory, order, and beauty, and the relation between the musical and rhythmic (i.e., 'linguistic') created universe and its ordinator, the eternally quiet God, as it is mediated by universal harmony.

A knot of sound and language, of time and beauty, a promise to be fulfiled in the unfolding itself, syllables are the best example, nay the epitome, of mortality – angels, indeed, read the face of God 'sine syllabis temporum' (*Confessions* 13.15.18).[79] Both evanescent and grounded, syllables exemplify the way mortality interacts through construction with eternity.

The Syntax of Love and Desire in Speech and Universe

The grammatical model for time, founded on the hinge of the syllable, creates for both speech and universe an internal necessity for a syntactical pattern. This syntax counteracts the irreducibility of time by articulating it into meaningful sentences and bestowing to it order and beauty. The rules of this syntax are rooted in love and desire.

In the recurrent comparison between the universe and a poem, Augustine articulates and consolidates two types of order: that of language and that of love. The *ordinata dilectio*, the map of signs and things with which Christians are called to interpret the discourse that leads them back to God, is inscribed in the speech of the universe as the desire, inherent in signs and things, to rush together to form an orderly whole. The pleasure (*delectatio*) that derives from the beauty (*pulchritudo*) of that order functions as a compass. Consider, for instance, the passage from the *Confessions* in which the temporal universe is described in terms of a syntactically organized sentence:

> Quae oriuntur et occidunt et oriendo quasi esse incipiunt et crescunt, ut perficiantur, et perfecta senescunt et intereunt: et non omnia senescunt et omnia intereunt. Ergo cum oriuntur et tendunt esse, quo magis celeriter crescunt, ut sint, eo magis festinant, ut non sint. Sic est modus eorum. Tantum dedisti eis, quia partes sunt rerum, quae non sunt omnes simul, sed decedendo ac succedendo agunt omnes universum, cuius partes sunt. Ecce

sic peragitur et sermo noster per signa sonantia. Non enim erit totus sermo, si unum verbum non decedat, cum sonuerit partes suas, ut succedat aliud. (4.10.15)

[Things rise and set: in their emerging they begin as it were to be, and grow to perfection; having reached perfection, they grow old and die. Not everything grows old, but everything dies. So when things rise and emerge into existence, the faster they grow to be, the quicker they rush towards non-being. That is the law limiting their being. So much have you given them, namely to be parts of things which do not all have their being at the same moment, but by passing away and by successiveness, they all form the whole of which they are parts. That is the way our speech is constructed by sounds which are significant. What we say would not be complete if one word did not cease to exist when it has sounded its constituent parts, so that it can be succeeded by another.]

Like in a reverse binocular, the emphasis shifts from the dispersion of the syllables to the grander discourse in which they are framed. Order and composition emerge in the unfolding, and unity supersedes fragmentation.

Nam et quod loquimur, per eundem sensus carnis audis et non vis utique stare syllabas, sed transvolare, ut aliae veniant et totum audias. Ita semper omnia, quibus unum aliquid constat (et non sunt omnia simul ea, quibus constat) plus delectant omnia quam singula, si possint sentiri omnia (4.11.17).

[The words we speak you hear by the same physical perception, and you have no wish that the speaker stop at each syllable. You want him to hurry on so that other syllables may come, and you may hear the whole. That is always how it is with the sum of elements out of which a unity is constituted, and the elements out of which it is constituted never exist all at the same moment. There would be more delight in all the elements than in individual pieces if only one had the capacity to perceive all of them.]

The order and composition of the single parts is a source of pleasure ('plus *delectant* omnnia quam singula') because order is beauty, and it is, in turn, love. In one of the many variations of the image of speech and universe as parallel ways of unfolding in time, the one we read in the eighth book of the *De natura boni* (399), Augustine argues that there is a kind of beauty ('quaedam in suo genere pulchritudo') in the succession of temporal things. A well-composed speech is beautiful ('sermo bene compositus pulcher est') because syllables and words pass by being born and dying. Accordingly, the beauty of the speech and universe, insofar as it is temporal and transitory, rests precisely in its necessity to 'sound and pass' within the universal order.[80]

According to Augustine, beauty is a matter of proportion and symmetry.[81] Just as a body is more beautiful than its single limbs, so too does beauty rest in the harmony of unity.[82] Beginning already with the early dialogue De ordine (386), which still bears a strong neo-Platonic imprint, the notion of order as beauty is central to Augustine's philosophy. The opening question of the dialogue posits the problem of order in terms of beauty and magnitude: why should the limbs of the flea be so beautifully and clearly disposed, while human life is troubled by inconstancy and turbulence? Order is unity and is managed by God, but the human being is short-sighted before the big picture – like someone who perceives only one tessera of a mosaic floor and, unable to understand the beauty of the whole, blames his own failure on the artist.[83] One should therefore strive for order, searching first among the 'shadows and traces' (2.15.43: 'umbras,' 'vestigia') of it in the sensible word, and retracing from them the clearer image of order as it is found in numbers.[84] The quest of the De ordine is sufficient to recognize the existence of order, yet not sufficient to practise it. The journey from disorder to order cannot be accomplished by reason alone.

Soon after the De ordine, Augustine glues the notion of order to that of love. As discussed before, love and order are brought together in the very first formulation of the uti/frui distinction in the De diversis quaestionibus, and the first book of De doctrina christiana is devoted to a description and systematization of the ordinata dilectio, the order of love that governs the universe. Dilectio, as explained in question 36 of the De diversis quaestionibus, defines the purest aspect of caritas, that which joins the human soul to God.[85] The order of love, then, represents both the trace of God in the universe and the map that allows for its interpretation.

The primary Augustinian image for universal order is the weight of love (pondus amoris), a gravity that drags every element, including the human soul, to its proper place.[86] Its most famous formulation is inscribed in one of the most powerful passages of the Confessions (13.9.10), where the transition from disorder to order entails for the elements a pacification of desire ('inquieta' ... 'quiescunt'):

Corpus pondere suo nititur ad locum suum. Pondus non ad ima tantum est, sed ad locum suum. Ignis sursum tendit, deorsum lapis. Ponderibus suis aguntur, loca sua petunt. Oleum infra aquam fusum super aquam attollitur, aqua supra oleum fusa, infra oleum demergitur; ponderibus suis aguntur, loca sua petunt. Minus ordinata inquieta sunt: ordinantur et quiescunt. Pondus meum amor meus; eo feror quocumque feror.

[A body by its weight tends to move toward its proper place. The weight's movement is not necessarily downwards, but to its appropriate position: fire tends to move upwards, a stone downwards. They are acted on by their respective weights; they seek their own place. Oil poured under water is drawn up to the surface on top of the water. Water poured on top of oil sinks below the oil. They are acted on by their respective densities, they seek their own place. Things which are not in their intended position are restless. Once they are in their ordered position, they are at rest. My weight is my love. Wherever I am carried, my love is carrying me.]

In a beautiful variation of this image in the *De civitate Dei*, Augustine explores the particular momentum of the soul: after recounting the universal desire (of cattle, trees, wind, water, flames) for a proper place and order ('locorum atque ordinis appetitus'),[87] he writes that the soul too desires its place – but its search requires a return toward its own beginning, which implies an orderly interpretation of universal desire. For the human soul, love is the weight that impels the creature to sift hurriedly ('currentes') through the chart of signs and things and collect clues of their desire for order, so that it can climb back toward God.

in his quidem rebus, quae infra nos sunt, quoniam et ipsa nec aliquo modo essent nec aliqua specie continerentur nec aliquem ordinem vel appeterent vel tenerent, nisi ab illo facta essent, qui summe est, qui summe sapiens est, qui summe bonus est, tamquam per omnia, quae fecit mirabili stabilitate, currentes quasi quaedam eius alibi magis, alibi minus impressa vestigia colligamus; in nobis autem ipsis eius imaginem contuentes tamquam minor ille evangelicus filius ad nosmetipsos reversi surgamus et ad illum redeamus, a quo peccando recesseramus. (11.28)

[as we run over all the works which He has miraculously established, let us consider His footprints, as it were, more deeply impressed in one place and more lightly in another, but distinct even in those things which are below us. For such things could not exist in any way, or be contained in any shape, or desire or sustain any order, had they not been made by Him Who supremely is, and Who is supremely wise and supremely good. Contemplating His image in ourselves, therefore, let us, like that younger son of the Gospel, come to ourselves, and arise and return to Him Whom we had forsaken by our sin.]

In another formulation of the image of the *pondus amoris*, contained in the sixth book of the *De musica*, the notion of delight (*delectatio*) – desire as pleasure, desire in sight of fulfilment – is described as the factor that gives order and direction to the soul ('delectatio ordinat animam'):

Non ergo invideamus inferioribus quam nos sumus, nosque ipsos inter illa quae infra nos sunt, et illa quae supra nos sunt, ita Deo et Domino nostro opitulante ordinemus, ut inferioribus non offendamur, solis autem superioribus delectemur. Delectatio quippe quasi pondus est animae. Delectatio ergo ordinat animam. *Ubi enim erit thesaurus tuus, ibi erit et cor tuum:* ubi delectatio, ibi thesaurus: ubi autem cor, ibi beatitudo aut miseria. Quae vero superiora sunt, nisi illa in quibus summa, inconcussa, incommutabilis, aeterna manet aequalitas? Ubi nullum est tempus, quia nulla mutabilitas est; et unde tempora fabricantur et ordinantur et modificantur aeternitatem imitantia, dum coeli conversio ad idem redit, et coelestia corpora ad idem revocat, diebusque et mensibus et annis et lustris, caeterisque siderum orbibus, legibus aequalitatis et unitatis et ordinationis obtemperat. Ita coelestibus terrena subiecta, orbes temporum suorum numerosa successione quasi carmini universitatis associant. (*De musica* 6.11.29)

[Let's not, then, be envious of things inferior to ourselves, and let us, our Lord and God helping, order ourselves between those below and those above us, so we are not troubled by lower, and take delight only in higher things. For delight is a kind of weight in the soul. Therefore, delight orders the soul. 'For where your treasure is, there will your heart be also.' Where delight, there the treasure; where the heart, there happiness or misery. But what are the higher things, if not those where the highest unchangeable undisturbed and eternal resides? Where there is no time, because there is no change, and from where times are made and ordered and changed, imitating eternity as they do when the turn of the heavens comes back to the same state, and the heavenly bodies to the same place, and in days and months and years and centuries and other revolutions of the stars obey the laws of equality, unity, and order. So terrestrial things are subject to celestial, and their time circuits join things together in harmonious succession for a poem of the universe.]

The metre of the poem of the universe, which connects lower and higher bodies, time and eternity, is the equality, unity, and order of the revolution of the stars. The soul partakes of this order through pleasure-desire. *Delectatio*, as Étienne Gilson and Isabel Bochet have remarked, is a very nuanced and lively concept in the works of Augustine.[88] It defines a 'connective' type of pleasure that joins the love and its object, a pleasure-desire that ordinates the direction of the soul on the same wavelength as the beautiful order of the universe. Delight is experienced in the whole, in the unity, in the poem, which shines through beyond the scattered parts. Just as a syllable cannot appreciate the beauty of the ensemble,[89] a single, transient part cannot experience the pleasure of being ordered. But loving earthly things as a means of searching for their superior order is difficult, because it requires a quest for the meaning hidden beyond the construction of words and things.[90] A Christian life itself becomes then a 'holy desire' – 'sanctum desiderium,' as Augustine describes it in a passage of his *Tractates on the First Epistle of John* (407). By postponing fulfilment, by both inflicting the hardships and offering the pleasures of the interpretation of signs and things, God stretches the soul and increases its capacity. Holy desire is hence a form of training that steers the soul away from the love of this world toward the path of an *ordinata dilectio*.[91] The end point of the search is beyond desire and above and outside order: God, the ever quiet, eternally present, simultaneously spoken Word – the recapitulation of the earthly syntax of language and love. The succession of sounds, syllables, and words, the rising and falling of earthly things, all eagerly rush on the evanescent slide of the present in order to be fully past and transferred into meaning. Only when the last word is pronounced does the speech make sense retrospectively in the silence resulting from the full stop.

Of all the many passages that Augustine devotes to silence, the most encompassing is the description of the ecstatic, suspended moment at Ostia in the ninth book of the *Confessions*. Augustine and his mother wish for an imaginary full stop that momentarily silences the syntax of the universe, so that they can contemplate the Word in its eternity and simultaneity. The vision of Ostia should be called indeed an 'audition,' its key words being *silere, tacere, dicere, loqui, audire*. One by one, signs and things 'give their speech' – always the same line, indeed, for the attentive listener ('quoniam si quis audiat, dicunt heac omnia: non ipsa nos fecimus, set fecit nos qui manet in aeternum') – and let their meaning unfold.

> Si cui sileat tumultus carnis, sileant phantasiae terrae et aquarum at aeris, sileant et poli et ipsa sibi anima sileat et transeat se non se cogitando, sileant somnia et imaginariae revelationes, omnis lingua et omne signum et quicquid transeundo fit si cui sileat omnino (quoniam si quis audiat, dicunt heac omnia: 'Non ipsa nos fecimus, sed fecit nos qui *manet in aeternum*') his dictis si iam taceant, quoniam erexerunt aurem in eum, qui fecit ea, et loquatur ipse solus non per ea, sed per se ipsum, ut audiamus verbum eius, non per linguam carnis neque per vocem angeli nec per sonitum nubis nec per aenigma similitudinis, sed ipsum, quem in his amamus, ipsum sine his audiamus. (9.10.25)

> [If to anyone the tumult of the flesh has fallen silent, if the images of earth, water, and air are quiescent, if the heavens themselves are shut out and the very soul itself is making no sound and is surpassing itself by no longer thinking about itself, if all dreams and visions in the imagination are excluded, if all language and every sign and everything transitory is silent – for if anyone could hear them, this is what all of them would be saying, 'We did not make ourselves, we were made by Him who abides for eternity' – if after this declaration they were to keep silence, having directed our ears to Him that made them, then He alone would speak not through them but through Himself. We would hear His word, not through the tongue of the flesh, nor through the voice of an angel, nor through the sound of thunder, nor through the obscurity of a symbolic utterance. He who in these things we love we would hear in person without their mediation.]

Yet this imaginary full stop is usually granted to the individual only at the end of life, when death retrospectively applies meaning to one's discourse. Nothing else can be said, but only then can what has been said so far be integrated and made sense of.

The Analogy

The link that fosters the connection between speech and universe, theory of language and theology is the analogy that Augustine draws between the two human words and the two Words of God. Augustine developed it over time and located it in the inner recess of the creature, that place 'more intimate than the inside' ('intimior intimo meo'), where the image of God resides. Although passing references to the analogy between the two sets of words are often found in Augustine's work, especially with respect to the two key speech acts of Creation and Incarnation,[92] it is only in the *De Trinitate* (Book 15) that the crux of his theory is fully articulated and explained: the notion of the interior human word.[93] Not only does it represent the missing link in the analogy between linguistics and metaphysics, but it also becomes a crucial actor in the extended analogy between the Trinity and the human soul – the process of anamnesis through which the *imago dei* inscribed inside of human beings is brought to light.

The notion of the interior word relies on the Pauline distinction between interior and exterior man. Accordingly, the human being is endowed with two types of word: the word of the mouth (*vox*, the exterior word, 'the word that sounds without,' a mere sound that has different outcomes in different languages); and the word of the heart (*verbum cordis*, the interior word, 'the word that shines within,' a word that belongs to no language and can be compared to interior truth). The word of the mouth is completely subordinate to the word of the heart, and the semiotic universe to which it pertains is inconsistent per se. Likewise, two Words belong to God: the Word *in principio*, which is coeternal with God, and the Word made flesh.

The relationship between the four w/Words is elucidated by Augustine in Book 15 of the *De Trinitate*. The proportion between the two sets of words is given by the system of likeness and unlikeness that governs every relationship between humankind and God, until a vision 'face to face' is allowed after death. First, he relates the interior human word to the Word *in principio* (15.10.19). In order to approximate the Word of God, one has to have an intuition of the inner human word of man in its 'purest' state, before images of its sounds become attached to it and revolve in the mind.

Quisquis igitur potest intellegere verbum, non solum antequam sonet, verum etiam antequam sonorum eius imagines cogitatione volvantur: hoc est enim quod ad nullam pertinet linguam, earum scilicet quae linguae appellantur gentium, quarum nostra latina est: quisquis, inquam, hoc intellegere potest, iam potest videre *per* hoc *speculum* atque *in* hoc *aenigmate* aliquam Verbi illius similitudinem, de quo dictum est: *In principio erat Verbum, et Verbum erat apud Deum, et Deus erat Verbum.*

[Whoever, then, can understand the word, not only before it sounds, but even before the images of its sound are contemplated in thought – such a word belongs to no language, that is, to none of the so-called national languages, of which ours is Latin – whoever, I say, can understand this, can already see through this mirror and in this enigma some likeness of that Word of whom it was said: 'In the beginning was the Word, and the Word was with God; and the Word was God.']

Next Augustine relates the exterior human word to the Word made flesh (15.11.20), the ratio of the analogy here being given by the semiotic quality of the human word as opposed to the performative quality of God's (*vox* versus *caro*).

Proinde verbum quod foris sonat, signum est verbi quod intus lucet, cui magis verbi competit nomen. Nam illud quod profertur carnis ore, vox verbi est, verbumque et ipsum dicitur, propter illud a quo ut foris appareret assumptum est. Ita enim verbum nostrum vox quodam modo corporis fit, assumendo eam in qua manifestetur sensibus hominum; sicut *Verbum Dei caro factum est,* assumendo eam in qua et ipsum manifestaretur sensibus hominum. Et sicut verbum nostrum fit vox, nec mutatur in vocem; ita Verbum Dei caro quidem factum est, sed absit ut mutaretur in carnem. Assumendo quippe illam, non in eam se consumendo, et hoc nostrum vox fit, et illud caro factum est.

[Hence, the word which sounds without is a sign of the word that shines within, to which the name 'word' more properly belongs. For that which is produced by the mouth of the flesh is the sound of the word, and is itself also called 'word,' because that inner word assumed it in order that it might appear outwardly. For just as our word in some way becomes a bodily sound by assuming that in which it may be manifested to the senses of men, so the Word of God was made flesh by assuming that in which He might also be manifested to the senses of men. And just as our word becomes a sound and is not changed into a sound, so the Word of God indeed becomes flesh, but far be it from us that it should be changed into flesh. For by assuming it, not just by being consumed in it, this word of ours becomes a sound, and that Word became flesh.]

The relationships between the four w/Words is represented in figure 1. This interlacing structure operates in analogy (the dotted arrow: between

Figure 1.1: Relationships between the four words/Words

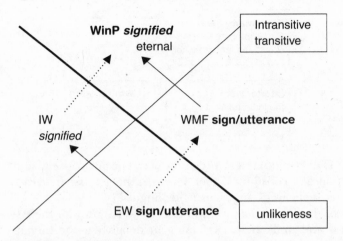

WinP: Word *in principio*
IW: interior word
WMF: Word made flesh
EW: exterior word

WinP and IW, and between EW and WMF), and in signification (between WinP and WMF, and between IW and EW). The two diagonal lines indicate two discriminants: the system of unlikeness keeps the realms of God and humankind discrete, and the opposition between transitive and intransitive (that is, between a word that stays with itself and one that unfolds in utterance) separates the uttered words from the non-uttered words. WinP, the absolute signified, which is only pointed to, and EW, the absolute sign, which only points are two 'pure' terms. In the middle are two hybrid terms, which both point and are pointed to (using a category from Augustine's theory of signs, we might say that they both belong to the realm of *translata*): IW points to WinP analogically and is pointed to by EW in terms of signification, while WMF points to WinP in terms of signification and is pointed to analogically by EW. The two hybrid terms in the figure above are also related when we consider WMF as the referent of IW. Christ, God's utterance, is in fact also the interior teacher of humankind, the consultant and the guarantor of the truth of the interior word.[94] The proportion between the two sets of w/Words can be written with a focus on the similarity between the middle terms as shown in

Figure 1.2: The proportion of the four words/Words

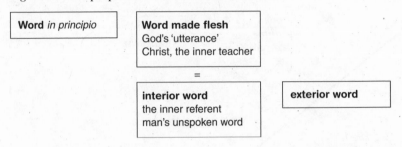

Figure 1.2.[95] The paradoxical Word produced performatively and unfolded semiotically constitutes, therefore, the hinge that holds together and seals the heart of Augustine's theolinguistics.

In Book 15 of the *De Trinitate*, Augustine deals at length with the system of likeness and unlikeness, explaining in detail how the human interior word mirrors God's and the ways in which they differ. As Augustine explains in chapters 8 and 9, likeness itself it twofold: according to Saint Paul's statement, it must be intended *per speculum* (through a mirror, that Augustine explains as an image) *in aenigmate* (a particularly obscure allegory, a likeness that is difficult to understand).[96] The likeness of the w/Words revolves around three main points:

- Both words can 'incarnate.' (The Word incarnates in flesh, the human word in sound.)
- They are coextensive with knowledge.[97]
- They pre-exist action.[98]

In the profound difference between human knowledge and God's knowledge, the aspect of unlikeness unfolds:

- The human word can be false; God's Word is truth (15.15.24).
- In the human word there is a revolving motion (*volubilis motio*) between thought of the thing and the word: therefore it is 'formable.' In contrast, the Word can by no means be called 'thought of God' (15.15–16).[99]
- Only the Word is eternal (15.15).

The system of likeness and unlikeness firmly divides the realms of God and humankind. As Augustine, following Saint Paul, states repeatedly, it collapses only when a face-to-face vision is granted. Then, not only the difficulty of likeness (the *aenigma*), but also some aspects of unlikeness will disappear.[100]

The likeness between the interior word and the Word *in principio* also revolves around the compact and instantaneous quality of their syntax. As discussed earlier, the Word of God with God is one that is 'said eternally and in which everything is said eternally' ('quod sempiterne dicitur et eo sempiterne dicuntur omnia,' *Confessions* 11.7.9). The discourse of the Word is beyond syntax: meaning is achieved 'simul et sempiterne,' with no need to unfold one word after the other until a whole sentence is uttered and 'makes sense' ('Nec finitur, quod dicebatur et dicitur aliud, ut possint dici omnia'). In the absolute signified, the sole and true recipient of the order of the *frui*, all things are contained (and, therefore, said and made) simultaneously and eternally. The word of the heart behaves in a similar way, though on a lesser scale. It is closer to thought than to the sign through which it is uttered.[101] As with the Word, the interior word is not diminished by uttering;[102] it is therefore 'non-transitive,' remaining in the interior self also when spoken. Finally, the interior word can be described as a simultaneous – although not eternal – combination of words, sentence, and discourse, which unfolds to the outside by means of a succession of signs/sounds.

The analogy between the interior word and the Word *in principio* rests on the consideration of the interior word in its purest sense: 'before the images of its sounds are considered in thought,' that is, before the isolated words ('imagines sonorum') start detaching themselves from the interior word and unfold into a sentence. Between the interior word in its purest sense (analogous to the Word *in principio*) and the utterance (analogous to the Word made flesh), stands a transitional phase of language, still interior, yet already scanned into discourse.[103] A lengthy passage from the *De catechizandis rudibus* (circa 400) clearly explains these features of the interior word. This passage (2.3) represents an important *locus* for the discussion of Augustine's theory of language, since it describes, step by step, the evolution from thought to utterance, enriching the standard explanation of the transit between *verbum* and *vox* with revealing details and outlining the actual threefold nature of the human word that is composed of a 'pure' interior word (which Augustine, as we shall see later, calls also *verbum intimum* in the *De Trinitate*), a 'linguistic' interior word, and the exterior word.

Augustine opens his treatise on 'Christian faith for beginners' with some remarks on the constitutional frustration of language: there is, inside the speaker, a much better speech than that which is uttered, a speech so satisfying that the speaker actually approaches it in terms of *frui* ('saepe *fruor* interius'). In the microcosm of language, the interior word is then as intransitive as the Word, not only because it does not leave the inner speaker, but also because it is not bound by the dimension of *uti*.

Nam et mihi prope semper sermo meus displicet. Melioris enim avidus sum, quo saepe fruor interius, antequam eum explicare verbis sonantibus coepero: quod ubi minus quam mihi motus est evaluero, contristor linguam meam cordi meo non potuisse sufficere.

[For my part, I am nearly always dissatisfied with my discourse. For I am desirous of something better, which I often inwardly enjoy before I begin to unfold my thought in spoken words; but when I find that my powers of expression come short of my knowledge of the subject, I am sorely disappointed that my tongue has not been able to answer the demands of my mind.][104]

This intellected word is compared to a flash of light (*coruscatio*) and later called a blow (*ictus*) in which all things to be said are contained in a non-organized fashion. The flash contains a whole speech (*locutio*), which then unfolds into an organized succession of words, which differs from it in duration (*tarda*), extension (*longa*), and quality (*longeque dissimilis*). While the slow speech unfolds, the intuition of it disappears ('dum ista volvitur, iam se ille in secreta sua condidit').[105] Between the quick disappearance of the interior flash and the slow and revolving exterior speech, there stands a crucial phase, the 'operative' aspect of interior language, which is suspended between interior and exterior man, and takes place on the support of memory, the fundamental tenet of Augustine's theory of time, the place where time at once passes and is held. The first blow of intuition imprints *traces* (*vestigia*), which subtend the speech but still belong to no language. These traces then join *syllables*, turning into constructed language.

tamen, quia vestigia quaedam miro modo impressit memoriae, perdurant illa cum syllabarum morulis; atque ex eisdem vestigiis sonantia signa peragimus quae lingua dicitur vel Latina, vel Graeca, vel Hebraea, vel alia quaelibet, sive cogitentur haec signa sive etiam voce proferantur; cum illa vestigia nec Latina, nec Graeca vel Hebrea, nec cuisque alterius gentis sint propria, sed ita efficiantur in animo ut vultus in corpore.

[nevertheless because it has stamped in a wonderful way certain imprints upon the memory, these endure for the length of time it takes to pronounce the words; and from these imprints we construct those audible symbols which are called language, whether it be Latin or Greek or Hebrew, or any other tongue, whether these symbols exist in the mind or are actually uttered by the voice, though these marks are neither Latin, nor Greek, nor Hebrew, nor peculiar to any other race, but are produced in the mind as is the expression of the face in the body.]

Interestingly, these traces resemble a secondary aspect of Augustine's theory of signs –facial expression – which in this context is considered more representative than uttered speech. For example, there is a word for anger in Latin, another in Greek, but they are not as immediate and 'international' as the face of an angry man ('apertus et manifestus vultus').[106]

The construction of language takes place in memory, where the non-organized, all-encompassing intuition meets the minimal unit of time, the syllable. There, the different languages are also stored. Between the initial *corruscatio* and the final *locutio* stands, therefore, a critical passage: when the intuition meets memory, it dives in time, it turns into a proto-sign, analogous in its immediacy to facial expression in the outer person. The *vestigium* is an evanescent sign: it shares with the flash of intuition the fact that it belongs to no language and that it is not yet syntactically organized, and shares with constructed language the fact that it starts aligning itself in time. While the *corruscatio* disappears, the *vestigium* is grounded, 'trapped' so to speak, in the short delays of syllables (*syllabarum morulis*) and, from there, in the familiar process of linguistic construction (words, sentences, speech). As such, the trace subtends utterance, following it syllable by syllable, whether words are actually uttered in sounds or just 'uttered in silence.' For Augustine, in fact, there is no difference between the actual sound (*vox*) and the thought of the sound (*cogitatione soni*).[107] The relation between the *vestigium* and the *syllaba* on the support of memory represents, therefore, the operative aspect of language, which can be figured as:

$$\text{Coruscatio} \leftarrow \text{vestigium} \leftrightarrow \text{syllaba} \rightarrow \text{locutio}$$
$$\text{memoria}$$

The interior word appears thus as a core of meaning, which contains in composition a whole sentence or speech. With the help of traces impressed in the memory (the operative syntactical structure that subtends language), the interior word emerges into memory and unfolds in time in a succession of syllables and words. In its purest sense, before it is 'thought in the fashion of sounds,' the interior word enigmatically mirrors the Word of God with God: as the Word, it is intransitive and is approached in terms of fruition as opposed to use. In its purest sense, as it is described at the end of the *De Trinitate*, the interior word is truly the word of the image of God ('verbum non de Deo natae, sed a Deo factae imaginis Dei') and it is perfectly equal to knowledge ('gignitur de scientia quae manet in animo, quando eadem scientia intus dicitur'). Hence, it is a true word.[108]

Love, Desire, and the Interior Word

The knot of interior word and knowledge is tied by love. Just as the syntax of the universe and of uttered speech is dictated and subtended by an order of love, so too is the birth of the interior word within the individual. This further connection between the system of language and that of love is found in the wider context of the trinitarian analogy, and in the role played by love and desire in the conception of the interior word.

The intimate trinitarian structure of Creation and creature may be regarded as the organizing principle of Augustine's philosophy,[109] and, although it pervades all of Augustine's texts, it is worked out in the difficult and tormented *De Trinitate* (399–421).[110] Traditionally, the work is divided into two sections. The first (Books 1–7) contains a description of the Trinity according to the scriptures and a defence of the trinitarian dogma; the second (Books 8–15) – the original core of the work – inquires into the possibility of human understanding of the Trinity through analogical approximations that are rooted in sensible experience and ruled by the system of likeness and unlikeness.[111] According to Augustine, both universe and the human being bear the structural imprint of the metaphysical Trinity. That trace, although feeble and hidden, becomes the most powerful means of apprehension and knowledge; through it, the human being may come to understand both its innermost interiority and its outermost referent.

Trinitarian analogies proliferate in the universe and in the exterior man,[112] but the best place to approximate the trinitarian relation is the innerness of the self. In the scriptural performative command 'let us make man in *our* image and likeness,' Augustine takes the plural to mean the Trinity itself. The *imago dei* inside of the human being is, therefore, trinitarian in structure, and although deformed by sin, it is never lost. Thus, through Christ and grace it can be reformed.[113] In the second section of the *De Trinitate*, Augustine guides his reader through an intricate interlacing of trinitarian analogies that includes the trinities of the exterior man and the more accurate trinities of the interior man. Trinities are born one from the other with an arpeggio-like progression. All the trinitarian analogies hold to the complex metaphysical strategy of the divine Trinity: the set of relations that God establishes to himself. Although resting on perfect coextensiveness, simultaneity, oneness, eternity, the one essence–three persons unity articulates itself by way of 'missions' (the more evident happenings of God on earth, such as Christ, the Gift of the Holy Ghost, etc.; Books 2–4) and 'processions' (the more cryptic way in which God differentiates himself within his unity; Books 5–7).

Augustine's exposition of the scriptural portrayal of divine relations is a complex and delicate one. An interesting example is the discussion of the scriptural names of the three persons in their relative positioning,[114] where the process of differentiation within unity emerges 'linguistically' as one of expression and binding. The first person, notoriously the most impenetrable, is known as the Father, the Principle, and the Unbegotten: Father in relation to the Son; Principle in relation to what proceeds from him (*De Trinitate* 5.12–14); and Unbegotten – here the discussion becomes more complex – as relative as Begotten (5.6–7). The second person is the most clearly relative and, at the same time, 'expressive': Son in relation to the Father; Word in relation to the mind that expresses it; and Image in relation to the likeness that it expresses.[115] The third person is circular and binding. Known scripturally only as the Holy Ghost, it is also called the Gift and Love. By considering what the terms *gift* and *love* mean in the scriptures, Augustine concludes that the Holy Ghost, the term that donates the gift and the love of God on earth, is Gift and Love within the Trinity. As the love that proceeds from and circulates between the Father and the Son, it acts as an embracing, binding factor between the two.[116]

The passage that perhaps most fully encompasses this complex web of internal relations in the Trinity is Augustine's explanation of Saint Hilary's definition of the Trinity: eternity in the Father, form in the Image, and use in the Gift ('*Aeternitas*, inquit, *in Patre, species in Imagine, usus in Munere*'). Augustine dwells in particular on the second and third terms. The notion of form (*species*) applies to the Son on account of the beauty arising from the perfect harmony, equality, and similarity be-

tween him and the Father.[117] The Son is thus the 'perfect word' ('verbum perfectum') of the Father. He is God's immutable knowledge/dis-
course, immune to time's necessary construction ('et ideo cum
decedant et succedant tempora, non decedit aliquid vel succedit scientiae Dei').[118] Then Augustine moves to describe the ineffable embrace,
the binding, between the Father and the Son. Hilary concisely calls the
third term 'use' (*usus*), while Augustine begins by calling it 'enjoyment'
(*perfruitio*). In order to reconcile the two sides of the order of love
Augustine modulates the vocabulary of love (*caritas, dilectio, delectatio*)
and counterpoints it with that of blessedness (*gaudius, felicitas, beatitudo*). The Holy Spirit is the sweetness that joins begetter and begotten,
which overflows Creation and leads creatures to rush toward (and happily rest in) their proper place.

> Ille igitur ineffabilis quidam complexus Patris et Imaginis non est sine per-
> fruitione, sine caritate, sine gaudio. Illa ergo dilectio, delectatio, felicitas
> vel beatitudo, si tamen aliqua humana voce digne dicitur, usus ab illo
> appellatus est breviter, et est in Trinitate Spiritus Sanctus, non genitus, sed
> genitoris genitique suavitas ingenti largitate atque ubertate perfundens
> omnes creaturas pro captu earum, ut ordinem suum teneant et locis suis
> acquiescant. (*De Trinitate* 6.10.11)

> [This ineffable embrace between the Father and the Image is, therefore,
> not without pleasure, without love or without joy. Consequently this love,
> this delight, this happiness, or this blessedness, if indeed it can be worthily
> expressed by any human word, is briefly defined as Use by the above-men-
> tioned writer. In the Trinity it is the Holy Spirit, who was not begotten but is
> the sweetness of the begetter and the begotten, pouring out on all crea-
> tures according to their capacity, His immense bounty and the fullness of
> His gifts, in order that they may keep their proper order and rest content
> in their proper place.]

The Holy Spirit is both *usus* and *fruitio*, transitive and intransitive. As
binding (*complexus*), it represents the syntax that holds together and
recapitulates the Trinity, yet it also spills over Creation and creature as
the order of love, which organizes the discourse of the universe. The
Holy Spirit is thus the glue (*gluten*) that internally binds the Trinity and
also links it to the created universe.[119] Here Augustine connects the construction of the universe – consisting of unity, form, and of the order
resulting from the physical weight of bodies and the weight of love and

of the pleasure (*delectatio*) in the soul – to the Trinity, of which it represents the trace.[120]

Of the three persons, the first is the most hidden (unbegotten) – a starting point (Principle), an 'a quo' (father); the second is clearly the most expressed (image, Word, Son); and the third is the most recapitulative (love, communion). On these last two rests the dynamic of the trinitarian analogy in the human being. But, although the divine Trinity is differentiated in its inner articulation into expression and binding, it remains irremediably unknowable in its simultaneity, coextensiveness, equality, and eternity. In other words, a 'linguistic' side (expression and binding) is hindered and contradicted by an 'ineffable' side. In contrast, in the trinitarian analogy inside the human being, which culminates in the trinitarian functioning of human thought, the strategy of expression and binding finds support in the two great markers of intelligibility: time and memory. On these transient supports, a veritable syntax is inscribed within the human being – a discourse that is bound together by love and, as such, approximates the inner, defiled *imago dei*.

In order to mirror the divine Trinity, albeit imperfectly ('per speculum in aenigmate'), the internal trinitarian structure is subject to certain constraints. It has to be, somehow, 'triune': the terms must be at the same time differentiated and equal, and they have to form a unity that works in terms of generation (the second term from the first) and procession (the third term from the first and second). The main difference between divine and human trinity stands in the divide between time and eternity and in the fact that while the three divine persons *are* God, the three terms are *part* of the human being but not the human being itself (15.7.11–13).

Augustine's point of departure is the scriptural trinity 'love, the beloved, and the lover' ('amor quod amatur et amans,' 8.10.14), which is the most enigmatic image when referring to the Trinity, and the lowest when referred to the creature.[121] Here love, like the third term in the Trinity, acts as a glue between the lover and the beloved: it joins ('copulat') or desires to join ('appetens copulari') the other two in its embrace. This self-reflecting Trinity generates all the others, love always acting as the means to cohere the other two terms. The process of trinitarian anamnesis begins here, producing, in addition to a number of 'minor' trinities, three main trinities: two in the interior man and, as a detour between them, one in the exterior man.

In order to shift to the second analogy, Augustine discusses a situation in which the mind loves itself (therefore being at the same time *amans* and *quod amatur*). But the mind, Augustine argues, cannot love itself unless it knows itself, and thus he extracts a second trinity: *amor, mens* (*amans*), *notitia* (*quod amatur*). This first trinity is somehow convoluted, and then the mind evolves it into the more accurate *memoria, intelligentia, voluntas,* which is posited for the first time at the end of Book 10 and constitutes, with its variations, the focus of the last Books (12–15). This trinity is the closest possible analogy to the divine within the human (15.5): in it God must be recalled, beheld, and desired in context of the system of likeness and unlikeness (15.20). Before discussing this latter trinity, Augustine enters into a quest for the 'trinity of the exterior man' – choosing vision among other senses and thus sorting the two tercets 'object, vision, attention of the mind' (11.2) and 'image in the memory, gaze of the mind and will' (11.7).[122] Not surprisingly, the transition from the first more convoluted to the second more accurate interior trinity happens via the word.

Augustine devotes the beginning of Book 9 to a discussion of the 'triune' quality of the first interior trinity – *mens, notitia et amor* – considering it an accurate approximation of the divine, since the three terms are one and equal.[123] Furthermore, since the components are connected by generation/expression and binding, this interior trinity holds to the dynamic strategy of the divine. Augustine begins by describing the generation of the second term from the first. The mind bears the knowledge of itself and of things *as a word,* that very inner word that is born from knowledge but does not detach itself when uttered ('atque inde conceptam rerum veracem notitiam tamquam verbum apud nos habemus et dicendo intus gignimus, nec a nobis nascendo discedit,' 9.7.12). This born/expressed knowledge of the mind within itself is the analogical image of the second person of the Trinity. As the Word in the Trinity is then uttered as Christ, so too is the interior word then transferred to the outside by means of signs, turning into the outer word.[124] As the divine Trinity is 'wrapped up' by the Holy Spirit, so too here binding is performed by love: the inner word is knowledge bound with love ('cum amore notitia').

> Verbum est igitur, quod nunc discernere et insinuare volumus, cum amore notitia. Cum itaque se mens novit et amat, iungitur ei amore verbum eius. Et quoniam amat notitiam et novit amorem, et verbum in amore est et amor in verbo, et utrumque in amante atque dicente. (*De Trinitate* 9.10.15)

[The word, therefore, which we now wish to discern and study is knowledge with love. Hence, when the mind knows and loves itself, its word is joined to it by love. And because the mind loves its knowledge and knows its love, then the word is in the love and love in the word, and both are in him who loves and who speaks.]

In the binding act of love, however, also lies the possibility of both (re)forming and undoing the inner trinity. Like the second person of the divine Trinity, the word has to be generated. The interior word, which rules human words and actions (both rightful and wrongful; 9.7.12), undergoes in fact a process of conception and birth. The first step, conception, happens in love, although love is split into the two opposites *caritas* and *cupiditas* – *caritas* being a rightful application of the order of love (when a creature is either used or enjoyed but in reference to the creator), and *cupiditas* being an abuse of the same order (when a creature is enjoyed per se).[125] The second step, the birth of the word, happens 'when the thought is pleasing': at this point love binds the word to the mind that generated it – the firmness of love's operation being underlined by the series 'coniungit,' 'complexu,' and 'costringit.'

Nascitur autem verbum, cum excogitatum placet, aut ad peccandum, aut ad recte faciendum. Verbum ergo nostrum et mentem de qua gignitur, quasi medius amor coniungit, seque cum eis tertium complexu incorporeo, sine ulla confusione constringit. (9.8.13)

[But the word is born when that which is thought pleases us, either for the purpose of committing sin or of acting rightly. Love, therefore, as a means, joins our word with the mind from which it is born; and as a third it binds itself with them in an incorporeal embrace, without any confusion.]

Depending on whether it is conceived in *caritas* or in *cupiditas*, the word can be born either in unity – a pacified, perfect word in which *voluntas*, the will, and *notitia*, the knowledge, are coextensive; or in fracture – an unbalanced word conceived in lust and born in attaining ('cupiendo concipitur, adipiscendo nascitur').[126] The word conceived *in caritate* follows a pattern of conception and birth that preserves the image of the divine Trinity, whereas the word born *in cupiditate* conceived as an abuse of the order of *frui* is projected in the outer realm of the signs, increasing its entropy and deforming and debasing the *imago dei*.[127]

In the final part of Book 9 and at the beginning of Book 10, Augustine closely considers the binding quality of love within the first trinitarian analogy. In order to mirror the divine Trinity, the third term must
proceed from the first two and not be generated from them. Augustine
explains the workings of love through the process of learning, which
can be summed up as 'desire triggers, love encloses.' Love is split in two:
as desire, it is linked to the first term (the mind, the 'father'); as love it is
linked to the second term (the generated knowledge/word, or, better,
the known word, the 'son'). Learning, as knowing, is a form of generation – as the similarity between finding (*reperire*) and generating (*parere*)
confirms.[128] Learning and knowledge are preceded by a desire inherent
in the mind itself. When something is unknown, the mind desires to
know it, to find it; to generate it – in other words, to *express* it ('Quae
autem reperiuntur, quasi pariuntur, unde proli similia sunt. Ubi nisi in
ipsa notitia? Ibi enim quasi expressa formantur'). This desire (*appetitus*)
proceeds ('procedit') from the seeker; it remains in suspense ('pendet
quodam modo') and restlessly tends toward its goal ('neque requiescit
fine quo intenditur'), until it joins ('copulatur') with the desired thing.
Desire – which can be called also *voluntas* or *studium* – is not love, but it
is of the same kind of love.[129] Desire is the love of the unknown; it is love
displayed in a tension that pursues the object and, once it has gained it,
encloses it in its own circular embrace and makes it the expressed offspring of the mind.

> Partum ergo mentis antecedit appetitus quidam, quo id quod nosse volu-
> mus quaerendo et inveniendo, nascitur proles ipsa notitia; ac per hoc
> appetitus ille quo concipitur pariturque notitia, partus et proles recte dici
> non potest. Idemque appetitus quo inhiatur rei cognoscendae, fit amor
> cognitae, dum tenet atque amplectitur placitam prolem, id est notitiam,
> gignentique coniungit. Et est quaedam imago Trinitatis, ipsa mens, et noti-
> tia eius, quod est proles eius ac de se ipsa verbum eius, et amor tertius, *et
> haec tria* unum atque una substantia. Nec minor proles dum tantam se novit
> mens quanta est; nec minor amor, dum tantum se diligit quantum novit et
> quanta est. (9.12.18)

> [A kind of desire, therefore, precedes the birth in the mind, and by means
> of it, that is, by our seeking and finding what we wish to know, an offspring,
> namely, knowledge itself is born. Therefore, that desire by which knowl-
> edge is conceived and born cannot be rightly called a 'birth' and 'off-
> spring'; and this same desire by which one yearns for the knowledge of the

thing becomes love of the thing when known, while it holds and embraces the beloved offspring, that is, knowledge, and unites it to its begetter. And so there is a certain image of the Trinity: the mind itself, its knowledge, which is its offspring, and love as a third; these three are one and one substance. The offspring is not less, while the mind knows itself as much as it is; nor is the love less, while the mind loves itself as much as it is.]

In Book 10 Augustine dwells on the example of learning through signs. The arguments of the *De magistro* (learning does not depend on signs but on things) and of the *De doctrina christiana* (the first step in the correct process of learning stands in the knowledge that signs are signs and as such necessarily point to something else) are enriched here by the notion of desire. Augustine explains that the reference for 'temetum,' an ancient and unusual word for 'wine,' is initially unknown. Precisely by being a sign, the unknown word alerts the desire of the mind. The fact that it is made up of letters and divided into three syllables, suggesting that this sound might indeed be a sign of something else, is enough to inflame the desire of the mind. The exterior word, the imperfect, limited, outer representation, generates the desire for perfect, coextensive, inner knowledge: the interior word.

Iam itaque oportet ut noverit signum esse, id est, non esse inanem illam vocem, sed aliquid ea significari; alioquin iam notum est hoc trisyllabum, et articulatam speciem suam impressit animo per sensum aurium. Quid amplius in eo requiratur, quo magis innotescat, cuius omnes litterae omniaque soni spatia nota sunt; nisi quia simul innotuit signum esse, movitque sciendi cupiditatem, cuius rei signum sit? Quo igitur amplius notum est, sed non plene notum est, eo cupit animus de illo nosse quod reliquum est. Si enim tantummodo esse istam vocem nosset, eamque alicuius rei signum esse non nosset, nihil iam quaereret, sensibili re, quantum poterat, sentiendo percepta. Quia vero non solum esse vocem, sed et signum esse iam novit, perfecte id nosse vult; neque ullum perfecte signum noscitur, nisi cuius rei signum sit cognoscatur. Hoc ergo qui ardenti cura quaerit ut noverit, studioque accensus insistit, num potest dici esse sine amore? (10.1.2)

[He must, for that reason, already know that it is a sign, namely, that it is not a mere sound, but that it signifies something. This word of three syllables is in other respects already known, and has impressed its articulated form on his mind through the sense of hearing. What more can be acquired for this greater knowledge, if all the letters and all the spaces of sound are already known, unless it shall have become known to him at the same time that it is a sign, and shall have moved him with the desire of knowing the thing of which it is the sign? Hence, the more a thing is known, but not fully known, the more the mind desires to know the rest. For if he knew that it was only a sound, and did not know that it was a sign of something, he would seek no further, since he had perceived the sensible thing in his consciousness as far as he could. But because he already knew that it was not only a sound, but also a sign, he wished to know it perfectly. But no sign is known perfectly if it is not known of what thing it is a sign. If anyone, therefore, applies himself with ardent diligence to know, and inflamed with zeal continues this search, can he be said to be without love?]

The sign (the 'unknown' *temetum*) moves the mind's desire, while the thing (the 'known' *temetum*) moves love, which binds together the mind and the knowledge, pointing to the greater significance of knowledge itself. What the mind loves and desires, then, is not the sign in and of itself, but the intuition that beyond it lies a web of signification, 'the beauty of a science that encloses the knowledge of all signs' and allows for communication.[130] A truly universal grammar is thus inscribed as a form of beauty ('peritiae pulchritudo') in the human being. The root of desire and that of language are one and the same.[131]

The same recapitulative strategy also applies to self-knowledge – the necessary *intentio* of the mind within itself – which promotes the transition to the second, more accurate, internal trinity: *memoria, intelligentia, voluntas*. Inherent in the mind is the desire to know itself, and self-knowledge is generated from this inherent desire. From both the mind and its object of desire (self-knowledge) proceeds the love that binds them. Just as the sign, by being a sign, activates the desire for learning the thing to which it refers, so too is there a trace impressed in the memory of the creature that activates the process of self-knowledge and of the attempted knowledge of God: the memory of the self is the memory of the lost image of God.[132] Although debased and disfigured, and risking a plunge into the abyss from which it was once rescued,[133] the image of God is immortally impressed in the creature. It is so powerful that it is able to join creature and Creator.[134] Hidden in the deepest interiority of the self, it elicits a desire to be known, thereby activating a productive process of reformation that leads from the 'deformis forma' to the 'forma formosa' (*De Trinitate* 15.8.14). This is the same place, a deepness

more hidden and secret than memory ('abstrusior profunditas memo-
. riae nostrae'), where the interior word in the purest sense – indeed a
verbum intimum – resides.

Sed illa est abstrusior profunditas nostrae memoriae, ubi hoc etiam primum cum cogitaremus invenimus, et gignitur intimum verbum, quod nullius linguae sit, tamquam scientia de scientia, et visio de visione. (*De
Trinitate* 15.21.40)

[But there is a more profound depth of our memory, where we also find
those contents which we think of for the first time, and where the inner
word is begotten which does not belong to the language of any nation, as it
were, knowledge of knowledge, vision of vision.]

Like in the language model outlined in the *De catechizandis rudibus*,
memory works as an interface between knowledge of the outside word –
since the signs are glued to it by love and become interior discourse –
and the anamnesis of the image of God, which surfaces toward it from
an even more interior layer ('intimior intimo meo'). Both knowledges
are summoned and articulated by desire. Memory, time, and articulated
interior language act therefore as the medium that glues together the
abstruse, abyssal profundities of the human being, where the intimate
word in its purest sense and the image of God reside and the transient
beauty and the necessary mortality of the uttered construction of speech
and universe.

The arduous discussion of the *De Trinitate* itself dissolves into prayer.[135]
After all the effort and the desire to understand, the quest is still unfulfilled. In commenting on the first epistle of John, Augustine remarked
that the life of the Christian – indeed his or her commitment – is desire,
which dilates the soul and makes it able to receive the vision of God. At
the end of the *De Trinitate*, desire and language converge. As long as one
speaks inwardly, one desires, and a prayer is a form of ever-burning,
extended desire directed toward God ('interior sine intermissione oratio, quae est desiderium').[136] Hence Augustine prays for more strength,
begging to be freed from the multitude of words and thoughts. He prays
ardently for a full stop that will put an end to all the words in order to
leave space for their unique and univocal meaning: the one w/Word
with which the blessed simultaneously and eternally praise God. 'Sine
fine dicemus': the unfolding one after the other of many words ceases

('cessabunt multa'), and one simultaneous word is uttered – a word
that, like the Word of God, has no need for succession and a full stop in
order to express its meaning – a word that 'makes' by saying: 'et in te
facti etiam nos unum.'[137] With this one word, desire as longing ceases
and becomes fulfilment.

Within Augustine's 'chain doctrine,' his linguistic thought has dragged
and conflated many links, so that, more than a link, it looks like the
chain itself. Augustine's reflection on language encompasses two syntaxes: one belonging to the most sacred and secret recess of the inner
man, the other belonging to the universe as an order of love that organizes signs and things. The Word/Christ is at the centre of both, and the
movement of desire connects them. In human language, which closely
mirrors the Word of God, a syntax of parallel order and construction
subtends speech syllable by syllable: it carries and harmonizes signs
through time and leads them to silence and meaning. In the same way,
the Word of God, a simultaneous and eternal discourse, subtends the
temporal universe 'thing by thing' and thereby realizes the beauty and
order of a discourse that must be interpreted through a grammar of
love (the distinction between use and enjoyment). God imparts order to
the poem of history, in which the Word made flesh plays a very special
role. As God's sign to humankind, Christ acts in history as a full stop: he
interrupts the endless linearity of time (as conversion interrupts linearity in the individual's life) and inserts there a pause from which meaning unfolds retrospectively as recapitulation. As the referent of human
knowledge and truth, Christ draws an unmistakable, unchanging line
between the 'true' word and the world of the Christian, and the fallen
word and the world of sin. While the syntax of speech and universe
progresses as a parallel construction of letters, syllables, words, and sentences (things, events, ages) and is directed and interpreted by a linear
notion of love (*ordo, pondus*), another syntax is at work inside the creature, one that works as a glue (*gluten*) and progresses by means of
expression and binding, which love seals circularly. The Trinity and the
interior man are articulated by a strategy of expression (the word) and
binding (love). The third term acts as a glue, providing internal recapitulation – the embrace between Father and Son, and between mind and
(self-) knowledge – and also the articulation toward the unfolding of
Creation as/and speech. In the inner creature, as in the universe, the
grammar of love and desire is inscribed.

2 Modistae: The Syntax of Nature

Movement and desire, and with them time and mortality, are still at stake when the notion of syntax is examined from the point of view of grammar – the bottom discipline in the medieval system of knowledge, and the inverse discourse with respect to theology, as it deals with words as opposed to the Word. Medieval grammatical thought waxes with Latin language and wanes with universal language. Among the disciplines of the medieval system of knowledge, grammar appears as both the most necessary and the most dormant, with two significant exceptions: an initial descriptive position, with the systematization of the rules of classical Latin by the last grammarians of antiquity, Donatus (fourth century) and Priscian (sixth century), who provided the centuries to come with the basic textbooks of grammar; and a normative conclusion with the quest for rules of a universal language within the same Latin language by the grammarian-logicians of the twelfth and thirteenth centuries. It is within this last burst of scholastic inquiry that syntax acquired a very prominent place in the theorization of the Modistae, a group of grammarians operating mostly in Paris at the end of the thirteenth century. Syntax is the main concern – and indeed the end point – of the linguistic theory of the Modistae, who conceived of words as components of speech and studied the way they interact syntactically through their *modi significandi*. This new grammar is a speculative science, its subject matter being the abstraction of a natural operation: the one, universal, and innate structure of language that is only later diversified into different languages, which are viewed as mere accidents of the substantial core. Although the writings of the Modistae are strictly technical, and none of them are particularly generous with extra-grammatical information, their system appears deeply rooted in logic and establishes a lively relationship with the new sciences flourishing in Paris upon the arrival of the 'new' Aristotelian texts.

The philosophical grammar of the Modistae is based upon the notions that reality and language are coextensive and that it is possible to cross from one to the other through a process in which the mind acts as a filter. Language formation is a three-step process that relies on the analogy between the modes of being (*modi essendi*), the modes of understanding (*modi intelligendi*), and the modes of signifying (*modi significandi*). The system of the *modi* both reinforces and alters the traditional correspondence between *res* and *verba*. What mind understands and language expresses is not the *res* itself, but one of its modes of being – the thing-as-noun, the thing-as-verb, etc. Consignification, not signification, is the rationale of the *modi*. Thus Modistic language captures and finalizes not the happening of one object/concept into one word, but what in mind and in reality is a discourse, an articulated mode of being and of thought.

Modistic grammar encompasses two core aspects: a process of language that leads from object (*res*) to syntactically operative expression (*pars orationis*), and a syntax proper that is divided into three hierarchically arranged steps (*constructio, congruitas, perfectio*). Language, then, results from the intersection of two linear forces: the horizontal progress of the *modi* (from *res* to *pars orationis*) intersects the vertical movement of syntax at the pivotal point of the *pars orationis*. The three modes are discrete and proportional. While they derive from one another, they do not disappear into each other. On the contrary, the movement of syntax is a vertical one – an ascension 'per gradus' (from *constructio* to *perfectio*) – that requires the former level to be incorporated and overcome by the latter. The composition of the two forces yields to a circular movement whose centre is the *pars orationis*, the intersection between the end point of the horizontal process (representing as such the form of the thing coming into expression) and the starting point of the ascension (representing as such the potentiality of syntax, a *constructibilis*).

Once brought to perfection, the system of language does not hark back to the thing itself but to the mind – the finality of grammar being the perfect expression of the concept. The mind integrates reality and language and grants the circle a new opening. Rather than a circle, then, Modistic language is best represented by a wheel, an image that conjures the idea of both a metaphysical uniform circularity and a phys-

Figure 2.1: The circular movement of language

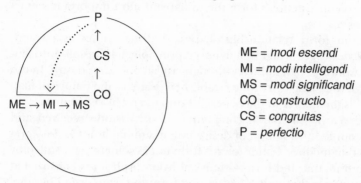

ME = *modi essendi*
MI = *modi intelligendi*
MS = *modi significandi*
CO = *constructio*
CS = *congruitas*
P = *perfectio*

ical, linear thrust forward.[1] Movement is indeed an important constituent of Modistic grammar. Albeit working on an abstracted, 'substantial' version of a universal language, the Modistae promote a language of accident (and therefore of movement and time), as opposed to one of substance, since late medieval grammar reinterprets the roles of noun and verb, the two most important parts of the speech, and installs the verb – as movement, succession, and *fieri* – at the centre of the sentence. Moreover, the Aristotelian model for motion, featured as a satisfaction of a potentiality between a principle and a terminus, sustains the Modistic notion of syntax.

In the course of this chapter's discussion I will emphasize the modalities by which reality becomes language and language shapes reality. With this, I by no means intend to portray the Modistae as extreme realists (which they were not), but rather aim to show how the osmotic relationship that grammar establishes with the rest of the system of knowledge (especially with logic and natural science) fosters a theory of language that is closely patterned after the laws of nature – and, on the other hand, how nature, seen from the perspective of grammar, appears as syntactically organized. More surprising than the reification of language, the 'linguistification' of reality takes place in Modistic theory. One particular device pervades Modistic syntax and trespasses and transcends its employment as terminology to become the primary blueprint of the new theory of language: hylomorphism. The way matter and form come together to form a composite in nature imprints and illustrates some crucial loci of the new grammar: the relation between noun and verb in morphology; the way syntax is constructed in reality; and the way

in which in *constructio*, the first and most crucial step of sentence formation, the two constructibles form the initial and most important syntactic microcosm.

The matter–form relationship shapes Modistic syntax as passion,
unorthodoxically governed by a material principle, and installs into language the workings of a hidden although crucial operator: desire. In the
first book of the *Physics*, Aristotle established desire as the nature of matter: matter is the matrix in the genesis of things, and its very nature is 'to
desire and yearn.'[2] Medieval commentators of Aristotle received and
partially modified this notion of desire by envisioning it not as a natural
operation that inclines matter toward form but as something instilled by
God in both matter and form.[3] Medieval hylomorphism is constructed
around the desire that unites matter and form to create order, by compelling everything to eventually find a proper place in the universe.
Albertus Magnus, for instance, associates the unfolding of desire with
motion: desire is a movement that mutually and exclusively joins matter
and form. Insofar as it represents the essence of motion, matter desires
to turn into a more perfect state.[4] Form, as the end point of the movement and the quenching of matter's desire, represents the 'desirable'
('appetibile') of the process.[5] Form desires neither matter nor transmu-
tation but the 'continuation' of the state of perfection:

> Adhuc autem non est desiderium nisi ad duo, scilicet ut continuetur esse,
> et hoc est desiderium rei perfectae, et ut transmutatio fiat ad esse, et hoc
> est desiderium rei imperfectae. (*Physica* 1.3.17)

> [Desire only tends toward two things: to continue, and this is the desire of
> the perfect thing, and to transmute into being, and this is the desire of the
> imperfect thing.]

Hylomorphic desire is then twofold: it is the lack that pushes matter
toward form and the extended fulfilment (as continuation of desire) of
form. In the Aristotelian-Scholastic construction of reality this desire
affects everything by continuously tightening the binding of matter and
form – it represents indeed the will of God happening on earth. In
grammar, desire moves matter and form, combining them into construction. Syntax then appears as an (any other) ineluctable necessity of
nature. As the force that compels material and formal elements to
cleave together and that yearns for the stability of the form, syntax represents the desire of language itself. The wheel of language is also a

wheel of desire: the final completion of the sentence is the culmination of a circular movement propelled by two kinds of desire: the linear appetite that unites matter and form, and the circular, recapitulative desire of the mind – the pleasure and fulfilment of language that takes place in communication.

The Modistae

The grammar of *modi significandi* can be described as a stream of thought that was rooted in the twelfth century and crossed into the thirteenth. It involves a wide corpus of authors, many unpublished, and many anonymous. G.L. Bursill-Hall, elaborating on the work by Jan Pinborg, has conveniently organized the history of grammar in the late Middle Ages into six periods and sets of authors, as follows:

1 Retention of old definition: Priscian and Donatus
2 Fusion of grammatical and logical termini: Abelard, Anselm, William of Conches, Gilbert de Poitiers, Hugh de St Victor, Berengar of Tours
3 Grammar established as autonomous, though logical terms preserved and incorporated into grammatical metalanguage: Petrus Helias
4 Introduction of the idea of a universal grammar: Jordan of Saxony
5 Refinement of a universalist concept and extension of the modus significandi, which served to refine the description of word-classes: Nicholas of Paris, Lambert of Auxerre, Robert Kilwardby
6 Synthesis of Modistae, producing a unified grammatical theory: Martin of Dacia, Boethius of Dacia, Michel de Marbais, Sigier de Courtrai, Thomas of Erfurt[6]

The grammatical thought of the twelfth and thirteenth centuries falls into two categories. 'Speculative grammar' is the broader, and at times elusive, term that embraces the evolution of grammatical thought from descriptive to normative and toward the notion of a universal language ruled by the modes of signifying. The term *Modistae*, on the other hand, connotes a relatively distinct set of authors who refined and systematized the *modi significandi* with an emphasis on syntax, developing a stable and homogeneous model between 1260/70 (with Martin of Dacia, the first 'official' Modista) and the first quarter of the thirteenth century (with Thomas of Erfurt, who probably wrote his treatise around 1310 and is traditionally considered the last Modista, while Sigier of Courtrai, who died in 1341, is considered almost an epigone). In reference to this later, more cohesive group, speculative grammarians are often collectively known as pre-Modistae. The grammar of the *modi significandi* had a long gestation, a quick consolidation, and was swiftly out-fashioned. In the years 1320–30, attacks on Modistic grammar came from different speculative trends and targeted the very foundation of their theory: the universality of language (against which the critics argued that universality belonged only to thought) as well as their non-economical explanations of linguistic facts.[7] Harsh criticism from both the realist and the nominalist side silenced for many centuries that grand and tortuous monument of grammatical thought.

In recent years, the Modistae have enjoyed renewed attention. Besides the sporadic (and philologically flawed) interest of philosophers of language such as Charles S. Peirce and Martin Heidegger (both of whom mistook Thomas of Erfurt's *Grammatica speculativa* as a work by Duns Scotus) and most recently of Jacques Derrida,[8] the Modistae have been studied by linguists and scholars of medieval philosophy and logic and have been considered under three main aspects. Substantial scholarly effort has been devoted to the admirable enterprise of editing, describing, and classifying the work of the Modistae down to the smallest technical detail.[9] The basics of this complex, recalcitrant, and often confounded system are now thoroughly outlined and the often unstable technical vocabulary that the Modistae employed has been elucidated. The modern project of systematizing Modistic thought was in part spurred by the enthusiasm in comparing and contrasting the Modistic theory of language with twentieth-century grammatical theory, especially Noam Chomsky's generative grammar.[10] However, there is now consensus that this comparison works only in the most general terms – namely around the idea(l) of a universal grammar that is located in the deep structure of a language and assumes different aspects on the surface. This notion, as many have pointed out, is commonplace in medieval thought, which just as easily makes Augustine a precursor of Chomsky. Nonetheless, such general terms are a fascinating indication of the similarities between pre-modern and postmodern quests for an ideal language. Finally, following de Chenu's illuminating input into the importance of the relationship between grammar and theology and de Rijk's monumental work on terministic logic and its relationship to grammar, scholars have laboured to contextualize the grammar of the *modi significandi* in the late medieval system of knowledge. Placing the Modistae in context in this way reveals the osmotic and lively participation of grammar in the late medieval system of knowledge.[11]

My examination of the Modistae here is based on both descriptive and interpretive trends. Rather than focusing on those sections of the treatises that are devoted primarily to rules, I will concentrate on the points where cracks appear in the system and links to a wider discourse are shown. I explore the Modistae as an intellectual system – not as a group of authors – and as the culmination of a complex progression of late medieval reflections on language and syntax. Repetition and analogy run through the laborious evolution of late medieval grammar, and originality is scarce and often sporadic, both among the Modistae themselves and the speculative grammarians who preceded them. Of great interest is the way in which the Modistae produced a homogeneous system by integrating many concepts that had been elaborated in various disciplines throughout the centuries – and that often have elusive origins – and the way in which the emphasis on syntax gives their work coherence. I will focus mainly on a set of seven authors: Martin of Dacia, author of *Modi significandi*; Boethius of Dacia, author of *Modi significandi sive quaestiones super Priscianum maiorem*; John of Dacia, author of a *Summa grammatica*; Simon of Dacia, author of *Quaestiones super secundum minoris Prisciani*; Radulphus Brito, author of *Quaestiones super Priscianum minorem*; Thomas of Erfurt, author of *Modi significandi sive grammatica speculativa*; and Sigier of Courtrai, author of *Summa modorum significandi*.[12] Notwithstanding the technical differences between specific authors, it is commonly believed that the Modistae's basic system is homogeneous and its founding issues held valid by all the grammarians. Within this group, Boethius dwells at greatest length on the theoretical problems of grammar, while Thomas presents a very unified theory that is considered a useful synthesis of the previous Modistae. For these reasons Boethius and Thomas are often viewed as representative of the whole group.

The general features of the treatises confirm the substantial unanimity of the grammarians. The titles themselves (either *Modi significandi* or *Quaestiones supra Priscianum/Donatum*) reveal one of the Modistae's basic qualities: the raw material for the grammarians still consists of the linguistic system of antiquity,[13] which is reduced to its bare bones through the logical proceeding of the *quaestio* and reinterpreted by the notion of *modi significandi*. Their discussions often cover first the justification of the new notion of grammar and the functioning of language (*de gramatica in generali*), then a description of morphology (*etymologia*) and, finally, syntax (*diasyntetica*).[14] Rather than offering the traditional description of grammar, the Modistae propose a *theory* of grammar, which relies on the existence of a core unchanging structure of language.

Thus, the Modistae target a universal grammar – a mirror image of reality – and are concerned with neither the array of different languages, nor with phonology. The differences between specific languages are considered mere accidents of the core system, and the sound part of the voice (*vox unde sonum* as opposed to *vox significativa*) is for them the domain of the natural scientist rather than the grammarian.

The end of the thirteenth century when the Modistae flourished in Paris was a period during which heated philosophical debate reached one of its all-time highs in Western culture. Although the channels through which a whole new Aristotelian corpus penetrated the heart of the West from Greece, Spain, Italy, and the Arabic world is still in part unknown, the panorama of its reception, assimilation, and later rejection in Paris is today very clear, and is considered one of the most crucial cultural transitions of Western thought.[15] The bulk of the new Aristotle – consisting of *logica nova* (*Analytics, Topics, Elenchi*), *libri naturales* (*Physics, De anima, De sensu et sensatu, De memoria et reminescentia, De generatione et corruptione, Parva naturalia*, just to mention the most relevant), and the new, enlarged version of the *Metaphysics* – was already available in Paris at the beginning of the thirteenth century. The thirties of the same century, however, saw a new set of translations and commentaries, mostly connected to the work of Averroes, which renewed intense interest and gave rise to a fracture among philosophers, between the most radical faction, known as Averroism or radical Aristotelianism, whose leaders were Sigier of Brabant and the Modista Boethius of Dacia,[16] and the supporters of a more orthodox Aristotelianism, mediated through faith, as Thomas Aquinas.

The history of Aristotle's reception in the West is understood mainly through the history of three sets of prohibitions of his texts. The first condemnation, dated 1210/15, mainly targeted the *libri naturales* and was reinforced in 1228/31, when Pope Gregory IX established a commission 'to purge the errors of Aristotle.' While the first two sets of prohibitions did not seriously challenge the interest in the 'new' Aristotle, the third set (13 propositions condemned in 1270; 219 propositions condemned in 1277) succeeded in banishing the most heterodox aspects of Aristotelianism from the university, and, one may add, from Western thought. The radical Averroistic propositions (and with them some Thomistic and more orthodox ones) targeted by the 1277 condemnation revolve mainly around issues derived from the reflection and commentary on Aristotle's *libri naturales* (chiefly the *Physics*) and the

De anima. The most delicate and dangerous 'heresies' addressed questions such as the eternity of the world, determinism, and monopsychism. Although ties between the Paris condemnations (7 March 1277) and the one that took place in Oxford eleven days later (18 March 1277) are not completely traceable, this latter set of propositions shows a considerable focus on problems of grammar. Among the thirty items condemned (not as heretical, but as 'manifestly false') by Archbishop Robert Kilwardby, himself a speculative grammarian, four pertain to grammar, nine to logic, with emphasis on the referential aspect of language, and the rest to natural science.[17]

Although radical Aristotelianism was not particularly concerned with grammar, and the Modistae were quite traditional and orthodox in their statements on grammar, which are narrowly concentrated on linguistic matter, still they appear not to be immune to the intense cultural debate happening around them. As we shall see in more detail, the grammarians were influenced by the complex cultural transaction surrounding them and revealed awareness of the texts of the new Aristotle and of the commentaries related to them, incorporating some of the ideas in their theory of language.

The relationships between grammar, logic, and the new sciences is suggestively illustrated by Henri d'Andeli's *La bataille des sept ars*, written in the second quarter of the thirteenth century.[18] The French trouvère describes a battlefield clash of two schools: Paris, where philosophy and logic have downgraded the study of the *auctores*, and Orléans, where grammar is still in the service of literature. On the side of Orléans we find Grammar, with Donatus, Priscian, and an army of classical *auctores*; on the side of Paris, Logic (with her 'champions' Plato and Aristotle), and the 'new' sciences (Physics and Medicine and 'Necromancy'[19]). The four sciences of *quadrivium* do not participate in the quarrel but are present on the battlefield, while Theology hides in a wine-cave. At the end of the battle Grammar is conquered and goes into exile but promises a victorious comeback within the next thirty years; a prophetic (although not timely) announcement of the humanistic refutation of scholastics.[20]

Grammar and the System of Knowledge

Grammar, according to the Modistae, bears a twofold meaning: on the one hand it is a synonym for language, while on the other it is a very well-defined area within the system of knowledge. Two founding principles are firmly embedded in the Modistae's understanding of grammar: grammar is universal and it is a speculative science. These tenets, which some Modistae take for granted, are derived from a century-long revision of the arrangement of the system of knowledge. The status of grammar as science and the notion of universal grammar are tightly connected, since in order to conform to Aristotle's definition of science, the study of grammar must turn its gaze to the necessary first principles of language that are applicable to all languages. The two themes can best be explored through the discourse of Boethius of Dacia. In the first part of his treatise, Boethius traces the foundations of the new grammar from the problem of the *inventio* of grammar to the justification of *modi significandi*, through twenty-seven *Quaestiones*.[21] The redefinition of the status of grammar within the system of knowledge and the notion of universal grammar are central (and related) statements in his introduction.

The notion of universal language is an acquisition of earlier speculative grammar. First discussed by William of Conches,[22] among the Modistae it is acknowledged by Boethius and John of Dacia with very similar arguments. Boethius begins his treatise by stating the philosophical and not the grammatical origin of grammar (*Quaestio* 1): as the *inventio* of grammar precedes grammar itself, the inventor cannot be a grammarian. Grammar, moreover, depends upon the system of reality (*natura rerum*), and its first principles (*modi essendi et intelligendi*) are the domain of the philosopher – 'philosophus,' which often presupposes 'naturalis' in Boethius, more precisely a 'metaphysicus' in John of Dacia (*Summa grammatica*, 69). The grammarian enters into play only when expression is at stake,[23] as he does not deal with the principles *in se*, but only insofar as they come together into a signifying process. The intimate connection between the system of reality and that of expression ensures the universality of grammar/language discussed in the second question. Since grammar depends upon reality, the core structure of language is the same for all languages.

> et quia naturae rerum sunt similes apud omnes, ideo et modi essendi et modi intelligendi sunt similes apud omnes illos, apud quos sunt illa diversa idiomata, et per consequens similes modi significandi, et ergo per consequens similes modi construendi vel loquendi. Et sic tota grammatica, quae est in uno idiomate, est similis illi, quae est in alio idiomate. (*Modi significandi*, 12)

> [and since the natures of things are similar for everyone, and the modes of

being and the modes of understanding are similar for all those people speaking different languages, by consequence the modes of signifying are also similar, as are the modes of constructing and speaking. And, therefore, the whole grammar of one language is similar to that of another.]

Different languages are mere accidents of a core structure: 'Ipsa enim una est necessario in specie, solum diversificata secundum diversas figurationes vocum, quae sunt accidentales grammaticae' (13: therefore [grammar] is necessarily of one kind and only diversified according to the different figurations of the voices that are the accidents of grammar). In order to reinforce the universality of grammar, Boethius later stresses the natural aspect of language-learning. In *Quaestio* 16, grammar is explicitly assimilated with language (*locutio*), and Boethius states that a universal grammar and the potentiality of language-learning are innate, whereas the learning of a specific language is accidental:

si homines aliqui in deserto nutrirentur, ita quod numquam aliorum hominum loquelam audirent nec aliquam instructionem de modo loquendi acciperent, ipsi suos affectus naturaliter sibi mutuo exprimerent et eodem modo. Locutio enim est una de operibus naturalibus, cuius signum est, quod instrumentum, per quod fit locutio, natura in nobis ordinavit. Et ideo, sicut naturaliter habet homo alias operationes naturales, sic et locutionem vel grammaticam, per quam potest homo exprimere conceptum intentum. Vide tamen quod licet latinus non intelligit grammaticam graeci nec e converso, hoc est, quod isti sunt modi accidentales grammaticae per doctrina habiti, et non per naturam. (*Modi significandi*, 61)

[if some people were raised in the desert – so that they never heard the language of others, nor received any instruction on how to speak it – they naturally would somehow find a way to express their affections with one another. Speaking is, in fact, one of the natural operations and the evidence of this is that nature granted in us the instrument through which speech takes place. And thus, as the human being naturally has the other natural operations, so too one has language and grammar through which one can express an understood concept. Nevertheless, you see that a Latin doesn't understand the grammar of a Greek and vice versa. It happens because these are accidental modes of grammar that are acquired by doctrine and not by nature.]

Boethius's argument for universal grammar is played out as a distinction between grammar as nature, the domain of a pure philosopher, and grammar as language, the domain of a *purus grammaticus*. The link between philosopher and grammarian, between reality and language, is to be found in the very backbone of language itself: the system of the *modi* (*essendi, intelligendi, significandi*), which organizes the relationship between *res* and *verba*.

Only a truly universal language can be the subject matter of grammar as a speculative science. The transition from grammar as an art to grammar as a science took place before the Modistae, although the two understandings still coexist in the writings of the pre-Modistae. Pinborg connects this transition with the appearance in Europe in the twelfth century of Aristotle's *Posterior Analytics* and Alfarabi's *Liber de scientis*, where the knowledge of language is divided into two sections; words and rules.[24] Alfarabi's Latin expositor Dominicus Gundissalinus (circa 1150) had already emphasized the key tenet of speculative grammar: the unchanging, 'universal' set of rules that underlies every language is constituted by syntax. Following Alfarabi, Gundissalinus divided the study of grammar into two sections: the science of the meaning of single words ('scientia intelligendi ad quid significandum singulè dictiones sint imposite'), which is learned naturally by children and varies with different languages; and the science that considers the rules underlying the words. This second grammar consists of syntax ('scientia ordinandi singulas dictiones in oracione ad significandum concepciones anime'), it is learned as an adult through schooling, and it is common to every language.[25] These unchanging rules of construction of speech, which are common to every language, properly make the *ars grammatica* a science.[26]

The pre-Modistae also posited grammar as a speculative, as opposed to active, science: its object is truth as opposed to action. The term *scientia speculativa* entered the system of knowledge with (Severinus) Boethius, as a translation of the Aristotelian distinction between theoretical and practical science, and it therefore entails universality, abstraction, and theory. Following Aristotle, Boethius's classification of speculative philosophy includes three sciences – *naturalis, mathematica,* and *divina* – hierarchically arranged according to degrees of abstraction and separation from nature: while natural science is fully implicated with matter and motion, mathematics begins the process of abstraction, and theology deals with forms that are abstracted and separated. The discourses of the three sciences are different: physics proceeds rationally (*rationabiliter*), mathematics disciplinarily (*disciplinariter*), and theology intellectually (*intellectualiter*). Boethius's classification is widely discussed throughout the Middle Ages and is maintained with certain variations.[27] Both the pre-Modistae and Modistae deemed the sciences of language to be speculative – albeit as 'auxiliary' and not 'necessary' like the three main speculative sciences.[28] For example, John of Dacia's *Divisio scientiae*, close in time and spirit to the Modistae, expounds the Boethian classification of the three main speculative sciences (24–34) and adds as auxiliary ('adminiculativae') to them the three sciences of language, which he also calls accidental ('accidentales') and rational ('rationales'), since they consider three *rationes* or 'intentions' of objects: construction ('modus construendi'), knowledge ('modus sciendi'), and persuasion ('modus persuadendi').

Boethius of Dacia posits grammar as a speculative, unified science that serves as the gateway to other sciences (*Quaestiones* 3–5). Grammar is considered a science because its subject matter fulfils two conditions: it is intellectual and has essential causes: the *modi significandi* and construction.[29] It is considered a speculative science, but not an essential part of philosophy, as the three main speculative sciences (*naturalis, mathematica, divina*): rather, it is introductory to the three main sciences.[30] Not only is grammar necessary for humans because it serves to introduce other sciences, which in turn lead human beings to blessed living (consisting of 'operatio boni,' 'cognitio veri,' and 'delectatio in utroque'), but grammar is also indispensable in and of itself because its principles are rooted in things – it is not merely an invention at the will of the grammarian. Moreover, it is a unified science because its subject matter is universal: 'ideo una est grammatica apud omnes, quamquam diversificata sit accidentaliter' (20: Therefore grammar is one for everybody, albeit diversified by accident). Even though grammar operates in terms of abstraction ('abstrahit ab omni sermone,' 25), it must still be considered a science of language, since it abstracts from the accidents of language and not from its essence.[31]

Boethius posits grammar as a science of language whose subject is syntax (*Quaestiones* 6–7).The minimal unity of grammar, the voice (*vox*), is not to be considered as sound, the domain of the natural philosopher, but as a sign of a thing connected to a *modus significandi*. Yet the subject of grammar is not even the expression (*dictio*) but the *iunctura orationum*, the joining, the culmination of words in context, into articulated discourse[32] – which in turn mirrors the way concepts are ordered in the intellect ('imitatur ordinationem intelligibilium apud intellectum').

The subject matter and final goal of grammar is therefore a weaving of words, the *sermo*, which correctly represents the concepts as understood by the mind.[33]

Finally, Boethius states that grammar shares with logic a double status within the system of knowledge (*Quaestio* 8). On the one hand it is a special science (*scientia specialis*) that teaches a specialized knowledge, yet on the other hand it is a common art (*ars communis*), knowledge of which is applicable to every art and science.[34]

The position of grammar within the system of knowledge is established in opposition to and participation with logic and the other speculative sciences, especially natural science – logic being the foremost science of language and discourse in this age of crisis of rhetoric, and physics being the science of things whose properties are captured in language. The other disciplines enter into play in two ways. On the one hand, and most explicitly, they trace the boundaries of grammar and establish which elements are of no concern to the grammarian. On the other hand, they implicitly enlarge its theoretical functions. The explicit discourse of the Modistae aims at keeping grammar discrete from the other sciences and at making it a self-sufficient realm – the workshop of an abstracted, artificial language. Nevertheless grammar at its roots is closely imbricated with logic, physics, and metaphysics, and these sciences substantiate its very structure.

The discourses of the different sciences are portrayed as parallel within the medieval system of knowledge: different sciences say different things about the same reality. Boethius illustrates the different operation of grammar, logic, and natural science by considering three different problems embedded in a sentence such as 'homo est animal': the grammarian is called to establish its congruity, the logician its property, and the natural philosopher its truth.[35] The three disciplines are kept discrete and diverging, but there are unmistakable if subtle relations among them.

The ties between grammar and logic are by far the most complex.[36] As with the other sciences in the system of knowledge, logic provides grammar with its discursive apparatus. Logic and grammar, then, are dangerously contiguous: they share the same metalanguage and the same subject matter. Moreover, late medieval grammar is itself a product of logic. It is only after the revival of logic in the tenth and eleventh centuries and within the frame of medieval Aristotelianism that the two fields are reunited, logic stripping and radically changing the premises of grammar, turning the *philologus* into a *philosophus*. Contemporary grammarians and logicians were quick to recognize a mutual interaction, yet at the same time were quick to point out the independence of the two disciplines. While asserting the independence of logic and grammar, Abelard in his *De dialectica* was the first to put forward again the reconciliation between Aristotle's notion of subject and predicate and Priscian's eight parts of speech (first provided by Boethius in his Commentary to the *De interpretatione*) after centuries in which logic and grammar were seldom considered conjointly.[37] It is by way of logic that grammar is later established as a speculative science with universal language as its subject matter; and it is the reciprocal influence of logic and grammar that brings syntax to the fore. It is helpful to recall de Rijk's comments on the two disciplines' mutual interest in syntax:

> The shift of the interest of the grammarians away from the primordial invention and imposition of the individual words to their syntactical functions seems to have found its counterpart in – and, no doubt, to have stimulated – the parallel development on the side of the dialecticians, when the latter in their theories of signification transferred their main interest from the original imposition of the words to the actual meaning of *this* word in *this* proposition as a result of its actual function in that proposition.[38]

Thirteenth-century grammarians and logicians took great pains to maintain the discreteness of grammar and logic. They argued that grammar and logic view language in two different ways (truth and falseness being the concern of logic, while grammar concerns the correctness of the sentence), that logic considers only two parts of the speech – *subiectum* and *predicatum* – whereas grammar considers eight, and so on. Although they were both grammarians and logicians, the Modistae were among the most zealous defendants of the boundaries between the two disciplines. As Irène Rosier points out, on some occasions the same problem would be approached differently, depending on whether they were acting as logicians or as grammarians.[39]

The greatest friction between grammar and logic takes place on the grounds of semantics. The grammarians distinguish between a grammatical meaning (*significatus generalis*) and a lexical, and as such, logical, meaning (*significatus specialis*). Where logic distinguishes between proper or improper, grammar discerns correct from incorrect: a fair share, until one gets to the shady ground of the so-called figures of construction (of which the standard example is the Ovidian 'turba ruunt,' an ungrammatical but successful expression) or to what can be termed 'figures of grammar' (a famous one, used by Petrus Helias, being 'Socrates habet sotulares hypoteticos cum categoricis corrigiis').[40] Medieval grammarians tended to concede something to logic and semantics when dealing with these particular cases. For instance, Petrus Helias posits a distinction between the congruity of the sentence *secundum vocem* (grammatical) and *secundum sensum* (intelligible, non-nonsensical). Roger Bacon and Robert Kilwardby distinguish two types of *perfectio*, the final completion of the sentence: a primary understanding (*ad intellectum primum* = grammatical) and a secondary understanding (*ad intellectum secundum* = semantic).[41] The Modistae, however, are the strictest on these issues. The divergence from logic seems to yield to a completely artificial and hypothetical system of language that allows even for improper statements. For Boethius, the grammarian doesn't know what to answer if asked whether the expression 'homo est lapis' is truer than 'homo est animal' (*Modi significandi*, 55). For Thomas of Erfurt the expression *cappa nigra* is both congruous and proper and is therefore acceptable to both the grammarian and the logician, while *cappa categorica* is only congruous and is therefore acceptable only to the grammarian.[42] When approaching different degrees of perfection, Thomas withdraws completely into grammar: a construction is perfect *secundum sensum* when both constructibles are expressed (as in 'ego lego') and *secundum intellectum* when one constructible is implied (as in 'lego').[43]

The schism between grammar and logic is, then, an extreme consequence of the influence of logic over grammar. Logic, forcing grammar toward abstraction – not only from language-in-use, but from meaning itself – eventually allows grammar to abstract itself from logic and to reach a different level of interpretation within language: with the new grammar, construction becomes an absolute principle disconnected from signification and judgment.

The issue of signification is also a point of interface between grammar and natural science.[44] In the convoluted *Quaestiones* 11 and 12, which are devoted to the special meaning of things (*res speciales; res predicamentales*), Boethius argues that grammar can exist without the *res speciales* – the subject matter of the other speculative sciences ('omnis res specialis aut est metaphysica aut naturalis aut mathematica,' 43) – because construction, its final goal, does not require a special understanding of the thing.[45] Grammar is therefore complete without reference to any special meaning. *Nihil* and *homo* are both simply nouns for the grammarian, and the pure grammarian cannot make a distinction between a construction as 'tonat' and a construction as 'currit,' nor can he decide whether one is more perfect than the other: the judgment would in fact rely on extra-grammatical information, i.e., the nature of thunder and lightening, with which the grammarian should not concern himself (46–7).

When it comes to the choice of a voice to signify the thing, both the grammarian and the natural philosopher are required to shift from the realm of things to the realm of language:

> Dicendum est ad hoc, quod purus grammaticus non potest imponere tales voces ad significandum, quae scilicet significant res speciales, nec etiam purus philosophus, sed debet esse uterque. Debet enim esse philosophus realis, ut possit considerare proprietates rerum a quibus modos significandi accipit, sub quibus vocem ad significandum imponit, et debet esse grammaticus, ut modos significandi possit considerare, et eos tales faciat, ut et ex eis possit causari constructio et omnes species eius. Unde si purus grammaticus esset, proprietates rerum non consideraret, et si purus philosophus esset, modos significandi et constructiones non consideraret, et ideo debet esser uterque, ut possit imponere voces ad significandum sub modis significandi designantibus proprietates circa res ipsas significatas. (*Modi significandi*, 50)

> [In this regard we have to say that the pure grammarian cannot impose these voices which signify the *res speciales* in order to obtain signification, but neither can the pure philosopher. There has to be a philosopher of nature that can consider the properties of things, from which one derives the modes of signifying, under which the voice is imposed in order to signify; and there has to be a grammarian that can consider the modes of signifying and use them to provide construction in all its aspects. Therefore, a pure grammarian would not take into consideration the properties of things, and a pure philosopher would not consider the modes of signifying and construction. Thus one must be both in order to impose voices to signification according to the modes of signifying that designate the properties that surround the signified things themselves.]

Natural science seems to interact only peripherally with grammar – in a liminal space prior to grammar proper, that of the *inventio* of grammar and of the *impositio vocis*. However, there is evidence that the 'new' science of nature interacts with the very core of grammar. At the beginning of his treatise, Thomas of Erfurt quotes the beginning of Aristotle's *Physics* as the authority in establishing grammar as science.[46] As Louis Kelly remarks, this quote orients the reader in two directions: on the one hand, and most explicitly, it supports the scientific validity of the universal presupposition of grammar-as-science; on the other hand, it points the reader to the relevance of physics in grammar.[47] Kelly has persuasively argued that much of the 'new' terminology that the Modistae apply to the definition of noun and verb is indeed indebted to Aristotle's *Physics*, via medieval commentators – as demonstrated by the use of terms such as *quies* (for the noun), *terminus, fluxus, successio, distantia* (the general mode of signifying of the verb, crucial for the completion of the sentence). Moreover, Kelly argues that the structure of construction itself, which implies a movement from a term *a quo* to a term *ad quem*, is patterned on the Aristotelian theory of motion, and that the verb, carrying the notion of distance (*distantia*), fully embodies the syntactic model of motion.[48]

The validity of the motus model for grammar has been both embraced and disputed by scholars, and there is consensus that its presence in grammar is pervasive but not systematic. Covington (76) notes that its influence was already visible in early to mid-thirteenth-century grammatical theories, that is, as soon as the *libri naturales* became available in northern Europe – proof of the grammarians' flexibility and eagerness in quickly adopting and adapting the new knowledge (the *libri naturales* and the tradition of Arabic and, later, Western commentaries). The attention that the grammarians show in many instances toward the *libri naturales* suggests that the impact of natural science on the new grammar is not merely terminological, and maybe that it is not univocal. It signals that when the grammarians pattern their theory of language on nature, they embrace a basic structure of nature as motion – as movement, change, alteration, transformation, birth, and decay; and they consider motion as a satisfaction of a potentiality propelled by the mutual desire of matter and form. What in nature is movement, in grammar is construction.

At the end of the process of integration, both grammar and physics are changed: on the one hand language truly appears like a movement, while on the other hand nature appears syntactically disposed and constructed. Reading the *Physics* with the grammarians in mind, one has the impression that nature is a giant discourse brought forth by movement and powered by difference and resistance.

The interaction between logic, natural science, and grammar is two-fold. As separate, distinct fields, the two sciences not only furnish grammar with metalanguage and working examples but serve to delimit the reach of grammar as a discipline. At the same time, however, logic and natural science are also at the very core of the new science of language – and heavily influenced by it. Syntax, the logic of the new grammar, becomes also the logic of nature.

Reality, Mind, Language

The most unified and mature Modistic account of the functioning of the process of language formation can be found in the initial chapters (1–6) of Thomas of Erfurt's *Grammatica speculativa*.[49] The process takes place in three 'spaces' (reality, mind, and finally language)[50] and happens on three tracks (elements, properties, faculties) according to a double state (active and passive). It leads from 'a thing as it is in nature' (*res*), through 'a thing as it is in the mind' (*conceptus*), to 'a thing as it is in language' (*dictio*), or more specifically, to 'a thing as it is in syntax' (*pars orationis*).[51] The operative aspect of the process moves from 'the properties of the thing as they are in nature' (*modi essendi*), through 'the properties of things as they are in the mind' (*modi intelligendi*), to 'the properties of things as they are in language' (*modi significandi*). Language formation also depends upon a faculty that is effective at all stages: the faculty of being (*ratio essendi*), the faculty of understanding (*ratio intelligendi*), and the faculty of signifying (*ratio significandi*).[52]

The same properties of the thing move in each space, and through the three spaces by leaps of difference: by being the same in terms of matter but different in terms of form, or the same in terms of form but different in terms of matter. The motor of the process of language is the interplay between an active and a passive state of the *modi*. While the mode of being is an absolute, the modes of understanding and signifying are diversified into active and passive. The inert, passive state describes the same property of the thing as it is in reality (*modus essendi*), as it is in the mind (*modus intelligendi passivus*), and as it is in language (*modus significandi passivus*).[53] In other words, in the passive state the material principle consists of the same properties of the thing, whereas the form is given by the three different *rationes* (*essendi, intelligendi,* and *significandi*).The passive state is not a concern for the grammarian, since it does not actively enter into the production of language or into its description. The active state – the phase where language formation actually unfolds – builds on the passive state by calling into play a different set of properties. The matter of the active state is the property of the intellect (*modus intelligendi activus*) and that of the voice (*modus significandi activus*). The forms of the active state, are, once again, the three different *rationes*.[54] Within each space, the passive and active states differ in terms of matter while agreeing in terms of form, since the same faculty (*ratio*) underlies both of them. The *ratio* itself is diversified into active and passive: through the active faculty the intellect understands the property of the thing and language signifies it, while it is by the passive faculty that the thing is understood and signified.[55]

Language formation takes place in a cross-meeting of the passive state in one space, with the active state in the other. The passive state provides the 'raw material' upon which the active state acts. Strictly speaking, the formation of the *dictio/pars orationis* occurs in the passage between the passive modes of understanding and the active modes of signifying: the rest can be considered a necessary corollary (modes of being) or a by-product (passive modes of signifying).[56]

The process of language is indeed a matter of consignification, as the active modes of signifying are powered by the faculty of consignifying (*ratio consignificandi*). Thomas postulates two different forms of signification bestowed upon the word by two faculties: the *ratio significandi*, which makes it a *dictio*, and the *ratio consignificandi*, which allows it to interact with other parts of speech.[57]

To summarize Thomas's laborious argument: in the absolute space of reality, the thing is endowed with a faculty of being (*ratio essendi*) and a property of being (*modus essendi*). In the intellect, informed by the faculty of understanding (*ratio intelligendi*), a concept (*conceptus*) is produced through a twofold mode of understanding (*modus intelligendi*). In the space of language, informed by the faculty of signifying and consignifying, the expression (*dictio*) and the syntactical unit (*pars orationis*) are produced through the modes of signifying (*modi significandi*). The production of language can be viewed as a movement that advances by leaps of difference. It unfolds within the three spaces by leaps of matter and form; it is kept uniform by the passive modes and accelerated by the active modes. The end point of the process – and the starting point of syntax – is consignification, which endows the word with all the links necessary to join other words in the combination of the sentence.

As this quick overview reveals, the Modistae are hardly innovators in philosophical terminology.[58] The triad *essendi: intelligendi: significandi* is

a commonplace model of cognition and signification in medieval philosophy. The notions of active and passive, matter and form are land-
marks of medieval Aristotelianism. *Ratio* and *modus* are also standard
and flexible terms, commonly found in the discursive apparatus of the
late medieval system of knowledge. The notion of *modi* (i.e., qualities,
properties of the object) *significandi*, from which the Modistae derive
their title, is current in medieval logic and theology, and it appears in
grammar around the time of Abelard.[59] It is consistently used by all the
speculative grammarians to define the parts of the speech, although it is
only with the Modistae that it acquires a specific syntactic value,[60]
describing the way a word functions syntactically: as we have seen, the
Modistae's *modi significandi* are indeed *modi consignificandi*.

Although their vocabulary may be derivative, the speculative grammarians were innovative in the way they utilized, integrated, and refined it,
synthesizing it into a stable and consistent model in which the notion of
modi accounts for every step of language, from its formation to its functioning in terms of syntax. The use of this vocabulary is not, I believe, a
mere 'descriptive device,' as Bursill-Hall holds.[61] The fact that grammar is
pervaded by the same principles that substantiate the whole late-medi-
eval system of knowledge doesn't necessarily mean that in grammar (as
opposed to other disciplines, say logic or natural science) those principles should be devoid of their impact. On the contrary, grammar – while
appropriating these principles by means of terminological osmosis, and
certainly bending them to its needs – is radically changed and influenced
by them.

The most laborious philosophical topic of speculative grammar is the
triad *esse: intelligere: significare*, the medium through which reality is mirrored in language. Early Modistae seem to creatively disagree quite a bit
on the subject, whereas later Modistae perpetuate the standard model
described above.[62] Martin of Dacia holds an extreme and 'pure' position. The three modes, not yet differentiated into active and passive, are
described as identical ('penitus idem'), differing only accidentally, since
the object is the same whether it is outside, intellected, or signified ('res
extra, intellecta et significata sunt una et eadem res').[63] This position
has the flaw, as Covington explains, of making the modes of signifying
'the real world properties that are consignified by words' (31), and
grammar the study of the properties of the object rather than the mechanism of language. Boethius accounts for the connection between the

modes of being, understanding, and signifying not through identity but rather through the notion of *similitudo* in his explanation of the similarities and differences between the three spaces (*Quaestio* 26).[64]

> modi essendi et intelligendi et significandi non sunt idem penitus, quia tunc, statim cum esset modus essendi rei, statim esset modus significandi in dictione illius rei, quod falsum est. Tamen modus significandi accipitur ad similitudinem modi intelligendi et modus intelligendi ad similitudinem modi essendi. Unde non oportet quod illa sunt idem penitus, quorum unum accipitur ad similitudinem alterius. (*Modi significandi*, 81)

> [the modes of being, of understanding, and of signifying are not exactly the same thing because, otherwise, there would be a mode of signifying as soon as there were a mode of being, which is false. Nevertheless the mode of signifying is acquired in the likeness of the mode of understanding, and the mode of understanding in the likeness of the mode of being. Hence it is not necessary that things that are derived by similarity be completely the same.]

With Boethius's solution, the *modi significandi* become 'the attributes of the word that makes consignification possible' (Covington, 31).[65] John of Dacia (*Summa grammatica*, 231–5) restates Martin's position but seems to add some subtlety by pointing out a distinction between the modes of signifying 'actively' and 'passively,' a distinction that is very similar to the one held by later grammarians.[66] In their work, the passive state grants a separation between reality and language, which were dangerously contiguous in the earlier formulation. It becomes a sort of reservoir for reality, from which the active state draws in order to turn reality into language. Later Modistae extend the passive state to the mind as well (dividing the *modi intelligendi* into *activi* and *passivi*), as seen in Thomas's standard model.[67] Thus, the grammarian no longer questions the differences among the three *modi*, but among *modi essendi, intelligendi passivi*, and *significandi passivi* (which are identical *materialiter* but differ in terms of form, and they are, therefore, Martin's three *modi*) on the one hand, and among *modi essendi, intelligendi activi*, and *significandi activi* (which differ in both matter and form) on the other.

This refinement of the model both grounds language in and disconnects it from reality. The grammarian is then able to withdraw entirely into the issues of grammar and is absolved from any responsibility regarding reality, since the passive modes are beyond his purview. The system of the active and passive modes becomes a filter between reality and language, creating a form of resistance between the two, on which (con)signification travels. Like a prism, the *modi* both heighten and obscure the connections among reality, mind, and language, so that language and the study of grammar are both clearly rooted in reality yet independent from it – or, òne may say, they are independent from reality *because* they are universally rooted in it.

Thus, the system of the *modi* shifts emphasis from signification to consignification. Whereas signification establishes a pure and somewhat rigid relation between the object and the expression, consignification consists in the plunging of language into act, time, and the process of unfolding.[68] As seen in the Introduction, consignification in the Middle Ages is often viewed as a degeneration with respect to signification. The Modistae, on the contrary, privilege the flexibility of consignification to the point of barely alluding to (or ignoring *tout court*) the traditional notion of signification: in the new, universal grammar, *significare* is already *consignificare*.

Certain authors make a distinction between two articulations of the voice. The first articulation (Priscian's *articulatio prima*) leads to signification, and it is explained as *impositio*, which, as we have seen, does not fall under the duty of the pure grammarian; the second articulation (*articulatio secunda*) leads to consignification.[69] Boethius suggestively views the two articulations as the progressive tightening of signification around the object: the voice is stolen away from undifferentiated existence ('ablata est eius indifferentia') and forced ('arctare,' to tighten, coincidentally one of the medieval etymologies for 'art')[70] first into a determinate meaning and then into the even tighter operation of the modes of signifying. Signification and consignification are simultaneous: when the voice is forced into signification, it is also tightened to and by a determined mode of signifying. The double articulation takes place simultaneously: 'cum vox in sua impositione ad determinatum significatum, artatur etiam ad determinatum modum significandi.'[71] While recognizing that signification 'naturally' precedes consignification, the Modistae bypass the problem of meaning through the *modi*. The system of the *modi* reinvents the relationship between language and reality: it is no longer a matter of how *this* thing is signified by *this* word, but of the way in which the properties of things, 'passively' constructed in reality, are actively constructed by language.[72]

The correspondence between reality and language, so artfully constructed by the grammarians, is challenged by the existence of expressions that do not exist in reality – such as negations (*nihil*), privations (*caecitas*), and fictions (*figmenta*, 'ut tragelaphus, chimaera et cetera talia')[73] – or that transcend reality (such as *deus* and the 'strangely' feminine *deitas*). The Modistae face this challenge by enhancing the role of the modes of understanding, positing and testing therefore the relation between language and knowledge, as the inexpressible turns eventually out to be the unknown – and, as such, the non-existent. Interestingly, the expressions that occupy the liminal spaces of existence are less functional than others in context, since they have fewer modes of signifying and cannot be properly unfolded in speech. Instances of full, 'healthy' signification, knowledge, and existence are inevitably tied to the fullness of syntactic articulation.

In *Quaestio* 20, Boethius states that there are two sorts of expressible things: those that have existence (*esse*) and therefore a mode of being outside of the mind (*extra animam*), and those that have existence and mode of being only inside the mind (*apud animam*). The mode of being belonging to the second type of thing is indeed the mode of understanding ('quia modus essendi talium rerum apud animam earum est modus intelligendi').[74] The truly inexpressible is something that doesn't have a mode of being inside the mind: 'Quaecumque modorum essendi apud animam habere non possunt, illum etiam modum significandi habere non possunt' (73: All things that cannot have a mode of being inside the mind, cannot have a mode of signifying).

John of Dacia (*Summa grammatica*, 201) stresses the fact that some non-being is still intelligible as *privatio entis*, lack of being, and therefore expressible ('non ens est intelligibile. Ergo non ens est significabile'). John describes non-being as threefold ('non ens dicitur tripliciter'). First, there is a non-being in act, i.e., a being in potency, like matter, for instance. Then there are fictions, non-beings both in potency and act, which can still be reconstructed through imagination: for example, the union of 'mountain' and 'gold' yields to a golden mountain in the imagination. Finally, there is a kind of non-being that is not in act, in potency, or in imagination: this non-intelligible non-being is inexpressible ('nullo modo cadit in intellectum nec per consequens significari potest per vocem').[75] Next to the non-being, John explores the other end of the spectrum of signification and the greatest crux of the relations between grammar and theology: the name and attributes of God.[76] The grammarian is tentative, but not defeated. God doesn't fall under the grasp of motion or imagination, yet His power, wisdom, and goodness can be known and signified through the way in which they shine through in his creatures. God is not fully nominable by one name, but by many.[77] Here John faces also an interesting problem deriving from Averroes' *Liber de causis*: God is inexpressible because he is 'inexplicable'; he cannot be narrated ('enarrare'), unfolded, and contained in articulated speech. Articulated discourse, as opposed to mere signification, represents the plenitude of expression, and John is forced to admit that what cannot be fully and perfectly (con)signified, cannot be fully known.[78] Hence (con)signification is essential to knowledge and an active part of knowing.

Thomas too grants a larger role to the intellect when it comes to negations and deity: the mind has the power to shift balances in consignification by detaching the properties of things from the things-as-they-are-in-reality and relocating them in different words: 'modus significandi ... potest accipi a proprietate rei alterius dictionis, et rei illius dictionis tribui.' If an entity, such as the separate substances, is unintelligible, the mind appropriates the properties of some other intelligible thing, creates from it the modes of signifying, and attributes them to the unintelligible thing.[79]

When testing the inferior (non-being) and superior (absolute being) limits of being, the grammarians are forced to grant more space to the interpretive and combinatory power of the intellect. Reality is, however, always in sight, as opposition, likeness, or combination.[80] When the connection to it is lost, language encounters the abyss of God (for which names proliferate without really grasping him) or that of the absolute, absolutely inexpressible, non-being. In both cases, knowledge is defeated along with signification.

The Parts of Speech: Permanence and Becoming

The entire Modistic system relies on the active modes of signifying. As Martin of Dacia puts it, one has to 'think modally,' to twist back each problem to the system of the modi ('modaliter intelligendum est,' 'retorquendum est ad modos') – a statement that Costantino Marmo correctly describes as a manifesto.[81] It is the system of the *modi*, and not single parts of speech, that dictates the modalities of signification: accordingly, realities of succession/becoming such as *motus* and *tempus* are signified under the quality of permanence, as nouns. *Ignis* and *ignitur* signify the same thing under the modes of stability and becoming. The modes of signifying shape the *pars orationis*, the real starting point for the grammarian, so that it can function in context and endow it with all the links that enable it to join other parts and find its position in a sentence.

The Modistae retain the traditional eight *partes orationis* (noun, pronoun, verb, participle, adverb, conjunction, preposition, and interjection), but they consider them as operative syntactical units. The *modus significandi* not only leads to the formation of the *pars* but also enters into the process of distinguishing and describing its qualities. A *pars* can be looked at in terms of its *modus essentialis*, which describes its essence, or in terms of its *modus accidentalis*, which describes its accidents, the ways in which it relates to other parts. One can examine what makes a *pars* different from the others (*modus specificus* or *absolutus*) or see what allows for a concord among the parts (*modus generalis* or *respectivus*). A number of sub-modes (*modi significandi subalterni*) allow for an even more detailed description of each part. The richer section of the Modistae's reflections covers the four declinable parts that are endowed with many more *modi* than the indeclinable components – in particular, it is intuitive that they have more accidental modes.[82]

The two most important parts of speech – noun and verb – are characterized by the two most significant combinatory factors in nature: permanence and becoming. The *modus* (*essentialis respectivus*) *entis* or *habitus* carries the notions of stability, permanence, substance, coherence, and presence, and is distinctive of noun and pronoun. The *modus esse* or *fieri* instead represents movement, becoming, action and passion, and accident, and identifies verb and participle. Noun and pronoun are kept discrete by the notion of determination (*modus apprehensioni determinatae/ indeterminatae*), while the notion of distance (*modus distantis/indistantis*) distinguishes verb and participle. Sigier of Courtrai provides a summary of the terminology for noun and verb. For the noun: 'Modus significandi essentialis generalis nominis est modus significandi substantiae, permanentis, habitus seu entis' (*Summa modorum significandi*, 96). For the verb: 'Modus autem significandi generalis essentialis verbi est modus significandi per modum fluxus, fieri, seu motus, seu esse' (108).[83] In approaching the two most important terms of logic and grammar in this way, the Modistae once again incorporate and modify the preceding philosophical terminology so as to privilege the system of the *modi* over the specificity of single parts.

The traditional Aristotelian definition that 'noun signifies substance' (in Priscian, 'substance with quality') is not dismissed by the grammarians but tuned toward the ideas of permanence and quiet rather than of substance, in order to avoid the paradox by which substance signifies 'accidentally.' The verb is traditionally understood as carrying the notion of action and passion and the extra-indication of time – so that, according to Aristotle and the logicians, the verb, along with other things, also always 'consignifies time,' therefore constituting a special part of speech. The Modistae, however, prefer a definition that itself includes the notion of motion, flux, becoming, and succession, relegating the notions of active/passive and tense to the accidental modes of the verb. In other words, they privilege the image and terminology of movement over that of time (time entering into the picture only insofar as it represents movement).[84] Not only do the Modistae thereby readjust the notions of noun and verb, but they also gently subvert the traditional balance of power within the sentence. The centrality of the notion of *habitus* and *fieri* suggests a question at the heart of the system of the Modistae: are they proposing a language of substance, as Aristotle did, or a language of accident and, therefore, of movement and time? Is· universal language, the core system whose accidents are languages, rooted in movement or stability, time or timelessness?

Traditionally the noun – 'signifying substance' – was considered the most important part of speech, in analogy with the primacy of substance in nature. Although not unanimous on the issue, the Modistae seem to value the verb as the most relevant part of the speech and grant more importance – 'dignity,' as they call it – to the verb/accident than to the noun/substance. This bold move is unquestionably dictated by syntactic concerns, i.e., the necessity of the verb for the perfect completion of a sentence. The pre-Modista Simon of Dacia (author of the *Domus gramatice*), for instance, seems initially to claim the supremacy of the noun ('substantia est dignior quam accidens. Ergo nomen est dignior verbum' [54: substance is more important than accident, therefore the noun is more important than the verb]), but he soon rectifies his position by stating that the noun is more important in 'being and signifying,' while the verb is more important in 'forming' (ibid.). Since the ultimate concern of grammar is not signification but construction, the verb is also indirectly promoted.

Boethius by contrast frames the issue in terms of the 'necessity' of the verb in the sentence and of the possibility for substance to be 'accidentally.' In *Quaestio* 31 he confronts the ancient grammarians' assertion that the noun is the first part of speech in both order and importance. This hierarchy of parts of speech is unnecessary insofar as the grammarian is concerned, insists Boethius, since such an order is not suggested by the voice ('ratione suae vocis'), meaning ('ratione significati'), or *modus significandi* ('ratione modi significandi specifici').[85] As we shall see in more detail later, Boethius undermines the traditional primacy of the noun, relying on the new take on signification brought about by the system of the *modi*, according to which accident can be signified by noun and substance by verb. Insofar as the grammatical trade is concerned, however, the verb is more important than the noun, since it is the necessary foundation of the sentence, and no other part can take its place.[86] This claim is axiomatic for Thomas of Erfurt, for whom the finality of language is the installation of distance within the sentence, that is, the presence of a verb, without which a sentence is incomplete.[87]

An inverted perspective of reality is at the basis of Sigier of Courtrai's grammatical sophisma 'Magistro legente pueri proficiunt,' which is devoted to the exploration of the problem of *regimen*, the government of the sentence, and to the discovery of the noblest part of speech.[88] Having stated that grammatical government must follow the cosmic *regimen* of reality according to the traditional notion of *similitudo*, Sigier rehearses the Aristotelian argument regarding the hierarchy of perfection and of operation: all things converge toward the most noble, which in turn directs and governs them. The *regimen* of nature tends toward God, who directs ('regit') all beings. All bodies are in turn governed by the heavenly body. Within the animal kingdom, man governs the other species; within man's body the heart has primacy; and within man's virtues the possible intellect directs all the others. By analogy, within the sentence, the multitude of the parts tends toward the one that complies and renders perfect ('complet') the sentence itself: the verb.[89] In Sigier's argument, *regimen* becomes the key word for cosmic operation and order: instead of grammar being patterned on nature, nature begins to look like a giant grammatical construction that tends toward God. Although seemingly ruled by a strict logic, Sigier's discourse reveals a macroscopic inversion between the starting point, the cosmos of God, and the end point, the cosmos of the verb. At the centre of the universe of language – portrayed as an analogy to the universe of God – stands not an *ens primum* but the verb. The universe of language, as opposed to the universe of God, is organized around movement, time, and becoming: the verb acts indeed as the 'mobile mover' of the sentence.

The notions of permanence and becoming bestow a new flexibility upon noun and verb, and enact and enhance the connection between grammar and the science of nature – the lowest and most tangible of the three speculative sciences. Thomas, for example, in discussing the essential mode of signifying of the noun, explains the distinction between permanence and becoming and relates them to the basic modes of nature, through the recollection of Averroes' commentary to the fourth book of *Physics*. There are in nature two very common properties ('in rebus invenimus quasdam proprietates comunissimas, sive modos essendi comunissimos, scilicet modum entis, et modum esse'), indeed the main modes of existence ('modi principales entium'), being and becoming, from which the grammarian derives the main parts of speech.[90] As nature, language is portrayed as a composite that results from the opposition of permanence and becoming, of substance and accident.[91]

The influence exerted by language and nature (and by grammar and natural science) is reciprocal. On the one hand, the grammarians reinvent through physics the roles and qualities of the parts of speech, so that grammar appears more and more as a microcosm of nature. On the other hand, the closeness between the two sciences raises problems in both, which the grammarians solve by providing a view of nature that appears more and more grammatically oriented. I will now examine two such creative encounters between the fields: the signification of the noun in Boethius and the notion of verb as succession in Thomas.

As mentioned before, ancient grammarians posited the noun as the primary part of speech, since it 'signifies substance,' and substance comes first in the order of nature. Boethius contradicts this argument by relying on the flexibility of consignification, stating that a noun doesn't always signify substance (as in the case of the word *nihil*) and that substance can also be signified by a verb (as in the case of the words *fire* and *burn*, where the same substance is signified under the mode of permanence and under the mode of becoming):

Quid enim prohibet verbum aliquando eandem substantiam significare, quam significat nomen, licet sub alio et alio modo significandi, ut patet in hoc nomine 'ignis' et in hoc verbo 'ignitur'? Licet enim ignis significat substantiam per modum habitus et 'ignitur' per modum fieri, unam tamen et eandem significant substantiam. (*Modi significandi*, 97)

[What hinders the verb from sometimes signifying the same substance which the noun signifies, albeit under a different mode of signification, as the noun 'fire' and the verb 'burn' show? Even though 'fire' signifies substance through the mode of permanence, and 'burn' through the mode of becoming, they signify one and the same substance.]

The noun does not signify substance but rather signifies the object in terms of substance (101: 'nomen autem rem suam significat per modum substantiae'), and the same thing can be signified in terms of accident. Later, Boethius explores the problem of the discordance ('repugnantia') between the modes of being and the modes of signifying. *Motus* and *tempus* belong in reality to the sphere of becoming, but this doesn't hinder their signification in terms of stability.[92] The evident existence of nouns such as *motus* and *tempus* calls for a closer look into their modes of being in order to find the reason why realities of becoming can be signified in terms of stability. In the case of *motus*, for instance, Boethius finds in reality a unity and simultaneity of essence that allows for motion to be signified in terms of permanence:

> modus significandi per modum habitus non repugnat ei, quod significatur per hoc nomen 'motus,' quia licet motus habeat successionem partium et ita habet modum essendi per modum fieri, et secundum hanc proprietatem sibi debetur modus intelligendi et significandi per modum fieri, istae tamen partes sunt indifferentes secundum essentiam. Ideo habent unitatem et simultatem essentiae, secundum quam proprietatem per modum habitus potest designari. Licent enim in motu sint partes succedentes, tamen in motu non sunt partes succedentes secundum diversitatem essentiae, sed est ibi simultas partium in unitate essentiae.' (*Modi significandi*, 102)

[The mode of signifying through the mode of stability is not opposed to that which is signified by this noun *motus*. Although movement involves a succession of parts and, therefore, it has a mode of being through a mode of becoming, and according to this property it deserves a mode of understanding and a mode of signifying through the mode of becoming, these parts are not distinguished according to essence. Therefore, they have unity and simultaneity of essence, a property which can be designated through the mode of stability. Although in movement parts are in succession, they are not in succession according to difference of the essence, but there is a simultaneity of the parts in the unity of essence.]

Levering on the flexibility of the *modi* in order to argue against the primacy of the noun, Boethius adds complexity and flexibility to nature itself. Since substance can be signified accidentally, and accident substantially, in the being of substance there must be a property (*modus essendi*) that leans toward accident, and vice versa. Thus, grammar provides an unconventional outlook on reality, which appears more and more disposed toward consignification.

The notion of succession, borrowed from the Aristotelian theory of motion (*Physics* 5.3) raises some very interesting questions within Thomas of Erfurt's discourse. The property of succession is a *modus essendi* that results in the general mode of signifying of the verb. Succession implies time and resistance (which, in the Aristotelian theory of motion, testifies to the non-existence of the void), but not everything exists in terms of succession. God and the Divine Intelligence, birth and decay, along with the illumination of the air, 'are' verbally, but their being does not have succession.[93] 'Deus est' is a fundamental dilemma for medieval epistemology, for it problematizes not only the existence of God but also the human capacity to understand Him. The grammarian acknowledges both problems and solves them by reducing eternity to difference. Thomas faces the objection that God and Divine Virtue are not beings in time by suggesting that succession and duration are also inscribed in eternity, as if the difference between time and eternity is not decided in terms of an opposition (eternity = absence of time) but in terms of a parallel (eternal succession vs. temporal succession). Human time – with its inherent features of succession and duration – becomes, in Thomas's discourse, a blueprint from which human beings can understand the superior succession and duration of eternity.

> Dicendum, quod licet esse Dei et intelligentiarum non sit successivum successione temporis, est tamen successivum successione aeternitatis; et licet aeternitas sit tota simul et perfecta possessio, secundum Boëtium; tamen, quia intelligimus ex istis inferioribus, ideo imaginamur ibi successionem et durationem aeternitatis per diversa spatia temporis. (*Grammatica speculativa*, 210)[94]

> [We have to say that even though the being of God and of the Intelligences is not successive in terms of the succession of time, it is successive in terms of the succession of eternity. Even though eternity, according to Boethius, is a simultaneous whole and a perfect possession, we understand it from these inferior things, thus we imagine the succession and duration of eternity through different spaces of time.]

Grammar cannot account for simultaneity and perfect possession, but it offers an earthly, 'verbal' perspective on the existence of God. Through the verb, eternity is expressed via a difference, and it becomes intelligible in the lowest spheres and in language as a difference of eternal successions. Indeed grammar constructs eternity into intelligibility as difference. [95]

Thomas observes that birth and decay, and the illumination of the sky, do not happen in terms of succession, yet we still say 'generatio, et corruptio et illuminatio aeris sunt, sive fuerunt.' In the process of generation and corruption it is possible, according to Thomas, to detect a kind of succession unfolding between time and the end-term of time ('inter tempus et terminus temporis,' 210). Similarly, in the production of light, succession is given by the resistance between two opposite terms, the term *a quo* and the term *ad quem*.[96]

The grammatical construction of God and nature elicits two different answers from the grammarian. In the case of God, he withdraws into the inferior perspective of the creature and activates the interpretative power of the intellect, as he does for the inexpressible. In the case of nature, he is prompted to find the homology between the construction of reality and that of language.

Syntax and Desire

The osmotic relation that is established between reality and language through the filter of the mind animates the Modistic discussion of the sentence. According to the Modistae, the articulation of the sentence exists in all three spaces (reality, mind, and language), yet only language is operative and explicit in terms of syntax, since it creates specific *partes orationis*, which are linked to each other in order to function in context. Through the system of the *modi*, reality, mind and language are rendered both coextensive and estranged, so that three equal but different constructions take place in them.

Boethius illustrates this point with a famous example in *Quaestio* 14. A thing and a concept can be signified by any part of speech, until it falls under the charge of a particular mode of signifying. Only in language the single notion of 'pain' can be unfolded variously into 'pain,' 'I suffer,' 'suffering,' 'painfully,' 'ouch!'[97] Even though syntax is activated only in language, reality and mind are themselves syntactically organized by the system of the *modi* – the sum of properties and faculties that describe the potentiality of the thing/concept to be turned into language. As Boethius later argues (*Quaestio* 24), there is a difference between thing and concept on the one hand, and property of the thing (*modus essendi*) and property of the intellect (*modus intelligendi*) on the other hand, The thing in itself and the concept in itself can signify without the modes of signifying, but eventually a selection is made, and a property (of being a noun, a verb, a pronoun, etc.) is chosen. The thing and the property are kept discrete both in reality ('quia proprietas, a qua accipitur modus significandi per essentiam a re differt') and in the mind ('intellectus rem ipsam et proprietatem eius bene distinguit').[98] Reality and mind, with their modes of being and understanding, are the remote, not perfect cause of construction, otherwise expression wouldn't be possible.[99] Only the modes of signifying organize speech in terms of *constructio*, the joining of two constructibles, yet they capture an articulation already existent in reality.

The language-oriented status of reality and mind is emphasized in the discussion on syntax. In *Quaestio* 27, Boethius argues that there are three kinds of constructions ('triplex est constructio'): the first in the things themselves ('constructio rerum per suas proprietates'), the second in the mind ('constructio intellectorum per suos modos intelligendi apud intellectum'), and the third in language ('constructio dictionum per suos modos significandi').[100] When dwelling on the construction of reality, Boethius argues that the syntax of reality is the relationship between substance and accident. A syntax is already inscribed in nature, where things are constructed by the continuous interplay of matter and form.

> Est enim quaedam constructio rerum per suas proprietates. Accidens enim per suam naturam et proprietatem, per quam non habet quod ipsum sit aliquod ens in se, sed in alio – universaliter enim essentia accidentis non sufficit in suo esse sed praeter essentiam accidentis exigitur subiectum ad hoc, quod accidens sit – per hanc ergo suam proprietatem et naturam unitur cum substantia, et habet substantia proprietatem huic proprietati correspondentem, eo quod habet naturam, ut sit quoddam ens in se et non in alio et in quo omnia alia; et ideo dicit Aristoteles, quod substantia est ens, quod non est in alio, sed omnia in ipso. (*Modi significandi*, 82–3)

> [There is, in fact, one kind of construction of things according to their properties. The accident, according to its nature and property, is not allowed to be a being in itself, but only in something else. Universally, in fact, it is not enough for the essence of the accident to be in itself, but for the accident to be, a subject is necessary, besides the essence of the accident. According to this property and nature (the accident) unites with the substance, and the substance has a property that corresponds to the accident's property, since it has such a nature that it is a kind of a being in itself

and not in something else, and all other things are in it. And so Aristotle says that substance is an *ens* which is not something else, but all things are in it.]

The syntax of reality is hence reflected in the modes of being. Boethius explains further that a construction such as 'Socrates runs' exists in language, in the mind, and in reality:

> Si enim dicam 'Socrates currit,' sicut in hoc sermone unum de altero enuntiatur congrue propter modos significandi dictionum proportionem ad invicem habentes, sic de necessitate prius fuit apud intellectum enuntiatum de eodem congrue propter modos intelligendi proportionem ad invicem habentes similes modis significandi dictionum, et aliquando etiam in re est constructio similis, ut cum cursus inest Socrati, inest sibi secundum proprietates similes istis modis intelligendi et significandi, quibus sibi sic inesse intelligitur et significatur. (*Modi significandi,* 83)

> [If I say 'Socrates runs' (as in this sentence one part is expressed from the other correctly according to the modes of signifying of the words that have a reciprocal proportion), necessarily in the same way the expression was enunciated in the intellect according to modes of understanding, similar to the modes of signifying of the words that have a reciprocal proportion. At a certain point in the thing there is a similar construction, since, as the running is inherent in Socrates, it is in him according to properties similar to the modes of understanding and signifying. Thus the fact that 'running' is in Socrates in this particular way is understood and signified.]

In other words, Socrates has some properties that allow for the running to be in him, and language frames into words what is already 'inevitably' constructed in reality.

Although the mind represents the crucial link between reality and language, the Modistae do not particularly develop the theme of mental syntax. Generally, they regard the mind as an intermediary between reality and language. The modes of signifying dwell in it, and the construction of language takes place in the encounter between the intellected properties of things and the active aspect of signification. Moreover, the mind is the propelling centre of the wheel of language, since the goal of grammar is to express a concept through a syntactic arrangement,[101] which in turns generates, as we shall see, a perfect understanding in the mind of the hearer. The notion of a mental syntax, one that takes place before and beyond the construction of language, is a tenet of the nominalist grammar of the fourteenth century. The idea of a mental language completely independent of the outcome in utterance is indeed one of the arguments that the adversaries of the Modistae used as a basis for their criticism of the Modistic system.[102]

Martin of Dacia seems to grant a special syntactical faculty to the space of intellect. When describing the process that leads the thing into expression, he argues that the intellect understands the thing by 'co-intellecting its properties' ('cointelligendo eius proprietates,' *Modi significandi*, 5).[103] In explaining the similarities and differences between the modes, Radulphus Brito mentions an 'esse cointellectum' alongside the 'esse consignificatum,' and describes a *ratio cointelligendi* that is inherent in the active mode of understanding, in the same way as the *ratio consignificandi* is related to the modes of signifying.[104] 'Co-intelligere,' itself a resounding theological word,[105] appears then to be in the intellect the counterpart of the 'consignificare' in language.

For the rest, the Modistae allude only briefly to construction in the intellect as a product of the *modi intelligendi*, giving to it equal weight as the construction in things and in language. It is the mind that weaves construction – otherwise, paradoxically, the words would 'construct' by themselves – but by means of the *modi significandi*, which are present in the mind as the efficient cause of construction.[106] The mind then appears as an intermediary between thing and discourse, and the construction that takes place therein is more similar, in terms of the order of words, to the construction of things than to that of language.[107]

It is only with John of Dacia that the issue of mental speech is approached at length, and interestingly, it is done so not from a strictly grammatical angle. Among the authors under consideration, John is the only one who approaches the question of why human beings speak. He does so while discussing the notion of *vox significativa* (the *dictio* considered under the aspects of sound and meaning). In this passage (*Summa grammatica*, 177–85), woven with references from Augustine, Aristotle, Plato, and their medieval commentators, John somewhat creatively applies to language the Aristotelian theory of perception and intellectual knowledge as laid out in *De anima* (with special reference to Book 2.8 and Book 3.3–4).[108] John begins by arguing that the imposition of the voice takes place in order to foster communication. The possible intellect contains many concepts and yearns for signs to express them. Once a concept has been intellected, a desire on the part of the intellectual power ('appetitus virtutis intellective') forces it into expression,[109] with the help of two powers: desire and imagination.[110] The desire for expression belongs to both animals and humans, but while the powers of desire and imagination are mostly indistinct and confused in the brutes, human concepts are complex and orderly and inspired by a stronger desire to be expressed ('voluntas exprimendi'). The capacity for articulated language is thus connected to a more intense drive toward expression. At this point, the intellect starts plotting and weaving the sentence:

> Cum igitur apud animam rationalem sint vocum intentiones et ymagina-tiones, consequenter apud eam fit excogitatio. Cogitat enim apud se, quem intellectum per quam vocem debeat significare, et sic patet quod vox men-taliter ante suam prolationem bene fit significativa. (*Summa grammatica*, 180)

> [Since in the rational soul there are desires and imaginations of voices, then the thought takes place therein. The soul considers within itself which concept should be signified by which voice. So it is clear that the voice becomes signifying well before its utterance.]

Later John specifies the nature of this desire: it is a cognitive force that compels the sensitive power toward expression.[111] Interestingly, this interior language, which is the locus of desire, is not described as a *verbum* (as it is for most of the medieval tradition, including Augustine and Aquinas) but as already a *sermo* ('mentalis,' 'intraneus') that then yields to *sermo exterior*.

> Et istum sermonem mentalem bene habent, qui a nativitate muti sunt, dummodo auditum habeant, si hoc possibile sit, et etiam illi, qui propter passionem aliquam vocem amiserunt. Cum ergo apud animam sit huius-modi sermo intraneus, considerandum est, quod ad eius similitudinem profertur sermo exterior, qui sensibilis est. Nam cum apud animam fit pre-cogitatio vocis, qua talem rem oporteat significari, tunc postmodum illi voci applicatur intentio significabilis sicut finis eius, quod est ad finem, et sic etiam bene fit vox significativa, cum profertur. (*Summa grammatica*, 180)

> [And this mental speech also belongs to those who are mute since birth, if they have the sense of hearing (if this is possible), and also to those who lost their voice due to some kind of accident. Since this internal speech is

in the mind, we have to consider that the exterior speech, which is sensible, is uttered in the likeness of it. In fact a pre-cogitation about the voice through which a certain thing has to be signified takes place in the mind. After that, a voice is applied to it (the *precogitatio*) toward the intention of signification, which is its goal; and then the signifying voice is created, when it is uttered.]

With John, the connections among the Aristotelian theory of perception, Modistic syntax, and the operation of desire in language are uncovered:[112] the mind plays the important role of creating desire and expectation in view of syntactic completion. As we shall see later, the theme of the mind's desire is more implicit in other authors, and it is often alluded to at the end of their explanations of linguistic syntax as a yearning toward articulation, which is quenched by the final completion of the sentence.

The Modistae's syntactical theory begins in reality and affects every step of their reflection on language. The web of the *modi significandi* prepares and enables each part of speech to perfectly function in syntax. No wonder, then, that the Modistae's discussions of the rules of syntax (*diasyntetica*) may upon a first reading appear more rushed than their discussions of morphology – at times they are not even extant.[113] The most comprehensive account of syntax is found once again in Thomas of Erfurt's *Grammatica speculativa*. Syntax, according to Thomas, is an application of the eight *partes orationis* to the passions of speech (*passiones sermonis*). Following Aristotle, Thomas recognizes four general principles of syntax: *principium materiale* (the constructibles, as 'matter' of the construction); *formale* (the union of constructibles); *efficiens* (divided into *intrinsicum*, i.e., the *modi significandi respectivi*, and *extrinsecum*, i.e., the intellect); and *finale* (the expression of a composite concept of the mind). The first of these three principles can be considered still related to morphology, and Thomas therefore deals in detail with only the three *passiones*. The progression toward a complete sentence (i.e., one that includes a verb) occurs by ascending through three grades of construction, which are hierarchically arranged: *constructio*, the union of constructibles; *congruitas*, which relies on the conformity among the constructibles; and *perfectio*, the completion of all the grammatical steps that looks back to the concept of the thing as it is 'perfectly' expressed in language.[114]

The crux of the Modistae's theory of syntax is *constructio*. Like *congrui-*

tas, it takes place between two (and only two) terms, whereas *perfectio*, the final completion, affects the whole speech.[115] Fundamentally, then, modistic syntax proceeds by means of binary sets – a dualism that is already pre-Modistic. Scholars account for this binary preference in three ways: Bursill-Hall attributes it to Scholastic dualism combined with syntactic theories of antiquity;[116] Marmo relates it to the Aristotelian-medieval theory of relation;[117] other scholars such as Kelly and Rosier identify in it the influence of the Aristotelian model of motion.[118]

Whether or not the motus model can account with precision for Modistic construction (the grammarians are not always consistent in their terminology), the relationship between the two basic elements, *dependens* and *terminans*, indeed appears as the satisfaction of the potentiality that creates a movement between two terms (*terminus a quo* and *ad quem* in physics; in grammar *principium* and *terminus* or *primum* and *secundum constructibile*). As Rosier very clearly points out, the two sets of elements must not be confused. The pair *principium–terminus* refers to movement, *principium* being 'the substance which is the point of departure of the act,' and *terminus* 'the substance which is the point of arrival of the act' (*La grammaire*, 137). The pair *dependens–terminans* in contrast refers to construction: *dependens* is the term in potency (the matter) in the relationship of government, and *terminans* is the term in act. In a construction such as 'Socrates reads,' the verb is the *dependens*, and Socrates is the *principium* with respect to the act and *terminans* with respect to the construction. In a construction such as 'he reads a book,' on the other hand, 'book' is the *terminus* of the act and the *terminans* of the dependence opened by the verb (*La grammaire*, 150).

It is my argument that the dualism inherent in Modistic construction is dictated by the fundamentally osmotic relation between language and nature. The way matter and form come together to make a composite in nature is employed by the Modistae to illustrate events in language – such as the difference and necessary attraction between the two principal parts of speech, and the existence of a syntax in reality. As nature 'constructs' itself through the interplay between a formal and a material principle, so language proceeds by means of binary agglomerates, until the verb inscribes the distance that is necessary for the completion of the movement. Hylomorphism is not a terminological device but rather the blueprint for *constructio* itself.

The most complete formulation of the interface between matter and form is found in Thomas. The *dependens* is an element in potency ('dependens accipitur ut quid in potentia'), while the *terminans* is in act ('terminans est ens in actu,' 280). The relationship between the *dependens* and the *terminans* mirrors an existing construction in nature – that of matter and form:[119]

> Relinquitur ergo, quod constructibilium unum sit dependens, alterum vero dependentia terminans: nam sicut ex materia et forma, quorum unum est in actu, alterum vero in potentia, fit per se compositum in natura; sic ex ratione dependendi et terminandi fit per se constructio in sermone. (*Grammatica speculativa*, 280)

> [What's left, therefore, is that one of the constructibles is a dependent and the other is the one which terminates that dependency. As a composite in nature is created by matter and form, of which one is in act and the other in potency; the construction in speech is created by the faculty of depending and terminating.]

As many have noticed, thirteenth-century grammarians connect the notion of dependency with that of *regimen*.[120] This rather violent grammatical relation implies that the two terms are not equal, but it is the *dependens* that governs the *terminans*, and not vice versa. If extracted from the discussion of grammar and compared to the wider philosophical background of thirteenth-century philosophy, this claim sounds strikingly unorthodox: a material principle (the *dependens*) governs a formal one (the *terminans*). A passion ('passio constructibilium') where the leading principle is a material one inevitably evokes a hotly debated topic in the philosophy of the period: Aristotle's theory of passion. As Maria Luisa Ardizzone explains, passion is a central notion in the texts of the 'new' Aristotle (*De anima, De generatione et corruptione, Physics*).[121] One of the categories, passion, is the foundation and the liaison between the theory of perception (*De anima, De memoria et reminiscentia, De sensu et sensato*) and the theory of matter (*Physics, De generatione et corruptione*). The general theory of passion is set forth in the *De generatione et corruptione*, where matter, 'the substrate which seeks form,' is defined as passive, thus making passion the central tenet of the process of birth and decay, and the leading principle for change and existence. The theory of passion and matter is connected to the (very unchristian) theory of the eternity of the world, as formulated by Aristotle and enhanced by Averroes: matter, with its property of being acted upon, rules generation and corruption, so that nothing new is generated, but everything progresses and exists according to transformation. Since it denies biblical Creation, the theory of the eternity of the world (eternity of matter) is one of the major targets of the 1277 condemnation. The orthodox tenet claims instead the supremacy of the formal principle over the material one.

As previously observed, in speculative grammar action and passion cease to be qualities of the verb, as they had been traditionally. Instead, action and passion become a principle of language, both as the interplay of the active and passive state in language formation and in the description of syntax, whose three stages represent three passions of speech. In *constructio*, the first, most crucial *passio*, matter takes over form, suggesting that at the heart of syntax the stability of the act is secondary to the unruly flowing of potentiality. Although, as we shall see, the sentence tends to formal perfection, in its minimal unit, matter governs form. Perhaps it is not just by chance that Radulphus Brito, one of the late Modistae, inverts these terms. Rudolph first agrees with the other grammarians by stating that when considered by themselves, the two constructibles are arranged like the two Aristotelian principles of nature: the *dependens*, like matter, is in potency, and it desires ('appetens') the *terminans*, which, like form, is in act:

> Ars imitatur naturae, ut dicitur 2^0 Physicorum. Sed in natura sufficiunt duo principia per se ut materia et forma … Ergo similiter erit in arte grammatica, quod sufficiunt duae partes orationis materialiter ad unam constructionem. Et huiusmodi constructibilia se habent ad similitudinem materiae et formae, quia ante actualem constructionem dependens secundum quod dependens est quid in potentia, quia est suae dependentiae terminum appetens. Terminans autem secundum quod terminans est quid in actu, quia est dependentiae terminus dans. (*Quaestiones*, 115–16)

> [Art imitates nature, as it is said in the second book of the *Physics*. Two principles are sufficient in nature, matter and form. Similarly, in the art of grammar, two parts of speech are materially sufficient for one construction. And thus, the constructibles are in the likeness of matter and form. Before the actual construction, the dependent, insofar as it is dependent, is something in potency, because it desires the terminus of his dependence. The *terminans*, insofar as it is terminant, is something in act, because it gives a terminus to the dependency.]

When the *dependens* and the *terminans* unite in actual construction, however, the balance switches: the *dependens* turns into a formal principle and the *terminans* into the material one. Being 'more constructible' than the terminant, the dependent 'works more' toward the syntactic arrangement of the construction: 'Licet ut actu sunt in constructione sit contrario modo, quia tunc dependens est formalius terminanti, quia plus operatur ad formam constructionis' (*Quaestiones*, 116: But it is the opposite when they are in act in construction, because then the dependent is more formal than the terminant, since it labours more in view of the construction). In reversing the traditional balance between matter and form, Rudolph might have indeed identified and rectified a position that, although located within the microcosm *constructio,* he perceived as untenable.[122]

The matter–form relationship – a feature of reality that language captures in the microcosm of construction – also unveils the workings of desire in language. Just as matter and form are mutually attractive in nature, so are the two principles of construction. The operations of the material *dependens* and formal *terminans* are defined in speculative grammar in the following terms: the *dependens* is forced by its own *modi significandi* to 'ask and expect' ('quod ratione alicuius modi significandi tantum petit vel exigit'), while the *terminans* is forced to 'give and allow' ('tantum dat vel concedit,' *Grammatica speculativa,* 280–2). These terms, viewed by Bursill-Hall as 'unsatisfactory notional criteria,'[123] indeed reveal traces of the discourse of desire. *Exigere, exigentia* are standard grammatical terms for the operation of construction, and are often replaced by *regimen.*[124] Kelly quotes one particularly telling definition given by Magister Jordanus, in which *exigentia* is defined as a compelling desire, indeed an (at)traction, toward construction. The desire of the dependent ('tractio vel desiderium') then perfectly portrays the desire of matter always yearning for form.

> Exigere est desiderare aliam dictionem ad perfectionem orationis; exigentia est tractio vel desiderium alterius dictionis ad perfectionem orationis; et dicitur exigere quasi extra se egere. (*The Mirror,* 183)

> [To demand is to desire another *dictio* in view of the perfection of the speech; exigentia is an attraction or desire for another *dictio* in view of the perfection of the speech; 'exigere' is, so to speak, going outside of oneself.]

In desiring termination, the material principle trespasses itself ('extra se egere'), joining the formal one to create a composite. It is hence desire that compels language toward articulation.

The operation of desire as attraction between constructibles also affects *congruitas*, the most elusive part of modistic syntax. While *constructio* requires only the 'absolute' union of the constructibles ('constructio requirit constructibilium unionem absolute,' *Grammatica speculativa*, 308), *congruitas*, the second passion of the speech, claims the correct union ('debita unio') of the constructibles. As previously discussed, the notion of *congruitas* is the place for great friction between grammar and logic, the Modistae being the most strenuous supporters of a purely grammatical, artificial system of language – one that allows for an expression such as *cappa nigra* (proper and congruous construction) as opposed to *cappa categorica* (congruous but improper, yet acceptable to the grammarian). The Modistae maintain that the correctness of a construction does not depend upon the special meanings of the words, but rather on the conformity of *modi significandi*. Congruity installs in syntax the notion of order: *ordinatio* is often synonymous with congruity, and one medieval etymology connects *con-gruitas* to the orderly flight of a flock of cranes (*grues*): as the cranes naturally follow one common behaviour in flight, so the word that enters into construction must adopt the features of the other constructibles.[125]

Congruitas is also the step that is less lenient to be related to the discourse of nature. While nature operates by means of opposition, language often works in terms of likeness and concordance.[126] The leading principles of *congruitas* are the notions of *similitudo* and *proportio* – concord and syntactic linkage, as explained by Bursill-Hall. *Similitudo* and *proportio* regulate the attraction between the constructibles and bestow order upon the sentence by creating a net of orderly correspondences between the modes of signifying.[127] As Kelly remarks (*The Mirror*, 184), the two terms are current in the scholastic theological discourse and 'come into the discussion of congruitas early in the thirteenth century. Indeed in syntax *proportio* and *similitudo* seem to be essential to the working of the *appetitus* for construction in the *dictiones*.'

In *constructio* and *congruitas*, desire is an active and linear force that pushes the sentence along. In *perfectio*, the third and last passion of the sentence, desire achieves the circular feature of fulfilment. Perfection, the desired fullness of everything, is the end point of the Aristotelian scholastic system. Once reached, perfection implies both the satisfaction and the continuation of desire, as seen, for instance, in Albertus Magnus's rewriting of the *Physics*. *Perfectio*, the final goal of grammar, considers for the first time a whole sentence/speech (*locutio, oratio*) and appears like the fulfilment of all the expectations of language. The pacification of the sentence relies mainly upon the presence of a verb, introducing *distantia* (difference, movement) in the sentence. The most immediate goal of the perfect construction is therefore the presence of a verb: a construction as 'homo albus' is still incomplete. Because it lacks distance, the mind cannot rest on it ('intellectus super compositionem primam non quiescit'). 'Homo est albus' is a perfect construction since it reaches the remote goal of perfection – the pacification of the intellect and the production of a perfect sense in the mind of the hearer.[128] In one of his rare non-technical descriptions, Martin of Dacia talks about the fluctuation, vacillation, and restlessness of the mind over the incomplete construction:

> Sed si proferatur suppositum solum ut *homo* vel *homo albus* vel dicendo *si Socrates currit,* fluctuat anima et vacillat et non quiescit, quia suppositum est nullius termini determinati in hac oratione. Licet enim sit per se stans absolute, tamen per comparationem ad animam, ut anima super aliquod perfectum quiescat, debet habere appositum, ut per ipsum finitetur et quiescat anima super orationem. (*Modi significandi,* 114)

> [If only the suppositum is expressed, as *homo* or *homo albus,* or when saying *si Socrates currit,* the mind fluctuates and vacillates and doesn't rest, because the suppositum is not of any determined term in this sentence. In absolute terms it stands by itself, but in relation to the mind, in order for the mind to rest on something perfect, it must have an appositum, so that it may be brought to termination by it and the mind can rest over the sentence.]

There are three requirements for the perfect construction: the presence of a verb, which provides *distantia*; the conformity of *modi significandi*; and the termination of every dependent ('quod nulla dependentia sit non terminata').[129] If complete, the sentence will reflect the three attributes of perfection as listed in Aristotle's *Metaphysics*: to have nothing absent, to have attained its finality, and to be able to generate something similar to itself (*Grammatica speculativa,* 314–16).

Perfection goes beyond grammar, connecting language again to the reality that generated it and to the mind that produced it. From the elaboration of the modes to the relationship of the different parts of speech, the interplay between matter and form, potency and act, has pushed language along in terms of movement. In *perfectio* language seeks fulfilment, the enjoyment and pacification that signal the peak and the continuation of desire. It takes place in communication, as the perfect construction quenches the expectations of not only the speaker, but also the hearer. As Thomas notes, there are different degrees of perfection, which can be measured by degrees of pacification in the mind of the hearer ('Nam ea magis perfecta est, quae magis quietat animum auditoris; et quae minus quietat, minus perfecta erit').[130]

All three stages of syntax are pervaded by desire. In *constructio*, the linear desire between the material dependent and the formal terminant establishes the supremacy of matter at the heart of modistic syntax. In *congruitas*, desire is featured as a form of order, regulated by *similitudo* and *proportio*. In *perfectio*, desire is twofold: the drive on the part of the intellect, which pushes the sentence forward until it is pacified by the presence of a verb; and the external desire of the hearer, which is pacified by the perfect construction. The fullness and fulfilment of the form, *perfectio* constitutes the culmination of a desire that continues desiring in communication. The movement of the sentence (and before and beyond it, the movement of constructed things and concepts) appears then as an initially linear and subsequently circular movement toward the stillness and the pleasure of a full stop.

Medieval metaphysics is formulated as a syntactic movement of desire toward God, the Aristotelian unmoving mover who organizes and subordinates the motions of the heavens through the desire he inspires in them. Interestingly, within the system of the Modistae, the 'god' of the sentence is the verb. Language, as a movement of desire, revolves around the verb-movement. Language as a movement of desire revolves, in the end, around itself.

3 Dante: The Syntax of Poetry

After theology and grammar, poetry is a 'third way' to knowledge within the highly unified medieval epistemological system. With theology, the connection between a word and the Word – language and 'n-squared language' – was in focus; with grammar, a language about language – the square root of language – was key. Poetry decomposes the two constituents of language (sound and meaning) and, by turning the first into its ruling pattern (rhythm and rhyme), offers a different perspective on the second. Where theology provided the idea of a hyperbolic approach to the truth through language, and grammar a parabolic trajectory between reality and expression, poetry proffers an elliptic perspective on language, since poetic language is always threatened by aphasia.

Theology and grammar establish the Cartesian axis for locating Dante's discourse on language/syntax. In my earlier discussions on theology, I stressed the idea of syntax as a cosmic order imparted by God on the universe. Regarding grammar, I have underlined the primacy of syntax in a process that leads co-extensively from thing to expression by means of leaps of desire between matter and form. In Dante, syntax emerges as an equally strong notion, one that is synonymous with both the operation of God in the universe and the way poetry, as redeemed language, reconstructs it. Moreover, in Dante's *Divine Comedy*, the three aspects of language (sound, sign, and meaning) become three structural notions, three spatial, temporal, and moral entities.

A fitting epigraph for a discussion of Dante's poetic and metaphysical linguistics is a line in canto 29 of the *Paradiso*, where cosmic order is described as a constructed sentence: 'concreato fu ordine e costrutto' (31: order was created and ordained).[1] The word *costrutto* means indeed 'syntactically ordained' – as Dante's usage in other passages confirms.[2]

The order that unfolds syntactically in the universe ('costrutto') is inherent in matter and form ('concreato').[3] While this order is simultaneously and eternally present to the inhabitants of heaven, the poet and the pilgrim must pattern it through the temporality of language and desire: this arduous path is the subject matter of the present chapter.

Dante's discussion of language is encompassed in all his work – albeit intermittently and often implicitly. From the often disregarded seeds of Vita Nova 6 and 15–16,[4] through the position of Convivio 1 and the core discussion of the De vulgari eloquentia, all the way to the conclusion in Paradiso 26, the problem of language is ever present and pressing to an author who, as all critics agree, automatically aligned his practice of poetry with theoretical reflection.[5] Throughout his work, Dante's theory of language is continuously reassessed and readjusted. The many contradictions that punctuate its development – nomina sunt consequentia rerum versus significatio ad placitum, the greater or lesser nobility of the vernacular with respect to Latin, the unstable and fluctuating meaning of gramatica and of 'volgare illustre,' the mystery of Adam's primiloquium, to name the most clamorous – are further proof that Dante approaches the problem of language from the point of view, and with the necessity, of a poet – namely a vernacular poet. There is always an urgent practical end to Dante's reflection on language: the problem of language is explicitly posed first and foremost as a question of craft and authorship, in terms of a strenuous defence of vernacular poetry..Yet the position and the articulation of the issue of language in its full practical force coincide with the poet's (implicit) attempt to re-inscribe it, rewrite it in a wider context, through which Dante intends to test the epistemological limits of language as a poetic tool, and to locate it within the dialectic of time and eternity.

While the Modistae considered a very uniform and unified stratum of language (the universal core of grammar belonging to every language), Dante operates on the superior and inferior borders of it: the language of God and the vernacular, i.e., the invisible referent and the external accident of the Modistae's system.[6] The main objective of Dante's theory and practice of language is to reconcile the two extremes. Poetry emerges as an antidote to the irremediable deterioration of human language after the Fall. Through music, poetry binds the fallen temporality of human language to the eternity of the Word of God. The actualization of this poetic potential is the Commedia, where the binding operation of terza rima supports a narrative where language, desire, signs, and bodies concur in the unfolding of meaning.

In his essay 'The Significance of Terza Rima,'[7] John Freccero has shown that the metrical aspect of the poem mirrors the functioning of three other aspects: the thematic (the forward motion of the pilgrim toward the point of departure of the narrative), the logical (narrative of conversion), and the metaphysical (God's way of writing narrative; Christian theory of history and biblical allegory). All four facets of the poem progress as a 'forward motion that moves toward its own beginning' (264) and, as such, they work according to the theological process of recapitulation, which implies 'the integration of the beginning into the end' (266).[8] In a truly Augustinian way, poetry – the syntax that binds and stabilizes fallen language through rhyme and rhythm – becomes the mirror of the order ruling personal and universal history.

In the *Comedy*, the discourse of language also intercepts that of desire. By structuring the three otherworldly realms in terms of loss (*Inferno*), lack (*Purgatorio*), and fulfilment (*Paradiso*), desire also interprets personal as well as universal history. A product of time and mortality, desire – like poetry – ends up defying it, by propelling the journey of the pilgrim and of the poet forward, beyond ineffability and pacification, in a place where silence is not any more a limitation but the sound of meaning itself.

Heavenly Refutations

Rather than rehearsing *in toto* the complex, well-known, and yet much debated arguments of the *Convivio* and the *De vulgari eloquentia*, I will present here some key aspects of the problem of language in these texts. I will first look at this issue *sub specie aeternitatis*, by focusing on two famous 'heavenly refutations' and reading two key passages from the prose works: *Convivio* 2.13 (the theory of rarity and density) and *De vulgari eloquentia* 1.4 (Adam's language) alongside their refutation in *Paradiso* 2 and 26. These provide a compact sketch of the evolution of Dante's thoughts on language, in terms of the widening of the gap between fallen human language and its transcendental counterpart, the language of God. In Dante's portrayal of this vexing disparity between mortal and divine language, a clear need emerges for something to hold together deteriorated human language and bind its irremediable temporality to eternity. Poetry functions precisely as this constructing, binding force. A 'synoptic' reading of *Convivio* and *De vulgari eloquentia* on the issue of Babel and the primacy of vernacular poetry[9] highlights the redemptive qualities of poetry, particularly its capacity to return language to an ideal state where names and things coincide.

Convivio *and the Heaven of the Moon: Grammar and Science*

The fluctuating meaning of the term *gramatica* is a notable terminological problem in Dante's linguistics.[10] In Dante's work the term seems to bear three meanings: that of science of language; that of artificial, 'universal' language,[11] fabricated by the human being in order to find a common ground of communication, albeit restricted to few; and, finally, that of the Latin language, including Latin grammar and Latin literature. Rather than considering these three meanings as contradictions – and arguing over which is which in the different passages – it is more useful to consider them as variations revolving around the same notion of *lingua regulata* (ruled language).

Dante holds that Latin – the *gramatica* of a specific intellectual community to which Dante belongs[12] – was up to a certain point a natural language. Spatial and temporal challenges compelled the *inventores gramatice facultatis*, the founders of grammar as a system of stability and rules, to look for its structural regulations. As a consequence, Latin was 'frozen' in a determinate state, which is still a temporal and local state, the language of the Roman *auctores*.[13] Bound by a system of grammatical rules, the *hic et nunc* Latin (or Greek) becomes an *'ubique et semper'* kind of language and is preserved from further deterioration and corruption so that a socially restricted group of people is able to use it as a form of communication.[14] In other words: (1) *Gramatica* is a natural language 'embalmed' by means of grammatical rules. It becomes an artificial language – universal but with spatial, temporal and social restrictions. (2) Latin is the grammatical language currently used by Dante and the intellectual community to which he relates spatially and temporally. (3) Grammar is the ensemble of rules that turn a natural language into an artificial one. Such rules are found within the natural language – as it is at a determinate time and place – and later imposed upon it from outside in order to prevent its growth and preserve its stability. Although very stable, *gramatica* (in all three versions) is not completely durable. But, in contrast to the vernacular's radical and unruly mutability, *gramatica* seems to obey a certain cyclicity, as its representation in the *Convivio* shows.

In *Convivio* (2.13.9–10), within the general comparison of heavens and sciences, Dante establishes a twofold relationship between Grammar and the Moon:[15]

Dico che 'l cielo della Luna colla Gramatica si somiglia, perché ad esso si può comparare [per due propietadi]. Ché se la Luna si guarda bene, due cose si veggiono in essa propie, che non si veggiono nell'altre stelle. L'una si è l'ombra che è in essa, la quale non è altro che raritade del suo corpo, alla quale non possono terminare li raggi del sole e ripercuotersi così come nell'altre parti; l'altra si è la variazione della sua luminositade, ché ora luce da uno lato e ora luce da un altro, secondo che lo sole la vede. E queste due propietadi hae la Gramatica: ché per la sua infinitade li raggi della ragione in essa non si terminano, in parte spezialmente delli vocabuli; e luce or di qua or di là, in tanto [in] quanto certi vocabuli, certe declinazioni, certe construzioni sono in uso che già non furono, e molte già furono che ancor saranno: sì come dice Orazio nel principio della Poetria, quando dice: 'Molti vocabuli rinasceranno che già caddero.'

[I say that the heaven of the Moon resembles Grammar because it may be compared to it; for if the Moon is closely examined, two things will be seen peculiar to it which are not seen in the other stars: one is the shadow in it, which is nothing but the rarity of its substance in which the rays of the Sun cannot terminate and be reflected back as in its other parts; the other is the variation of its luminosity, which shines now on one side, now on the other, according as the Sun looks upon it. These two properties Grammar possesses; for because of its infinitude the rays of reason are not terminated, especially in the particular of words; and it shines now on this side, now on that, insofar as certain words, certain declensions, and certain constructions are now in use which formerly were not, and many were formerly in use which will yet be in use again, as Horace says at the beginning of his Poetics, when he says: 'Many words shall be born which have long since fallen out of use.']¹⁶]

In this passage Dante discusses two features of Grammar, its infinity and its cycles, in connection with two features of the heaven of the Moon, moon spots and moon phases. On the natural science side of the comparison, the first of the two issues (moon spots) deals with a theoretical problem of principles (rarity/density as a principle of the moon spots) related to *matter*, the second with an applied/empirical problem (moon cycles) related to *time*. This twofold structure is reflected in the presentation of Grammar. The theoretical issue of the infinity of grammar (= rarity of the moon) is followed by the historical/applied issue of the cycles of language, the rise and fall in time of words, declensions, and constructions. As rarity/density is a question of quantity of matter, so too is the 'infinity' of grammar a question of quantity of linguistic matter – especially in terms of lexicon ('spezialmente de li vocabuli'), as Dante points out. It is the uncontrollable quantity of isolated words that keeps the rays of reason from fully embracing Grammar ('li raggi de la ragione in essa non si terminano'). On the other hand, moon phases suggest and prompt a reflection on the cyclical quality of language, which Dante considers in terms of both lexicon and syntax, even though the quotation from Horace ('molti vocabuli rinasceranno che già furono') brings the focus back to isolated words. Interestingly, in this formulation a linear trajectory (termination) intersects a circular one: thus, the potentially subversive idea of a limitless vocabulary is partially corrected by the notion of cyclical return, providing in the end the image of an 'elliptical' science.

This passage is considered problematic by critics since it implies instability for the ruled language too,[17] an issue upon which Dante remarks again in *Convivio* (4.6.3), when he refers to the Latin verb *auieo* as 'un verbo molto lasciato dall'uso in gramatica' (that has very much fallen out of use in Latin), thereby proving that cyclicity applies to the ruled language as well. A more flexible notion of *gramatica*, one that takes into consideration its ties with a natural language 'frozen' by a set of rules, might ease the asperity of this passage, and help understand grammar as a system of rules that is unchangeable in the sense that it doesn't allow addition and subtraction, but is not so solid as to avoid internal alterations.

In *Paradiso* 2 (48–148), Dante rewrites the 'material' explanation of moon spots *sub specie aeternitatis* through Beatrice's long refutation of the Averroist theory of rarity and density. Traditionally considered an arid doctrinal canto, *Paradiso* 2 appears today to be one of the epistemological pillars of the canticle – and not by chance Dante opens it by spurring his readers with an Ulysses-like oration (2.1–18), which sanctions the redemption of rational knowledge.[18] Since Bruno Nardi's masterful explanation of the canto,[19] the modern reader is aware that the problem here is not the evaluation of the moon spots, in itself a minor issue, but the cosmic order – and with it, the modality of Creation and indeed God himself, a discourse that runs throughout *Paradiso* to the very threshold of the Empyrean.

Moreover, in canto 2 the reader is for the first time faced with the problem of interpretation *sub specie aeternitatis*, after the first canto had brought forth the suspicion that the 'trasumanar' entailed a disempowerment of the 'significar.'[20] When the pilgrim asks Beatrice 'ma ditemi: che son li segni bui / di questo corpo, che là giuso in terra / fan di Cain favoleggiar altrui?' (49–51: but tell me, what are the dusky marks of this body which there below on earth cause folk to tell the tale of Cain?), the problem of the sign (and of its correct interpretation) is raised again[21] – still from an earthly perspective ('là giuso'), but on the verge of rebounding to more significant ends, later in the same heaven, with Beatrice's explanation of condescension as signification in canto 4 – a point to which I shall return.

Within the *pars destruens* of her long refutation, Beatrice highlights the inherent dangers of the Averroistic theory: were the moon spots caused by the rarity and density of matter on the moon (i.e., by means of the quantity and not the quality of the matter), the same evidence could be applied to all the heavens and testify to the intensity of brightness of all the stars:

> Se raro e denso ciò facesser tanto,
> una sola virtù sarebbe in tutti,
> più e men distribuita e altrettanto. (2.67–9)

> [If rarity and density alone produced this thing, one single virtue, more or less or equally distributed, would be in all.]

The whole system of the heavens would therefore be reduced to one principle: a material principle as opposed to a formal one. Quite the reverse, unity and uniqueness are granted – within Beatrice's *pars construens* – only to Angelic Intelligence in the Empyrean. Divine Virtue, once transmitted to the heaven of the fixed stars through the 'filter' of the Primum Mobile, becomes diversified by the heavenly bodies according to their specific qualities. The operation of the Angelic Intelligence is one of unfolding ('spiega') and of binding (emphasized by the equivocal rhyme 'lega'):

> E come l'alma dentro a vostra polve
> per differenti membra e conformate
> a diverse potenze si risolve,
> così l'intelligenza sua bontate
> multiplicata per le stelle spiega,
> girando sé sovra sua unitate.
> Virtù diversa fa diversa lega
> col prezïoso corpo ch'ella avviva,
> nel qual, sì come vita in voi, si lega.
> Per la natura lieta onde deriva
> la virtù mista per lo corpo luce

come letizia per pupilla viva.
Da essa vien ciò che da luce a luce
par differente, non da denso e raro;
essa è formal principio che produce,
conforme a sua bontà, lo turbo e 'l chiaro. (2.133–48)

[And as the soul within your dust is diffused through different members
and conformed to different potencies, so does the Intelligence deploy its
goodness, multiplied through the stars, itself circling upon its own unity.
Divers virtues make divers alloy with the precious body it quickens,
wherein, even as life in you, it is bound. Because of the glad nature whence
it flows, the mingled virtue shines through the body, as gladness does
through a living pupil. Thence comes what seems different between light
and light, not from density and rarity. This is the formal principle which
produces, conformably with its own excellence, the dark and the bright.]

Although the system of corespondence between heavens and sciences is
not resumed in the *Paradiso*, Giuseppe Mazzotta has demonstrated the
tacit presence of Grammar in the heaven of the Moon, by pointing out
the crucial similarity between sacrifice and signification in cantos 3–5
and the emphasis given to the principle of allegorical representation in
canto 4.[22] On the basis of this oblique presence of Grammar in the *Paradiso* version of the heaven of the Moon, I suggest that the heavenly refutation might still entail a rethinking of its principles. With the argument
against the theory of rarity and density, the argument for the infinity of
Grammar might fall as well. *Sub specie aeternitatis*, then, Grammar would
not be considered infinite in quantity of linguistic matter. Since a higher,
more transcendental principle than quantity of matter is required to
explain moon spots, a stronger organizing principle than the quantitative infinity of the subject matter – particularly visible in terms of lexicon
('spezialmente ne li vocabuli') – is required for Grammar.
   A formal organizing principle is needed for grammar as well, something capable of 'unfolding' and 'binding itself' with the 'linguistic matter,' as the diversified angelic virtue binds itself with the heavenly bodies
('virtù diversa fa diversa lega'). In this context, then, the individual
words are not to be considered in terms of quantity, but in terms of quality: in grammatical terms, not as words but as *parts of speech*. It is my argument that this unchangeable yet potentially multiform first principle is
syntax, the universal, common core of language – as opposed to lexicon,
loose matter that needs to be bound together.

In *Paradiso* 2, Dante addresses and refutes only the first, and theoretical, feature of the moon as described in *Convivio* (moon spots), and does not allude to the second, and temporal, feature (moon phases). Bringing this back to the context of Grammar, it seems that by breaking up the argument of *Convivio* 2 and dealing only with the first part (density/rarity and infinity of grammar) and not the second (lunar phases and cycles of language), Dante widens the gap between the theoretical principle of language (where a stronger organizing principle is opposed to quantity of lexicon) and its application, its happening in history.

Adam's Language: De vulgari eloquentia *(1.4) and* Paradiso *(26)*

The second refutation *sub specie aeternitatis*, regarding the language first used by Adam, is a *locus classicus* of the discussion of Dante's theory of language. All scholars agree that it points to a further deterioration of human language and a greater diversion of the human from the divine.[23] The heavenly refutation, however, might concern not only Adam's actual first word, but the quality itself (semiotic vs. non-semiotic) of the language used by the first speaker. In the *De vulgari eloquentia*, Dante states that the first, joyful word pronounced by Adam is the name of God – *El* – in the form either of a question or of a response to an unuttered stimulus coming from God:

> Rationabiliter ergo credimus ipsi Ade prius datum fuisse loqui ab Eo qui statim ipsum plasmaverat.
> Quid autem prius vox primi loquentis sonaverit, viro sane mentis in promptu esse non titubo ipsum fuisse quod 'Deus' est, scilicet *El*, vel per modum interrogationis vel per modum responsionis. Absurdum atque rationi videtur orrificum ante Deum ab homine quicquam nominatum fuisse, cum ab ipso et in ipsum factus fuisset homo. Nam sicut post prevaricationem humani generis quilibet exordium sue locutionis incipit ab 'heu,' rationabile est quod ante qui fuit inciperet a gaudio; et cum nullum gaudium sit extra Deum, sed totum in Deo, et ipse Deus totus sit gaudium, consequens est quod primus loquens primo et ante omnia dixisset 'Deus.'
> (1.4.3–4)

> [Therefore it is reasonable to believe that the power of speech was first given to Adam, by Him who had just created him. As to what was first pronounced by the voice of the first speaker, that will readily be apparent to anyone in their right mind, and I have no doubt that it was the name of

God or *El*, in the form either of a question or of an answer. It is manifestly absurd and an offence against reason, to think that anything should have been named by a human being before God, when he had been made human by Him and for Him. For if, since the disaster that befell the human race, the speech of every one of us has begun with 'woe!,' it is reasonable that he who existed before should have begun with a cry of joy; and, since there is no joy outside God, but all joy is in God, and since God Himself is joy itself, it follows that the first man to speak should. first and before all have said 'God.']

As many have noticed, and as Zygmunt Barański has elaborated, Dante, in order to emphasize his point on Adam's *primiloquium*, revisits – or rather omits and manipulates – with a great deal of originality various major linguistic events of the Book of Genesis. Of those, the most puzzling omission is his silence about Adam naming the animals, while the craftiest displacement is his misogynistic dismissal of the dialogue between Eve and the serpent.[24] Rather than common nouns in isolation or the sinful speech of a woman, Dante selects the ultimate sign, the name of God,[25] as the first bit of semiotic communication in response to the mysterious summons of the air. [26]According to Barański, the omissions from Genesis 'highlight the structure of Dante's argument, with its movement from divine giving to divine punishment, and from proper to improper use of language – a structure which displays the centrality in his thought of the relationship between language and ethics' (113–14).

Interestingly, Dante's strategic rewriting aims at disconnecting God's gift (indeed a dowry, *dos*, as Barański notices on page 107) from any sense of purpose or necessity. It is not employed in naming or dialogue: it is an act of pure joy ('inciperet a gaudio'), which is God himself ('ipse Deus totus sit gaudium'). The utterance of His name represents the primal instance of the creature's enjoyment of God: in Augustinian terms, it belongs to the order of *frui* and not of *uti*. In the unfolding of this supremely selfless gift ('in explicatione tante dotis'), God is glorified, and a trace of this first linguistic happiness is impressed in the human being as the joy that is perceived each time the faculty is actualized:

> licet Deus sciret, immo presciret (quod idem est quantum ad Deum) absque locutione conceptum primi loquentis, voluit tamen et ipsum loqui, ut in explicatione tante dotis gloriaretur ipse qui gratis dotaverat. Et ideo divinitus in nobis esse credendum est quod in actu nostrorum effectuum ordinato letamur. (1.5.2)

[even if God knew (or, rather, foreknew, which is the same thing where God is concerned) the first speaker's conception without his having to speak, yet He still wished that Adam should speak, so that He who had freely given so great a gift should be glorified in its employment. And likewise, we must believe that the fact that we rejoice in the ordered activity of our faculties is a sign of divinity in us.]

That first joyful utterance represents, therefore, a true *imago dei* ('divinitus in nobis') inside the speaker, presumably obfuscated, but not erased, by the subsequent fall of language. Like for the other faculties, for postlapsarian language too, the memory of the initial happiness is not recollected through one disconnected act of language – as the joy of 'El' is substituted by the anguish of 'heu!' – but through the experience of the order that presides over it every time it is unfolded ('in actu ordinatu laetamur'). In the orderly binding of words, and not in words themselves, the potential redemption of language resides.

Adam's language is later explained as a *forma locutionis* (1.6.4), co-created ('concreata') with the soul, with which Adam's lips fabricated the first Hebrew words.[27] In *Paradiso* 26, Dante has Adam himself refuting the *De vulgari eloquentia* by making him not only the user, but also the maker of his own language, authoritatively defining the language he 'used and shaped' (114: 'l'idioma ch'usai e che fei'). As Nardi first noted, Dante here alludes to the medieval debate on whether or not Adam's language was of divine origin, and upholds a non-traditional position.[28] Adam explains that while the faculty of speech is a work of nature, language, since its inception, has been a mutable system:

La lingua ch'io parlai fu tutta spenta
innanzi che a l'ovra inconsummabile
fosse la gente di Nembròt attenta:
ché nullo effetto mai razïonabile,
per lo piacere uman che rinnovella
seguendo il cielo, sempre fu durabile.
Opera naturale è ch'uom favella;
ma così o così, natura lascia
poi fare a voi secondo che v'abbella. (26.124–32)

[The tongue which I spoke was all extinct before the people of Nimrod attempted their unaccomplishable work; for never was any product of reason durable forever, because of human liking, which alters, following the heavens. That man should speak is nature's doing, but whether thus or thus, nature then leaves you to follow your own pleasure.]

Adam denies any degree of stability even to Hebrew, pointing out that the language he used was already extinct prior to Babel. Even the name of God, the sign of all signs, was subjected to the fluctuations of time. It first was *I* and only then *El*.

> Pria ch'i' scendessi a l'infernale ambascia,
> *I* s'appellava in terra il sommo bene
> onde vien la letizia che mi fascia;
> e *El* si chiamò poi: e ciò convene,
> ché l'uso dei mortali è come fronda
> in ramo, che sen va e altra vene. (26.133–8)

[Before I descended to the anguish of Hell the Supreme Good from Whom comes the joy that swathes me was named *I* on earth; and later He was called *El*: and that must needs be, for the usage of mortals is a leaf on a branch, which goes away and another comes.]

The explanations for the two names of God are diverse and convincing.[29] While *El* is traditionally understood as the most typical of the Hebrew names for God, *I* can be interpreted as a simple letter, a number, a shortened form for *Ia*. More significantly, such an open signifier represents, as Barański observes, 'a perfect synthetic example of the instability of human linguistic creation.'[30] Particularly worth noting is what is entailed in the passage from one letter (*I*) to two letters (*El*): the passage from the one to the many. This is a crucial movement for the medieval mind, which conceived of eternity as wholeness and mortality as fragments.[31] It implies generation (*El* derives from *I*); generation implies corruption (*I* falls out of use to make space for *El*); corruption implies death; and death, in the absence of redemption, implies damnation.

Line 134 – '*I* si chiamava in terra il sommo bene' – also deserves particular attention. *I* – the most abbreviated, compact, and therefore most encompassing sign for God – is used *on earth* (at least until Adam's death). 'In terra' seems indeed to suggest that the use of this primal, seminal sign – and therefore the use of all signs – is a consequence of the Fall, leaving open the hypothesis that communication in Eden happened without signs. Certainly Dante does not openly state that there were no signs in Eden: 'on earth' can be understood as 'in Eden' or 'on earth after the Fall.' Yet when Adam says 'before I was sent down to hell's torments,' it seems likely that he is referring to his life after the Fall (930 years) rather than prior to it (seven hours). Whether or not he is stating that Eden was a space untouched by human signs, it is clear that Dante reassesses his theory of language with a focus upon the Fall. Adam's refutation downplays Babel's role as a turning point in the history of (fallen) language and locates the cause of language's 'fickleness' within language itself.

It is, however, important to keep in mind the context in which Dante depicts the inconsistency and mutability of language. The cameo involving Adam is set as the completion of the pilgrim's cycle of exams on the three theological virtues that began in canto 24, and right at the end of the celebration of charity: that is, divine love, redemptive love.[32] With Adam, the reader is reminded of the Fall, the event that pulled human beings away from God and created unlikeness between the Maker and his creature. [33]A few lines earlier, however, Dante had rehearsed for his readers the other side – the positive, constructive side – of salvation history. When John asks the pilgrim to mention the 'teeth by which this love grips' him (49–50: 'sì che tu suone / con quanti denti questo amor ti morde'), Dante answers,

> ché l'essere del mondo e l'esser mio,
> la morte ch'el sostenne per ch'io viva,
> e quel che spera ogne fedel com'io (58–60)

[the being of the world and my own being, the death that He sustained that I might live and that which every believer hopes]

Creation, Incarnation, Resurrection: the Fall is one and the same narrative as these events. In this narrative, the Fall is just the beginning of salvation, and Adam is one with Christ, Eve one with Mary, as other instances in the *Paradiso* recall.[34] Fall from grace and redemption are united through love. The same is true for language, only the act of love that saves language is poetry.[35]

Finally, it is worth noting that the four passages discussed so far are cross-connected by (almost) the same quotation of Horace's *Ars poetica* in *Convivio* 2 and *Paradiso* 26. The passage on Grammar and the heaven of the Moon in *Convivio* ends with a semi-literal translation of *Ars poetica* 70–2: 'multa renascentur quam iam cecidere, cadentque / quae nunc sunt in honore vocabula, si volet usus, / quem penes arbitrium est et ius et norma loquendi' (many terms that have fallen out of use shall be born again, and those shall fall that are now in repute, if Usage so will it, in

whose hands lies the judgment, the right and the rule of speech). In
Paradiso 26 Adam 'quotes' lines 60–2 of the same passage: 'ut silvae foliis
pronos mutantur in annos, / prima cadunt; ita verborum vetus interit
aetas, / et iuvenum ritu florent modo nata vigentque' (as forests change
their leaves with each year's decline, and the earliest drop off: so with
words the old race dies, and, like the young of human kind, the new
born bloom and thrive).[36] Dante's use of Horace deserves some attention: the neighbouring passages are employed when speaking about
ruled language in the *Convivio* and natural language in *Paradiso* 26. And
indeed Horace satisfies both cases, being a classic ('grammatical')
author, who talks about his language as natural. Moreover, Horace refers
to language as applied to the poetic craft, which appears therefore as the
space in which the contradictions of both grammatical and natural language are reconciled.

The four passages discussed here bring into sharp relief the contrast
between the irremediably fallen human language and the seemingly
unreachable language of God. However, Dante also seems to draw attention to the need for a strong binding notion between the two realms – a
bind that is stronger than the materiality of language in the *Convivio* and
the artificiality of grammar in the *De vulgari eloquentia*. Poetry, it seems,
can fill this need, serving as a flexible order – a syntax – that might
descend, or better, condescend to human language and reconcile and
redeem it. The necessity for this inner poetic bond is already evident in
Dante's discussion of Babel as a (not yet disempowered) turning point in
the dynamic relationship between the death and rebirth of human language – the lowest point of the Fall and the first step into redemption.
The arguments that connect the first book of the *Convivio* to the first
book of the *De vulgari eloquentia* trace a trajectory that leads from fragmentation to binding.[37]

The Pros and Cons of Babel

Dante introduces the episode of Babel[38] in the *De vulgari eloquentia* by
framing it within the perspective of salvation history's *pars destruens*, and
in one synthetic statement knits it closely to the Fall and the Flood as the
third and last punishment for the outburst of human pride:

> O semper natura nostra prona peccatis! O ab initio et nunquam desinens
> nequitatrix! Num fuerat satis ad tui correptionem quod, per primam pre-
> varicationem eluminata, delitiarum exulabas a patria? Num satis quod, per

universalem familie tue luxuriem et trucitatem, unica reservata domo, quicquid tui iuris erat cataclismo perierat, et [que] commiseras tu animalia celi terreque iam luerant? Quippe satis extiterat. Sed, sicut proverbialiter dici solet, 'Non ante tertium equitabis,' misera miserum venire maluisti ad equum. (1.7.2)

[Oh human nature, always inclined towards sin! Engaged in evil from the beginning, and never changing your ways! Was it not enough to correct you that, banished from the light for the first transgression, you should live in exile from the delights of your homeland? Was not enough that, because of the all-pervading lust and cruelty of your race, everything that was yours should have perished in a cataclysm, one family alone being spared, and that the creatures of earth and sky should have had to pay for the wrongs that you had committed? It should indeed have been enough. But, as we often say in the form of a proverb, 'not before the third time will you ride'; and you, wretched humanity, chose to mount a fractious steed.]

Babel is figured as the lowest and last step of the fall of human beings and their dispersion in space and time. According to Dante, language determines the national identity of people and not vice versa,[39] but even people belonging to the same group speak different languages in different times. In the episode of Babel, the birth of different languages is presented as a form of *contrapasso*, the harsher the punishment the higher the hierarchy of operation belonging to each group. Only the Jews, who abstained from building the Tower, are spared the destruction of their language, so that the birth of the Redeemer could happen in a language of grace and not confusion (1.6.6). However, another dispersion – still figured in terms of a punishment – awaits the Hebrew language with the diaspora ('antiquissima locutione sunt usi usque ad suam dispersionem' [1.7.8: (the Jews) used this most ancient language until the time of their dispersal]).

After Babel, humankind is therefore left with: (1) a completely isolated, rarefied language of grace; (2) an unruly natural language fragmented into the various vernaculars and dispersed in space and time; and, as a fully human antidote to this dispersion, (3) an artificial language, *gramatica*. However, the insertion of the vernacular within the triplex biblical episode of the same Fall also entails its inscription into a process of redemption that has to go through the Caudine Forks of history, through its maze, its miseries, and its desperation. By tearing down language completely with the destruction of the Tower of Babel, Dante puts it on the path to salvation through history. And it is indeed within the pit of history, from the abyss of a region of (linguistic) unlikeness, that the constructive quality of poetry rescues the vernacular.

The notion of the deterioration of language through time represents the textual link between the *Convivio* and the *De vulgari eloquentia*: while suggesting the problem of language's temporal dispersion in the *Convivio*, Dante declares that he will be writing a booklet on the vernacular.[40] At this point in the *Convivio* Dante stresses the higher nobility of Latin in light of its fixity, as opposed to the vernacular's mutability:[41]

> Per nobilità, perché lo latino è perpetuo e non corruttibile, e lo volgare è non stabile e corruttibile. Onde vedemo nelle scritture antiche delle comedie e tragedie latine, che non si possono transmutare, quello medesimo che oggi avemo; che non aviene del volgare, lo quale a piacimento artificiato si transmuta. (1.5.7–8)

> [Because of its nobility, for Latin is eternal and incorruptible, while the vernacular is unstable and corruptible. Thus in the ancient Latin comedies and tragedies, which cannot undergo change, we find the same Latin as we have today; this is not the case with the vernacular, which, being fashioned according to one's own preference, undergoes change.]

In Dante's condemnation of the vernacular's variability, however, there is also subtle praise for the flexibility of the new linguistic tool, 'lo quale *a piacimento artificiato* si transmuta,' which can be translated more literally as '[vernacular] changes by being elaborated according to taste.' Besides time and space, craft also accounts for the vernacular's mutability. It is precisely this threefold flexibility – as opposed to the fixity and partial universality of Latin – that begins to grant the vernacular some 'beauty,' a very humble variety of beauty indeed, born out of the love that individuals and the small community bear for their own language. As a result of its punctual presence in time and space and to its malleability, the vernacular creates a bond within the individual (since it is immediately 'united' to his mind)[42] and within the community:

> E così lo volgare è più prossimo quanto è più unito, [e quello è più unito], che uno e solo è prima nella mente che alcuno altro, e che non solamente per sé è unito, ma per accidente, in quanto è congiunto colle più prossime persone, sì come colli parenti e [colli] propî cittadini e colla propia gente. (1.12.5)[43]

[And so a man's vernacular is nearest to the extent that it is most closely related to him, for it is in his mind first and alone before any other; and not only is it related to him intrinsically but accidentally, since it is connected to those persons who are nearest to him, that is, his kin, his fellow citizens, and his own people.]

The affection that the individual – which Dante begins to consider both as individual and as author, 'naturalmente e accidentalmente' (1.10.6) – bears toward one's own language spurs one to find beauty in it against the other languages (both Latin and the natural languages), even in the simplest, most straightforward usages of prose.[44] However, the individual/author and the vernacular, bound together by their 'friendship,' share a desire for preservation and stability, which only poetry can grant through the binding system of rhyme and rhythm ('legar sé con numero e con rime'):[45]

Anche, è stato meco d'uno medesimo studio, e ciò posso così mostrare. Ciascuna cosa studia naturalmente alla sua conservazione: onde, se lo volgare per sé studiare potesse,' studierebbe a quella; e quella sarebbe aconciare sé a più stabilitate, e più stabilitate non potrebbe avere che [in] legar sé con numero e con rime. E questo medesimo studio è stato mio, sì come tanto è palese che non dimanda testimonianza. Per che uno medesimo studio è stato lo suo e 'l mio: per che di questa concordia l'amistà è confermata e acresciuta. Anche c'è stata la benivolenza della consuetudine, ché dal principio della mia vita ho avuta con esso benivolenza e conversazione, e usato quello diliberando, interpetrando e questionando. (1.13.6–8)

[Furthermore, it has had the same purpose as I myself, and this I can show as follows. Everything by nature pursues its own preservation; thus if the vernacular could by itself pursue anything, it would pursue that; and that would be to secure itself greater stability, and greater stability it could gain only by binding itself with meter and with rhyme. This has been precisely my purpose, as is so evident that it requires no proof. Consequently, its purpose and mine have been one and the same, so that through this harmony our friendship has been strengthened and increased. There has also been a sense of benevolence born of familiarity; for from the beginning of my life I have looked on it with benevolence and been intimate with it, and have used it in deliberating, explaining, and questioning.] ·

Civil (*diliberando*), intellectual (*interpretando*), and philosophical (*questionando*) activity lead to friendship with the vernacular, yet only poetry manages to bind language within a system of rules (number and rhythm) and to secure it within a system of stability. This is an important turning point in the dynamic of fall and redemption and eternity and time in which the vernacular is put under the aegis of Babel: poetry, by stabilizing and preserving the vernacular, turns it into a 'grammar'[46] – without annihilating the vitality of the natural language. In other words, inserting the vernacular – the lowest point of dispersion, the beginning of human history in terms of the spatial and temporal dislocation of the nations – into an eschatological framework (the Fall, the Flood, Babel) allows it to be recognized as a flexible tool for the new poetry, which in turn grants it stability and order. Importantly, however, poetry serves as more than a means to preservation: it leads the vernacular into redemption.

After closely dialoguing on the issue of language, the two works follow their own independent directions. In the *De vulgari eloquentia*, the search for a more stable, more 'grammatical' vernacular soon strays into poetry.[47] The second book of the treatise outlines a 'grammar of poetry' – a comparative grammar indeed – in which the way poetry constructs the vernacular into stability is explored in the context of the already grammatical (Latin) or more established (Provençal) languages and poetry. Although the interruption of the *De vulgari eloquentia* does not allow us to fully interpret Dante's position, the pre-eminence given to poetry is clear.

> Sed quia ipsum prosaycantes ab avientibus magis accipiunt et quia quod avietum est prosaycantibus permanere videtur exemplar, et non e converso – que quendam videntur prebere primatum –, primo secundum quod metricum est ipsum carminemus. (2.1.1)

> [But, because writers of prose most often learn the vernacular from poets, and because what is set out in poetry serves as a model for those who write prose, and not the other way about – which would seem to confer a certain primacy – I shall first expound the principles according to which the illustrious vernacular is used for writing poetry.]

The beginning of Book 2 represents another point of convergence (and this time a point of agreement) between the treatise on language and the *Convivio*. In using the rare term *avientes* (binders of words) to refer to poets, Dante is implicitly making reference to his discussion of the word *author* in *Convivio* 4.6.3–5. According to Albert Ascoli, this passage is crucial to understanding Dante's construction of poetic authority in opposition to the authorities of power and knowledge and in the mirror of the 'absolute' authority of God.[48] Dante provides two distinct etymologies: one that applies to authority in general (< *autentin* = worth of faith and obedience), and another that applies only to poets (< *auieo* = to bind words together).

> Questo vocabulo, cioè 'autore,' sanza quella terza lettera C, può discendere da due principii: l'uno si è uno verbo molto lasciato dall'uso in gramatica, che significa tanto quanto 'legare parole,' cioè 'auieo.' E chi ben guarda lui, nella sua prima voce apertamente vedrà che elli stesso lo dimostra, ché solo di legame di parole è fatto, cioè di sole cinque vocali, che sono anima e legame d'ogni parole, e composto d'esse per modo volubile, a figurare imagine di legame. Ché, cominciando dall'A, nell'U quindi si rivolve, e viene diritto per I nell'E, quindi si rivolve e torna nell'O: sì che veramente imagina questa figura: A, E, I, O, U, la quale è figura di legame. E in quanto 'autore' viene e discende da questo verbo, si prende solo per li poeti, che coll'arte musaica le loro parole hanno legate. (4.6.3–4)

> [This word, namely 'auctor' without the third letter C, has two possible sources of derivation. One is a verb that has very much fallen out of use in Latin and which signifies more or less 'to tie words together,' that is, 'auieo.' Anyone who studies it carefully in its first form will observe that it displays its own meaning, for it is made up only of the ties of words, that is, of the five vowels alone, which are the soul and tie of every word, and is composed of them in a different order, so as to portray the image of a tie. For beginning with A it turns back to U, goes straight through to I and E, then turns back and comes to O, so that it truly portrays this image: A, E, I, O, U, which is the figure of a tie. Insofar as 'author' is derived and comes from this verb, it is used only to refer to poets who have tied their words together with the art of poetry (music).]

The etymology *auieo* singles out poets as 'binders of words,' who graft stability onto fallen human language by way of the rules of poetry, namely rhyme and rhythm. This quality is imparted to poetry by music, an art ('arte musaica'), which responds to an abstract science that mirrors in turn the even and eternal movements of the stars and their harmonious interaction.[49] The intimate connection between poetry and music – evident in Dante's definition of poetry as 'fictio rhetorica musicaque poita'

(*De vulgari eloquentia* 2.4.3: verbal invention composed according to the rules of poetry and music)[50] – enables poetry to act as syntax in the way that Augustine theologically, and the Modistae scientifically, understood it: a set of rules, a structure, a thread, that harmonizes the corruptible word of humankind with God's eternal one.

Moreover, as Dante describes it, the etymology *auieo* – a bundle of vowels that both *means* and *is* 'binding' – harks back to his first fleeting reflection on language, *Nomina sunt consequentia rerum*:[51]

> lo nome d'Amore è sì dolce a udire, che impossibile mi pare che la sua propria operatione sia nelle più cose altro che dolce, con ciò sia cosa che li nomi seguitino le nominate cose, sì come è scripto: 'Nomina sunt consequentia rerum.' (*Vita Nova* 6.4)

> [The name of Love is so sweet to hear that it seems impossible to me that the effect itself could be in most things other than sweet, since names follow from the things they name, as the saying goes: 'Names are the consequences of things.']

This 'legalization' of the relation between signs and things is later recalled in the complex architecture of interpretation that surrounds the names of Beatrice and Giovanna-Primavera, in which Cavalcanti plays the part of a baffled *impositor*, and which signals that the problem of language in Dante is, since its inception, projected into transcendence.[52] As Maria Corti explains (*Dante a un nuovo crocevia*, 70–6), there is no contradiction between the 'realism' of the *Vita Nova* and the later endorsement, in the *De vulgari eloquentia*, of the traditional scholastic notion of *significatio ad placitum*, the conventional relationship between sign and thing.[53] Dante carries out his reflection on language on two levels: the level of human history, through which *significatio ad placitum* runs, and the transcendental level, where *nomina sunt consequentia rerum*.[54] A first glimpse of this double level can be found as early as in *Vita Nova* through the experience of love poetry, but its full implicit theorization – or better, its own writing, the inscription itself of this double principle – is the *Commedia*.

Language and Languages: The Parallel Episodes of *Inferno* 26–27 and *Paradiso* 15–17

The contradictions and harmonization that mark Dante's theory of language in the *Commedia* can be exemplified by examining two 'puzzles' of language(s) in the episodes of Ulysses/Guido da Montefeltro and Cacciaguida, according to the principle of the 'parallel episodes' formulated by Amilcare Iannucci.[55] Iannucci shows how the critical frame of mind that compels Dante always to reflect, punctually and locally, on his own poetry, and that marks Dante's oeuvre before the *Commedia*, does not vanish in the poem. Besides the letter to Cangrande della Scala, auto-exegesis within the poem is carried out in a subtle yet substantial way, through a technique of 'testimony' or 'parallel passage,' which Dante borrows from biblical exegesis. By establishing precise inner references Dante creates 'parallel episodes' that, although apparently distant, shed light onto each other. My hypothesis here is that in *Inferno* and *Paradiso* Dante inserts two summaries of his reflection on language and style – one that points to contradiction, antagonism, and obscurity, and the other that points to harmonization and coexistence. In the *Inferno*, the realm of the deviated sign, stiff *gramatica* and unruly vernacular argue in a grotesque way, whereas in the *Paradiso*, the realm of the redeemed sign, they peacefully coexist, sustained by their relationship to true meaning.

The episode of Ulysses opens with the famous lines in which Virgil bids the eager pilgrim to hold his tongue and let him do the speaking because 'the Greeks' might disdain his speech:

Lascia parlare a me, ch'i' ho concetto
ciò che tu vuoi; ch'ei sarebbero schivi,
perch'e' fuor greci, forse del tuo detto. (73–5)

[Leave speech to me, for I have understood what you wish – and perhaps, since they were Greeks, they would be disdainful of your words.]

Modern commentators agree that this is not a matter of language but of style:[56] Virgil is here addressing the heroes with the formalities and the language of the 'alta tragedìa,' using the 'parola ornata' (*Inferno* 2.67) that makes him such an appealing guest of hell and a fitting guide for the pilgrim. It is worth recalling, however, that in the *De vulgari eloquentia* the poetry of antiquity is perceived as solid and honourable exactly because it is written in the *lingua regulata*, whereas the challenge of the medieval poet is precisely to find a (largely hypothetical) vernacular strong enough to support high poetry,[57] that 'illustrious' and elusive vernacular amidst the wide and for the most part dissonant variety of Italian dialects. As spoken in one of those dialects, though – the 'garrulous' Lombard[58] – Virgil's supposedly lofty and ornate *licentia* ('la licenza del dolce poeta,' 28.3) is overheard in the next canto by Guido da Montefeltro, who addresses the Roman poet:

> O tu a cu' io drizzo
> la voce e che parlavi mo' lombardo,
> dicendo 'Istra ten va, più non t'adizzo' (19–21)

> [O you to whom I direct my voice and who just now spoke Lombard, saying
> 'Now go your way, I do not urge you more']

Guido manages to annoy Virgil to the point that he elbows Dante forward: 'Parla tu; questi è latino' (33: You speak: he is Italian).

Style and language go hand in hand, as the *De vulgari eloquentia* shows: in the eight bolgia, *alta tragedìa* (+ *gramatica*) and *sermo humilis* (+ Lombard dialect) clash to create a parodic, if not disconcerting, effect on the reader.[59] The message here conveyed by Dante is no doubt a moral one: in hell (and paradigmatically in the pouch of evil counsellors, who bent their speech to sin), there is no difference between the 'parola ornata' and the *sermo humilis*: they are both stained by sin, and thus they both turn grotesque. This strategy is applied elsewhere in the eighth circle by aligning characters, as opposed to languages, in order to increase the comic effect of estrangement and the sense of linguistic entropy: the best example is the quarrel between Master Adam and Sinon in canto 30 but think also of the uneven diptych, in the same canto, of Mirra and Gianni Schicchi; or think of cantos 18 (Venedico Caccianemico and Jason, Alessio Interminelli and Taide), or even 28 (Mohamed and Dolcino).

In the episode involving Cacciaguida, Dante surveys the possibilities of language through interplay rather than conflict. One can count at least four 'versions' of language(s) used by Cacciaguida.[60] In welcoming Dante, he begins with three lines in Latin, a patchwork of Virgilian and biblical reminiscences (15.28–30):

> O sanguis meus, o superinfusa
> gratïa Deï, sicut tibi cui
> bis unquam celi ianüa reclusa?

> [O blood of mine, o lavish grace of God! To whom was Heaven's gate ever
> twice opened, as to thee?]

In order to thank God for Dante's arrival (15.37–48), Cacciaguida continues with the inner language of heaven, which is incomprehensible to Dante because it is a language made of things as opposed to words:

Indi, a udire e a veder giocondo,
giunse lo spirto al suo principio cose
ch'io non lo 'ntesi, sì parlò profondo (15.37–9)

[Then, a joy to hearing and to sight, the spirit added to his first words things I did not comprehend, so deep was his speech.]

Cacciaguida's language is not understandable to Dante until it meets 'the sign' – which is at the same time 'the limit' and 'the word' – of human intellect ('lo segno del nostro intelletto,' 45).

né per elezïon mi si nascose,
ma per necessità, ché 'l suo concetto
al segno d'i mortal si soprapuose.
E quando l'arco de l'ardente affetto
fu sì sfogato, che 'l parlar discese
inver' lo segno del nostro intelletto,
la prima cosa che per me s'intese,
'Benedetto sia tu,' fu, 'trino e uno,
che nel mio seme se' tanto cortese!' (15.40–8)

[nor did he conceal himself from me by choice, but of necessity, for his conception was set above the mark of the mortals. And when the bow of his ardent affection was so relaxed that his speech descended toward the mark of our intellect, the first thing I understood was, 'Blessed be Thou, Three and One, who show such favor to my seed.']

When he talks about his ancestors and Florence in his own times, Cacciaguida's address to Dante – 'non con questa moderna favella' (16.33: not in this our modern speech) – is unanimously understood by critics as referring to an archaic version of the Florentine vernacular, although there is no trace of it in Cacciaguida's actual speech. Finally, in order to explain the obscure meaning of the prophecies previously heard by Dante, Cacciaguida uses a 'chiaro e preciso latino,' as opposed to the obscure language prior to the Incarnation, a redeemed discourse, one that has met in Christ the inner referent:[61]

Né per ambage, in che la gente folle
già s'inviscava pria che fosse anciso
l'Agnel di Dio che le peccata tolle,
ma per chiare parole e con preciso
latin rispuose quello amor paterno,
chiuso e parvente del suo proprio riso. (18.31–6)

[In no dark sayings, such as those in which the foolish folks once ensnared themselves, before the Lamb of God who takes away sins was slain, but in clear words and with precise discourse that paternal love replied, hidden and revealed by his own smile.]

With respect to languages – we might call it the 'exterior word' side – it is easy to recognize in this episode the two possibilities described in the *De vulgari eloquentia* and the *Convivio*. Latin is treated as *gramatica*, a language whose artificial quality is stressed by the montage of classical and biblical sequences, which makes Cacciaguida's first utterance almost a *cento*. On the other hand, the mention of the ancient Florentine later testifies to the mutability of the vernacular in time. As for language – the 'interior word' side – readers are faced on the one hand with the incomprehensible language of heaven, a primal language made of things, which is above the 'sign' of human intellect; and on the other hand, with a redeemed language that has met time and history, and therefore has been confused and obfuscated by human sin and later redeemed through Incarnation. This language is therefore able to convey the truth to humankind – clearly and precisely.[62] Thus four possibilities of language stand effortlessly juxtaposed in the episode, testifying to the binding quality of poetry *sub specie aeternitatis*.

It may not be by chance that the harmonization of human speech in all its versions (from a quasi-direct communication with God to the fluctuating vernacular, through *gramatica* and redeemed language) should happen in the heaven of Mars, which in the *Convivio* is also the heaven of Music.[63] As seen in the preceding section, music fulfils the desire of the natural language to be supported by a system of stability. In the heaven of Mars/Music, human language in both versions (the fallen and diffuse vernacular and the rigid and artificialized *gramatica*) sees its desire fulfilled – and even surpassed: not only stability, but appeasement and redemption await it in paradise, through a fluid and graceful composition of its centrifugal forces. Through Christ's sacrifice in history and in the mirror of God in heaven, language 'means' again, thanks to the binding quality of poetry.

The complex interplay of language, desire, and poetry is a constant throughout the *Commedia*: it certainly does not lodge in this episode alone but spans the whole poem from the beginning of *Inferno* through to the vision of God. The way language and desire participate in the syntax of poetry in the poem results in a very wide dynamic, which I will sketch next by tracing the interconnected maps of language and desire in the poem – the backbone of the constructive quality of poetry.

A Map of Language

Since the three canticles show different language strategies, which turn into theological and moral marks of the three realms, the problem of language in the *Comedy* has to be posited in different ways: in terms of utterance in the *Inferno*, in terms of sign in the *Purgatorio*, and in terms of meaning in the *Paradiso*. Five aspects are relevant in drawing the map of language in the poem: soundscape, communication, sign imparted by God, the relationship between signs and bodies, and the relationship between poetry and language.[64]

Inferno is the realm of *vox unde sonum*, of sound unrelated to meaning, the place of the distortion of language, in both utterance and internal order. The inscription on the gates of hell – the early, and only, sign imparted by God to signal without appeal the content of the forthcoming realm – represents the 'dead' – indeed petrified – 'letter' of sin. As John Freccero has shown, the inscription brackets the whole realm within a tight and dead-end structure of irony.[65] From now on, the bodies themselves of the sinners – wounded, metamorphosed, and torn apart as to signify peremptorily the reasons for their condemnation – bear the sign of Divine Justice, which nails to endless, useless repetition the deadly literality of sin.

When the pilgrim enters the gates of hell, his sight is impaired by darkness, and his first, painful perception of the new realm is acoustic: 'quivi sospiri, pianti ed alti guai / risonavaŋ per l'aere sanza stelle' (3.22–3: here sighs, laments and loud wailings were resounding through the starless air). Throughout the *Inferno*, many other first impressions are delegated to the sense of hearing, because there is conspicuous lack of light. The *sottofondo* of *Inferno* is inarticulate noise, which roars and echoes throughout the cantos in different sound shapes, and it is thus described in canto 3:

Diverse lingue, orribili favelle
parole di dolore, accenti d'ira,

voci alte e fioche, e suon di man con elle
facevano un tumulto il qual s'aggira
sempre in quell'aura sanza tempo tinta,
come la rena quando turbo spira. (25–7)

[Strange tongues, horrible outcries, utterances of woe, accents of anger,
voices shrill and faint, and the beating of hands among them, were making
a tumult that swirls unceasingly in that dark and timeless air, like sand
when a whirlwind blows.]

These seemingly paratactic variations on the very notion of utterance
('lingue,' 'favelle,' 'parole,' 'accenti,' 'voci,' 'suono') provide an immediate, profound impression of the deterioration of language in *Inferno*.
The focus is initially on language, albeit 'diverse lingue,' as if to point out
that any common core of language is lost, that the pilgrim has entered a
post-Babelic realm.[66] The next term is 'favelle,' an unmarked word in
Dante's usage, that registers the transition between a notion of language
and a less specified idea of 'way of speaking.' Then we turn to 'parole,'
which suggests the idea of a word in isolation, a powerless word: 'parole
di dolore' indeed suggest interjections, the most isolated of the grammatical categories. Then the focus shifts to 'accenti' – interestingly an
hapax in Dante, which signals that the word has become an inflection –
and then to 'voices,' which surely are not meaningful signs, but unrelated sounds; and in fact they are measured by loudness and weakness
('voci alte e fioche') and are almost indistinguishable from the following
sound of clapping hands. The final result, 'tumulto,' has no relationship
to, and yet is the outcome of, the initial 'diverse lingue': when its common core is lost, language quickly deteriorates, slides away from meaning into confusion.

Linguistic confusion is not solely characteristic of the background,
however. 'Anima sciocca / anima confusa' (stupid soul, confused soul,
31.70, 74) – the epithet with which Virgil addresses the giant Nimrod,
the conceiver of the tower of Babel[67] – can be applied to each and every
one of the damned and represents the blueprint for language and communication in hell. Upon hearing Nimrod's meaningless utterance, Virgil first advises the giant to play his horn instead of speaking ('tienti col
corno, e con quel ti disfoga'), since his language is devoid of meaning,
and then discourages the pilgrim from attempting communication,
since the giant is locked in his linguistic solitude ('Lasciànlo stare e non
parliamo a vòto; / ché così è a lui ciascun linguaggio / come il suo ad

altrui che a nullo è noto').[68] At the very bottom of hell, as well as at its gates, there is no distinction between sound and language.

The famous infernal riddles of language – Plutus' *Pape satan, pape Satan, aleppe!* (7.1) and Nimrod's *Raphèl maì amècche zabì almi* (31.67), the former a montage of deformed Greek and Hebrew words, the latter a distortion of Hebrew words (as the most common interpretation goes)[69] – constitute the perfect linguistic match to the damned bodies in hell. The wounded, torn, cleft, metamorphosed expressions concisely sum up important linguistic features of hell: sin disfiguring the soul of language (interior word) also affects its body (utterance); and in *Inferno* not only the natural language is debased, as shown in canto 3, but even grammar (Greek) and the most sacred of languages (Hebrew) are challenged as bearers of stable meaning, as the intelligible but horribly inverted *Vexilla regis prodeunt inferni* (34.1) later reinforces.

Moreover, at the bottom of hell the discourse on language dovetails, as is customary in Dante's work, with that on poetry. At the beginning of the next canto, the poet laments the lack of 'le rime aspre e chiocce' (32.1: harsh and grating rhymes) – where 'chioccia' interestingly recalls Plutus' voice ('cominciò Pluto colla voce chioccia' [7.2: Pluto began with a clucking voice). This seems to suggest that a fitting description of the last circle's horror could be woven only in the fashion of Nimrod's and Plutus' wretched utterances. The poet only glimpses and then rejects the 'dark side' of poetry, choosing instead to support his failing natural language, which is reverting to the utmost infantile inexperience ('lingua che chiami mamma o babbo') with the severity and stability of the ancient ruled poetry dictated by the Muses ('Ma quelle donne aiutino il mio verso / ch'aiutaro Anfione a chiuder Tebe').[70]

The degeneration of language in *Inferno* not only compares to physical punishment: it 'feels' like it. The distorted, 'divorced' relationship between the interior and the exterior word is represented as a form of violence that is akin to, although not always as graphic as, the cruelty that disfigures the aerial bodies. As Leo Spitzer's masterful reading shows,[71] canto 13 is by far the clearest representation of linguistic violence in *Inferno*, because of the peculiar status of the suicides.[72] For them, the relationship between body and soul is not only distorted but indeed completely severed, and therefore new bodies, 'monstrously hybrid' (147), are born in the wood. In the same way, their speech is a hybrid of words and blood, as confirmed by the singular verb *usciva* in the line 'usciva insieme parole e sangue' (came out words and blood together), later restated as 'soffi con sangue doloroso sermo' (blow forth with blood your doleful speech). The speech of the suicides is thus portrayed as a purely physical act, a semi-human device; it trespasses the corporeality of sound, and becomes thicker matter: speech becomes body. Spitzer points out that the production of language in this episode is indeed part of the *contrapasso*, and he draws attention to the lines where the Harpies, scratching the bushes in the suicides' wood, 'fanno dolore, e al dolor fenestra' (102: give pain, and to the pain an outlet): 'the tyranny of the need of self expression by language, the self-mutilating sadistic power of speech which while seeming to give consolation only aggravates the wound – this has never been more powerfully symbolized, nay, more graphically depicted than in this macabre episode' (155). Although nowhere else in *Inferno* is the tyranny of language posed with such clear evidence as in canto 13, Spitzer's conclusion can be extended to the whole canticle.

To further underscore this point, let us briefly return to cantos 26–7. As discussed before, in the bolgia of the fraudulent counsellors, style and language challenge each other in a grotesque fight (the *gramatica* of ancient high style versus the dialect of *sermo humilis*). Another *tessera* can be now added to the problem of language in these cantos, by noting that the mechanism of language itself is jammed somewhere, and the result is the subversion of its external configuration. The (at once metaphorical and literal) tongues of fire, in which the trapped souls of Ulysses, Diomedes, and Guido da Montefeltro painfully give utterance (since their voice cannot find 'via né forame' [course or outlet]) represent a monstrous, abnormal device for speaking that is also cruelly ironic, considering the sin punished in the bolgia is 'fraud by words.' After the long description of the slow and torturous utterance, the first word spoken by Ulysses (the heavy-sounding 'Quando') is craftily placed at the end of the verse, and the line-pause that follows it allows the reader to fully appreciate, and indeed to experience, the fatigue involved in the act of speaking:

Lo maggior corno de la fiamma antica
cominciò a crollarsi mormorando,
pur come quella cui vento affatica;
indi la cima qua e là menando,
come fosse la lingua che parlasse,
gittò voce di fuori, e disse: 'Quando (26.85–9)

[The greater horn of the ancient flame began to wag, murmuring, like one

that is beaten by a wind; then carrying to and fro its tip, as if it were a
tongue that spoke, it flung forth a voice and said: 'When]

These huge burning tongues are indeed language torture-machines, as
is clear from the comparison with the Sicilian bull – the cruel brass cast
built by the Athenian artisan Perillus for Phalarys, the tyrant of Agri-
gento; when it is heated around the victim, human screams transform
into the bellowing of a bull.[73] The doleful words of the damned wander
ineffectually and painfully through the fire, indeed sounding like it ('in
suo linguaggio si convertïan le parole grame'), until they manage, with a
desperately athletic 'guizzo,' to force the tongue to speak:

> così, per non aver via né forame
> dal principio nel foco, in suo linguaggio
> si convertïan le parole grame.
> Ma poscia ch'ebber colto lor viaggio
> su per la punta, dandole quel guizzo
> che dato avea la lingua in lor passaggio,
> udimmo dire: 'O tu a cu' io drizzo (27.13–19)

[thus, having at first no course or outlet in the fire, the doleful words were
changed into its language. But after they had found their way up through
the tip, giving it the same vibration the tongue had given in their passage,
we heard it say, 'O you to whom I direct]

These examples, together with the dysfunctional language of the cantos of the Thieves, make clear that the disfigured language of the *Inferno*
moves ever closer to meaningless noise (*vox unde sonum*), in accordance
with the trend of the soundscape and as highlighted by the occasional
linguistic enigma (*Inferno* 7 and 31). Moreover, in the assimilation to
lower nature (wind, fire, plant, animal), these utterances seem to suggest
the possibility of a subhuman form of communication in hell, one that is
strictly denied by the *De vulgari eloquentia*,[74] but here might be implied
even by Ugolino's 'bestial segno' (32.133) at the bottom of hell.[75]

In *Purgatorio*, the realm of human language, both the exterior and the
interior word enjoy an unmarked facility, on a *sottofondo* of chanted
prayer, which itself hovers between words and music. Beginning with the
cardinal '*In exitu Isräel de Aegypto*' (2.46), every episode in the *Purgatorio* is
given a tune, so to speak, by a few (usually Latin) words from the *incipit*

of a liturgical chant (prayer or psalm), which evokes both a melody and
a whole text (as 2.48 warns: 'con quanto di quel salmo è poscia scripto'
[with the rest of that psalm as it is written]). Purgatory's evoked soundscape must have been overwhelming to the medieval reader; for the
modern reader, often disconnected from the practice of chanted prayer,
the best place to approximate it is perhaps the description of the *Te Deum*
that the pilgrim hears after passing the door of purgatory. Here, the
alternate balance of words and melody, whether instrumental or
chanted,[76] impairs the hearing of single words, but not the understanding of the well-known text:

> Io mi rivolsi attento al primo tuono,
> e '*te Deum laudamus*' mi parea
> udire in voce mista al dolce suono.
> Tale imagine a punto mi rendea
> ciò ch'io udiva, qual prender si suole
> quando a cantar con organi si stea;
> ch'or sì or no s'intendon le parole. (9.138–45)

> [I turned attentive to the first note, and '*Te Deum laudamus*' I seemed to
> hear in a voice mingled with sweet music. What I heard gave me the same
> impression we sometimes get when people are singing with an organ, and
> now the words are clear and now are not.]

In purgatory – historically and theologically a new realm,[77] the place
for a reconciliation between humankind and God as well as for redemption through Christ's passion – language, too, is reconciled: free of
obstructions, language glides flawlessly from the inside to the outside,
and languages exist effortlessly side by side. Hence the seamless dialogues between Sordello and Virgil and between Statius Virgil and
Dante, and the cameo on Arnaut Daniel, 'miglior fabbro del parlar
materno' (26.117).

Arnaut's beautiful excerpt is also one of the strongest reminders that
the discourse of the *Purgatorio* is also – and most conspicuously – a discourse on poetry,[78] which in turn entails, as the *De vulgari eloquentia*
shows, a reflection on poetic language. The discussion of poetry seems at
first glance to be established in terms of the condemnation of earthly
poetry (indeed Dante's own) in canto 2, with the powerful matching of
the salvific, polysemic '*In exitu Isräel de Aegypto*' and the retarding and
self-complacent 'Amor che ne la mente mi ragiona.'[79] However, together

with souls, bodies, and language, earthly love poetry embarks here on a process of purgation, especially in the 'cantos of the poets' (21–6). The love poetry confronts its own shortcomings and unravels its knots, going through a gentle *contrapasso*, as is the case with Arnaut's lines, a patchwork of Provençal poetry bent and twisted toward spiritual meaning, where 'affina' (26.148), a technical term of the *trobar*, becomes the very operation of the redeeming fire ('nel foco che li affina').[80]

The purgative process of the love poetry is especially significant when considering Patrizia Pizzorno's suggestive interpretation of Matelda in cantos 28–9 as a personification of the canzone placed in the Garden of Eden.[81] One is indeed tempted to call it a plenary indulgence, the best example of the reconciliation of sacred and earthly song (both Latin and vernacular), as if the whole quest of the *De vulgari eloquentia* had been purged and redeemed – if one considers that Matelda as canzone sings a psalm acting both 'come donna innamorata' (a sentence that, as commentators point out, carries a strong echo from Cavalcanti's *Rime*) and as a quite bucolic nymph:[82]

> Cantando come donna innamorata,
> continüò col fin di sue parole:
> '*Beati quorum tecta sunt peccata!*'
> E come ninfe che si givan sole
> per le salvatiche ombre, disïando
> qual di veder, qual di fuggir lo sole,
> allor si mosse (29.1–7)

> [Singing like a lady enamored, she continued at the end of her words, '*Beati quorum tecta sunt peccata!*' and, like nymphs who used to wend alone through the woodland shades, this one desiring to see and that to avoid the sun, she moved]

Purgatory is also the realm where God's intervention through signs is most keenly manifested. Without entering into a discussion of the whole symbolic apparatus of the canticle,[83] let us recall that each terrace is characterized by a set of signs (visual, acoustic, or visionary), which have a twofold goal: on the one hand, they provide the purging souls with *exempla* for their process of expiation; on the other, they introduce and progressively connect them – both Dante and the souls – to the 'higher' language of *Paradiso*. Interestingly, these meaningful signs are initially externally supplied to the purging souls ('visibile parlare' of cantos 10 and 12; the aerial voices of cantos 13 and 14; and the visions of cantos 15 and 17) but end up as the language of the souls themselves (as when the souls cry out the examples in cantos 18, 20, 25, and 26). The speaking trees of cantos 22 and 24, which provide examples of temperance (22.130–54) and of gluttony (24.103–29), can be read as the specular opposite of the 'uttering bushes' of *Inferno* 13. Not only do the lively, fruit-bearing trees of *Purgatorio* demonstrate flawless speech, but their speech also provides a set of signs that points to the ultimate meaning of salvation and eternity. Moreover, dreams – a thick language always in need of interpretation – are also part of the symbolic structure that guides the upward progress of the pilgrim.[84]

The complex symbolic apparatus of the second realm becomes denser toward the top of the mountain, with the maximum concentration in cantos 28–33. Barański has shown that at the summit of purgatory Dante the poet actively engages himself and his readers in a discussion of the tradition and modalities of semiosis.[85] Eden, portrayed in the *De vulgari eloquentia* as poor (virtually pure) of signs, becomes in the *Commedia* the theatre for the loudest symbolic representation and for the most intense moment of reflection on the nature of signification.

Finally, bodies too participate in the lively process of signification throughout the *Purgatorio*. Besides *contrapasso*, distinctly less remarkable than in the *Inferno*, the body at times becomes a blank page upon which signs of salvation are inscribed. Manfred's wound (canto 3) represents an early example: as John Freccero has shown, it bears the inscription of both human history and salvation history.[86] Another forehead, however, participates actively in the process of signification: that of the pilgrim on which the seven *P*s are inscribed upon admission into purgatory and then successively erased at each terrace. As a further example, Manuele Gragnolati has shown that in the skeletal countenance of the gluttons, one reads not only 'omo,' as the text suggests, but indeed 'ecce homo':[87] the suffering Christ is inscribed in the sufferance of the purging souls, a 'signed guarantee' that their pain is productive and redemptive. Just as physical punishment is painful but not desperate in purgatory, so the interpretation of the complex and polysemic signs of this realm is difficult but never impossible. With poetry, language too is resurrected from the dead (1.7: 'Ma qui la morta poesì resurga' [But here let dead poetry rise again]) – and its soul and body cooperate once again in the production of meaning.

In the midway realm of redeemed time and history, language maintains a flawless, effortless balance between sign and meaning. The reader, together with the pilgrim and the souls, is invited to explore the lively richness of signification and interpretation that leads them all, step by step, sign by sign, syllable by syllable, one word after the other, to a loud Eden of reconciliation. Like the language of the scriptures and sacraments, like the wounded body of Christ, the signs of *Purgatorio* enjoy the double status of both being, and pointing to, a higher reality. Like the Incarnation itself, as well as the scriptures and sacraments, they are signs of reconciliation between human beings and God, and yet they have to be transcended in order to achieve blessed life. Within the fictional plan of the poem, they must be physically surpassed in order to continue the ascent; from a temporal and eschatological perspective, they have to be temporally *past* in order fully to unfold their meaning. Pushing my reading a little further, I suggest that the whole of *Purgatorio* is a single sign, one gigantic act of pointing: after all, it is the realm that at the end of time – at the full stop of history – will disappear and be transcended, just like human language, the scriptures, and the Christ event in history itself.

In the *Paradiso*, the frustration of poetic language is employed to portray – among other things – the extreme, excessive facility of communication in heaven. Language in *Paradiso* 'hides' because of its own fullness of meaning, as light hides behind its brightness. The *sottofondo* of paradise is polyphonic music ('la dolce sinfonia di Paradiso,' 21.59), which, as explained in Justinian's words, has the advantage of granting diversity within unity:

Diverse voci fanno dolci note;
così diversi scanni in nostra vita
rendon dolce armonia tra queste rote. (6.124–6)

[Diverse voices make sweet music, so diverse ranks in our life render sweet harmony among these wheels.]

The 'different voices,' which share a common core of language, are the specular opposite of the radically non-communicative 'different languages' of *Inferno* 3. Being part of such a choir, the voices of the blessed are a mere recreational tool (a 'trastullo') in heaven.[88] Language – both in terms of utterance and thought – is indeed unnecessary, since the blessed enjoy perfect knowledge in the mirror of God, where the enigma of language is lifted.[89] As discussed before, the inner language of paradise – the language of Cacciaguida's prayer, for instance – is a language of 'things' as opposed to words, and is therefore incomprehensible to the pilgrim until it meets the sign of human intellect.

In paradise, even God's signs are put forth only for the pilgrim's facilitation and enjoyment: one need only recall the speaking eagle in the heaven of Justice,[90] a triumphant *son-et-lumiéres* show, which mixes together in one majestic metamorphosis signs, letters, sentences, singular and plural, and more – so that no element of semiosis or grammar is stable anymore. In an excess of self-productivity, the eagle's utterance, flowing effortlessly through the hollow neck,[91] exhibits for the reader yet another hidden sign (the acrostic LUE of lines 115–41). This fluid set of signs that interprets itself in the making is the specular opposite of the petrified inscription on the gates of hell (also a product of Divine Justice). The intelligibility of this mutant language is provided by its transcendental syntax, which belongs to the Augustinian order of enjoyment: the souls, the initial signs of light that compose the speaking eagle, are joyfully 'conserte' (joined in order, interwoven, from *con-serere*, the same root word as in *sermo*) in the sweet fruition ('il dolce frui,' 20.1–3) of God.

Whether coming from the blessed or directly from God, language exists in heaven only as a part of condescension, as Beatrice explains in canto 4:

Qui si mostraro, non perché sortita
sia questa spera lor, ma per far segno
de la celestial c'ha men salita.
Così parlar conviensi al vostro ingegno (37–40).

[These showed themselves here, not because this sphere is allotted to them, but to afford sign of the celestial grade that is last exalted. It is needful to speak thus to your faculty.]

Condescension is a performance staged by the blessed souls to meet Dante's shortcomings, the limitation of the sign. It can be considered a sort of 'performative speech act,'[92] in that, by 'affording the sign,' by bending 'inver lo segno del nostro intelletto' (15.45), they *are* in the different heavens. Since the pilgrim, bound by mortality, is not able to receive the simultaneity and wholeness of the Empyrean's blessedness all at once, condescension spells it out for him in signs. The transient quality of condescension is accentuated by the knowledge – which the reader acquires as early as canto 4 – that as soon as the pilgrim has left one heaven, the souls (the signs, the words) desert it too and return to their seat in the Empyrean, where their meaning resides. Condescension, as a sentence, spells and places each syllable and word 'one after the other' and then surpasses it in order to rush toward the full stop of meaning.

This movement is connected to desire: over and over in *Paradiso* the same plot is staged, where Dante refrains from formulating a question because he (rightly) thinks that the souls already know what he wants to ask, but they beg him to ask anyway, in order better to fulfil heavenly love and desire (and for the canticle/poem to be written). See, for instance, canto 15, where Cacciaguida first restates the argument for the superfluity of language even at the level of the Augustinian interior word, since God is the mirror 'in which, before you think you display your thought' (15.63). But there is a need for utterance in *Paradiso*, both on the part of the blessed and of the pilgrim:

> ma perché 'l sacro amore in che io veglio
> con perpetüa vista e che m'asseta
> di dolce disïar, s'adempia meglio,
> la voce tua sicura, balda e lieta
> suoni la volontà, suoni 'l disio
> a che la mia risposta è già decreta! (64–9)

> [But in order that holy love, in which I watch with perpetual vision, and which makes me thirst with sweet longing, may be the better fulfilled, let your voice confident and bold and glad, sound forth the will, sound forth the desire, whereto my answer is already decreed!]

In order for heavenly desire to be fulfilled, the pilgrim's desire must be uttered, either by the pilgrim himself or by the blessed speaker. The ascending, vertical desire of the pilgrim meets the condescending circular desire of the souls in the writing of the poem itself. The two desires meet in language, in the *sign* ('per far segno'), and the canticle, which unfolds through their encounter, spells out both desires, activating in turn the desire of the reader.

An interaction among the three desires is staged in canto 5: 'Ecco chi crescerà li nostri amori' (105: Lo one who shall increase our loves), exclaim the souls in the heaven of Mercury upon seeing Dante, meaning that the conversation with the pilgrim justifies condescension and increases heavenly love. Dante, in turn, is animated by an intense desire to know about the souls, and, in order better to describe the desire of the pilgrim, the poet appeals to the reader's own desire and to the deep disappointment – the 'anguished craving,' a mix of infernal loss and purgatorial lack – the reader would experience in the event of a sudden interruption of the canticle:

> Pensa, lettor, se quel che qui s'inizia
> non procedesse, come tu avresti
> di più savere angosciosa carizia;
> e per te vederai come da questi
> m'era in disio d'udir lor condizioni. (5.109–13)

[Think, reader, if this beginning went no further, how you would feel an anguished craving to know more, and by yourself you will see what my desire was, to hear of their conditions from them.]

In the *Paradiso*, therefore, language appears more and more as a function of desire – the only 'real character' of the canticle, the hinge around which the converging discourses of the sign and the body unfold.

The map of language in the *Divine Comedy* unfolds along polar extremes: from distortion to lucidity; from physical act to pure intellectual act; from mere noise (*vox unde sonum*), through sign (*vox unde signum*), to pure meaning. In contrast to the effortless flow of language in *Purgatorio*, both *Inferno* and *Paradiso* present, in opposite ways, the problem of a language in dissolution: both canticles are threatened by silence. The pathology of language is readily diagnosed in *Inferno*, where, as we have seen, a certain amount of physical pain is connected to utterance, and language is a form of 'arch-punishment' – a wound that forces the damned to utter a narrative of pain and loss. The disturbance of language in *Paradiso* is less evident at first sight because we are so accustomed to thinking of linguistic failure in terms of ineffability – a problem that affects both poetry and the system of language.[93] Both canticles, however, are affected by parallel and equally serious language disorders.

Notably, the two diametrical linguistic afflictions (excess of sound versus excess of meaning) affect Dante 'the listener' in the same way as each other, as is shown by two parallel but reverse lines. In the midst of the anguished linguistic confusion of canto 24 of *Inferno*, Dante expresses his bewilderment as 'sì com'io *odo* quinci e non *intendo*' (74: not only do I hear without understanding). Confronted with the sublime music of

Paradiso 14, Dante is described as 'come ... colui che non *intende* e *ode*' (126: one who understands not but hears). Ultimately, in both cases, Dante's access to meaning is obstructed, but the specular nature of the different problems causing the lack of comprehension is brought into relief with the aid Roman Jakobson's description of two types of aphasia – similarity disorder and contiguity disorder.[94] According to Jakobson, selection and combination are the two main features of speech. *Selection* operates at the level of the code (of lexicon) and works in terms of substitution, similarity, and alternation. *Combination* operates at the level of the context (of syntax) and works in terms of contexture, contiguity, and alignment. Thus, 'The addressee perceives that a given utterance (message) is a combination of constituent parts (sentences, words, phonemes) selected from the repository of all possible constituent parts (the code)' (75). Accordingly, Jakobson describes two types of aphasia. *Similarity disorder* (78–84) involves a deficiency in selection. For patients affected by this disorder, words in isolation mean nothing, and the only way to cope with this disturbance is to refer isolated words to the syntactical context. Moreover, 'In this type of language disturbance, sentences are conceived as elliptical sequences to be supplied from antecedent sentences' (78). Similarity disorder hinders the production of synonyms, leading to a loss of the capacity of naming (which is, as Jakobson points out, a loss of metalanguage) and restricts the patient to one language at the point that 'the idiolect becomes the sole linguistic reality' (82). The opposite disturbance – *contiguity disorder* (85–9), also called agrammatism – consists in the loss of the syntactical structure underlying words; i.e., the loss of the capacity of combination. It confines patients to a 'telegraphic style.' Interestingly, the impairment of the syntactical structure also affects the phonemic aspect of language. Contiguity disorder makes the patient relapse to an infantile stage of linguistic development and, in some cases, may even lead to *aphasia universalis*, 'the total loss of the power to use or apprehend speech' (88).

The context of these two lines shows that the same effect on the listener is provoked by two different features of the message: disconnection as opposed to excessive density. The problem of hearing and not understanding in *Inferno* is connected to a voice ill-suited for forming words ('a parole formar disconvenevole'):

onde una voce uscì de l'altro fosso,
a parole formar disconvenevole.
Non so che disse, ancor che sovra 'l dosso

fosse de l'arco già che varca quivi;
ma chi parlava ad ire parea mosso.
Io era vòlto in giù, ma li occhi vivi
non poteano ire a fondo per lo scuro;
per ch'io: 'Maestro, fa che tu arrivi
de l'altro cinghio e dismontiam lo muro;
ché, com'io odo quinci e non intendo,
così giù veggio e neente affiguro.' (24.65–75) *

[a voice, ill-suited for forming words, came out from the next ditch. I do
not know what it said, though I was already on the crown of the arch that
crosses there, but he who was speaking seemed to be moving. I had turned
my eyes downward, but because of the darkness my keen gaze could not
reach the bottom; wherefore I said: 'Master, pray, go on to the next belt,
and let us descend the wall, for from this point not only do I hear without
understanding, but I look down and make out nothing.']

Standing on the brink of the Thieves' pouch, it is tempting to ascribe the
speech disturbance to the language organs themselves, since they have
been turned into a snake mouth and tongue during metamorphosis,
causing the damned to whistle and to spit.[95] However, the adjective *disconvenevole* – *hapax* in the *Divine Comedy* – seems to describe the disparity
between the interior word and its utterance, as if an obstacle were inter-
jected in the natural flow of the speech. Outside of the *Comedy*, the word
disconvenevole can be found in the first book of the *Convivio*, where Dante
justifies his choice to use the vernacular over Latin in writing commentary to the poems. Convenience or, better, 'cautela di disconvenevole
ordinazione' (1.5.2), is the first of the three reasons (followed by
'prontezza di liberalitade' and 'naturale amore della propria loquela')
for his choice of the vernacular. *Disconvenevole* is always paired and con-
trasted with a notion of order,[96] and suggests therefore that the language
problem of canto 24 should be interpreted as a subversion of the structure that underlies words: the voices of the damned are ill-suited for
forming words because some internal order has been subverted and
impaired. Contiguity disorder, the loss of the syntactical structure underlying words, best describes the dysfunction of the system of language 'a
parole formar disconvenevole' (ill-suited to forming words).

The second half of the specular pair of problems that causes Dante to
'hear but not understand' is also quite interesting. It follows the vision of
the Cross in the heaven of Mars, and of the body of Christ flashing on

it.[97] From the Cross a hymn also issues forth, but because the verbal music that the pilgrim hears is dense, its meaning is incomprehensible. Dante manages to capture only a few isolated words ('Resurgi' e 'Vinci'), yet he 'falls in love' with the heavenly speech, and even though it lacks selection of words, there is a binding element in it that holds the listener with sweet bonds:

s'accogliea per la croce una melode
che mi rapiva, sanza intender l'inno.
Ben m'accors'io ch'elli era d'alte lode,
però ch'a me venìa 'Resurgi' e 'Vinci'
come a colui che non intende e ode.
Io m'innamorava tanto quinci,
che 'nfino a lì non fu alcuna cosa
che mi legasse con sì dolci vinci (14.122–9).

[a melody gathered through the cross which held me rapt, though I followed not the hymn. Well I discerned it to be of lofty praise, for there came to me: 'Rise' and 'Conquer,' as to one who understands not, but hears; by which I was so moved to love that till then nothing had bound me with such sweet bonds.]

Jakobson's notion of a similarity disorder applies here since there is a loss of the capacity of selection, which is a problem of syntax without words. The internal structure of language, its core meaning, prevails over the external aspect, and binding prevails over selection. Since all the possible selections are simultaneously present in the mirror of God, there is no need for utterance outside of condescension – no need to name and distinguish what is already and eternally evident and bound together in the discourse of God.

How do the two canticles 'cope' with their language disorders? Or rather, what is the poetic antidote to aphasia? For the *Paradiso*, condescension can be understood as a form of selection: as explained in canto 4, condescension is the 'affording of the sign' ('per far segno') and therefore implies the choice of some particular words/signs among all the possible combinations, thus allowing the simultaneous articulation of the heavens to unfold and become explicit: 'così parlar conviensi al vostro ingegno,' one word after the other. In the *Inferno*, on the other hand, the dis-order and dissolution of the speech of the damned is given what Jakobson calls 'contexture, contiguity and alignment' by participation in the *contrapasso*. As noticed by Spitzer, language is a form of arch-punishment in hell: not only is utterance painful, but further torture is inflicted on the souls by condemning them to organize and utter their doleful narrative of loss.

While only the *Purgatorio* traces a proper sentence made of an orderly and hierarchically arranged set of signs, in the *Inferno*, lost and fallen words and a lexicon without syntactic structure are given contexture by the *contrapasso*; in the *Paradiso*, simultaneous syntax (the Augustinian 'Word of God in which everything is said') is given selection by condescension, and while the latter renders more perfect heavenly love and desire, the former perfects infernal pain. The map of language in the poem resembles therefore an ellipse. The human/temporal movement of language as described in *Purgatorio* revolves around and always maintains a constant sum-distance from the two foci, the blind/mute spots of the aphasic systems of language of *Inferno* and *Paradiso*: sound decaying and meaning dissolving into silence.[98]

A Map of Desire

The thread of the *desiderio/disio* family (*desiderare, desiderio, desideroso, disiare, disio, disianza*) is widely represented in the *Divine Comedy*, increasing from nineteen occurrences in *Inferno*, to twenty-nine occurrences in *Purgatorio*, and fifty-nine in *Paradiso*, and is complemented by the more physical *brama* and *appetito*; the all-encompassing *voglia*, which identifies a large range of notions (from the lowest physical desire to will); and the less represented, but equally variable *talento*. The rich and nuanced verbal spectrum of the word *desire* in the poem as well as the complex system of desire in the *Paradiso* have been explored in depth by Lino Pertile.[99]

Dante's most conspicuous reflection on desire outside of the *Comedy* is found in the *Convivio*, a text that can be described as a production of desire, which is inscribed in its very first line: 'Sì come dice lo Filosofo nel principio della Prima Filosofia, tutti li uomini desiderano naturalmente di sapere' (As the Philosopher says at the beginning of the First Philosophy, all men by nature desire to know). It is the third and fourth treatises of the *Convivio*, however, that concentrate most heavily on the issue of desire. *Convivio* 3 mainly explores the desire for knowledge, a natural appetite of the human soul. It provides, therefore, an earthly perspective on desire, a 'degree zero' notion of it, not yet complicated by theologisation.[100] In *Convivio* 4 the theme of desire is connected to ethics with a comparison between desire for knowledge and desire for wealth.[101] In this context, Dante describes desire as a pyramidal structure, where the base is the ultimate desire (for God) and the tip the minimal desire.[102] With an image that beautifully fits the *Commedia*'s system of desire,[103] Dante depicts the wanderings of soul's desire toward God as the drive that pushes the pilgrim forward on the road:

> E però che Dio è principio delle nostre anime e fattore di quelle simili a sé (sì come è scritto: 'Facciamo l'uomo ad imagine e simiglianza nostra'), essa anima massimamente desidera di tornare a quello. E sì come peregrino che va per una via per la quale mai non fue, che ogni casa che da lungi vede crede che sia l'albergo, e non trovando ciò essere, dirizza la credenza all'altra, e così di casa in casa, tanto che all'albergo viene; così l'anima nostra, incontanente che nel nuovo e mai non fatto cammino di questa vita entra, dirizza li occhi al termine del suo sommo bene, e però, qualunque cosa vede che paia in sé avere alcuno bene, crede che sia esso. (4.12.14–15)

> [Now since God is the cause of our souls and has created them like himself (as it is written, 'Let us make man in our own image and likeness'), the soul desires above all else to return to him. And just as the pilgrim who walks along a road on which he has never traveled before believes that every house which he sees from afar is an inn, and finding it not so fixes his expectations on the next one, and so moves from house to house until he comes to the inn, so our soul, as soon as it enters upon this new and never travelled road of life, fixes its eyes on the goal of its supreme good, and therefore believes that everything it sees which seems to possess some good in it is that supreme good.]

No transitory object of desire is, however, able to provide fulfilment for the pilgrim, and just as there are roads that are good and others that are bad, so too are there right and wrong ways of following the path of desire.[104]

Knowledge and God are also the main tracks of desire in the poem. As Pertile has shown for the *Paradiso*, the ascent of the pilgrim takes place along with a succession of doubts staged as desire and answers that satisfy it; however, 'the satisfaction of each doubt increases both his knowledge and his desire to know.'[105] Desire for knowledge is therefore one of the motors of the journey. Throughout the poem one can track a consistent connection between this driving desire and the acts of speaking and listening. Within this framework, desire can be understood on the one hand as the formulation in the mind of a question or an answer before it is actually uttered and, on the other hand, as the capacity for receiving a piece of information through language. This linguistic desire is mostly distinctive of the pilgrim and is characterized as an interior word – the already formulated but not yet articulated, not yet uttered language of the heart. In *Inferno* 10, for instance, Virgil promises to answer both the pilgrim's spoken question and his unuttered one: 'il disio ch'ancor mi taci' (18: the wish which you hold from me). In *Purgatorio* 26, the refined and courtly question about Arnaut's name is formulated as a 'graceful place' carved in Dante's desire – where desire describes the interior word from the point of view of the listener: 'Io mi fei al mostrato innanzi un poco / e dissi ch'al suo nome il mio disire / apparecchiava grazioso loco' (137–9: I moved forward a little towards him that had been pointed out to me, and said that for his name my desire was making ready a grateful place). When Cacciaguida explains the relation between the blessed souls' condescending desire for speech and the pilgrim's ascending one, he orders Dante to let his voice clothe with sound his desire to speak (15.68: 'la voce tua sicura, balda e lieta suoni la volontà, suoni 'l disio' [sound forth the will, sound forth the desire]). Later in this episode, the articulation between exterior and interior word is figured as a dynamic between desire and its flame, whereas the balance between the drive toward knowledge and its satisfaction is described as a thirst-to-water ratio:

> Per che mia donna: 'Manda fuor la vampa
> del tuo desio' mi disse 'sì ch'ella esca
> segnata bene de la interna stampa
> non perché nostra conoscenza cresca
> per tuo parlare, ma perché t'ausi
> a dir la sete, sì che l'uom ti mesca.' (17.7–12)

[Wherefore my lady said to me, 'Put forth the flame of your desire, so that it may issue imprinted well by the internal stamp; not in order that our knowledge may increase through your speech, but that you may learn to tell your thirst, so that one may pour out drink for you.']

All desires in the poem bend toward and are encompassed by the overarching desire for God, which supports, animates, and directs the narrative. As the structural blueprint of each canticle, the desire for God assumes a peculiar nuance in each realm, portraying the specificity of the canticle itself in terms of loss (*Inferno*), lack (*Purgatorio*), and fulfilment (*Paradiso*). As such, there are striking similarities between this structural notion of desire and the system of language in each canticle. As I have shown, the relationship between sign and meaning is characterized as loss in *Inferno*, where sign is disfigured into mere sound; as longing in *Purgatorio*, where a balanced yet temporally contingent sign is inserted on the path of redemption, where it awaits the fullness of signification; and finally as fulfilment in *Paradiso*, where sign is transfigured and annihilated into pure meaning.

With the important exception of canto 5, where we also find the highest condensation of the term *desire*, the notion of desire in *Inferno* appears mainly in connection with the problem of language and knowledge.[106] The structural notion of desire as loss is carried by the famous line in which Virgil describes the punishment of limbo, where he and other great souls of antiquity dwell, punished 'only' by desire for their 'non-sin' of not having had the chance of being Christian for historical or geographical reasons:

Per tai difetti, non per altro rio
semo perduti, e sol di tanto offesi
che sanza speme vivemo in disio. (4.40–2)

[Because of these shortcomings, and for no other fault, we are lost, and only so far afflicted that without hope we live in longing.][107]

'Disio' translates here the classical notion of desire, *desiderium* (< *de-sideribus*), the understanding of desire as mourning, which refers mainly to the regret for something or somebody that does not exist anymore and is lost forever; it indicates an irreplaceable loss. But desire here translates also the theologians' *poena damni:* an ur-punishment underlying all the other punishments in hell (where *poena sensus* is added to *poena damni*). Desire without hope is the fittest Ur-*contrapasso* for those who were unable or unwilling to undo the original loss/desire initiated by the Fall.

In canto 3 we learn that the damned souls are spurred on Charon's boat by a strange desire. In Virgil's words,

'Figliuol mio,' disse 'l maestro cortese,
'quelli che muoion ne l'ira di Dio

tutti convegnon qui d'ogne paese;
e pronti sono a trapassar lo rio,
ché la divina giustizia li sprona,
sì che la tema si volve in disio.' (3.121–6)

['My son,' said the courteous master, 'those who die in the wrath of God all come together here from every land; and they are eager to cross the stream, for Divine Justice so spurs them that their fear is changed to desire.']

On the shores of the Acheron, Divine Justice appears almost as a character, inspiring in the damned the quite 'unnatural' desire to rush toward their punishment, to desire what they fear most. After this desperate flight, Divine Justice becomes the structure of hell itself, and every desire within it a form of loss. The 'punishment of loss' is connected to the Fall,[108] to which human language also is connected (in some versions of the story to which, as we have seen, Dante may have turned in *Paradiso* 26) in terms of loss of the direct communication with God and the necessity of interpolating a sign between thing and meaning. As structures of loss, both language and desire constitute the Ur-*contrapasso* of hell. As the sign in *Inferno* is disfigured and deflected from its relation to meaning, turning into mere sound, so desire's trajectory's toward knowledge and/or God is foreclosed. Moreover, speech becomes a tyrannical need, an open wound through which a narrative of hopeless desire is painfully uttered.

In *Purgatorio* the notion of desire is equally balanced between desire for speech and knowledge, desire as a natural appetite of the human soul, and desire for God. At the heart of the canticle stands the discussion of the theory of love, which uncoils in a set of circularly arranged cantos (16–19).[109] Following Marco Lombardo's explanation of free will (16), in canto 27 Virgil describes the whole system of virtues and sins and the structure of the realm in terms of a correct understanding of love and therefore of desire. This calls for an explanation of the nature of love, in canto 18, within which the definition of desire is provided. Desire is the fourth and last step in the process of love, following the spontaneous movement of the soul toward a likable object, the abstraction and 'knowledge' of the image, and the bending of the soul toward the image itself.[110] It is then that the soul tries to join the beloved object by means of desire, a 'moto spiritale' compared to fire:

Poi, come 'l foco movesi in altura
per la sua forma ch'è nata a salire
là dove più in sua materia dura,
così l'animo preso entra in disire,
ch'è moto spiritale e mai non posa
fin che la cosa amata il fa gioire. (18.28–33)

[Then, even as fire moves upward by reason of its form, being born to ascend thither where it lasts longest in its matter, so the captive mind enters into desire, which is a spiritual movement and never rests until (as long as)[111] the thing loved makes it rejoice.]

Love and desire are figured as natural movements, unmarked per se, that can be turned toward good or evil;[112] and it is left to *libero arbitrio* to restrain and order the natural impulse.[113] The remark on free will sets a circular seal upon this dense set of cantos, although a conclusion on the always imminent danger of unrestrained desire is staged in the dream of the Siren at the beginning of canto 19.[114]

Structurally, purgatory aims precisely at redirecting wrongful desire toward a better end, at 'torcere in suso'[115] (turning upwards) – or, better, at twisting through some violent and painful strength – the desire of the souls. In the second realm, the desires of the repentants that in life were linearly and fragmentedly scattered toward earthly matters are unified and aimed toward heaven, in a communion and concord of desire shared also by the pilgrim.

Poi disse un altro: 'Deh, se quel disio
si compia che ti tragge a l'alto monte
con buona pïetate aiuta il mio.' (5.85–7)

[Then said another, 'Ah, so may that desire be fulfilled which draws you up the lofty mountain, do you with gracious pity help my own.']

Indeed, desire in *Purgatorio* pushes the souls in opposite directions. Like at the beginning of *Inferno*, Divine Justice inspires in the souls the 'unnatural' desire of undergoing punishment, which counterbalances the will toward blessedness. However, whereas in hell the desire for punishment is the only force at stake, aimed at overcoming fear and plunging the souls into damnation, here two linear forces keep the soul suspended, like a compressed spring, until the knowledge of being cleansed counteracts the downward force, and the soul, experiencing a sudden lightness, can soar toward heaven. In Statius's words

De la mondizia sol voler fa prova,
che, tutto libero a mutar convento,
l'alma sorprende, e di voler le giova.
Prima vuol ben, ma non lascia il talento
che divina giustizia, contro voglia,
come fu al peccar, pone al tormento. (21.61–6)[116]

[Of its purity the will alone gives proof, which takes by surprise the soul, wholly free now to change its convent, and avails it to will. It wills indeed before, but the desire consents not, which Divine Justice sets, counter to the will, toward the penalty, even as it was toward the sin.]

At the same time, the movement of desire is figured as a return, a *nostos* of the soul. Purgatorial desire – a spiral that combines the upward/downward push and the circularity of the return – is best portrayed by the famous beginning of canto 8, which describes the longing and nostalgia of the sailor and of the pilgrim.

Era già l'ora che volge il disio
ai navicanti e 'ntenerisce il core
lo dì ch'han detto ai dolci amici addio;
e che lo novo peregrin d'amore
punge, se ode squilla di lontano
che paia il giorno pianger che si more. (1–6)

[It was now the hour that turns back the longing of the seafaring folk and melts their heart the day they have bidden sweet friends farewell, and that pierces the new pilgrim with love, if he hears from afar a bell that seems to mourn the dying day.]

The piercing, nostalgic desire of the purgatorial navigator holds its course steadily toward the homeland, harking back to Augustine's pilgrim in the *De doctrina christiana*. Like in Augustine's work, signs in *Purgatorio* belong to the order of *uti*: they are the vessels that carry the pilgrim to the homeland (God/meaning), to which his desire points.[117] *Purgatorio*, organized around a spiral structure of desire, and itself serving as a gesture of pointing, contains a system of language as signs – the

mark and the limit of human experience – lacking, and therefore longing for the fullness of meaning.

Heavenly desire is firmly rooted in cosmology and closely governed by
God's will: it is the mover of the heavens,[118] and it is therefore connected to eternity.[119] As Piccarda explains in canto 3, the very essence of
heavenly desire is to be constantly and uniformly fulfilled.[120] Pertile
argues that desire, as a longing for God in the pilgrim and as fulfilment
in the blessed souls, is the driver of dramatic action and of the narrative
pattern in *Paradiso*, as well as the mover of representation in the last canticle. Thus Pertile describes the paradoxical quality of desire in heaven:

> Dante's Paradise, then, is hardly the kingdom of quiet and immobility we
> might have expected; indeed it is perennial motion, desire and ardour,
> hunger and thirst – not, however, of a human kind, for this motion does
> not aim anywhere, it is in itself perfect, it is the tangible form of perfect
> love; this desire, hunger and thirst are constantly alive and constantly
> replenished. In Heaven the soul is not fed and satisfied once for all, its
> desire extinguished for ever and ever; but as it reaches God, desire and ful-
> fillment, perfectly balanced and simultaneous, become a timeless mode of
> being that is forever present.[121]

As Caroline Bynum beautifully puts it, in the mystic experience on earth,
and in heaven for the blessed, desire is 'now.'[122]

As discussed earlier, the *Paradiso* unfolds through signs by means of a
doubled desire, the ascending desire of the pilgrim and the condescending desire of the souls. While on the blessed souls' part the movement of
desire, like the circular revolution of the heavens, is simultaneously stimulated and fulfilled, that of the pilgrim is 'terminated' – constructed and
brought to perfection – only in the last cantos. In *Paradiso* 31, where the
pilgrim crosses the divide between time and eternity and reaches the
final goal of his pilgrimage, St Bernard,[123] Dante's guide through the
very last stretch of his journey, thus welcomes him: 'Al terminar lo tuo
disiro / mosse Beatrice me dal loco mio' (65–6: to terminate your desire
Beatrice urged me from my place). A long journey of desire comes to an
end in the Empyrean. Almost imperceptible and figured as loss in
Inferno, felt as a steady lack in *Purgatorio*, desire is conspicuous and crucial to the *Paradiso*, where it becomes at the same time more intense and
more fulfilled the closer we get to the vision of God. The peak of the pilgrim's desire is described in lines 46–8 of canto 33, as a sort of introduc-

tion to the arduous set of images that approximate the final vision:

> E io ch'al fine di tutt'i disii
> appropinquava, sì com'io dovea,
> l'ardor del desiderio in me finii.[124]

[And I who was drawing near to the end of all desires, raised to its utmost, even as I ought, the ardour of my longing.]

The pilgrim's desire is 'terminated' only in the final image, where his desire and will are granted to wheel around with the heavens, enjoying for a moment what the blessed souls enjoy by default: fulfilment, the circular and eternal version of desire.

> ma già volgeva il mio disio e 'l *velle*
> sì come rota ch'igualmente è mossa,
> l'amor che move il sole e l'altre stelle. (33.143–5)[125]

[but already my desire and my wheel were revolved, like a wheel that is evenly moved, by the Love which moves the sun and the other stars.]

Language, Desire, and the Poem

In the *Paradiso* the reader gradually comes to understand that the challenging writing of the canticle is itself a plot woven with language and desire. As Teodolinda Barolini has shown, the poetic strategy of the *Paradiso* is empowered by that very 'disagguaglianza' that makes of the pilgrim a 'creature of difference' as opposed to the equal eternity of heaven.[126] Barolini stresses that 'as the poem heads toward the *uguaglianza* of its ending, as it is deprived of the fuel of *disagguaglianza*, it stutters' (219). Early 'stutterings' of the poem are the Cristo-rhymes in cantos 12 and 14, whereas the recurrent jumps signal the failure of its poetic motor. The first of these jumps provides a concise example for examining the interplay among language, desire, and the poem.

Canto 17 opens with a moment of suspended silence – following Cacciaguida's revelation of Dante's exile – in which both the actors ponder their interior word, Cacciaguida with satisfaction, Dante with preoccupation.[127] Beatrice breaks the silence by rekindling Dante's desire toward the final goal (4–6), and in her eyes the pilgrim catches a glimpse of such a heavenly beauty that, for a moment, it satisfies his every desire. That very moment corresponds to an interruption within the poem ('io qui l'abbandono').

Io mi rivolsi a l'amoroso suono
del mio conforto; e qual io allor vidi
ne li occhi santi amor, qui l'abbandono:
non perch'io pur del mio parlar diffidi,
ma per la mente che non può redire
sovra sé tanto, s'altri non la guidi.
Tanto poss'io di quel punto ridire
che, rimirando lei, lo mio affetto
libero fue da ogne altro disire,
fin che 'l piacere etterno, che diretto
raggiava in Bëatrice, dal bel viso
mi contentava col secondo aspetto. (7–18)

[I turned round at the loving sound of my comfort, and what love I then saw in the holy eyes I leave here untold; not only because I distrust my own speech, but because of memory, which cannot return on itself so far unless Another guides it. This much of that moment I can retell, that as I gazed upon her my affection was freed from every other desire so long as the Eternal Joy that shone direct on Beatrice satisfied me from the fair eyes with its reflected aspect.]

The momentary absence of desire marks a hiatus in the narrative, which Beatrice is able to overcome by spurring Dante to listen to the other souls – to reactivate language and desire – since heaven does not 'terminate' in her eyes (19–21): 'Volgiti e ascolta; / ché non pur ne' miei occhi è paradiso' (Turn and listen, for not only in my eyes is Paradise). The satisfaction of desire implies, therefore, the silence of the poetic word. The poet represents his own writing as a production of the desire of the pilgrim: the more it approximates fulfilment, the more it vanishes into silence.

As the internal and poetic language fade and fail, a powerful substitute of the sign facilitates the hardest part of the spiritual and poetic ascent. Besides desire for language and desire for God, there is another desire that is shared equally by the pilgrim and the blessed and that pushes the poem forward, especially in its final part: the desire for body.[128] A close connection between words and bodies is established as early as De vulgari eloquentia 1.3.1, where language is described as a uniquely human operation due to the *grossitia* and *opacitas* (heaviness and density) of the mortal body, which hinders the communication between minds.[129] In both *Inferno* and *Purgatorio*, bodies reflect the trend of language: in hell the aerial bodies represent the disrupted, 'dead letter' of sin; in *Purgatorio*, both the souls' aerial bodies and the pilgrim's actual body start to function as signs that point to a higher meaning. In the *Paradiso*, bodies enter even more conspicuously into the issue of representation and become crucial and irreplaceable actors in the dynamic of language and desire.

In canto 22, Dante begs Benedict to show himself 'con immagine scoverta' (60: in your uncovered shape). Benedict, in response, delays Dante's 'high desire' to the Empyrean, where every desire is completed:

> Ond'elli: 'Frate, il tuo alto disio
> s'adempierà in su la ultima spera,
> ove s'adempion tutti li altri e 'l mio
> Ivi è perfetta, matura e intera
> ciascuna disïanza.' (22.61–5)

> [Whereon he, 'Brother, your high desire shall be fulfilled up in the last sphere, where are fulfilled all others and my own. There, every desire is perfect, mature and whole.']

'Perfetta,' 'matura,' and 'intera' should not be taken in this context as an emphatic repetition for the wholeness of the Empyrean's fulfilment. Rather they describe, I believe, three degrees of the construction of desire – a construction that brings desire from fragmentation to fullness. As such, they can be compared, in reverse order, to the three steps of construction as proposed, for instance, by Thomas of Erfurth (see chap. 2). 'Intera' suggests that desire in the Empyrean is complete in all its parts or, more specifically, that it is a wholeness made of parts;[130] it recalls *constructio*, the gathering of the constructibles. 'Matura' conveys a sense of growth, of the congruous melting together of the parts that make desire whole, a disposition to fullness; it recalls *congruitas*, the second step of construction, the correct union of the constructibles themselves. The disposition of 'matura' is terminated in 'perfetta,' perfectly describing the paradox of blessedness in heaven, where desire is simultaneously stirred and fulfilled;[131] it recalls *perfectio*, the third and last passion of the sentence, characterized by the presence of a verb and the 'termination' of all the open dependences. This quenches the expectation of language by leading the sentence toward the stillness of a full stop and, in the silence that follows it, to the reconstruction of the initial meaning. In the context of *Paradiso* 22, the three steps of construction describe the perfection of desire in the empyrean as related to the vision of the glorified body: the syntax of desire in *Paradiso* therefore passes through the vision of, if not yet through the reunion with, the resurrection body.

In the *Paradiso* we witness the dissolution of the aerial body, which steadily vanishes into the garment of light, but the issue of the body itself does not disappear; on the contrary it is reinforced by the discussion of the resurrection body. Rooted in the doctrine of Incarnation (canto 7), the doctrine of Resurrection is explained in canto 14, where Solomon's speech on the privileges and improvements to the resurrection body (14.36–57) is followed by a burst of desire for the dead body itself on the part of the blessed souls:

> Tanto mi parver sùbiti ed accorti
> e l'uno e l'altro coro a dicer 'Amme!'
> che ben mostrar disio d'i corpi morti:
> forse non pur per lor, ma per le mamme,
> per li padri e per li altri che fuor cari
> anzi che fosser sempiterne fiamme. (61–6)

[So sudden and eager both the one and the other chorus seemed to me in saying 'Amen,' that truly they showed desire for their dead bodies – perhaps not only for themselves, but also for their mothers, for their fathers, and for the others who were dear before they became eternal flames.]

This passage reveals to the reader a vestige of lack in heaven: the desire for the dead body cannot, in fact, be immediately fulfilled, but rather must be delayed until the end of time.[132] By functioning as lack, the desire for body can be compared to the desire for signs: it articulates a discourse that is active in the Empyrean and carries the canticle along all the way to the vision of God.

Dante the pilgrim is also animated by the desire for seeing, if not for joining with, the resurrection body, as first stated in his request to see Benedict 'con imagine scoverta' in canto 22. Benedict's deferral of Dante's 'high desire' to see the glorified body is addressed again in canto 30, where the expression 'alto disio' (70) is used for the second time in the canticle to describe the pilgrim's yearning before the river of light. Soon after, the metamorphosis of the celestial river/garden begins to reveal to the pilgrim the two heavenly courts (30.91–6). What the pilgrim sees at the end of the masquerade of light are 'visi a carità süadi, / d'altrui lume fregiati e di suo riso, / e atti ornati di tutte onestadi' (31.49–51: faces all given to love, adorned by the light of Another, and by their own smile, and movement graced with every dignity). Although still quite undefined, these are not the shades of the other canticles, but the first real faces to appear in the poem as they will appear on judgment day (30.44–5).

With a stunning invention Dante places *bodies* in the Empyrean – the incorporeal heaven outside time and space.[133] These bodies, however, are signs of resurrection, the real bodies of the blessed being dust on earth – 'terra in terra,' as John tells the pilgrim in canto 25 (124), reminding him that only Christ and Mary ascended to heaven with their bodies. As *signs*, the bodies in the last heaven map eternity for the pilgrim into intelligibility. Like the body of Christ in history, the function of the glorified bodies in the Empyrean is to be a sign. As such, their presence directs the pilgrim toward the final leg of his journey, and opens the ground for a glimpse in the final vision of 'la nostra effigie' (33.131) itself, the Word made flesh.[134] In canto 32, after the pilgrim is handed over to Bernard, the 'terminator' of his desire(s), Dante sees these bodies arranged in order in the 'candida rosa' according to the rules of contiguity (binding) and hierarchy (government) – indeed just as in a sentence, which Dante and Bernard spell out by the unfolding of one body-sign after the other. Significantly, this sentence is marked by a full stop ('qui farem punto'), connecting the eternity of the Empyrean to the temporality of the poem:

Ma perché 'l tempo fugge che t'assonna,
qui farem punto, come buon sartore
che com'elli ha del panno fa la gonna. (32.139–41)[135]

[But because the time flies that brings sleep upon you, we will stop here, like a good tailor that cuts the garment according to his cloth.]

The time allotted to the mortal pilgrim and to the poem is elusive at this point. The syntax of signs and bodies that has carried the pilgrim this far must be subverted, the rules of grammar 'bewildered.' In order for the pilgrim to perceive, and for the poet to represent, the Word in its simultaneity as opposed to its unfolding, syntax needs to be unbound. This is precisely what Bernard achieves when he begs the Virgin to unbind the clouds of mortality that tie the pilgrim: 'perché tu ogne nube li disleghi / di sua mortalità' (33.31–2) – in a prayer that is a truly Augustinian 'stretching' of desire. The poem and the universe switch places at the end of the last canto. As the pilgrim, unbound from mortality, perceives the universe as bound together by love and arranged in God's volume (85–6: 'legato con amore in un volume, / ciò che per l'universo si squaderna'), the Augustinian Word in which everything is uttered eternally and simultaneously, the poem appears 'squadernato.' As with the Sibyl's leaves in the wind, the syntactic order of the sentence is lost and the vision of God is approximated by means of a parataxis of ineffability and vision.[136]

In summary, in the interplay between the discourse of the sign and that of the body in *Paradiso*, desire – initially featured as a desire for the sign – powers condescension: by bending 'inver lo segno del nostro intelletto' (15.45: toward the mark of our intellect), the blessed souls execute a performative speech act that, as a syntax, carries the pilgrim to the heaven where their meaning resides. As early as canto 14, however, the plot of the body starts interlacing with that of the sign,[137] and it acquires further significance in canto 22, where it is presented as a promise that will be fulfilled in the Empyrean. In the last and only heaven, where every desire is 'perfect, mature and whole,' the sign starts to dissolve into meaning, and language as a consequence stutters and reaches a stop – then the glorified body emerges from light to sustain the syntax of the poem all the way to the final vision. The blessed, who condescended as signs, re-ascend as bodies in order to unfold there a new discourse that makes intelligible for the pilgrim the absolute incorporeality of the Empyrean. The syntax/desire of signs and bodies together allow the reaching of a full stop and the following recapitulation, and also allow the pilgrim to integrate the beginning ('La gloria di colui che tutto move' [1.1: The glory of the All-Mover]) into the end ('L'Amor che move il sole e l'altre stelle' [33.145: the Love which moves the sun and the other stars]).

The 'literal' full stop of the movement of language and desire we have been tracing so far suggests that we resume the grammatical analogy proposed before and extend it to the whole poem. The last word of the poem – 'stelle' – mirrors and encapsulates the full stops of the previous canticles. The ending of *Inferno* 'e quindi uscimmo a riveder le stelle' (34.139: and thence we issued forth to see again the stars) represents the full stop of the Christian individual, the achievement of the point zero within the dialectic of death and rebirth, which started for Dante in the 'selva oscura' and was completed at the bottom of hell ('io non mori' e non rimasi vivo' [34.25: I did not die and I did not remain alive]). In grammatical terms, it represents *constructio*, the gathering of evidence. The last line of *Purgatorio* – 'puro e disposto a salire a le stelle' (33.145: pure and ready to rise to the stars) – represents a full stop of time and history redeemed through Incarnation and recalls *congruitas*, the maturity and correctness of the construction. The ending of *Paradiso* – 'l'Amor che move il sole e l'altre stelle' (33.145: The Love that moves the sun and the other stars) – marks the achievement of absolute meaning, which encompasses all the previous full stops, as well as the full stop of a poetic language that – in John Freccero's words – 'represents non-representation without falling ... into silence' (211). It brings the poem to *perfectio*, to stillness and to recapitulation, and hands it, in turn, to the desire of the reader.

Epilogue

The themes of syntax and desire are very well represented in twentieth-century thought – in philosophy, linguistics, psychoanalysis, and theology. Like in the Middle Ages, contemporary syntax and desire can be read as flexible concepts that hold together and secularly 'redeem' the split, disrupted, or disintegrated self. Syntax is a prominent feature of a God-like language (the reverse of the medieval language-like God) that shapes (and even 'creates') both the self and the world. Desire is a feature/fixture of a self that tries, more desperately than successfully, to overcome its finitude and lack – indeed finitude-as-lack. Transcendence has been marginalized but not entirely abandoned by the secularism of late modernity, seeming to reappear as a cosmic black hole, where the lines of language and desire intersect. That hole is often named poetry, and/or worded by it.[1]

While in the Middle Ages syntax and desire appear to collaborate in the construction of a path of meaning that leads back to the syntactical and emotional Absolute, in contemporary reflection, the two forces are often staged as opposite – that is, revolutionary disjunctive desire disrupts normative conjunctive syntax. On the one hand, construction is viewed as the constriction of (linguistic and/or metaphysical) desire; on the other hand, desire disrupts that very order of which syntax is perceived as the linguistic invigilator. My aim is to show that this staged animosity is not irreconcilable. The opposition between syntax and desire springs from the fact that desire is indeed featured as counter-syntax, a skewed, 'disorderly' order in which meaning, the carrying structure of linguistic syntax, is barred and annihilated.

In this epilogue I will explore some aspects of both 'constructionist' and 'anti-constructionist' (terms that help me avoid the strictures of too many -isms) theories of language and desire, both separately and conjointly. Poetry is the hinge between the two sections of this epilogue and, in my argument, the only possible juncture between the discourses of syntax and desire. Ruled by a tighter syntax than that of ordinary language (the paradoxical, 'paradigmatic' order of rhyme and rhythm), yet simultaneously a stretched, diseased, absolute, and non-analysable language, poetry is not, as it is almost trite to say, the language of desire. It is, as Dante saw it, the desire of language.

'I am afraid we are not rid of God, because we still have faith in grammar'

Nietzsche's statement in *Twilight of the Idols* frames with caustic precision the scenario of twentieth-century reflection on language. It is acknowledged that much of twentieth-century linguistic thought holds to a metaphysics of language that affects even the most secular thinkers.[2] Language is indeed the god of a century that strived to rid itself of God. It is approached through a *via positiva* as a bridge toward the unknown and through a *via negativa* as a leap into silence. Like the Augustinian God, twentieth-century language is paradoxically located in the 'intimior intimo' and 'superior summo.' Like God, language is inscribed like a cipher in both the innermost self and in the universe. The growing complexity of the readings of the internal relations of the semiotic triangle make it a sort of a secular trinity of God-language. Contrary to what happens in the religious trinity, here the aspect of splitting and separation seem to prevail over binding, leaving all the pressure and weight on the signifier.

My aim here is to trace some aspects of a subcategory of the contemporary metaphysics of language: the metaphysics of syntax. As I do in the main chapters, which focus on the medieval context, here too I intend to keep the understanding of syntax open and flexible, one that circulates between language and 'the world' and is more akin to a notion of order (as combination and/or construction) of single elements, of which grammatical syntax is just an example and a reduction. I am interested in how a notion of order is formulated, starting from or culminating in language and, on the other hand, in how many standard features of grammatical syntax – such as combination, construction, order, universality, binding, government, and meaningfulness – transcend the limits of this discipline and posit wider questions to language and to the 'world.' Grammar, according to the authors I examine, always means something other than its traditional meaning; it is just the front window of a busy workshop in which other thoughts operate.

The metaphysics of syntax is a disguised metaphysics, one that works with and promotes articulation, difference, relation, and interval. It allows the insertion of meaningful moments of silence between the words/things of its discourse, but still brings discourse toward the definitive silence of the full stop that recapitulates god-meaning.

I begin by sketching three very different 'constructionist' hypotheses, three different positions and locations of syntaxes: as the extreme cipher of the world (Wittgenstein's logical form), on the surface of language in between the abstract and the particular (Saussure's syntagmatic), and in the universal recess of the mind (Chomsky's syntax). In all three cases, but with particular emphasis in Wittgenstein's and Chomsky's theories, some kind of syntax is both the subject matter and the strategy of the theory. The three theories of language I examine are the polemical target and/or the platform for 'anticonstructionist' theories of language and desire, to which I then turn my attention. In anti-constructionist thought (whether or not it is de-constructionist), syntax often emerges as the anti-subject matter: not by chance has deconstruction, one of the consequences of post-structural thought, been compared to a negative theology.[3]

An unconventional and fascinating image of syntax emerges from Wittgenstein's *Tractatus Logico-Philosophicus* – the extreme and most interesting outcome of the merciless test that logic imposed to the coherence of language, a trend initiated by Wittgenstein's predecessors, Frege and Russell. The *Tractatus*, the 'final solution' of the problems of philosophy, obtained through some 'unassailable' and 'definite' truths, is, instead, the liquidation of philosophy itself.[4] The coextensiveness of the world and language – not ordinary language but a logically trained, or rather one should say logically 'violated' language – leads philosophy into silence.

Totality, which presupposes arrangement and combination, as opposed to the solitude and fragmentation of objects/words, is the target of the *Tractatus*. The 'totality of facts,' 'arranged in logical space' determines the world (1, 1.11, 1.13). Facts, in turn, are given by 'states of affairs,' combinations of things. As G.E.M. Anscombe notices, *Sachverhalt* (translated in the 1922 edition as 'atomic fact') means literally 'situation' and etymologically suggests 'hold of things,' which later Wittgenstein explains with the image of links in a chain.[5] The way situations are arranged in the logical space is presented by a picture: that is, a model of reality that displays what cannot be depicted, its pictorial form, its common grounds, so to speak, with reality (*Tractatus* 2.1–3.1). The logical picture of a fact is a thought (3), a proposition, which is expressed through projection in a propositional sign (3.11–3.13).

Language too is a totality, comprising propositions (4.001), which are articulated, and in which the elements (words) stand in a determinate relation to one another (3.14, 3.141, 3.142). Propositions, like arrows, arrange the elements (names), which are like points (3.144), cannot be dissected any further,[6] and mean only in the 'nexus' ('Zusammenhange') of the proposition (3.3). The nexus is not merely a grammatical one. The single elements in fact resist logic's order, and confusion arises from the different modes of signification of some words (such as in the sentence 'Green is green,' where the first is a person and the last an adjective [3.323]). In order to harness this tendency to disorder, the philosopher must use a language governed by a logical syntax (3.325), in which 'the meaning of a symbol should never play a role' (3.33). It is within human capacity to construct a language prior to meaning. However, everyday language, in which words play more freely with the possibilities of signification, is not a good tool for the logic of language; instead it disguises it, just as clothing hides the form of a body.[7] Like a tableau vivant, the words arranged into a proposition present a state of affairs (4.0311). Like pictures, 'propositions can represent the whole of reality, but they cannot represent what they must have in common with reality in order to be able to represent it – logical form' (4.12). Propositions mirror, show, display the logical form, but don't represent it (4.121).

This is the framework – minutely discussed in the *Tractatus* – that establishes the coextensiveness of world and language, their co-participation in the logical form, and leads to the famous corollary that 'the limits of my language mean the limit of my world' (5.5571) and to the final appeal to silence. The very structure of the *Tractatus*, as much as its content, has instructed the reader to confront the truth of the impossibility of a metalanguage and the fact that language can only show but not say the logical form that it shares with the world – leading in turn to the conclusion that 'what we cannot speak about we must consign to silence' (7). The structure of the *Tractatus*, under the strict command of logic, leaps into the unknown. In the very act of transcending the ladder that has led him or her so high, the careful reader is allowed one final recapitulative gaze backwards on the author's propositions (his pictures that display but don't say):

6.54. My propositions serve as elucidations in the following way: anyone who understands me eventually recognizes them as nonsensical, when he has used them – as steps – to climb up beyond them. (He must, so to speak, throw away the ladder after he has climbed up it.)

He must transcend these propositions, and then he will see the world aright.

Taken by themselves, the propositions are nonsensical. However, inserted in a wider discourse – their order and combination, i.e., the ladder – they are meaningful. Their meaning is 'said' by silence. Thus, the *Tractatus*'s structure realizes another form of syntax and parallels the logical syntax of language, although it runs in the opposite direction, that of the re-production of meaning. While the logical syntax of language constricts language away from meaning in order to display its co-participation in the logical form, the structure of the text forces the propositions into an order and a hierarchy that progress toward a full stop, a final halt that allows for a recapitulation of meaning. In the light of this superorder, propositions act like points and their nexuses like arrows. Meaning, stripped from the single words, is restored to the whole – and it leaps into silence.

As it is well known, Wittgenstein himself broke that silence ten years after the *Tractatus* by producing a wide-ranging and lively corpus of unpublished writings in which he considerably readjusted and partially rejected the positions of his book – abandoning the earlier severity in favour of a more flexible and multifaceted vision of language.[8] Central to this evolution is the replacement of logic with grammar at the core of philosophy (not linguistic grammar, but, as logic, a metaphysically apt discourse that can express the essence of things, with focus on language use).[9] In its stringency, however, the *Tractatus* remains the best rational approximation of the closeness of language and the world through the notion of syntax. A quintessential and abstract form of connection, Wittgenstein's logical form violates language, forcing it to resemble the world. Its structure, which is mirrored in the structure of the text, restores in abstraction language's meaning-producing function and projects it into a 'superior order.'[10]

Some years before Wittgenstein elaborated the logic system of the *Tractatus*, Ferdinand de Saussure established the foundations of contemporary linguistics through the lectures later collected in the *Cours de linguistique générale*.[11] Both an heir to and overcomer of nineteenth-century historical and comparative linguistics – which established and systematized the unstable and uncertain heritage of the Indo-European language, the positivistic interpretation of a pre-Babelic language – Saussure initiated a sense of creative fragmentation within the twentieth-century study of language by proposing a linguistics based on dichotomies such as *langue–parole*, synchronic–diachronic, signifier–signified, syntagmatic–associative. As Giulio Lepschy observes, each of these four cardinal dichotomies created a revolution in the traditional study of language.[12] Through the formulation of the arbitrariness of the relation between signified and signifier, language becomes an autonomous system, disconnected from the 'world' by its very arbitrariness – so that there is no further need to inquire into the relationship between the sign and the 'world.' The *langue–parole* couple distinguishes between an abstract, generalizing, and social aspect of language, and a concrete, particular, individual one. The synchronic–diachronic dichotomy imagines two possible ways of considering language, as a stable model or as an evolutionary one. Finally, the co-presence of syntagmatic (horizontal, based on contiguity) and associative (vertical, based on similarity) relations establishes a new grammar within language.

These dichotomies are flexible rather than exclusive and aim at the enrichment and not the reduction of the problem of language. The resulting fragmentation yields a combinatory interplay between different facets of language rather than to their restriction; fragmentation always maintains the complexity, freedom, and even inscrutability and irreducibility of language, language in act, languages in view. Although one can say that Saussure promotes a synchronic linguistics based on *langue*,[13] diachrony and *parole* are engaged in a constant, creative, and unexpected interplay with them and with the other couplets. Even besides the four cardinal dichotomies, Saussure's reflection on language is constantly powered by twin, hermaphroditic couplets, which simultaneously imply exclusion and combination. The system of language is indeed a great combinatory game – chess unsurprisingly being a frequently employed instructive image. There is no identity without difference,[14] no unity without combination – as the famous example of the combination of thought and sound in language demonstrates: language is a piece of paper in which the recto is thought and the verso is sound; one cannot 'take a pair of scissors and cut one side of paper without at the same time cutting the other.'[15]

Difference, then, is the real operator of a linguistic system: 'dans la langue, il n'y a que différences' (166), so that a linguistic system can be summed up as a series of differences of sound combined with differ-

ences of ideas. Their matching creates a system of values, which constitutes the actual bond between the phonic and mental elements.[16] The
notion that a system of differences regulates language is also evident in
Saussure's antidote for the fundamentally chaotic quality of language.
According to Saussure, the linguistic sign holds to two fundamental principles. Creativity and the constant evolution of language are lodged in
the first primordial feature of the linguistic sign: its 'radical' arbitrariness, the connection between signified and signifier.[17] The second
founding principle is seemingly obvious, but the whole mechanism of
language depends on it: because of its auditory nature, the linguistic sign
is temporal and therefore linear, in that it represents an extension,
which is measurable solely in the dimension of a line.[18]

Affected by the chaotic input given by the sign's arbitrariness, language rests on a precarious balance between order and chaos. Since the
central quality of the sign, its arbitrariness, bears confusion and dispersion, the linguist has to work with a view to limiting arbitrariness and
introducing order:

> Everything that relates to language as a system must, I am convinced, be
> approached from this viewpoint, which has scarcely received the attention
> of the linguists: the limiting of arbitrariness. This is the best possible basis
> for approaching the study of language as a system. In fact, the whole system
> of language is based on the irrational principle of arbitrariness of the sign,
> which would lead to the worst sort of complication if applied without
> restriction. But the mind contrives to introduce a principle of order and
> regularity into certain parts of the mass of signs, and this is the role of rela-
> tive motivation. (182)

While some signs are and remain completely arbitrary (and therefore
unmotivated), others can be relatively motivated: that is, their arbitrariness can be recognized and scaled in degrees (181).

What brings relative stability to the sign is the sum of the syntagmatic
and associative relations. Syntagmatic relations are realized *in praesentia*
upon the support of extension and are created and conditioned by the
temporality and linearity of signs. Associative relations are realized in
absentia upon the support of memory.[19] Syntagmatic and associative sol-
idarities contribute to the motivation of the signs: *dix-neuf* is less unmotivated than *vingt* because it recalls in succession the terms that compose it
and associates with *dix-huit* and *soixante-dix*; *poirer* recalls both *poire* syntag-
matically and *cerisier* associatively. Intuitively, and interestingly, the moti-

vation of the sign 'is always more marked if the syntagmatic analysis is more straightforward and the meaning of the constituent units more obvious' (181): that is, the associative *cerisier, pommier* relies on a syntagmatic strategy (*ceris-ier; pomm-ier*).

Of the two principles of the linguistic sign, then, the first appears as a bearer of chaos and the second of order. Once the per se arbitrary element is immersed into a series, a system of differences can be activated, which traps the chaotic spin within a partial structure of order. The combination of syntagmatic and associative relations – always simultaneously active in every linguistic act – creates a form of grammar that is much more flexible and representative than the traditional one. Syntagmatic and associative are hence the axes upon which the linguistic fact is identified.[20] Interestingly, while the associative belongs to the abstract side of *langue*, the syntagmatic enjoys an in-between, undecided position that allows it to interact with both *langue* and *parole*.

As an example of the shortcomings of traditional grammar, Saussure takes syntax. Syntax is syntagmatic, but not all of the syntagmatic relations are syntactical (188). Grammar must be rebuilt upon a 'different and superior principle,' that is, the distinction and combination of syntagmatic and associative relations.[21] Order in language is given by the harmonious interplay of syntagmatic and associative relations, which counterbalance the chaotic spin impressed on it by the arbitrariness of the sign. Traditional grammar is unable to account for this complexity and needs to be replaced by a superior principle, an order in which the phonic and verbal element is actively involved, motivated, 'constructed' by its surroundings, a structure that encases the chaos of the single within the syntax of the whole.

From Saussure's systematization of language stemmed, from the 1920s onwards, various schools of structural linguistics and – at a later time and with different goals – the cultural practice of structuralism.[22] Notwithstanding their recognized differences, both structural linguistics and structuralism rely on Saussure's principles of the inevitability of language's entropy and the necessity for reconfiguration and support. Both work in terms of abstraction, with the aim of uncovering strategies of order and creating models for and from language, which may then account for the inherent entropy of a given linguistic or cultural system, and focus on aspects of organization, coherence, and structure of the text.[23] With structuralism as a cultural practice, moreover, the 'rules' of language are once again extended to the 'world.' This move both maintains and explodes Saussure's predication: language, extracted and rescued by Saussure from the tyranny of the world, returns to it as a quasi-absolute ruler.

The linguistic studies of the second half of the twentieth century were characterized by a focus on syntax and by a search for a 'theory of syntax' that exists prior to the actual use of language – a quest that, although very technical in appearance, is guided by wider philosophical issues such as the possibility of universal grammar, the problem of universals, and the relationship between language and mind. Generative grammar, the most conspicuous linguistic trend since the 1950s, encompasses a wide and fragmented corpus of scholarly activity, but is inextricably linked to the work of its best-known scholar, Noam Chomsky, who places philosophical concern at the forefront. Chomsky's theory of language is totalizing in both presuppositions and scope, and it aims at framing both the creative and the regular aspects of language. Although Chomsky acknowledges the centrality of the creative aspect of language – which has limitless possibilities and therefore is an instrument of free thought and expression – his theory presupposes a notion of a universal grammar and aims at defining a limited set of rules that is capable of accounting for and explaining the capacity for language that is inherent in every speaker and every language, focusing on competence ('the speaker-hearer's knowledge of his language') as opposed to performance ('the actual use of language in concrete situations').[24]

Universal grammar, a notion borrowed and modified from the Cartesian linguistics of the Port Royal grammarians,[25] is an innate device for language acquisition, is common to all humans, and is defined 'as the system of principles, conditions, and rules that are elements or properties of all human languages not merely by accident but by necessity ... biological, not logical, necessity.' Universal grammar expresses 'the essence of human language,'[26] and it is the sole invariant aspect of language(s) and speakers: each human language conforms to it, differing only by accidental properties. Universal grammar is not to be confused with universal language, or with the deep structure of language,[27] or even with grammar itself. As a theory of language, 'universal grammar is not a grammar, but rather a theory of grammars, a kind of metatheory or schematism for grammar.'[28] In other words, universal grammar adds a further level of abstraction to grammar, which already is an abstraction from language, a language about language: universal grammar is indeed the metatheory of a metalanguage. As G. Graffi puts it, 'The concept of universal grammar ... is both the starting point of the research and its ultimate goal.'[29] A metaphysical hypothesis, universal grammar springs forth from and soars into transcendence.

Universal grammar, the before and beyond of language, in turn links language to cognition. Language, being the most isolated and 'isolable' of the cognitive systems, may in fact provide great insight into the cognitive capacity of the mind. Indeed grammar, in Chomsky's sense, can be envisioned as the abstraction par excellence of and toward the widely unknown cognitive capacity of the mind: it encompasses the idea of a restricted set of rules that can account for every interface between the mind and the outer world, as it is implied, for instance, in the possibility of a 'grammar of vision.'[30] The human being is viewed as working in terms of grammar(s) possibly interrelated among each other (and, therefore, holding to an even prior Ur-grammar?) and inscribed as a cipher in the very core of being.

A quasi-metaphysical white whale, the sole invariant principle of language, universal grammar preserves the course for a continuously evolving corpus of theory. Chomsky's linguistic thinking from the 1950s to the 1990s is marked by continuous adjustments and refinements to the hypothesis of universal grammar, mostly according to criteria of simplicity. At least six major phases, springing one from the other, can be traced: Logical Structures of Linguistics Theory, Standard Theory, Extended Standard Theory, Government and Binding Theory, the Minimalist Program – the key question of the final phase being 'How perfect is language?'[31] Although the terminology and economy of Chomsky's theory has been modified over the years, some basic features remain the same. One is the premise that grammar is innate and not subject to semantic constraint. This is proven by the existence of 'an intuitive sense of grammaticalness' through which the speaker can recognize as grammatical a 'meaningless' sentence such as 'colorless green ideas sleep furiously' and as merely meaningless (and not grammatical) its syntactically dishevelled version 'furiously sleep ideas green colorless.'[32] Not only is syntax autonomous from semantic (or any other) concerns,[33] but it is also the only creative aspect of language, where creativity 'is predicated on system of rules and forms, in part determined by intrinsic human capacities. Without such constraints, we have random and arbitrary behavior, not creative acts.'[34]

The basics of Chomsky's formulation – as expressed, for instance, in the Standard Theory – include the theory that any grammar consists of three components: a syntactic component, which has to do with sentence formation and represents the sole autonomous and creative aspect; a semantic component, which deals with sentence interpretation; and a phonetic component that is connected with sentence pronunciation. These three components interact within the two interrelated structures of language: 'an abstract deep structure that expresses the content of a sentence' and 'a fairly concrete surface structure that indicates its form.'[35] The syntactic component produces and binds together both structures, since it consists of a base that generates deep structures and a transformational component (a set of transformational rules) that allows for the mapping of the same deep structure into surface structure, the visible, sensible (phonetic) aspect of the sentence. The farther one moves away from the base, the more diversified language(s) become(s), yet the creative aspect of language does not lie in its diversified surface structure but rather in its universal syntactic core. Semantic and phonetic components are, in fact, merely interpretive, while the creative aspect of grammar belongs solely to the syntactic component.[36]

Changing terminology and focus notwithstanding, Chomsky's theory of language boils down to the study of a complex and abstract modality of nexuses (the transformations) between the three structures and the three components.[37] Syntax, however, is not merely one of the components; it is also what generates and performs the act of binding and combination between the various sides of language. It is language's creator, mediator, and binder – indeed a triune linguistic god. Moreover, true to the tautology that turns theology into a 'logology,'[38] syntax is not only the central autonomous and creative aspect of this language theory but also the very strategy of the theory itself.

Chomsky's theory of language has been at the centre of linguistic debate for almost fifty years. Although his work is very technical and for the most part accessible only to experts in the field, its presuppositions and primary tenets have nonetheless been subject to lively discussion within wider intellectual circles. Standard critiques accuse Chomsky's theory of 'totalitarianism' and target its abstraction, its disregard for actual language use, and its tendency to reduce (and, thus, to impoverish) the complexity of language(s) and their social and ideological charge. Most damningly, it has been argued that the principles of Chomsky's universal grammar are suspiciously similar to those of English grammar.[39] The critiques to which I will now turn focus on the role of syntax as the invigilator and enforcer of a failing metaphysics, and emphasize the need to reconceptualize syntax (or disrupt it *tout court*) in order to reinvent the relations among language, the self, and the world in a looser yet truer way.

In *Philosophy in the Flesh*,[40] Lakoff and Johnson provide a radical rewriting of the Western philosophical tradition on the basis of three findings in the field of cognitive science: the inherent embodiment of the mind; the fact that 'thought is mostly unconscious'; and the metaphorical quality of abstract concepts.[41] According to the second generation of cognitive science, the founding philosophical questions of Western thought are posited according to an understanding of 'reason' as disembodied and transcendental. However, the very metaphorical nature of such questions – a nature that is not different from that of ordinary thought – shows precisely the opposite: reason is embodied; evolutionary; universal but not in a transcendental sense; unconscious; metaphorical (as opposed to literal); and engaged (as opposed to dispassionate).[42] One such illuminating metaphor, 'Language is thought,' substantiates Chomsky's theory of language, which the two authors discuss at the end (469–512) of their critical summary of Western philosophical development (including Greek philosophy, Descartes, and Kant). Interestingly, syntax is perceived as the culmination of a distorted philosophical thought.

Johnson and Lakoff begin by targeting the Cartesian presupposition of Chomsky's theory, which establishes language as the essence of being human, and the formalist presupposition, which establishes syntax as the essence of language, as something that 'creates from nothing external to itself' (475). Syntax ends up being the non-evolutionary essence of the human being, which needs to be pursued in a scientific way irrespective of other non-essential aspects of language (as, for instance, semantics).[43] Thus,

> There is a reason why 'language' for Chomsky does not include poetic language and why his 'linguistic universals' do not include a consideration of the sensuality of language, of poetic universals and of the universal capacity to form imagery and metaphor and express them in language. (479)

Feasible critiques of Chomsky's philosophical syntax come from both neuroscience (which contends that Chomsky's theory of syntax is physically impossible because it does not take into consideration the neural input on the abstract model, 480) and descriptive grammar (which demonstrates that the universal model of syntax is unable to account for many aspects of language in act and language learning, 480–1). However, according to Johnson and Lakoff, it is imperative to base the challenge of the Chomskian project primarily on its philosophical presuppositions, which make it immune to external (semantic and pragmatic) interference. When the Cartesian and formalist a priori structure is removed, strong tenets such as the autonomy of syntax (483–6) and the notion of grammaticality (486–94) appear less tenable. The research springing from cognitive science instead proposes an understanding of syntax as structured 'to express meaning ... in accordance with communicative strategies ... in accord with the deepest aspects of culture ... arising from aspects of the sensorymotor system (479).[44] The focus of cognitive linguistics, as far as syntax is concerned, is the notion of 'grammatical construction,' fundamentally embodied and polysemous, consisting of complexes of neural connections between conceptual and phonological categories. Cognitive philosophy of language, as a broad practice, aims at freeing the study of language from any a priori philosophy, and to reconceptualize such investigations under a very different (although no less 'totalitarian') intent: to 'become applicable to every human endeavor.'[45]

The notion of syntax as the 'universal' ordering agent also hides some ideological risks, namely that syntax might operate within language as a 'repressive' force, silencing diversity and subversion. Julia Kristeva's critique of syntax as a constituent part of the symbolic order is particularly incisive in this sense.[46] In her work, which has a clear structuralist and psychoanalytical perspective, the Lacanian subject, ruled and barred by language, is rescued by an operation à la Jakobson – that is, by listening to the articulated polysemy of poetry.[47] According to Kristeva, linguistics and the philosophy of language are too concerned with providing and defining unified systems and often overlook the fact that language is the product of a speaking subject that is split. Hence language, too, is necessarily split into two spheres (dispositions): the *symbolic* (space of the consciousness, of the father, of 'meaningful,' articulated, and ruled language) and the *semiotic* (an undetermined, non-posited space of the unconscious, akin to the unrepresentable Platonic *chora*;[48] of the mother-as-body, of an unruly and subversive language). The semiotic – polysemic and disruptive of both syntactic and symbolic laws – represents the truly revolutionary aspect of language; it defies and subverts symbolic closure. An ethically conscious linguistics, then, should have as its subject matter 'poetic language' – not the language of poetry, but a complex operation in which the dynamic interaction of the semiotic with the symbolic, usually screened out in ordinary language, is active and visible – a language that is 'truer' the farther away it stands from symbolic construction and constriction.[49]

Poetic language contains both language and its otherness; it is regular/regulated language indented, wounded, and delimited by its own transgression. The otherness in poetic language is the 'unfathomable,' and it is mirrored in the irreducible maternal body, childhood language, psychotic language, and silence. Kristeva's poetic language, suspended and stretched between syntactic totalitarianism and psychotic elision, is a language of polysemy, rhythm, repetition, and sound-pattern; it is a shocked, shaken language in which, if one listens carefully, one perceives a primal cry of silence. The birth of these irreducible fragments into symbolic law is usually supervised and dictated by syntax, which annihilates the unspeakable by erasing and condemning anomalies in language. Poetry, however, rescues childhood language by reinstating those anomalies over symbolic language.

In the essay 'From One Identity to Another' (1975),[50] after addressing the shortcomings of the philological attitude, which envisions language as an organic identity having only one meaning and an 'opaque' historical subject, Kristeva cites the revolution of structuralist linguistics in destabilizing language's unidirectional signification through highlighting the instability and precariousness of the relationship between signifier and signified, and thus bypassing the centrality of the speaking subject. However, the structuralist breach toward a space of freedom in language is foreclosed by the resurfacing of the Cartesian subject within generative grammar, which uses 'that subject to justify the generative, recursive functions of syntactic trees' (128). Kristeva identifies the philosophical presuppositions of this closure in Husserl's consideration of syntax as the guarantor of transcendental Being. Thus 'the *predicative* (syntactic) operation constitutes this judging consciousness, positing at the same time the signified *Being* (and therefore, the object of meaning and signification) and the *operating consciousness itself*' (129–30). Operating consciousness, founded on syntax, fulfils a 'thetic' (i.e., 'positing') function: it posits Being, the signified object, and the ego.

In Kristeva's formulation, syntax marks a contrast between the symbolic and the semiotic aspect of language. The semiotic is precisely what escapes consciousness and is connected to the non-signifiable maternal body. The symbolic, operating through nomination, sign, and syntax, homogenizes and annihilates the semiotic's radical heterogeneity and confines it to a prior (childhood language) or marginal (psychotic discourse) phase. Syntax, as the foundation of thetic consciousness, becomes therefore the major perpetrator of the repression of the maternal body and, as a consequence, the supporter of symbolic order and 'social concord.'[51]

Albeit constantly threatened by psychosis and fetishism, poetic language 'works as an incest' in the economy of signification by levering on the semiotic cracks of language.[52] There are, then, two kinds of writers for Kristeva: the 'rhetorician,' fascinated by the symbolic function, merely tickles the semiotic possibilities of language; the 'stylist,' on the other hand, disrupts and re-invents language through the semiotic. One of the main subversive tools is precisely the disruption of syntax through rhythm: as an example, Kristeva suggests Céline's 'sentential rhythm' in *Death on the Installment Plan*, specifically the three dots that isolate phrases as they become more and more independent from the central verb within the sentences (141–5).

Although they approach the Chomskian theory of syntax from very different perspectives, the structuralist/psychoanalytical and cognitive science critiques both reveal two (related?) omissions from the predominant theory of language of the second half of the century: the body, the traditional victim of the Cartesian culture, and poetry. Both critiques point to the fact that an embodied or body-related language (and, as such, a poetic language) is not sufficiently accounted for – indeed it is actively repressed – by Cartesian syntax. While the opposition between body and syntax is deeply embedded in the 'original' Western split between body and mind, the incompatibility between syntax and poetry might be only superficial.[53] 'Colorless green ideas sleep furiously' – Chomsky's famous example of the minimum degree of grammaticality located in syntax irrespective of meaning – is perhaps the luckiest of a long tradition of variations on a theme of grammaticality vs. meaning.[54] Chomsky's example is more well-known and more frequently quoted then others because it is – unwillingly? – poetic. It has been employed in poetry, for instance in John Hollander' s *Coiled Alizarine*: 'Curiously deep, the slumber of crimson thoughts: / While breathless, in stodgy viridian / Colorless green ideas sleep furiously.'[55] Chomksy's 'line' is poetic in sound pattern (gr*ee*n ... sl*ee*p) and in imagery, based as it is on figures such as oxymoron (colourless green) and synaesthesia ('green ideas' recall almost immediately Rimbaud's green vowel and/or Marvell's 'green thought').[56] If read as verse, it is poetically meaningful, and it could easily fit, for instance, Kristeva's notion of poetic language, which challenges the standard relations of signification. Although it doesn't recognizably scan in regular metre, it does retain a rhythm. Heidegger's claim that 'thinking goes its ways in the neighborhood of poetry'[57] might be not so far-fetched a match for Chomsky's poetic/syntactic line.

Poetry – a declining cultural practice in our times? – offers a special outlook on the problems of language. An extreme state of language, a 'diseased' language one may call it – a language that declines and conjugates itself into music, dreams, and silence – poetry constitutes a locus of reflection (and redemption?) for the problems of language in various fields. The radicalness of poetry-as-language is one of the cornerstones of twentieth-century poetry (with special evidence in the avant-garde), most of which strives to bring to light the ontological power of language in opposition to and/or in participation with the common use of language. In twentieth-century poetics – and poetic practice in very different ways – language emerges as an absolute: it is not a means, but the goal; it is not a form of communication or a substitute for the ideas; it is the thing itself. As T.S. Eliot puts it, 'The poet's direct duty is to his language.'[58]

When philosophers or linguists engage the 'problem of language' with poetic concerns, a new, uncommon perspective seems to emerge, and poetry frequently appears as an outlet for the shortcomings of language. Almost by definition an act of trespass upon linguistic and epistemological limits, poetry is featured as positive, 'poietic,' performative, and creative. It is viewed as a way of actively and unconventionally engaging silence (the anti-matter of language) into the creation of meaning. Ruled by the even more restrictive syntax of rhyme and rhythm, poetry dissolves language (and the world's) order, reinventing fixed relations of meaning. Although ephemeral – *because* ephemeral and evasive, poetry reconstructs and eventually melds into transcendence; indeed at times it appears to be the only existing metaphysics.

At the beginning of the century, the trespassing of philosophical language into a poetic voice is a common strategy in Nietzsche's work. To disrupt God and grammar is, for Nietzsche, to transcend toward music and metaphor (and madness). In the hands of the oracular voice of the poet-philosopher, language breaks free from traditional constraints and becomes energy, creation, truth.[59]

'Where word brakes off, no thing may be.' Stefan George's line echoes as a refrain throughout Heidegger's reflection on language.[60] The ontological disposition of language – the house of Being (both as position and repository) – actively flows into silence through poetry. Heidegger's Being is truly founded in poetic language – the sole authentic and creative word, the word that posits the world by plunging into and emerging from silence.

The uncanny and unconventional side research of Saussure – by some perceived in stark contrast to his scientific investigations into linguistics –

involves the search for a secret (almost sacred) and quasi-sectarian water-
mark of the poetic trade – the words under the words, the anagrams that
obscure and yet attest to the existence of a further message in the verse.[61]
In Latin (and neo-Latin), Greek, and Sanskrit poetry, Saussure discovered inner combinations of syllables and phonemes that resulted in an
embedded message – often a proper name or the name of a god. The anagram (hypogram, paragram) is an element captured in the syntagmatic
sequence that disrupts and challenges syntagmatic linearity. As Roman
Jakobson explains, 'Besides being linearly employed as sense-discriminat-
ing elements in the service of higher, grammatical units, speech sounds
are invested with their own, plenipotentiary task as verse components.'[62]
An obscure, deviated syntagmatic element, the anagram disrupts the sign
and shows the existence of a further order within poetry, one that joins
sound and thing without being a sign.

Saussure's silent and tentative search represents an important connection to one of the strongest cross-fertilization of linguistics and poetics:
Jakobson's notion of 'the grammar of poetry.'[63] As it is well known, Jakobson extended Saussure's notion of associative (renamed 'paradigmatic'
by Hjelmslev) and syntagmatic relations to the whole panorama of literature and cultural practice. His reading of poetry as paradigmatic, resting
on the paradigmatic trope of metaphor (as opposed to syntagmatic
prose, which rests on metonymy), reveals a fascinating projection of the
paradigmatic into the syntagmatic. Poetry reveals a distinctive grammar
at all levels: not only does the poetic function introduce an ambiguity
into the semantic function,[64] but sound patterns and rhythm also distort
and reinvent traditional grammar. In Jakobson's words, 'In poetry similarity is superimposed on contiguity, and hence "equivalence is promoted
to the constitutive device of the sequence."'[65] Metre and rhyme project
an associative relation onto the syntagmatic structure: for instance,
rhyme, a typical associative relation between two words, becomes the 'syntax' of the poem.

In his studies on aphasia,[66] Jakobson notes that metonymy, the figure
of speech based on contiguity, is most representative of similarity disorder, the type of aphasia that is connected to the loss of the lexical capacity,
whereas metaphor, based on similarity, is distinctive of contiguity disorder, which entails the loss of the syntactic structure underlying words. At
the end of his study, Jakobson extends the two patterns of aphasia – albeit
in less extreme versions, in the forms of style, habit, and fashion – to
branches of the 'science of signs' (psychology, linguistics, poetics, semiotics, etc.). Jakobson turns to literature to show how metonymic and met-

aphoric patterns work in different authors and passages, concluding with a very interesting observation:

> The principle of similarity underlies poetry; the metrical parallelism of lines, or the phonic equivalence of rhyming words prompts the question of semantic similarity and contrast; there exist, for instance, grammatical and anti-grammatical but never agrammatical rhymes. Prose, on the contrary, is forwarded essentially by contiguity. Thus, for poetry, metaphor, and for prose, metonymy is the line of least resistance and, consequently, the study of poetical tropes is directed chiefly toward metaphor. (95–6)

Jakobson's conclusion implies that there is a line of 'maximum resistance' for poetry, and that it runs at the syntagmatic level. In his own work Jakobson explores this line by highlighting the relevance of the 'figures of grammar' in poetry, side by side with the figures of speech and the figures of sound, and by exploring the 'grammatical texture' of a poetic text.[67] However, the syntagmatic – as the line of maximum resistance for poetry – may function at a level different from that of a grammatical trope. Resistance, as Paul de Man formulates it,[68] is a notion almost akin to physics: it is the force of opposition that makes something visible and knowable. To pursue syntagmatic resistance in poetry might therefore mean exploring the ways in which poetry is syntax. And indeed poetry copes with contiguity disorder not only through the proliferation of metaphors, but also through a new system of order – the syntax of metre and rhyme, which disrupts and reinvents the traditional relations of language by eliminating and reconfiguring sanctioned differences.

Poetry, a language constantly threatened by silence – the linguist's aphasia, the logician's end point, and the philosopher's beginning – reveals the possibility of a new syntax and the restoration of a different, if not primal, meaning. The examples discussed show that poetry interacts with language by constructing a new order of both signification and syntax. Saussure's anagrams reveal that poetry, by bypassing the sign, establishes a different, more obscure, but also more direct relation between sound and meaning. Jakobson's notion of the grammar of poetry demonstrates that poetry eliminates the difference between the syntagmatic and the paradigmatic level, by projecting similarity onto linearity. Finally, the poetic analysis of Chomksy's example illustrates that poetry disrupts the traditionally understood relation between syntax and meaning. Poetry – language ruled and organized by rhetoric and music – appears to be able to restore language to its primal, elusive, hypothetical unity. A question hence arises: is poetry located at the level of that intuitive recognition that sanctions the existence of a universal grammar inside the human being? Is the essence of the human being and the unrepresentable cipher of language and the world poetic?

Desidero, ergo sum

The adventures of the other victim of Cartesian syntax (as a theory of language and a cultural practice), the body, are best explored through the interlacing of the discourses on language and desire in contemporary psychoanalysis, philosophy, and gender theory. Desire, as poetry, both disrupts the sanctioned order of language and the world and constructs new, unusual, hidden, and displaced meanings.

Rooted in psychoanalysis, the theme of desire emerges with force in twentieth-century reflection, and inspires discussion of crucial issues such as knowledge, power, identity, order, and subversion. Like language, desire is the 'identity card' of an irremediably split subject. Desire plays a central and controversial role in the dynamics between self and other (Other, others) by connecting and/or disconnecting these two sides in two conflicting ways. On the one hand, desire is often perceived as the power of attraction within the relationships of difference: desire is glue, a fluid movement that holds together disparate fragments. On the other hand, it is described as a marginal, disconnective notion: the victim of the repression brought about by symbolic order, desire is itself fragmented – a non- or poorly representable, irreducible, non-syntactic, revolutionary discourse hidden in margins, lacunae, and silences, only intermittently emerging through gaps and fissures. Linguistically, then, desire is represented by either discourse or an 'absolute,' absolutely irreducible word/sign.

An immovable fixture of the (speaking) subject, desire is featured as a recapitulative discourse that brings the subject back (or close) to its own Beginning, a term that twentieth-century reflection has tried to de-capitalize and 'make embodied.' Metaphysical desire is, however, always present – indeed it hides in the very formulation of desire as lack, which implies an other (which inevitably turns out to be an Other). While ancient and medieval philosophers strived to suppress the chaotic, 'passionate' spin of desire and to put it on the road of a supernal itinerary, contemporary philosophers try to reclaim disorder and irreducibility for desire. As a syntax, however, desire is truly a juncture of the two sides and implies them both.

The antecedent of much of twentieth-century reflection on desire is Hegel's formulation of desire as constitutive of the subject. In *Subjects of Desire*,[69] Judith Butler has lucidly traced the history of Hegel's reception and criticism in structuralist and post-structuralist thought. As Butler remarks at the beginning of her work, desire – 'immediate, arbitrary, purposeless, and animal' – is traditionally perceived as the enemy of Western philosophy, the antithesis of the detachment that is thought to be the philosophical condition, or at least its aim. Desire as a challenge to order 'often signaled philosophy's despair' (1–2), and since it could not be bypassed, it needed to be tamed. One instance of such domestication, and a very powerful one, takes place in Hegel's *Phenomenology of Spirit*, where desire is posited as 'a permanent principle of self-consciousness'[70] and a guarantor of the metaphysical position of the unified subject. Butler anchors Hegel's 'drama of desire' in the mobility of his rhetoric, which asserts 'the elusive nature of both the grammatical and the historical subject' (18).[71] Desire ('Begierde,' akin to animal appetite, 33) appears almost 'causally' on the stage of the subject's consolidation between consciousness and self-consciousness. As the voracious movement of the subject toward the world ('Life'), desire becomes also the recapitulative movement toward the self, which sanctions the external position of the self with respect to the world. In the dialectic between lord and bondsman, where desire is both superseded and preserved, Butler reads a complication of the drama of desire – one that calls into play the notions of body and interdependence and creates a new version of desire that 'seeks metaphysical satisfaction through the articulation of the subject's historical place in a given community' (58).

According to Butler, Hegel's narrative of desire and the subject reveals the 'ecstatic' quality of the Hegelian subject at a point of no return to identity; it provides, in sum, 'a definition of displacement, for which there is no final restoration' (xv). The subsequent reception and criticism of the Hegelian subject of desire certainly presses upon this crack between subject and identity, stressing the subject's 'growing instability, its placelessness, its imaginary solutions, its various strategies for escaping its own inevitable insubstantiality. The desire to create a metaphysically pleasurable fictive world, fully present and devoid of negativity, reveals the human subject in its metaphysical aspiration as a maker of false presences, constructed unities, merely imagined satisfactions' (185).

Although rooted, as Butler shows, in nineteenth-century philosophy, the contemporary notion of desire is generally considered an invention of psychoanalysis, due to Freud's intuition that the birth into society and into language comes at the expense of the constriction and denial of conflicting desires. By setting up the Oedipal problem as the repression of the 'unlawful' desire for the mother, Freud establishes desire as a nostalgic lack. However, it is with Lacan's powerful rewriting of Freud's thought, and the grafting of Saussure's and Jakobson's linguistics upon it, that language and desire emerge as the sole directories of the new science.[72] With Lacan, lack, 'la manque à être,' is turned into an irremediable loss, not referring to any initial plenitude but indeed to initial non-existence, or to the mere phantasmatic existence of both meaning and the object of desire. At the same time, however, desire is formulated as an omnipotent, all-driving force, which, crucially, excludes fulfilment. Lacan frames desire as a form of construction/constriction and articulation – a syntax, yet one that does not unfold meaning in a traditional, linear direction but rather through a trompe l'œil, a self-reflecting geometry. Like Möbius's strip or Escher's ladders, the articulation of the syntax of desire results in an irreducibly three-dimensional structure, infinitely revolving onto itself. It becomes the black hole, lined by signifiers, where meaning gets lost.

Lacan credits Freud's theory of dreams for bringing to light the function of desire with respect to language: he calls Freud the first 'grammarian of desire.'[73] Lacan strives to unveil the specificity of desire as opposed to love, need, and demand. Paradox and parataxis are always present on the stage of Lacan's (non-)definition of desire – as in the famous description of desire as 'paradoxical, deviant, erratic, eccentric, scandalous' (690). All the Latin prefixes indicating exceptionality and solitude concur to configure desire: abs- (disconnection); non- (opposition), para- (beyond), ex- (outside), and de- (deviation). Although not undetermined, desire is later described as 'absolute and enigmatic, necessarily in impasse, unsatisfied, impossible, unrecognized.'[74]

Desire is a scandal precisely because it cannot be domesticated amongst its kin (love, need, and demand): it does not represent yet another declension of the vocabulary of love, but it is the result of the subtraction between its terms ('le désir n'est ni l'appétit de la satisfaction, ni la demande d'amour, mais la différence qui résulte de la soustraction du premier à la seconde'). An absolute condition, desire ties self and Other into a situation of pure loss ('la pure perte'). By not conforming to – indeed by defying – the concreteness of love, need, and demand, desire peremptorily prohibits fulfilment.[75]

Desire is twofold: it operates both from within the symbolic net, which is the sole evidence of existence for the psychoanalytical subject, and from without. Desire is both the explicit syntax of the symbolic order and the irreducible presupposition of it. The interaction between language and desire takes place very early in the life of the psychoanalytical subject. The mirror stage, the 'drama' of the self's identification with external images of itself, sanctions the entrance of the subject into the fictional line ('une ligne de fiction') of the symbolic order. The mirror stage is both a construction and a stricture. It constructs the ego into a subject and leads it from fragmentation into a rigid armour of totality, but it also marks an irreducible rupture that will permanently affect the subject, situating it in a discourse that the subject will be able to join only intermittently, indeed asymptotically.[76] The symbolic is the realm of language – of the unconscious, which works like language – and of a radical intersubjectivity that binds the subject to the other(s). The binding is provided by desire, since the mirror stage sanctions the entrance into a realm of mediated desire (the desire of the Other), which shapes human knowledge.[77] This step is inevitable and 'predestined': even before its birth and after its death, the human being is enveloped by a net of symbols, 'a presence made of absences' (276), a 'servitude and grandeur' in which the living being is trapped. The pulse, the conflict – the life, so to speak – of this net of symbols is given by desire.[78] Psychoanalysis thus unravels and spells out the complex discourse of language-embodied desire. In doing so, it asserts an old metaphysics, by individuating inside of the human being the imperative of language, which, as the Word, is both creative law and gift ('l'impératif du verbe comme la loi qui l'a formé à son image ... le don de la parole').[79]

Lacan's symbolic realm derives from a radical and creative interpretation of Saussure's and Jakobson's linguistics. The richness and fluidity of this aspect is best explored in the essay 'L'instance de la lettre dans l'inconscient, ou la raison depuis Freud' (493–527), where 'the letter' is to be understood as the structure of language as it emerges from the psychoanalytical examination of the unconscious. Saussure's linguistics is (de)ciphered and altered by Lacan through the famous algorithm S/s ('signifiant sur signifié'), which sanctions the primacy of the signifier over the signified and the existence of a barrier of resistance between the two. The signifier does not merely represent the signified: it generates it (497–8). The structure of the signifier is articulated and its units undergo a double condition 'of being reduced to ultimate differential elements and of combining the latter according to the laws of a closed order' (501). The order that governs the signifier conjures the image of the signifying chain as 'rings of a necklace that is a ring in another necklace

made of rings' (502). Here Lacan challenges two assumptions of traditional linguistics: that signification is undivided and achieved in the sum
of signifiers, and that it is linear. The signifier 'works' meaning through
anticipation: it projects itself ahead of the signified.[80] The incessant sliding ('glissement incessant') of the signified under the signifier does not
follow a linear pattern but rather coalesces in the form of the 'lignes de
force,' compared to those that the mattress-maker traces on the fabric
around the 'point de capiton.'[81] Moreover, as poetry reveals, the signifying chain is a polyphony,[82] in which the main themes are engendered by
the horizontal thrust of metonymy, the connection between signifier and
signifier, and metaphor, the substitution between signifiers (505–7). Metaphor establishes a poetic, creative effect ('un effet ... de poésie ou de
création') that transcends the resistance of signification by 'crossing the
bar.'[83] Metonymy rests on the sliding nature of the process of signification, creating a desire for something missing and asserting the irreducibility of the relationship between signifier and signified by reaffirming
the presence of the bar.[84] The reference value of signification is invested
with desire. Metonymy indeed nails into its rails the enigma of desire:

> Et les énigmes que propose le désir à toute 'philosophie naturelle,' sa
> frénésie mimant le gouffre de l'infini, la collusion intime où il enveloppe le
> plaisir de savoir et celui de dominer avec la jouissance, ne tiennent à nul
> autre dérèglement de l'instinct qu'à sa prise dans le rails – éternellement
> tendus vers le *désir d'autre chose –*, de la métonymie. (518)

> [And the enigmas that desire – with its frenzy mimicking the gulf of the
> infinite and the secret collusion whereby it envelopes the pleasure of know-
> ing and of dominating in jouissance – poses for any sort of 'natural philos-
> ophy' are based on no other derangement of instinct than the fact that it is
> caught in the rails of metonymy, eternally extending toward the *desire for
> something else.*]

Lacan's understanding of metaphor and metonymy is clarified in two
sections of *Seminar III* (243–70) and exhibits a strong influence from
Jakobson, but with interesting twists. Metaphor is poetic ('là où la métaphore cesse, la poésie aussi,' 247). Metonymy is not directly related to
prose as Jakobson understands it, but to 'realism' ('la métonymie anime
ce style de création qu'on appelle, par opposition au style symbolique et
au langage poétique le style dit réaliste,' 260). Although staged as opposite – indeed referring to opposite functions of the speech ('la parole

fondatrice et les mots de passe,' 261) – metaphor and metonymy share a syntagmatic substratum, of which metonymy sets the rules: 'La métony-mie est au départ, et c'est elle qui rend possible la métaphore' (259). It is the signifying structure that grants qualification to the metaphor, which is unthinkable without articulation.[85] Psychoanalysis thus reveals a radical fracture in the Saussurian algorithm and turns it into a trap in which the subject is both caged and exiled by the inexorable finesse of the endless play of metaphors and metonymies.[86] This fracture leads Lacan to rewrite the Pauline dictum: although it is true that the letter kills and the spirit enlivens, there is nowhere else that the spirit can live but in the letter (509).[87] In this fracture desire is nested.

As Malcolm Bowie remarks, Lacan is always clear in defining what desire is *not* ('not an instinct, not a quasi-biological "libido," not a vari-able flow of neural energy or excitation, not an appetite, not the con-cealed source from which appetites derive and not, as it had been for the later Freud, the life principle itself,' 122), but he is less ready to define what desire *is*. Interpreting the complex and skewed geometry that cir-cumscribes desire somewhere between need and demand, Bowie con-cludes, 'On each occasion desire, announced at the outset as a term in search of definition, is conscientiously removed from view during the defining process: it is not a state or a motion but a space, and not a uni-fied space but a split and contorted one' (137). Desire is never defined in itself but as an articulation, the structure of which is given by subject, other, and language, and its 'non-coordinable' coordinates by need and demand.

The closest Lacan comes to providing a definition of desire is section 9 ('articulons pourtant ce qui structure le désir') of the last part of 'La direction de la cure,' where he warns that 'il faut prendre le désir à la lettre' (620):

> Le désir est ce qui se manifeste dans l'intervalle que creuse la demande en
> deçà d'elle-même, pour autant que le sujet en articulant la chaîne signifi-
> ante, amène au jour le manque à être avec l'appel d'en recevoir le complé-
> ment de l'Autre, si l'Autre, lieu de la parole, est aussi le lieu de ce manque
> ... C'est aussi, passions de l'être, ce qu'évoque toute demande au-delà du
> besoin qui s'y articule, et c'est bien ce dont le sujet reste d'autant plus pro-
> prement privé que le besoin articulé dans la demande est satisfait. (627)

> [Desire is what manifests itself in the interval demand excavates just shy of
> itself, insofar as the subject, articulating the signifying chain, brings to light

his lack of being with his call to receive the complement of this lack from the Other – assuming that the Other, the locus of speech, is also the locus of this lack ... Those passions of being are, moreover, evoked by any demand beyond the need articulated in that demand, and the more the need articulated in that demand is satisfied, the more the subject remains deprived of those passions.]

In the first part of the definition, the relation between subject and Other is worked out by means of a parallelism that hinges on the Other:

(a) subject, (b) language, (c) lack (which points to Other)

:

(a1) Other, (b) language, (c) lack (which points to subject)

This can be read as a chiasmus, where language acts as a reflecting surface in the middle of the tide of lack that drowns self and other:

(a) subject, (b) language, (c) lack

:

(c) Other (as seat of lack), (b) language, (a) subject (of lack).

No linear geometry can truly capture this exchange, which is akin to the trompe l'œil geometry of the Möbius strip, patiently and implacably enclosing the infinite in a three-dimensional movement.

Desire is the elusive force that travels on the signifying chain. Lacan ingeniously traps it in what looks like a cunning syllogism:

- si le désir est en effet dans le sujet de cette condition qui lui est imposée par l'existence du discours de faire passer son besoin par les défilés du signifiant;
- si d'autre part, comme nous l'avons donné à entendre plus haut, en ouvrant la dialectique du transfert, il faut fonder la notion de l'Autre avec un grand A, comme étant le lieu de déploiement de la parole ...
- il faut poser que, fait d'un animal en proie au langage, le désir de l'homme est le désir de l'Autre (628).

[• if desire is an effect in the subject of the condition – which is imposed on him by the existence of discourse – that his needs pass through the defiles of the signifier;
- and if, as I intimated above, by opening up the dialectic of transference,

we must establish the notion of the Other with a capital O as being the
locus of speech deployment ...
- then it must be posited that, as a characteristic of an animal at the mercy
of language, man's desire is the Other's desire.]

But desire remains elusive because the signifying chain properly belongs
neither to the subject nor to the Other: notwithstanding articulation,
desire remains irremediably ungraspable. It is like the electron in physics: one can never determine desire's position and speed at the same
time. Elsewhere, Lacan 'elliptically' expresses the paradox of the articulation of desire, articulated because it is non-articulable: 'que le désir soit
articulé, c'est justement par là qu'il n'est pas articulable' (804). In other
words, as a 'logical form' of the unconscious word, desire is 'shown' but
not 'said' in language.

A consequence of desire's mobility and paradoxical articulation – oxy-
moronic and surprising at a first reading – is the fact that desire emerges
as a negative absolute, an absolute loss. Framed by figures of nothingness
('rien,' 'haine qui va nier,' 'indicible'), desire is a seal, the painful brand-
ing of the signifier on the subject's shoulder.[88] Only the signifier itself
might be able to absolve it and redeem it, 'give the subject back its
desire,' but the signifier is trapped within itself. Desire is therefore the
very impossibility of this redeeming word.[89]

In a later essay ('Subversion du sujet et dialectique du désir dans
l'inconscient freudien'), Lacan discusses how the traditional, 'Hegelian'
subject is challenged by psychoanalytical desire. The balance between
desire and knowledge – the fact that the traditional subject 'knows what
it wants' (802) – is withdrawn, and the subject's existence is exiled in an
uncomfortable dimension, indeed a tense, one that captures precisely
the anticipatory-yet-foreclosed operation of language and desire: the
future anterior (808). Other nuances are added to the non-definition of
desire: opacity, margin, and vertigo.[90]

Finally, the irremediable function of language and desire as loss is
both sanctioned and redeemed in the connection between Lacan's theory of language and desire with gender and sexuality – one of the best-
known dynamics of Lacan's thought. As Bowie explains, Lacan turns psychoanalysis from the science of sexuality into an 'eroticized science of
meaning' (121) that revolves around one main signifier, the phallus, and
features desire paradoxically as undivided and specified, genderless and
masculine.[91] With a move worthy of a medieval grammarian, Lacan turns
sexual copulation into the logical copula.[92] The phallus, the signifier of

signifiers, the organizer of the discourse of desire, is then the emblem of a supreme loss. The unmoving mover of the discourse of language and desire is locked into a void.

Next to the phallus stands another invigilator of the symbolic order: the metaphor of metaphors, the Name-of-the-Father. As metaphor, the Name-of-the-Father crosses the division between signifier and signified, but it also fills a potentially catastrophic hole in the symbolic universe.[93]

The battle of desire is eventually fought in transcendence. A petrified, menacing idol, the phallus is defied, albeit occasionally, by an equally transcendental transposition: jouissance, that which 'amounts to no use' (*Seminar XX*, 10), a momentary absence of desire that becomes 'a central redeeming notion' (Bowie, 149). While the phallus is 'the image of vital flux as it passes through generation' (808), jouissance is the only true 'god,' the absence of which makes the universe vain (819). In its feminine version, it may even assume the God face of the Other; at the end of 'God and Woman's jouissance,' Lacan famously posited this view as a question.[94] The oppressive signifier and its Ur-metaphor (a metaphor that creates nothingness) are defied by the non-signifying (or paradoxically signifying) jouissance. Indeed in Lacan's metaphysics of desire and the Word, jouissance takes the place of the Word-made-flesh, the embodied and redeeming moment, which 'makes sense' of speech and universe.

Lacan's subject is trapped in a cage made of language and desire. The syntagmatic chain, in its continuous, continuously unreferred unfolding, represents the bars of the cage, while desire is the mysterious 'electrical' force that runs through them, without ever being locatable. Desire exists only on the support of articulated language and at the same time defies it by refusing articulation. In a truly 'negative theology of desire,' desire is everywhere and nowhere to be found. In the very construction of the cage, however, a tiny escape route appears: desire points to margins, and the margin shows the glimpse of a vertigo, in which desire subverts its own cage.

Nested in the vertiginous peripheries of the cage, the unrepresentable, irreducible, and unfathomable desire becomes in subsequent theorization the locus for the reconstruction of repressed identities – in terms of gender, sexuality, power, etc. Desire, placed ontologically in the beyond and outside, becomes yet another proof of existence: 'I desire, therefore, *I* exists,'[95] not only as a symbolic subject but also as a subversive subject (I desire, therefore *I* exists in such-and-such form[s]). Subsequent reflections on desire have also searched for the fulfilment excluded by Lacan's theorization and have tried to rescue or reconceptualize the lacking/lost object of desire. This rescue operation of desire necessarily rests on language, in the subversion of the dominant male discourse and syntax.

Lacan's non-gendered yet masculine desire is the polemic and constructive target of many aspects of feminist theory. In this complex and often dissonant discourse, the richness of which I by no means can capture in such a brief excursus, one voice clearly emerges, demanding that the question of desire be rephrased, with its focus on woman and/or body, and to re-tailor it as 'her' desire – a desire that refuses to be defined as lack and to be articulated into the symbolic order. In feminist discourse, desire becomes poetic, multiple, plural, subversive, and especially much more bodily than it is linguistic. It is also a desire that (paradoxically) strives to free itself from the imprisoning web of the signifiers and to reach again toward the signified. Desire seeks a new meaning (albeit one often left conveniently undefined) and a new, non-tyrannical (because less orderly) syntax. Thus, the discourse of desire often merges with the issue of the paternal and repressive function of articulated language, which is central to feminist debate. It revolves around two positions: a 'humanist' perspective (see, e.g., the work of Monique Wittig), which sees language as neutral per se in gender terms and therefore potentially subversive of the repressive discourse, especially when crafted and reworked by committed writing; and a more radical perspective that sees syntax as always bearing the imprint of paternal law.[96]

As we have previously seen, Julia Kristeva creatively engages the Lacanian theory of desire by positing the relevance of the semiotic as the negative space of the (negative) symbolic. In its semiotic disposition, language becomes a positive space for the emergence of 'poetry,' the intermittent, irreducible language of desire, and a redeeming space for the recovery of the beloved maternal body. Kristeva is often criticized, however, for having featured the female semiotic space as the mirror image of the male symbolic discourse.[97] In contrast, in her manifesto *Ce Sexe qui n'en est pas un*, Luce Irigaray cautions against understanding woman's desire (and, thus, woman's pleasure) through the blueprint of man's desire, so that it becomes both an inevitable loss (the desire to possess something equivalent to the male organ) and a mirror-image of male desire (the desire of being desired). Irigaray argues for a radical difference between male and female desire – the latter being, as Freud saw it, a cryptic and mysterious language submerged by Western phallo-logocentric logic. Irigaray describes female desire as multiple and therefore capable of carrying multiplicity into language by 'disconcert[ing] the

fidelity to a single discourse.'[98] Accordingly, Irigaray argues for the existence of two syntaxes: a masculine discursive and political syntax rooted
in language[99] and a more elusive feminine syntax that originates in the
body and stretches toward (feminine) language. Feminine syntax is
based on proximity, parataxis, and seems to refuse government:

> What a feminine syntax might be is not simple nor easy to state, because in
> that 'syntax' there would no longer be either subject or object, 'oneness'
> would no longer be privileged, there would no longer be proper meanings,
> proper names, 'proper' attributes ... Instead, that syntax would involve
> nearness, proximity, but in such an extreme form that it would preclude
> any distinction of identities, any establishment of ownership, thus any form
> of appropriation. (134)

Desire is characterized as plural also in Hélène Cixous's *Prénoms de per-
sonne*, where it is explored as a feature of writing.[100] Here too feminine
desire is perceived as a bridge providing access to the recapitulation of
meaning. The writing that is a production of desire reveals a plurality in
contrast to the homogeneity of Western master-ideology – it is the
unfolding of the 'resistance' of desire that overcomes the oppression of
the signifier in favour of the signified, but through the invention of a
'new' meaning. Desire can then be the subversive and destructive yet
simultaneously vital force that permeates literature like an energy.[101]

For Monique Wittig, too, literature is a potential Trojan horse inside
the fortification of language-as-power; it is a war machine that has the
capacity to disrupt norms and conventions and to restore the submerged
polysemy of languages and desires.[102] Writers have the power to plunder
traditional meaning from language and work with and on a 'raw material.' According to Wittig, this possibility of subversion, which is inherent
in language, is so powerful that it can affect the strongest grammatical
repressive brand, 'the mark of gender,' and can universalize the point of
view of the locutor/s – as Wittig attempts to do with the pronoun *elles* in
Les Guérrillères.

In *Gender Troubles*[103] Judith Butler proposes a different strategy to
counteract the universalistic claims of masculine discourse – which,
according to Butler, feminist discourse tends to mimic with an equally
totalizing gesture that fails to shatter the structures of the 'heterosexual
matrix' regulating sex, gender, and desire. The normative structure of
gender rules out as non-existent (as 'developmental failures' or 'logical
impossibilities,' 17) gender identities that escape cultural intelligibility

and 'literalizes' desire by pinning it to specific body parts. It therefore needs to be challenged by an imaginary desire located in an 'altered bodily ego'[104] and by yet another subversive act of body/language: the performative, which lodges in the present of the act the ontological status of gender, and, through parody, shows the inconsistency of any notion of 'original.'[105]

The connective and articulate function of desire, together with the hypothesis that the syntax of desire might indeed produce an unconventional and revolutionary meaning, is at work also when the theme of desire is explored in connection to power, in the work of thinkers such as Michel Foucault and Gilles Deleuze. In particular, a significant resetting of the relationship between power, desire, and discourse is at the core of Foucault's *History of Sexuality*.[106] Foucault outlines how the 'repressive hypothesis' is challenged by the reconstruction of a discourse of power-knowledge-pleasure, which governs human sexuality. Desire can be understood according to two conflicting positions with respect to power: as a natural, rebellious energy ('énergie sauvage, naturelle et vivante') that needs to be tamed and repressed by power; and as a law in and of itself, which already contains the strategy of power (108–9). Both positions hold to the same representation of power as a juridico-discursive logic (a logic founded upon the enunciation of the law), whereby desire-as-repressed aims at 'liberation,' and desire-as-law aims at 'affirmation.'[107] The notions of repression and law need to be bypassed and challenged in order to bring to light a structure of power as a complex strategy, made up of a multiplicity of 'rapports de force,' which are, as in any discourse, at certain times connective and at others disjunctive.[108] As power is multiple and mobile, so must its subversion be. There is not merely a single locus of supreme rebellion that represents the 'soul' of the resistance; there are 'resistances,' which are 'possible, necessary, improbable, spontaneous, savage, solitary, concerted, rampant, violent, irreconcilable, quick to compromise, interested or sacrificial.'[109] Resistances exist and act within the strategic field of power by adhering to a specular discursive mode: they break, displace, regroup, cut, and remodel the discourse of power; they create their own syntax and chase their own meaning. Rather than focusing on one repressed (or self-repressed) desire, Foucault invites his readers to look for a constellation of desires. Each point of resistance is like a word, specific in itself and partly irreducible yet branching toward others – together they constitute a revolutionary sentence that runs under the discourse of power and needs to be unearthed.

This complex map of power and desire led Foucault to a change of direction in his work, as explained in the introduction to the second volume of the *History of Sexuality*. In order to examine sexuality as an experience, it is necessary to dislodge the idea of sexuality as invariant, and therefore to destabilize the ontology of the desiring subject (and of the subject *tout court*). In place of a theory of desire, Foucault proposes the analysis of practices of desires – that is, practices of selves and bodies ('une herméneutique de soi') that have led subjects to decipher themselves as subjects of desire. In other words, we must study the complex 'jeux de vérité' that constitute the genealogy of 'l'homme du desir.'[110] Hence *pleasures* rather than desires are Foucault's object of inquiry[111] – a radical move away from a notion of desire as lack or loss.

Marxist thought has long called attention to the constant creation of desires and needs that is one of the key strategies of capitalism, which nonetheless hides the potential of its own disruption.[112] One particularly strong formulation of desire as revolutionary is contained in Deleuze and Guattari's *Anti-Oedipus: Capitalism and Schizophrenia*.[113] Psychoanalysis and capitalism are the joint target of the authors' critique, which establishes a parallel between desiring-production and social production.[114] The theme-image is that of a machine, and the focus is on production as opposed to representation. The book opens with an almost apocalyptic image of organs-as-machines plugged into other machines.[115] Desire gives 'organicity' to these metonymic fragments – it is a connective force that 'couples continuous flows and partial objects that are by nature fragmented and fragmentary' (5). Desiring machines work according to three forms of energy (*libido* or 'énergie de prélèvement,' *numen* or 'énergie de détachement,' and *voluptas* or 'énergie residuelle') and according to three types of synthesis (connective, disjunctive, and conjunctive).[116] They function in an intermittent way; indeed, they operate by constantly breaking down.[117] On the one hand, they organize the body as a whole (an organism), while on the other hand, they rely on the dis-organization (or anti-organization) of the body: the 'body without organs,' the 'unproductive, sterile, unengendered, unconsumable' (8) surface upon which desiring production takes place. This frozen body is the locus of the breakdown of the machines and the very presupposition of their functioning. In the political parallel, the body without organs is the capital.[118]

Desire is traditionally posited as lack, and market societies replicate this strategy, which means that the need springing from the object-as-missing condemns desire production into a mere production of fantasies. Deleuze and Guattari invert this argument: what is lacking in desire is not the object but the subject.[119] Three errors mark the conventional understanding of desire, turning desire into the fear of lacking something: lack, law and the signifier (111). With respect to signification, Deleuze and Guattari argue that desire is a 'point-sign' that once again strives for an unconventional reproduction of meaning. It is both non-signifying in the unary discourse of the symbolic and polyvalent in the intermittent yet flowing process of production.[120] There is a reason, then, why desire is repressed at both the psychic and social levels – a repression so powerful that desire is led to desire its own repression (105):

> If desire is repressed it is because every position of desire, no matter how small, is capable of calling into question the established order of a society: not that desire is asocial, on the contrary. But it is explosive; there is no desiring machine capable of being assembled without demolishing entire social sectors. Despite what some revolutionaries think about this, desire is revolutionary in its essence – desire, not left wing holidays! – and no society can tolerate a position of real desire without its structures of exploitation, servitude, and hierarchy being compromised. (116)

Few voices escape lack, law, and signifier, and as for Kristeva, they are inevitably psychotic and artistic.[121] Psychoanalysis has brought the process of repression to light, but has also committed the ominous mistake of nailing the notion of the production of desire into representation, thus creating a self-referential system of beliefs (296). A new kind of analysis is required truly to reverse repression: schizoanalysis. Both desiring-production and social production are schizophrenic; schizophrenia is their limit, their osmotic border, the very reason why they exist in a mutual relationship (8).[122] The task of the schizoanalyst – the mechanic, and not the interpreter of the desiring machines (338) – is then to explore the schizophrenic margins in order to recapture productive desire as opposed to desire as lack and as representation.[123] In their formulation of desire, Deleuze and Guattari come the closest to a notion of plenitude (fulfilment): although it doesn't seem to produce its own satisfaction, this desire that is not lacking and not at loss, is indeed productive of itself and never ceases.

Although post-Lacanian explorations of desire focus and rely on the extreme and revolutionary aspects of desire, they nonetheless attempt to 'domesticate' it – that is, to extract desire from Lacan's system of extreme loss and impossible redemption, and to exploit desire as a constructive force for the self. Desire traces syntaxes, ones that are unconventional and defying paternal law and language. Desire, the opposite of sanctioned meaning, constructs meanings.

In both Lacanian and post-Lacanian thought, the transcendental aspect of desire is often in sight, but nowhere is the notion of metaphysical desire articulated quite so clearly as in René Girard's formulation of 'mimetic desire.' The 'human face of God,' the role of the Word made flesh is here assumed by the mediator – who satisfies (and thus annihilates) the need for divinity. Indeed, in Girard's formulation, it is desire that creates god, and not the contrary – as the mediator becomes progressively divine at the expense of the object.

In Girard's *Desire Deceit and the Novel*,[124] Don Quixote, who bestows upon Amadis the choice of his objects of desire, is the prime example of the notion of 'triangular desire,' which guides Girard's excursus on the modern novel – from Cervantes to Flaubert, to Stendhal, to Proust, to Dostoevsky, etc. The straight, 'spontaneous' line that connects the subject and object of desire is complicated by the presence above the line of the mediator, who 'radiates' toward both the subject and the object. The triangle, a figure that can be altered in many ways but still retains its identity, becomes therefore a 'systematic metaphor,' a heuristic metaphor indeed, for a model that lies well beyond the novel and the intricacies of human relations and ventures toward the limits of transcendence. Depending on the distance between the subject and the mediator, mediation can be external (the spheres of subject and mediator not entering into contact) or internal (the two spheres penetrating each other, 9).[125] The mediator has a twofold role: on the one hand it imparts prestige on the object of desire (17); on the other it necessarily acts as an obstacle to it. In the external type of mediation this creates a link of worship between subject and mediator; in an internal one, one of hatred.[126] In both types of mediation, however, the object is soon transfigured into an illusion generated by the hero's imagination ('the mother') and the mediator ('the father,' 23). Its role becomes less and less important, and the desire for the object (which is the desire of the mediator) transforms itself into the desire for the mediator.

Girard maintains that the persistence of the model of triangular desire throughout literature shows that each case is the individualization of the 'metaphysical meaning of desire' (55) – the desire that informs an infinite variety of desires and that is a novelistic rephrasing of the Christian desire for God.[127] Mediation, by installing transcendence into desire, is a way of bypassing the problem of divinity.[128] Novelistic desire, rooted in transcendence, modifies the space of desire: it turns it from 'Euclidean' into 'Einsteinian,' showing that the straight line is after all a circle.[129]

Metaphysical desire has powers of abstraction: the object progressively loses value at the point of vanishing, while the mediator progressively expands and eventually turns into the target of desire.[130] Thus, 'as the role of the metaphysical grows greater in desire, that of the physical diminishes in importance. As the mediator draws nearer, passion becomes more intense, and the object is emptied of its concrete value' (85). Just as with any god, however, the mediator runs the risk of falling from the pedestal at the very moment that it is closest to the object of desire (89). Other features of metaphysical desire are to be contagious and to redouble symmetrically when it is shared, creating two specular opposite triangles enchained by a double mediation (99), which in turn is a generator of desire. In it and through it, desire circulates and regenerates itself. This overproduction, the overflow of desire, however, has its shortcomings. The very vitality of desire needs to be curbed and controlled in the novel. The novelist is someone who, like some of his or her heroes, has been 'cured of metaphysical desire' (233): the opposite of the philosopher, and a modern god.[131] Triangular desire – an omnivorous and self-reproducing model – overflows from novel to novel, emerging as a universal structure, a kind of transcendental hypertext that writers embody in different ways.[132]

Conclusion

In our overview of contemporary reflection on syntax and desire, many aspects shine through that suggest a reading of the two terms as forces that mend the ragged edges of the bleeding wound that is the modern self. Syntax is often depicted as a menacing, totalitarian, and imposed order, yet many aspects of it deny this kind of reading. Considering syntax under the aspect of temporality, for example, makes it less threatening. Construction takes place in time, performing while unfolding.[133] Although the routes that it follows are restrictive and mandatory, a route is also new each time it is travelled – each order is unique, and each constructed meaning is singular: it is the one that appears in the tracing and disappears into silence following its own traces. Moreover, order is not necessarily the synonym of repression or the opposite of chaotic vitality. Syntax may also appear as an order that is not so much imposed upon linguistic dispersion as it is created out of fragmentation itself, akin to that 'order out of chaos' that contemporary theories of self-organization investigate in science and nature.[134]

More than an affirmative reading of the inherent aspects of syntax, the discourse of desire provides syntax with supreme flexibility and positive potential. Variously framed, desire always seems to overflow its boundaries and to branch toward an unreachable before and beyond. In this sense, it is truly disconnective, irreducible, unrepresentable, literally 'absolute.' Entrapped but at the same time made visible by a despotic signifier, desire is the result of the very resistance of language. Although exceeding language, desire *is* language: in its connective, syntagmatic, metonymic, performative, discursive, novelistic aspects, it is the trace of an articulated but unfathomable language, and of submerged languages.

Anything but disorderly, desire indeed emerges as a syntax: whether repressive or revolutionary, it depends upon the status of the traditional subject, which is vanishing while growing more and more fluid, more quixotic, and increasingly detached from predicate and object. Lack and loss figure prominently in contemporary discussions of desire, whereas fulfilment is more elusive. When it appears on the stage of desire, fulfilment is connected either to a challenge to the order of the signifier – as in the momentarily and 'useless' suspension of jouissance and the schizophrenic notion of production – or to a projection into the order of the signified – as in the novelistic-metaphysical cure. Postulating desire as fulfilment might therefore entail a reinstatement and reconceptualization of meaning into articulated language – not the universal/ontological presupposition but as the subtending (punctual yet extensive) force of each act of desire – a meaning that is 'now' at every moment, but that is also invented while desiring. This may be the true revolution of the syntax of desire.

Notes

Introduction

1 For the complex polysemic interplay surrounding 'that which was already in the beginning' – involving the Hebrew *dabar*, the Greek λόγος and ῥῆμα, and the Latin *sermo* and *verbum* – see S. Vecchio, *Le parole come segni: Introduzione alla linguistica agostiniana* (Palermo: Novecento, 1994), 26–50.

2 'Sicut enim aliquis errans in via eget alicuius regimine ut ad viam redeat et per viam certus eat, sic dictiones pleraeque in constructione positae, per aliquam incertitudinem quam habent circam suam significationem, egent aliarum coniunctione dictionum a quibus regantur, id est ab illa incertitudine quam habent removeantur et certum quid significare monstrentur.' (Just as someone who gets lost on a journey needs the guidance of someone else in order to return to the right road and proceed with certainty, in the same way many words placed in syntactic structure, because of some inherent uncertainty about their meaning, require the addition of other words to govern them, i.e., to free them from the uncertainty that they bear and show that they mean something specific.)

See C.H. Kneepkens, 'Magister Guido's View on Government: On Twelfth-Century Linguistic Thought,' *Vivarium* 16 (1978): 108–41; and M.A. Covington, *Syntactic Theory in the High Middle Ages: Modistic Models of Sentence Structure* (Cambridge: Cambridge University Press, 1984), 15. I adopt here Covington's translation.

3 See J. Freccero, 'The Significance of Terza Rima,' in *Dante: The Poetics of Conversion*, ed. R. Jacoff (Cambridge, MA: Harvard University Press, 1986), 258–71.

4 Refrain in *Analecta hymnica medii aevi* quoted by E.R. Curtius, *European Literature and the Latin Middle Ages* (New York: Harper & Row, 1963), 42.

5 See R.H. Robins, *Ancient and Medieval Grammatical Theory in Europe* (London:

Bell, 1951), 2. Here Robins is referring to the initial remarks of J.R. Firth's
'The Semantics of Linguistic Science,' *Lingua* 1 (1949): 393–404.

6 For an overview on the medieval thought on language and grammar, see
Robins, *Ancient and Medieval Grammatical Theory* and his *A Short History of Linguistics*, 3rd ed. (London: Longman, 1990); and A. Maierù, 'Medieval Lin-
guistics,' in *History of Linguistics*, vol. 2, *Classical and Medieval Linguistics*, ed.
G. Lepschy (London: Longman, 1994), 134–315. For interpretations of the
role of grammar in medieval culture, see Curtius, *European Literature and the
Latin Middle Ages*; R.H. Bloch, *Etymologies and Genealogies: A Literary Anthropol-
ogy of the French Middle Ages* (Chicago: University of Chicago Press, 1983); J.M.
Gellrich, *The Idea of the Book in the Middle Ages: Language Theory, Mythology and
Fiction* (Ithaca: Cornell University Press, 1985); J. Ziolkowsky, *Alain of Lille's
Grammar of Sex: The Meaning of Grammar to a Twelfth-Century Intellectual* (Cam-
bridge, MA: Medieval Academy of America, 1985); and B. Cerquiglini, *La
Parole médiévale: discours, syntaxe, texte* (Paris: Minuit, 1981).

7 *Institutio Oratoria* 1.4.2.

8 See ibid., 2.1.4. Both passages are quoted in Curtius, *European Literature and
the Latin Middle Ages*, 42.

9 This basic model is derived from Curtius, *European Literature and the Latin
Middle Ages*, 36–54. Local and temporal variations to the basic model are
important and impressive on both the grammatical texts and the set of
authors, and the state of our knowledge does not allow to full understand
them. For the grammatical texts, let one example suffice. Priscian's *Institutio
grammatica* was studied without interruption in Italy throughout the early
Middle Ages; it appeared in Ireland in the seventh century but crossed the
Alps only with the Carolingian grammarians. See V. Law, 'Linguistics in the
Earlier Middle Ages: The Insular and Carolingian Grammarians,' *Transactions of the Philological Society* 83 (1985): 171–93.

10 V. Law, *Grammar and Grammarians in the Early Middle Ages* (London: Longman, 1997), xi.

11 On this point, see Gellrich, *The Idea of the* Book, 100.

12 *Enarrationes in Psalmos* 138, 20. See also *Sermo* 299.6: 'nec quaerant grammatici quam sit latinum, sed christiani quam verum.'

13 See, for instance, the studies in V. Law, ed., *History of Linguistic Thought in the
Early Middle Ages* (Amsterdam: Benjamins, 1993), and the already quoted
Law, *Grammar and Grammarians*.

14 *Metalogicon* 3.2: 'Unde ex opinione plurium idem principaliter significant
denominative et ea a quibus denominantur, sed consignificatione diversa.
Aiebat Bernardus Carnotensis, quia *albedo* significat virginem incorruptam,
albet, eandem introeuntem thalamum, aut cubantem in toro, *album* vero,

eandem sed corruptam. Hoc quidem quoniam albedo ex assertione eius simpliciter, et sine omni participatione subiecti ipsam significat qualitatem, videlicet coloris speciem disgregativam visu. Albet autem eandem principaliter, et si participationem personae admittat. Si enim illud excutias, quod verbum hoc pro substantia significat, qualitas albedinis occurret, sed in accidentibus verbi personam reperies. Album vero eandem significat qualitatem, sed infusam commixtamque substantiae, et iam quodam modo magis corruptam.' (Whence many say that while derivative words and the words from which they stem, signify fundamentally the same thing, they differ in their simultaneous secondary meanings (*consignificatio*). Bernard of Chartres used to say that 'whiteness' represents an undefiled virgin; 'is white' the virgin entering the bedchamber, or lying on the couch; and 'white' the girl after she has lost her virginity. He used this illustration because, according to him, 'whiteness' denotes the quality itself simply, without any participation of a subject, that is [it denotes] merely a certain kind of color, which pierces one's vision. 'Is white' basically denotes the same quality, but admits of some participation by a person. For if one inquires as to what this verb denotes relative to a substance, the answer is the quality of whiteness, but in the accidents of the verb one will also discover a person. 'White' signifies the same quality [whiteness], but, as infused into and mixed with a substance, and in a way still more impure.) Translation of the *Metalogicon* is taken from *The Metalogicon of John of Salisbury*, trans. D.D. McGarry (Berkeley: University of California Press, 1971). This passage is quoted by R.W. Hunt, *The History of Grammar in the Middle Ages*, ed. G.L. Bursill-Hall (Amsterdam: Benjamins, 1980), 25; Gellrich, *The Idea of the Book in the Middle Ages*, 104; and Maierù, 'Medieval Linguistics,' 279. A concurrent contemporary example from the *Notes Dunelmenses*, quoted by Vineis and Maierù (178 and 279) is the less suggestive example of *lectio, legit, lector*, where *lectio* is a lesson outside of the house ('lectio significat lectionem quasi extra domum posita'), *legit* signifies the entering into the house ('legit significat eandem intrare domum'), and *lector* refers to a man who stays inside the house ('lector de eadem agit ut de manente et quiescente in domo').

15 Gellrich (*The Idea of the Book in The Middle Ages*, 104, 118) argues that for John and Bernard the signification 'sine participatione subiecti' represents the purity of pre-babelic language.

16 For the medieval tradition of the commentary on the *Song of Songs*, see D. Turner, *Eros and Allegory: Medieval Exegesis of the Song of Songs* (Kalamazoo, MI: Cistercian Publications, 1995).

17 On the theme of desire in the Middle Ages, see J. Leclerq, *The Love of Learning and the Desire for God* (New York: Fordham University Press, 1974), and

Monks and Love in Twelfth-Century France (Oxford: Oxford University Press, 1979); F.C. Gardiner, *The Pilgrimage of Desire: A Study of Theme and Genre in Medieval Literature* (Leiden: Brill, 1971); J. Kristeva, *Tales of Love*, trans. L.S. Roudiez (New York: Columbia University Press, 1987), 83–187; and Turner, *Eros and Allegory*. For an analysis of the notion of desire from antiquity to the twentieth century, see C. Dumoulié, *Le désir* (Paris: Colin, 1999).

For the theme of desire in connection with resurrection, see C. Bynum, *The Resurrection of the Body in Western Christianity, 200–1336* (New York: Columbia University Press, 1995). Bynum points out that desire becomes, within the Platonic tradition of the Middle Ages, the very proof for resurrection, since 'God would not leave soul forever with its desire either for immortality or for body unfulfilled' (236). Throughout her book Bynum highlights the notion of desire as a 'metaphysical cement binding body to soul' (253). On the proof of existence through desire, see also R. Bodei, *Ordo amoris: Conflitti terreni e felicità celeste* (Bologna: Mulino, 1991), 157n13.

18 When discussing disorder (*perturbatio*) in Book 4 of the *Tusculanae disputationes*, Cicero lists *desiderium* under the heading 'pleasures' (together with malice, rapture, ostentation, anger, rage, hate, greed): '*desiderium* libido eius, quod nondum adsit, videndi' (4.9) (*longing* is the lust of beholding someone who is not present). Interestingly, *desiderium* has linguistic implications: 'Distinguunt illud etiam, ut libido sit earum rerum, quae dicuntur de quodam aut quibusdam, quae κατηγορήματα dialectici appellant, ut habere divitias, capere honorem: indigentia rerum ipsarum est, ut honorum, ut pecuniae.' (They distinguish another sense of longing and make it almost mean lust of the predicates affirmed of a person or persons (the terms used by the logicians being κατηγορήματα), as for instance a man longs to have riches, to obtain distinctions; while greed is lust of the actual things, as for instance of distinctions, of money.) Translations are taken from *Tusculan Disputations*, trans. J.E. King (Cambridge, MA: Harvard University Press, 1927).

In '"La punta del disio": Storia di una metafora dantesca,' *Lectura Dantis* 7 (1990): 3–28, esp. 6, L. Pertile points out a concurrent term, especially in later romance derivation (as, for instance, in the Italian *desio*): *desedium*, which is in turn connected to the classical Latin *desidia*, which describes a negative *otium*, inertia, sloth, negligence, but also the pleasure deriving from it – a lazy pleasure, enjoyment without labour.

19 Bynum, *The Resurrection of the Body*, 339. For heavenly desire, see 278–317; for the mystic experience, 319–43.

20 Although unknown to the Middle Ages, the work of the poet-philosopher Lucretius provides a prime example of this contrast. The *De rerum natura* opens with a celebration of cosmic/reproductive desire ('Alma Venus'), and

later ventures into a condemnation of desire as an obstacle to the philosopher (bk. 4), who needs to learn to love without desire.

21 *In Evangelium Ioannis* 26.4: 'Porro si poetae dicere licuit: "Trahit sua quemque voluptas," non necessitas, sed voluptas; non obligatio, sed delectatio, quanto fortius nos dicere debemus trahi hominem ad Christum, qui delectatur veritate, delectatur beatitudine, delectatur iustitia, delectatur sempiterna vita, quod totum Christum est?' (Moreover, if it was allowed to a poet to say, 'His own pleasure draws each man,' not need, but pleasure, not obligation but delight, how much more forcefully ought we to say that a man is drawn to Christ who delights in truth, delights in happiness, delights in justice, delights in eternal life – and all this is Christ?) Translations are taken from *Tractates on the Gospel of John*, trans. J.W. Rettig (Washington, DC: Catholic University of America Press, 1988–93).

22 G. Vattimo, *Al di là del soggetto*, 4th ed. (Milan: Feltrinelli, 1991), 75.

23 On these points, see G.C. Lepschy, *La linguistica del Novecento* (Bologna: Il Mulino, 1992), 45–6.

24 See, for instance, R. Jakobson, *Main Trends in the Science and Language* (London: Allen & Unwin, 1973), 50: 'We may state that among all the information-carrying systems, the genetic code and the verbal code are the only ones based upon the use of discrete components which, by themselves, are devoid of inherent meaning but serve to constitute the minimal senseful units, i.e., entities endowed with their own, intrinsic meaning in a given code.' For the various perspectives in which this language has been interpreted – Peircean, Saussurean, Chomskian, information science, post-structuralist, etc. – see C. Hemmeche and J. Hoffmeyer, 'From Language to Nature: The Semiotic Metaphor in Biology,' *Semiotica* 84 (1991): 1–42; and L. Kay, *Who Wrote the Book of Life? A History of the Genetic Code* (Stanford: Stanford University Press, 2000).

1. Augustine: The Syntax of the Word

1 E. Gilson, *Christian Philosophy of Saint Augustine* (New York: Random House, 1960), 236.

2 Augustine's texts are quoted from *Patrologia Latina*, vols. 32–45.

3 Interesting chapters in the study of Augustine's theory of language and sign are R.A. Markus, 'Saint Augustine on Signs,' *Phronesis* 2 (1957): 60–83; M. Colish, 'St Augustine: The Expression of the Word,' in *The Mirror of Language* (New Haven: Yale University Press, 1958), 8–81; A. Schindler, *Wort und Analogie in Augustins Trinitätslehre* (Tubingen: Mohr, 1965); R. Simone, 'Semiologia Agostiniana,' *La cultura* 7 (1969): 88–117; M.W. Ferguson, 'Saint

Augustine's Region of Unlikeness: The Crossing of Exile and Language,'
Georgia Review 29 (1975): 842–64; D.W. Johnson, '*Verbum* in Early Augustine,'
Recherches augustiniennes 8 (1972): 3–53; L. Alici, *Il linguaggio come segno e come
testimonianza: Una rilettura di Agostino* (Rome: Studium, 1976); D. Daniels,
'The Argument of the *De Trinitate* and Augustine's Theory of Signs,' *Augustinian Studies* 7 (1977): 33–54; T. Todorov, 'The Birth of Western Semotics,'
in *Theories of the Symbol,* trans. C. Porter (Ithaca: Cornell University Press,
1982), 15–59; M. Baratin, 'Origines stoïciennes de la théorie augustinienne
du signe,' *Revue des études latines* 59 (1981): 260–8; M. Baratin and F. Desbordes, 'Sémiologie et métalinguistique chez saint Augustin,' *Langages* 65
(1982): 75–89; E. Vance; 'St Augustine: Language as Temporality,' in *Mervelous Signals: Poetics and Sign Theory in the Middle Ages* (Lincoln: University of
Nebraska Press, 1986), 34–50; C. Ando, 'Augustine on Language,' *Revue
des études augustiniennes* 40 (1994): 45–78; S. Vecchio, *Le parole come segni:
Introduzione alla linguistica agostiniana* (Palermo: Novecento, 1994), 26–50; G.
Antoni, *La prière chez saint Augustin: d'une philosophie du langage à la théologie
du verbe* (Paris: Vrin, 1997); and L. Ferretter, 'The Trace of the Trinity: Christ
and Difference in Saint Augustine's Theory of Language,' *Literature and Theology* 12 (1998): 256–67.

For a closer discussion of particular issues or works, see also B. Darrel Jack-
son, 'The Theory of Signs in St Augustine's *De doctrina christiana,*' *Revue des
études augustiniennes* 15 (1969): 9–49; M.D. Jordan, 'Words and Word: Incar-
nation and Signification in Augustine's *De doctrina christiana,*' *Augustinian
Studies* 11 (1980): 177–96; R. Williams, 'Language, Reality and Desire in
Augustine's *De doctrina,*' *Journal of Literature and Theology* 3 (1989): 138–58; P.
Pulsiano, 'Language Theory and Narrative Patterning in *De civitate Dei,*
Books XV–XVIII,' in *The City of God: A Collection of Critical Essays,* ed. D.F.
Donnelly (New York: Lang, 1995), 241–52; R.A. Markus, 'Signs, Communica-
tion and Communities in Augustine's *De doctrina christiana,*' and D. Dawson,
'Sign Theory, Allegorical Reading and the Motions of the Soul in *De doctrina
christiana,*' both in '*De doctrina christiana': A Classic of Western Culture,* ed.
D.W.H. Arnold and P. Bright (Notre Dame: University of Notre Dame Press,
1995), 97–108 and 123–41; C. Ando, 'Signs, Idols and the Incarnation in
Augustinian Metaphysics,' *Representations* 73 (2001): 24–53; and J.M. Norris,
'Augustine and Sign in *Tractatus in Iohannis Euangelium,*' in *Augustine Biblical
Exegete,* ed. F. Van Fleteren and J.C. Schnaubelt (New York: Lang, 2001), 215–
31.

Many of these works quote and discuss at length passages from the *De dialectica, De magistro, De doctrina christiana, De Trinitate,* and *De catechizandis rudibus,* which I also quote and discuss. For the sake of brevity, I won't recall

these essays every time, unless they are strictly related to my argument at that point.

4 See Simone, 'Semiologia,' 95, and Baratin, 'Origines,' 266.

5 Todorov, *Theories of the Symbol*, 15. Accordingly, Todorov builds his chapter on 'The Birth of Western Semiotics' in terms of pre-Augustinian tradition and Augustinian synthesis.

6 See Todorov, *Theories of the Symbol*, 56–9; and U. Eco, *Semiotics and the Philosophy of Language* (London: Macmillan, 1984), 33–4.

7 H.I. Marrou, *Saint Augustin et la fin de la culture antique*, 4th ed. (Paris: Boccard, 1958), 15.

8 For a summary of the scholarly positions on the grammarian vs. theologian debate, see Vecchio, *Le parole come segni*, 20–6. The term *theolinguistics* was coined by H. Arendt, quoted in Vecchio, 25. On the passage from the logical to the theological 'word,' see also J. Henningfeld, 'Verbum-Signum: La définition du language chez saint Augustin et Nicholas de Cues,' *Archives de philosophie* 54 (1991): 255–68.

9 Vecchio, *Le parole come segni*, 23: 'Agostino non fu un filosofo di formazione linguistica, né un teologo dalle frequentazioni ermeneutiche; fu propriamente un linguista, che fece germinare la propria ricerca in direzioni differenti da quelle a cui la linguistica dei secoli successivi ha finito coll'abituare il lettore occidentale. Fu, se vogliamo, un linguista "impuro," ed è come tale che sta anch'egli, con altri, all'origine della linguistica occidentale.'

10 Johnson, 'Verbum in Early Augustine,' 28. On the complexity of the early Christian notion of Λόγος, see Vecchio, *Le parole come segni*, 26–50.

11 As does his theory of language, Augustine's theory of love and desire pervades all his work and is substantiated by both scriptural and pastoral concerns. A very helpful survey of the main *loci* of Augustine's doctrine of *caritas*, as well as of its controversial reception, is D. Dideberg, 'Caritas: Prolégomènes à une étude de la théologie augustinienne de la charité,' in *Signum Pietatis: Festgabe für Cornelius Mayer*, ed. A. Zumkeller (Wurzburg: Augustinus-Verlag, 1989), 369–81.

Important chapters in the exploration of the themes of love and desire in Augustine are H. Arendt's dissertation 'Der Liebesbegriff bei Augustin' (1929), recently translated and published along with her revisions in *Love and Saint Augustine*, ed. J.V. Scott and J.C. Stark (Chicago: University of Chicago Press, 1996); A. Nygren, *Agape and Eros*, trans. S. Watson (London: SPCK, 1938); J. Burnaby, *Amor Dei: A Study of the Religion of St Augustine* (London: Hodder & Stoughton, 1938); R. Holte, *Béatitude et Sagesse: St Augustin et le problème de la fin de l'homme dans la philosophie ancienne* (Paris: Études augustiniennes, 1962), esp. 207–94; O. du Roy, 'L'experiénce de l'amour et l'intelligence de la foi trinitaire selon Saint Augustin,' *Recherches augustiniennes* 2 (1963): 415–55; D. Dideberg, *Saint Augustin et la première Épître de saint Jean: Une théologie de l'agapè* (Paris: Beauchesne, 1975); O. O'Donovan, *The Problem of Self Love in St Augustine* (New Haven: Yale University Press, 1980); I. Bochet, *Saint Augustin et le désir de Dieu* (Paris: Études augustiniennes, 1982); S. Nicolosi, 'La filosofia dell'amore in Sant'Agostino: Dalla comunicazione alla comunità,' *Orpheus* 4 (1983): 42–66; R. Canning, 'The Unity of Love for God and Neighbor,' *Augustiniana* 37 (1987): 38–121; J. van Bavel, 'The Double Face of Love in Augustine,' *Louvain Studies* 12 (1987): 116–30; R. Bodei, *Ordo amoris: Conflitti terreni e felicità celeste* (Bologna: Mulino, 1991); and J.M. Rist, 'Will, Love and Right Action,' in *Augustine: Ancient Thought Baptized* (Cambridge: Cambridge University Press, 1994), 148–202.

For connections between theory of love and theory of language, see Williams, 'Language, Reality and Desire in Augustine's *De doctrina*'; W. Babcock, '*Caritas* and Signification in *De doctrina christiana* 1–3,' in '*Doctrina christiana*': *A Classic of Western Culture*, ed. D.W.H. Arnold and P. Bright, 145–63; Antoni, *La prière chez saint Augustin.*

12 *De civitate Dei* 14.28: 'Fecerunt itaque civitates duas amores duo, terrenam scilicet amor sui usque ad contemptum Dei, caelestem vero amor Dei usque ad contemptum sui. Denique illa in se ipsa, haec in Domino gloriatur.' (Two cities, then, have been created by two loves: that is, the earthly by love of self extending even to contempt of God, and the heavenly by love of God extending to contempt of self. The one, therefore, glories in itself, the other in the Lord.) Translations of the *De civitate Dei* are taken from *The City of God*, trans. R.W. Dyson (Cambridge: Cambridge University Press, 1998).

13 Translations of the *De Trinitate* are taken from *The Trinity*, trans. S. McKenna (Washington DC: Catholic University of America Press, 1961). This translation has been recently revised and published as *On the Trinity: Books 8–15*, ed. G.B. Matthews (Cambridge: Cambridge University Press, 2002).

14 For a closer discussion of Augustine's vocabulary of love and desire, see Burnaby, *Amor Dei*, 92–100; and Bochet, *Saint Augustin et le désir de Dieu*, 36, 143, 148, 277.

15 At the beginning of his book, Bodei argues that Saint Paul's split between flesh and spirit is turned, with Augustine, into a struggle between two wills. See the chapter 'I nodi della volontà' in *Ordo amoris*, 53–90.

16 See Bodei, *Ordo amoris*, 112: 'L'amore "incolla" il passato (come memoria del bene, riminescenza di una beatitudine e di un ordine di missione che Dio ci ha consegnato sin dal nostro *initium* terreno) e il futuro (come compimento dell'attesa di immortalità, appagamento di un desiderio che abbiamo sempre oscuramente avvertito) al presente temporale, facendo tralucere in esso

in esso il riflesso di un'eterna presenza a se stessi, di una esperienza come *memoria sui*, ordinata ed orientata verso il fine.' See also 168.

17 Of the seven *Disciplinarum libri*, only the *De musica* is completed and definitely attributed to Augustine. In the *Retractationes* (1.5), Augustine claims to have finished only the book on music and the *De grammatica*, which he subsequently lost. As for the other five books on dialectics, rhetoric, geometry, arithmetic, and philosophy, the bishop says he drafted only the beginnings and lost them anyway. The authenticity of the *De dialectica* has often been questioned, although scholars today are inclined to attribute it to Augustine. For a discussion of the authenticity of *De dialectica*, see its critical edition: *De dialectica*, ed. J. Pinborg, trans. B.D. Jackson (Dordrecht: Synthese Historical Library 16, 1975). For the question of authenticity and for an examination of the significance of dialectics in Augustine's work, see J. Pepin, *Saint Augustin et la dialectique* (Villanova, PA: Villanova University Press, 1976). For a discussion of the semiotic system described in this early work, see also Baratin, 'Origines'; Rist, 'Words, Signs and Things,' in *Augustine: Ancient Thought Baptized*, 23–40; and Todorov, *Theories of the Symbol*, 37–9. On Augustine and the liberal arts tradition, see Marrou, *Saint Augustin et la fin de la culture antique*.

As for the completed but lost *De grammatica*, tradition handed down two grammatical texts attributed to Augustine: the *Regulae Aurelii Augustini* and the *Ars Augustini pro fratrum mediocritate breviata*. Marrou (*Saint Augustin et la fin de la culture antique*, 571–6) considered them two independent epitomes of the lost original work. V. Law, in 'St Augustine's *De grammatica*: Lost or Found?' *Recherches augustiniennes* 19 (1984): 155–83, convincingly argues that the fundamental differences between the *Regulae* and the *Ars breviata* hinder a definite derivation from a common source. Law also argues that a better claim to authenticity can be granted to the *Ars breviata*, a text that shows a strong imprint of Donatus' *Ars minor*, but also some technical similarities to Augustine's grammatical theory as it emerges from other works, as well as thematic similarities to Augustine's writings. For Augustine 'as grammarian,' see G. Bellissima, 'Sant'Agostino grammatico,' *Augustinus Magister* 1 (1954): 35–42.

18 'Ego vero didici admonitione verborum tuorum, nihil aliud verbis quam admoneri hominem ut discat.' Translations of the *De magistro* are taken from *The Teacher*, trans. P. King (Indianapolis: Hackett, 1955).

19 *De magistro* 10.34: 'In quo tamen signo cum duo sint, sonus et significatio, sonum certe non per signum percepimur sed eo ipso aure pulsata, significationem autem re, quae significatur, aspecta.' (Now there are two elements in the sign: the sound and the signification. We don't perceive the sound by the

sign, but when it strikes the ear. We perceive the signification, however, by
seeing the thing signified.)

20 Johnson ('*Verbum* in Early Augustine,' 33–4) notices in this passage the
absence of the connection between signs/words, and Christ/Word of God –
an absence so striking that it has often led scholars to misquote the passage.
Johnson claims that Augustine is avoiding the use of *Verbum* here and in
other early works, precisely because the doctrine of 'words,' from which the
notion of 'the Word' was to spring, was still an unsafe space of reflection. On
this point, see also Vecchio, *Le parole come segni*, 44–6. For the interior
teacher, see also J. Pepin, 'Le problème de la communication des consciences chez Plotin et saint Augustin,' *Revue de métaphysique et morale* 55
(1950): 128–48. As we shall see later in this chapter, in *Confessions* 11.7.10,
the interior teacher is explicitly related to Christ.

21 It is well known that the Augustinian doctrine of illumination by the inner
teacher is a Christian adaptation of the platonic theory of recollection. As
Gilson points out (*Christian Philosophy*, 75), the translation of the platonic
doctrine contains a very important shift in terms of time, since the Augustinian 'memory of the present' substitutes the platonic 'recollection of the
past.'

22 The question of the polysemy of the sign with respect to the context in which
it is uttered represents perhaps one of the most interesting and lively parts of
the dialogue. By rejecting the notion of definition, since it bestows the
'power of truth' to man as opposed to the inner teacher, Augustine leaves
ample space for ambiguity and interpretation in the sign: an opening that
can be viewed as the starting point of the *De doctrina christiana*. See *De magistro* 13.43: 'Sed his accedit aliud genus, sane late patens, et semen innumerabilium dissensionum atque certaminum: cum ille, qui loquitur eadem
quidem significat, quae cogitat, sed plerumque tantum sibi et aliis quibusdam; ei vero, cui loquitur, et item aliis nonnullis non idem significat. Dixerit
enim aliquis audientibus nobis, ab aliquibus belluis hominem virtute super-
ari; nos ilico ferre non possumus et hanc tam falsam pestiferamque sententiam magna intentione refellimus: cum ille fortasse virtutem vires corporis
vocet et hoc nomine id quod cogitavit enuntiet, nec mentiatur, nec erret in
rebus, nec aliud aliquid volvens in animo mandata memoriae verba contexit,
nec linguae lapsu aliud quam volebat sonat, sed tantummodo rem quam
cogitat, alio quam nos nomine appellat: de qua illi statim assentiremur, si
eius cogitatione possemus inspicere, quam verbis iam prolatis explicataquae
sententia sua, nondum nobis pandere valuit. Huic errori definitiones mederi
posse dicuntur, ut in hac quaestione, si definiret quid sit virtus; eluceret

aiunt non de re, sed de verbo esse controversiam: quod ut concedam, quotusquisque bonus definitor inveniri potest? Et tamen adversus disciplinam definiendi multa disputata sunt; quae neque hoc loco tractare opportunum est, nec usquequaque a me probantur.' (There is another class in addition to these [the other possibilities of ambiguity in the sign], one that is widespread and the source of countless disagreements and quarrels: when the speaker does signify the selfsame thing he's thinking about, but for the most part only to himself and to certain others, whereas he doesn't signify the same thing to the person to whom he's speaking and again to several other persons. For example, let someone say in our hearing, that man is surpassed in virtue by some brute animals. We immediately can't bear this, and with great vehemence we refute it as false and harmful. Yet perhaps he's calling physical strength 'virtue' and enunciating what he was thinking about with this name. He would be neither lying nor in error about things. Nor is he reeling off words committed to memory while turning something else over in his mind. Nor does he utter by a slip of tongue something other than he wanted. Instead, he's merely calling the thing he's thinking about by another name than we do; we should at once agree with him about it if we could look into his thinking, which he wasn't yet able to disclose to us by the words he had already uttered in expressing his views. They say that definitions can remedy this kind of error, so that in this case if the speaker were to define what 'virtue' is, he would make it plain, they say, that the dispute is over the word and not the thing. Now I might grant this to be so. Yet how many people can be found who are good at definitions? In any event, there are many arguments against the system of definitions, but it isn't opportune to discuss them here; nor do I altogether approve them.)

23 The first and second book, and part of the third, were written in 396–7, while the last part of the third book, and the fourth book, a handbook of Christian rhetoric, were added later in 426. For an overview of the possible reasons for the interruption, see C. Kannengiesser, 'The Interrupted *De doctrina christiana*,' in *'De doctrina christiana': A Classic of Western Culture*, 3–13.

24 Translations from the *De doctrina christiana* are taken from *On Christian Teaching*, trans. R.H. Green (Oxford: Oxford University Press, 1997).

25 *De doctrina christiana* 1.2.2: 'Omnis doctrina vel rerum est vel signorum, sed res per signa discuntur. Proprie autem nunc res appellavi, quae non ad significandum aliquid adhibentur sicuti est lignum, lapis, pecus atque huiusmodi cetera; sed non illud lignum quod in aquas amaras Moysen misisse legimus, ut amaritudine carerent, neque ille lapis, quem Iacob sibi ad caput posuerat, neque illud pecus quod pro filio immolavit Abraham. Hae nam-

que ita res sunt, ut aliarum etiam signa sint rerum. Sunt autem alia signa, quorum omnis usus in significando est, sicuti sunt verba. Nemo enim utitur verbis nisi aliquid significandi gratia. Ex quo intellegitur, quid appellem signa: res eas videlicet, quae ad significandum aliquid adhibentur. Quamobrem, omne signum etiam res aliqua est; quod enim nulla res est, omnino nihil est. Non autem omnis res etiam signum est. Et ideo in hac divisione rerum atque signorum, cum de rebus loquemur, ita loquemur etiamsi earum aliquae adhiberi ad significandum possint, non impediant partitionem, qua prius de rebus, postea de signis disseremus, memoriterque teneamus id nunc in rebus considerandum est quod sunt non quod aliud etiam praeter se ipsas significant.' (All teaching is teaching of either things or signs, but things are learnt through signs. What I now call things in the strict sense are things such as logs, stones, sheep and so on, which are not employed to signify something; but I do not include the log which we read that Moses threw into the bitter waters to make them lose their bitter taste, or the stone which Jacob placed under his head, or the sheep which Abraham sacrificed in place of his son. These are things, but they are at the same time signs of other things. There are other signs whose whole function consists in signifying. Words, for example: nobody uses words except in order to signify something. From this it might be understood what I mean by signs: those things which are employed to signify something. So every sign is also a thing, since what is not a thing does not exist. But it is not true that every thing is also a sign. Therefore in my distinction of things and signs, when I speak of things, I shall speak of them is such a way that even if some of them can be employed to signify they do not impair the arrangement by which I will treat things first and signs later. And we must be careful to remember that what is under consideration at this stage is the fact that things exist, not that they signify something else besides themselves.)

26 Translations from the *De Genesi contra Manicheos* are taken from *On Genesis*, trans. R.J. Teske (Washington, DC: Catholic University of America Press, 1991), 47–141. See also *De Genesi ad litteram* 8.27 (49–50), where Augustine discusses the modality of the communication between God and Adam and acknowledges both an angelic and a mediated way. The mediated-semiotic way, however, seems distinctive of the moment after the sin: 'si modum quaerimus quomodo ista locutus sit Deus, modus quidem ipse a nobis proprie comprehendi non potest: certissime tamen tenere debemus, Deum aut per suam substantiam loqui, aut per sibi subditam creaturam; sed per substantiam suam non loqui nisi ad creandas omnes naturas, ad spiritales vero atque intellectuales non solum creandas, sed etiam illuminandas, cum iam

possunt capere locutionem eius, qualis est in Verbo eius quod *in principio erat apud Deum, et Deus erat Verbum, per quod facta sunt omnia.* Illis autem qui eam capere non possunt, cum loquitur Deus, nonnisi per creaturam loquitur, aut tantummodo spiritalem, sive in somnis, sive in ecstasi in similitudine rerum corporalium; aut etiam per ipsam corporalem, dum sensibus corporis vel aliqua species apparet, vel insonant voces. Si ergo Adam talis erat, ut posset capere illam locutionem Dei, quam mentibus angelicis per suam praebet substantiam; non dubitandum est quod eius mentem per tempus moverit miro et ineffabili modo, non motus ipse per tempus, eique utile ac salubre praeceptum veritatis impresserit, et quae transgressori poena deberetur, ea ipsa ineffabiliter veritate monstraverit: sicut audiuntur vel videntur omnia bona praecepta in ipsa incommutabili Sapientia, quae in animas sanctas se transfert ex aliquo tempore, cum ipsius nullus sit motus in tempore. Si autem ad eum modum Adam iustus erat, ut ei adhuc opus esset alterius creaturae sanctioris et sapientioris auctoritas, per quam cognosceret Dei voluntatem atque iussionem, sicut nobis Prophetae, sicut ipsis Angeli; cur ambigamus per aliquam huiusmodi creaturam ei esse locutum Deum, talibus vocum signis quae intellegere posset? Illud enim quod postea scriptum est, cum peccassent eos audisse vocem Domini Dei ambulantis in paradiso, quia non per ipsam Dei substantiam, sed per subditam ei creaturam factum est, nullo modo dubitat qui fidem catholicam sapit.' (if we ask how God spoke them [the words in Genesis to Adam], we cannot understand precisely how he did so. Nevertheless, we should hold it for certain that God speaks either through His substance or through a creature subject to Him, but that he does not speak through His own substance except in two cases: first, in creating the whole universe, and, second, in not only creating but also illuminating spiritual and intellectual creatures when they are able to grasp His utterance, which is His Word, *who was in the beginning with God, and the Word was God, and through the Word all things were made.* But when God speaks to those who are unable to grasp His utterance, He speaks only through a creature. Now he may employ a spiritual creature exclusively, in a dream or ecstasy, using the likeness of material things; or he may speak through a corporeal creature, as the bodily senses are affected by a form that appears or the sound of a voice that is heard. If Adam, therefore, was in such a state that he was able to grasp the utterance of God which He makes present to the minds of angels through His own substance, there should be no doubt that God moved Adam's mind in a mysterious and unaccountable manner, without Himself being moved in time, impressing upon Adam's mind a useful and salutary precept of Truth, and in the same Truth revealing the punish-

ment awaiting the transgressor. It is thus that all good precepts are heard or
seen in unchangeable Wisdom, which at times enters holy souls, although
Wisdom itself does not move in time. But if the justice of Adam was such that
he also needed the authority of another creature holier and wiser through
which he would come to know God's will and command, as we have needed
the prophets and they needed the angels, why do we doubt that God spoke
to him through some such creature in a language which he could understand? When Scripture says that when our first parents had sinned they
heard the voice of the Lord as He walked in Paradise, no one who holds the
catholic faith has any doubt that this was not done by means of that very substance of God himself but by means of a creature subject to Him.)

   Translations from the *De Genesi ad litteram* are taken from *The Literal Meaning of Genesis*, trans. J.H. Taylor (New York: Newman, 1982). On the Augustinian position about language in Eden and after the Fall and with respect to
Babel, see U. Duchrow, '*Signum* und *Superbia* beim jungen Augustin (386–
390),' *Recherches augustiniennes* 7 (1961): 369–72; J. Fyler, 'St Augustine, Genesis and the Origin of language,' in *St Augustine and His Influence in the Middle
Ages*, ed. E. King and J. Schaefer (Sewanee, TN: Press of the University of the
South, 1988), 67–98; Ando, 'Augustine on Language,' 64–8; Antoni, *La prière
chez saint Augustin*, 39–44; and Vecchio, *Le parole come segni*, 73–82.

27 *De doctrina christiana* 2.4.5: 'ista signa igitur [voces et litterae] non potuerunt
communia esse omnibus gentibus peccato quodam dissensionis humanae,
cum ad se quisque principatum rapit. Cuius superbiae signum est erecta illa
turris in caelum, ubi homines impii non solum animos, sed etiam voces dis-
sonas habere meruerunt.' (These signs could not be shared by all nations,
because of the sin of human disunity by which each one sought hegemony
for itself. This pride is signified by the famous tower raised towards heaven at
the time when wicked men justly received incompatible languages to match
their incompatible minds.)

   A more extensive account on Babel is found in *De civitate Dei* 16.4–6.

28 *De doctrina christiana* 3.7.11: 'Et si quando aliqui eorum illa tamquam signa
interpretari conabantur, ad creaturam colendam venerandamque refere-
bant. Quid enim mihi prodest simulacrum, verbi gratia, Neptuni non ipsum
habendum deum, sed eo significari universum mare vel etiam omnes aquas
ceteras quae fontibus proruunt?' (If any of them ever tried to interpret these
statues as signs, they related them to the worship and veneration of the created order. For what good is it, I ask, that (for example) an image of Neptune is not thought of as a god in itself, but considered to represent the
whole sea or all the other kinds of watercourse that flow from springs?)

29 *De doctrina christiana* 3.5.9: 'Ea demum est miserabilis animae servitus, signa pro rebus accipere, et supra creaturam corpoream oculum mentis ad hauriendum aeternum lumen levare non posse.' (It is, then, a miserable kind of spiritual slavery to interpret signs as things, and to be incapable of raising the mind's eye above the physical creation so as to absorb the eternal light.)

30 For a discussion of the Augustinian view of the (pagan, Jewish, and Christian) relationship between sign and referent in terms of idolatry and of the corrective role of Christ, see C. Ando, 'Signs, Idols and the Incarnation in Augustinian Metaphysics.'

31 *De doctrina christiana* 3.9.13: 'Hoc vero tempore posteaquam resurrectione Domini nostri manifestissimum indicium nostrae libertatis inluxit, nec eorum quidem signorum, quae iam intellegimus, operatione gravi onerati sumus, sed quaedam pauca pro multis eademque factu facillima et intellectu augustissima et observatione castissima ipse Dominus et apostolica tradidit disciplina, sicuti est baptismi sacramentum et celebratio corporis et sanguinis Domini. Quae unusquisque cum percepit, quo referantur imbutus agnoscit, ut ea non carnali servitute, sed spiritali potius libertate veneretur. Ut autem litteram sequi et signa pro rebus quae his significantur accipere, servili infirmitas est; ita inutiliter signa interpretari male vagantis erroris est.' (But at the present time, when a brilliant demonstration of our freedom has been revealed in the resurrection of our Lord, we are not oppressed by the tiresome necessity of attending to signs, even the signs which we now understand. Instead of many signs there are now but a few signs, simple when performed, inspiring when understood, and holy when practised, given to us by the teachings of our Lord himself and the apostles, such as the sacrament of baptism and the celebration of the Lord's body and blood. When an individual understands these, he recognizes with an inner knowledge what they relate to, and consequently venerates them not because of any carnal slavery, but because of his spiritual freedom. And just as it is a mark of servile weakness to follow the letter and accept the signs rather than the things signified by them, so it is a mark of badly disguised error to interpret signs in an useless way.)

32 Williams, 'Language, Reality and Desire in Augustine's *De doctrina*,' 142–3.

33 I prefer here the more literal translation of *propria* as 'proper' and *translata* as 'transposed' to the translator's 'literal' and 'metaphorical.'

34 Todorov, *Theories of the Symbol*, 51. According to Todorov, then, 'with Augustine, the very definition of "transposed" is new: the term no longer refers to a word that changes meaning, but to a word that designates an object which in turn carries a meaning' (52). This is part of Augustine's effort to 'broaden

the category of transposed meaning so that it can include Christian allegory.' Todorov also remarks that 'the opposition is better formulated in *On the Trinity*, where Augustine conceives of two types of allegory (that is, transposed signs), the one based on words, the other on things ... Another attempt at subdividing the category of transposed sign leads, later on, to the well known doctrine of the four meanings of Scripture' (ibid.).

35 For the distinction between use and enjoyment, see O. O'Donovan, '*Usus* and *Fruitio* in Augustine, *De doctrina christiana* 1,' *Journal of Theological Studies*, n.s. 33 (1982): 361–97; and W. O'Connor, 'The Uti/Frui Distinction in Augustine's Ethics,' *Augustinian Studies* 14 (1983): 45–62. For two different ways of connecting the uti–frui distinction with Augustine's theory of language, see Williams, 'Language, Reality and Desire in Augustine's *De doctrina*,' and Todorov, *Theories of the Symbol*, 40–1.

36 *De diversis quaestionibus octoginta tribus*, 30: 'Frui ergo dicimur ea re de qua capimus voluptatem; utimur ea quam referimus ad id unde capienda voluptas est. Omnis itaque humana perversio est, quod etiam vitium vocatur, fruendis uti velle atque utendis frui; et rursus omnis ordinatio, quae virtus etiam nominatur, fruendis frui et utendis uti.' (Therefore we are said to enjoy that from which we derive pleasure. We use that which we order toward something else from which we expect to derive pleasure. Consequently every human perversion [also called vice] consists in the desire to use what ought to be enjoyed and to enjoy what ought to be used. In turn, good order [also called virtue] consists in the desire to enjoy what ought to be enjoyed and to use what ought to be used). Translations from the *De diversis quaestionibus* are taken from *Eighty-three Different Questions*, trans. D.L. Mosher (Washington, DC: Catholic University of America Press, 1982).

37 *De doctrina christiana* 1.27.28: 'Ille autem iuste et sancte vivit, qui rerum integer aestimator est. Ipse est autem qui ordinatam habet dilectionem.' (The person who lives a just and holy life is one who is a sound judge of these things. He is also a person who has ordered his love.)

38 *De doctrina christiana* 1.31–2: 'Quapropter adhuc ambiguum esse videtur, cum dicimus ea re nos perfrui quam diligimus propter seipsam, et ea re nobis fruendum esse tantum, qua efficimur beati, ceteris vero utendum. Diligit enim nos Deus, et multum nobis dilectionem eius erga nos divina Scriptura commendat. Quomodo ergo diligit? Ut nobis utatur an ut fruatur? Sed si fruitur, eget bono nostro, quod nemo sanus dixerit. Omne enim nostrum bonum vel ipse vel ab ipso est. Cui autem obscurum vel dubium est, non egere lucem rerum harum nitore quas ipsa illustraverit? Dicit etiam apertissime Propheta: *Dixi Domino: Dominus meus es tu, quoniam bonorum*

meorum non eges. Non ergo fruitur nobis, sed utitur. Nam si neque fruitur neque utitur, non invenio quemadmodum diligat. Sed neque sic utitur ut nos; nam nos res quibus utimur ad id referimus ut Dei bonitate perfruamur; Deus vero ad suam bonitatem usum nostrum refert.' (There is still an element of uncertainty here. I am saying that we enjoy a thing which we love for itself, and that we should enjoy only a thing by which we are made happy, but use everything else. God loves us (and the divine scripture often commends his love towards us), but in what way does he love us – so as to use or to enjoy us? If he enjoys us, he stands in need of our goodness, which only a madman could assert; for all our goodness either comes from him or actually consists of him. It is not quite clear and beyond all doubt that light does not stand in need of the brightness of the things which it illuminates? The prophet says very clearly, 'I said to the Lord, 'you are my Lord, since you don't stand in need of my goodness.' So God does not enjoy is, but uses us. [If he neither enjoys us nor uses us, then I fail to see how he can love us at all.] But he doesn't use us in the way that we use things; for we relate to things which we use to the aim of enjoying God's goodness, whereas God relates his use of us to his own goodness.)

39 See on this Todorov, *Theories of the Symbol*, 41: 'The articulation between signs and things is further developed through the articulation between two basic processes, use and enjoyment. This second distinction is located in fact within the category of things; but things used are transitive, like signs, and things enjoyed are intransitive.'

40 J.L. Austin, *How to Do Things with Words* (Cambridge, MA: Harvard University Press, 1975), 6. For a reformulation of the problem of the performative and the ensuing discussion, see J. Derrida, 'Signature, Event, Context,' in *Margins of Philosophy*, trans. A. Bass (Chicago: University of Chicago Press, 1982), 307–30; and *Limited Inc.* (Evanston, IL: Northwestern University Press, 1988).

41 For a detailed discussion of Creation, see Gilson, *Christian Philosophy*, 189–209.

42 E. Vance, 'Augustine's Confessions and the Grammar of Selfhood,' *Genre* 6 (1973): 1–28, 8. See also 7: 'The cosmos exists, Augustine says, through and in the spoken word of God. Augustine's cosmology is modelled, in other words on the performance of oral discourse, on *enunciation*. God, to use modern terms, is competence, the creation is his performance ... Since enunciation is corporeal, God articulated the universe upon the inchoate matter of the abyss, upon the "infirmity" that preceded his word. The creation is a process of differentiation, just as our language occurs as phonetic differentiation within disorganized sound. Spatially, the word-as-message is a

disc, a circle at whose center is Jerusalem, where the word (*Verbum*) was made flesh.'

43 Translations are taken from *Confessions*, trans. H. Chadwick (Oxford: Oxford University Press, 1991).

44 The passage is pointed out by Johnson ('*Verbum* in Early Augustine,' 42), whose translation I adopt here.

45 The evolution of Augustine's thought on the problematic connections Word/Creation, Word/Christ, and word/language is quite tormented. As a general statement one can say that Augustine's thought evolves from being very troubled by the semiotic 'pollution' to solving it, by narrowing it down to one main problem: temporality. As a specimen I will examine the evolution of this problem around the passage 'fiat lux' within the three commentaries on Genesis: the early *De Genesi contra Manichaeos* (389), the first, unfinished *De Genesi ad literam liber imperfectus* (393), and the later *De Genesi ad literam libri XII* (404). In the first commentary Augustine doesn't bring up any linguistic issue in order to explain the line; he rather dwells on the problem of the incorporeal vs. corporeal nature of that light (1.3.7). The linguistic analogy is raised in the explanation of 'fiat lux' within the incomplete commentary on Genesis. The troubles inherent in a linguistic interpretation are evident throughout the passage, to begin with the statement that God uttered the sentence 'ineffably' (i.e., in a way that cannot be said); to the question whether the Word was said to the Son, or the Word was the Son himself, precisely by being spoken; to the blame of impiety on the thought that the word of God could be compared to the word of man, later figured as a 'perturbation' of the spiritual mind: 'Deum dixisse: *Fiat lux*, non voce de pulmonibus edita, nec lingua et dentibus, accipere debemus. Carnalium sunt istae cogitationes: secundum autem carnem sapere, mors est. Sed ineffabiliter dictum est: *Fiat lux*. Utrum autem hoc quod dictum est, Filio unigenito dictum est, an idipsum quod dictum est, Filius unigenitus est, quod dictum Dei Verbum dicitur, per quod facta sunt omnia, quaeri potest: dum tamen illa absit impietas, ut Verbum Dei unigenitum Filium quasi vocem prolatam sicut a nobis fit, esse credamus. Verbum autem Dei, per quod facta sunt omnia, nec coepit esse, nec desinet; sed sine inchoatione natum, Patri coeternum est. Quare hoc quod dictum est: *Fiat lux*, et si coepit et destitit dici, magis Filio dictum est hoc verbum, quam ipsum est Filius. Et tamen etiam hoc ineffabiliter; nec carnalis imago subrepat in animum et intellectum pium spiritalem conturbet' (*De Genesi ad literam imperfectus liber* 5.19). (We ought to understand that God did not say, 'Let there be light' by a sound brought forth from the lungs or by the tongue and teeth. Such

thoughts are those of carnal persons, and to be wise in accord with the flesh is death. 'Let there be light' was spoken ineffably. One can ask whether what was spoken is the only-begotten son. For what was spoken is called the Word of God, by whom all things were made. Only let us banish the impiety of believing that the Word of God, by whom all things were made does not begin to be nor cease to be, but it is born without beginning and is coeternal with the Father. Hence, if 'let there be light' begins and ceases to be said, this Word is rather spoken to than Word that is itself the Son. And yet this is said ineffably. Let no carnal image creep in the mind and disturb the pious understanding.) Translations are taken from *On Genesis*, trans. R.J. Teske, 145–88.

Facing the same passage in the later *De Genesi ad litteram* (1.2.4–6) the reader gains the impression that Augustine is acquainted with, and thus less troubled by, the problem of language. Language doesn't seem to pose a threat anymore, once it has been narrowed down to one single issue: temporality. Augustine, therefore, is in the position to ask a number of rhetorical questions about language, which show the absurdity of a certain type of inquiry, such as 'Was it a bodily voice? And if so, in which language was it uttered? What was God's language before Babel? Who was there to listen?' etc. Afterwards, he carefully addresses the problem of temporality exclusively: 'Cum enim de illo dicitur: *Omnia per ipsum facta sunt*; satis ostenditur et lux per ipsum facta, cum dixit Deus, *Fiat lux*. Quod si ita est, aeternum est quod dixit Deus, *Fiat lux*; quia Verbum Dei Deus apud Deum, Filius unicus Dei patri coaeternus est: quamvis Deo hoc in eterno Verbo dicente creatura temporalis facta sit. Cum enim verba sint temporis, cum dicimus: Quando et aliquando ; aeternum tamen est in Verbo Dei, quando fieri aliquid debeat: et tunc fit quando fieri debuisse in illo Verbo est, in quo non est non est quando et aliquando, quoniam totum illud Verbum aeternum est' (*De Genesi ad literam* 1.2.6). (When it is said of the Word, *All things have been made through Him*, it becomes quite clear that light was made through Him when God said, *Let there be light*, and so this utterance of God is eternal. For the Word of God, true God in the bosom of God and the only Son of God, is coeternal with the Father; and yet through this utterance of God in the eternal Word, creation has been brought about in time. It is true that the words 'when' and 'sometime' refer to time, but the when of something that must be created is eternal in the Word of God; and it is created when in the Word there is an exigency for its creation. But in the Word Himself there is no when and no eventuality, because the Word is in every way eternal.)

46 Quoted by Gilson, *Christian Philosophy*, 339.
47 For a complete account of Augustine's Christology, see J. van Bavel, *Recherches sur la christologie de saint Augustin* (Fribourg: Éditions universitaires, 1954). For remarks on Christ as *signum*, see Williams, 'Language, Reality and Desire in Augustine's *De doctrina*,' and Norris, 'Augustine and Sign in *Tractatus in Iohannis Euangelium.*'
48 Quoted by van Bavel, *Recherches*, 24n41.
49 An overview of Augustine's doctrine of Incarnation can be found in M.R. Miles, *Augustine on the Body* (Missoula, MT: American Academy of Religion Dissertation Series, 1979).
50 See, for instance, *De Trinitate* 4.21.31: 'Si autem quaeritur ipsa incarnatio quomodo facta sit, ipsum Verbum Dei dico carnem factum, idest hominem factum, non tamen in hoc quod factum est conversum atque mutatum, ita sane factum ut ibi sit non tantum Verbum Dei et hominis caro sed etiam rationalis hominis anima, atque hoc totum et Deus dicatur propter Deum, et homo propter hominem.' (But if it is asked how the Incarnation itself was brought about, I reply that the Word of God itself was made flesh, that is was made man. It was not, however, turned or changed into that which was made, but made indeed in such a way that there would be in it not only the Word of God and the flesh of man, but also the soul of a rational animal; and this whole is called God on account of God and man on account of man.)
51 On this point, see also Vecchio, *Le parole come segni*, 10–12. And consider also this other passage from the *Commentary on the Gospel of John* (also quoted by Vecchio): 'Domini quippe facta non sunt tantummodo facta, sed signa. Si ergo signa sunt, praeter id quod mira sunt, aliquid profecto significant; quorum factorum significationem invenire, aliquanto est operosius, quam ea legere vel audire.' (For the deeds of the Lord are not only deeds but signs. If, therefore, they are signs, besides the fact that they are wonders, they assuredly signify something; and to find the signification of these deeds is considerably more laborious than to read or hear them.)
     On Jesus' words and deeds, see also Norris, 'Augustine and Sign.' For miracles as signs, see F. Fernandez Ramos, 'Los signos en los *Tractatus in Ioannem*,' *Augustinus* 33 (1988): 57–76.
52 I extract and modify the notion of 'dual sign' from M. Riffaterre, *The Semiotics of Poetry* (Bloomington: Indiana University Press, 1978), 81–114. On pages 88–9, Riffaterre defines dual signs as signs that work simultaneously in two texts: the mimetic, syntagmatic text (in our case, the text of man in time) and the semiotic paradigmatic text (in our case, the eternal text of God, definitely non-semiotic but yet paradigmatic).

53 See *Confessions* 13.15.18. The text of man is the sacred scripture, the 'firmament,' that now extends as a skin, but will eventually be folded into a volume ('At quis nisi tu, Deus noster, fecisti nobis firmamentum auctoritatis super nos in Scriptura tua divina? *Caelum* enim *plicabitur ut liber,* et nunc sicut pellis extenditur super nos'). But the angels read already in a very different book, not unfolding in syllables of time, a book that doesn't close: '*Laudent nomen tuum, laudent* te supercaelestes populi angelorum tuorum, qui non opus habent suspicere firmamentum hoc et legendo cognoscere verbum tuum. *Vident* enim *faciem* tuam *semper,* et ibi legunt sine syllabis temporum, quid velit aeterna voluntas tua. Legunt, eligunt et diligunt; semper legunt et numquam praeterit quod legunt. Eligendo enim et diligendo legunt ipsam inconmutabilitatem consilii tui. Non clauditur codex eorum nec plicatur liber eorum.' (Let the peoples above the heavens, your angels, praise you. They have no need to look up to this firmament and to read so as to know your word. They ever 'see your face' and there, without syllables requiring time to pronounce, they read what your eternal will intends. They read, they choose, they love. They read, and what they read never passes away. By choosing and loving they read the immutability of your design. Their codex is never closed, nor is their book ever folded shut.)

The two texts are also wonderfully portrayed at the end of Dante's *Paradiso* (33.85–7): 'Nel suo profondo vidi che s'interna / legato con amore in un volume / ciò che per l'universo si squaderna.' (In its depth I saw ingathered, bound by love in one single volume, that which is dispersed in leaves throughout the universe.)

54 See Miles, *Augustine on the Body,* 113; and H.I. Marrou, 'Le dogme de la résurrection des corps et la théologie des valeurs humaines selon l'enseignement de saint Augustin,' *Revue des études augustiniennes* 12 (1966): 111–36.

55 For the notion of *sacramentum* as sign in Augustine, see H.M. Féret, '*Sacramentum – Res* dans la langue théologique de saint Augustin,' *Revue des sciences philosophiques et théologiques* 30 (1940): 218–43; and Vecchio, *Le parole come segni,* 127–32. See in particular 130–1: '"I segni" – scrive infatti – "quando riguardano le cose divine si chiamano *sacramenta*" (*E*138, 1, 7). Questa è l'altra grande novità linguistico-semiologica: aver collocato nella categoria dei segni, oltre alle parole anche i "sacramenti." In forza di questa decisione semiologica la posizione agostiniana diventa lo snodo principale del passaggio della dottrina sacramentaria dalla ricchezza e fluidità della posizione patristica (con rinvio all'intero "mistero" della salvezza e al Cristo suo centro) alla restrizione e rigidità della sistemazione della prima scolastica (attenta alla casualità e agli effetti del singolare segno-"sacramento"), alla quale Tommaso d'Aquino tentò senza successo di reagire.'

For a discussion of sacraments in connection to Austin's notion of the performative, see J.A. Appleyard, 'How Does a Sacrament "Cause by Signifying?"' *Science et esprit* 23 (1971): 167–200.

56 *In Evangelium Ioannis* 27.2: 'se prout voluerunt ita intellexerunt, et more hominum, quia poterat Iesus, aut hoc disponebat Iesus, carnem quia indutum erat Verbum, veluti concisam distribuere credentibus in se.' (but just as they wanted, and in a human way, so they understood that Jesus could, or that he was proposing, because the Word had been clothed in flesh, to cut himself up, as it were, and distribute himself to those believing in him.)

57 *Ordo amoris*, 176. For a slightly different perspective, see Augustine's *Confession*, and Vance, 'The Grammar of Selfhood,' 13: 'Hence, the authenticity of Augustine's conversion is marked not by a conclusion of a discourse about himself, but rather by its interruption and by the intrusion of God's own grammar, his own fiction (*poesis*): centered now upon the universal Word, Augustine's text becomes gloss and marginalia.'

58 In the case of the infant, signs cling to desire and don't yet have a relationship to reality ('similia voluntatibus meis, non enim veresimilia'): 'et ecce paulatim sentiebam, ubi essem, et voluntates meas volebam ostendere eis, per quos implerentur, et non poteram, quia illae intus erant, foris autem illi nec ullo suo sensu valebant introire in animam meam. Itaque iactabam membra et voces, signa similia voluntatibus meis, pauca quae poteram, qualia poteram: non enim erant veresimilia' (1.6.8). (Little by little I began to be aware where I was and wanted to manifest my wishes to those who could fulfill them as I could not. For my desires were internal; adults were external to me and had no means of entering my soul. So I threw my limbs about and uttered sounds, signs resembling my wishes, the small number of signs of which I was capable but such signs as lay in my power to use: for there was no real resemblance.)

In the case of the child (1.8), a more complex interplay of bodily and verbal signs leads to language learning, which is still nevertheless located in the interior man/child, and still marked by an incorrect application of the order of love. In both cases the child's wishes (*voluntas, voluntates*) carry a notion of lacking and therefore wanting. The imbalance of signs first and of words later is due to a misuse of the order of love. Language, and later in the *Confessions* the whole ladder of education, remains detached from 'true' meaning and restricts humans to the realm of signs, being indeed the first step into the 'stormy society of human life.'

'Non enim eram infans, qui non farer, sed puer loquens eram. Et memini hoc, et unde loqui didiceram, post adverti. Non enim docebant me maiores

homines praebentes mihi verba certo aliquo ordine doctrinae, sicut paulo
post litteras, sed ego ipse mente, quam dedisti mihi, Deus meus, cum gemiti-
bus et vocibus variis et variis membrorum motibus edere vellem sensa cordis
mei, ut voluntati pareretur, nec valerem quae volebam omnia nec quibus
volebam omnibus. Prensabam memoria, cum ipsi appellabant rem aliquam
et cum secundum eam vocem corpus ad aliquid movebant, videbam et
tenebam hoc ab eis vocari rem illam, quod sonabant, cum eam vellent ostendere. Hoc autem eos velle ex motu corporis aperiebatur tamquam verbis naturalibus omnium gentium, quae fiunt vultu et nutu oculorum ceteroque
membrorum actu et sonitu vocis indicante affectionem animi in petendis,
habendis, reiciendis, fugiendisve rebus. Ita verba in variis sententiis locis suis
posita et crebro audita quarum rerum signa esse paulatim colligebam
measque iam voluntates edomito in eis signis ore per haec enuntiabam. Sic
cum his, inter quos eram, voluntatum enuntiandarum signa communicavi et
vitae humanae procellosam societatem altius ingressus sum' (1.8.13). (Yet I
was no longer a baby incapable of speech but already a boy with power to
talk. This I remember. But how I learnt to talk I discovered only later. It was
not that grown-up people instructed me by presenting me with words in a
certain order by formal teaching, as later I was to learn the letters of the
alphabet. I myself acquired this power of speech with the intelligence which
you gave me, my God. By groans and various sounds and various movements
of parts of my body I would endeavor to express the intentions of my heart to
persuade people to bow to my will. But I had not the power to express all
that I wanted nor could I make my wishes understood by everybody. My
grasp made use of memory: when people gave a name to an object and
when, following the sound, they moved their body towards that object, I
would see and retain the fact that that object received from them this sound
which they pronounced when they intended to draw attention to it. Moreover, their intention was evident from the gestures which are, as it were, the
natural vocabulary of all races, and are made with the face and inclination of
the eyes and the movements of other parts of the body, and by the tone of
voice which indicates whether the mind's inward sentiments are to seek and
possess or to reject and avoid. Accordingly, I gradually gathered the meaning
of words, occurring in their places in different sentences and frequently
heard; and already I learnt to articulate my wishes by training my mouth to
use these signs. In this way I communicated the signs of my wishes to those
around me, and entered more deeply into the stormy society of human
life.)

59 For a close reading of these passages, see B. Stock, *Augustine the Reader: Medi-*

tation, Self-Knowledge and the Ethics of Interpretation (Cambridge, MA: Harvard University Press, 1996), 75–111.

60 It is interesting to notice the double meaning of the verb *indicare*, which means 'to point to' but also 'to reveal,' 'to show,' 'to tell a story.' By 'indicating,' Augustine points out to Alypius both his own event of conversion and the book; and Alypius discloses his own thoughts ('indicavit'), reads, and is converted soon after.

61 *De Genesi ad literam imperfectus liber* 13.38: '*Et sint in signis et temporibus, et in diebus, et in annis.* Videtur mihi hoc quod dixit, *in signis,* planum fecisse illud quod dixit, *et in temporibus;* ne aliud acciperentur signa, et aliud tempora. Haec enim nunc dicit tempora, quae intervallorum distinctione aeternitatem incommutabilem supra se manere significant, ut signum, id est quasi vestigium aeternitatis tempus appareat.' ('And to be as signs for times and for days and for years.' It seems to me that when the Scripture said, 'for times' it explained the words 'as signs.' We should not interpret the signs as something other than times. For the Scripture is now speaking of these times that by their distinctive intervals convey to us that eternity remains immutable above them so that time might appear as a sign, that is, a vestige, of eternity.)

62 For Augustine's theory of time and memory, see Gilson, *Christian Philosophy,* 189–96; R. Jordan, 'Time and Contingency in St Augustine' (1955), reprinted in *Augustine: A Collection of Critical Essays,* ed. R.A. Markus (New York: Doubleday, 1972), 255–79; Ferguson, 'Saint Augustine's Region of Unlikeness'; P. Ricoeur, 'The Aporias of the Experiences of Time: Book 11 of Augustine's *Confessions,*' in *Time and Narrative* (Chicago: University of Chicago Press, 1984), 1:5–30; G. O'Daly, *Augustine's Philosophy of Mind* (Berkeley: University of California Press, 1987), esp. 131–61; D.W. Polk, 'Temporal Impermanence and the Disparity of Time and Eternity,' *Augustinian Studies* 22 (1991): 63–82; J. Coleman, *Ancient and Medieval Memories* (Cambridge: Cambridge University Press, 1992), 81–111; and Stock, *Augustine the Reader,* 207–42.

For theories of time in antiquity and the Middle Ages, see R. Sorabji, *Time, Creation and the Continuum: Theories in Antiquity and the Early Middle Ages* (Ithaca: Cornell University Press, 1983).

63 On this point, see Ricoeur, 'The Aporias,' 25–31.

64 See Vecchio, *Le parole come segni,* 112.

65 *Confessions* 11.14.17: 'Praesens autem si semper esset praesens nec in praeteritum transiret, non iam esset tempus sed aeternitas. Si ergo praesens, ut tempus sit, ideo fit, quia in praeteritum transit, quomodo et hoc esse dici-

mus, cui causa, ut sit, illa est, quia non erit, ut scilicet non vere dicamus tempus esse nisi quia tendit non esse?' (Yet if the present were always present, it
would not pass into the past: it would not be time but eternity. If then, in
order to be time at all, the present is so made that it passes into the past, how
can we say that this present also 'is'? The cause of its being is that it will cease
to be. So indeed we cannot truly say that time exists except in the sense that
it tends towards non-existence.)

66 For the spatial metaphor, see Ricoeur, 'The Aporias,' 13; and Ferguson,
'Saint Augustine's Region of Unlikeness,' 853–5.

67 *Confessions* 11.26.33: 'inde mihi visum est nihil esse aliud tempus quam disten-
tionem: sed cuius rei, nescio, et mirum, si non ipsius animi.' (that is why I have
come to think that time is simply a distention. But of what is it a distention? I
do not know but it would be surprising if it is not that of the mind itself.)

68 *Confessions* 11.27.34: 'Metiamur plane et dicamus quanta [vox] sit. Sed adhuc
sonat nec metiri potest nisi ab initio sui, quo sonare coepit, usque ad finem,
quo desinit. Ipsum quippe intervallum metimur ab aliquo initio usque ad
aliquem finem. Quapropter vox, quae nondum finita est, metiri non potest,
ut dicatur, quam longa vel brevis sit, nec dici aut aequalis alicui aut ad aliquam simpla vel dupla vel quid aliud. Cum autem finita fuerit, iam non erit.
Quo pacto igitur metiri poterit? Et metimur tamen tempora, nec ea, quae
nondum sunt, nec ea, quae iam non sunt, nec ea, quae nulla mora extend-
untur, nec ea, quae terminos non habent. Nec futura ergo nec praeterita nec
praesentia nec praetereuntia tempora metimur et metimur tamen tempora.'
(Evidently we may at that stage measure it by saying how long it [the vox]
lasted. But if it is still sounding, it cannot be measured except from the starting moment when it began to sound to the finish when it ceased. What we
measure is the actual interval from the beginning to the end. That is why a
sound which has not yet ended cannot be measured: one cannot say how
long or how short it is, nor that is equal to some other length of time or that
in relation to another it is single or double or any such proportion. But when
it has come to an end, then it will already have ceased to be. By what method
then can it be measured? Nevertheless, we do measure periods of time. And
yet the times we measure are not those which do not yet exist, nor those
which already have no existence, nor those which extend over no interval of
time, nor those which reach no conclusion. So the times we measure are not
future nor past nor present nor those in the process of passing away. Yet we
measure periods of time.)

69 *Confessions* 11.27.35: 'Quid ergo est, quod metior? Ubi est qua metior brevis?
Ubi est longa, quam metior? Ambae sonuerunt, avolaverunt, praeterierunt,

iam non sunt; et ego metior fidenterque respondeo, quantum exercitato sensu fiditur, illam simplam esse, illam duplam, in spatio scilicet temporis. Neque hoc possum, nisi quia praeterierunt et finitae sunt. Non ergo ipsas, quae iam non sunt, sed aliquid in memoria mea metior, quod infixum manet.' (What is it, then, which I measure? Where is the short syllable with which I am making my measurement? Where is the long which I am measuring? Both have sounded, they have flown away; they belong to the past. They now do not exist. And I offer my measurement and declare as confidently as a practised sense-perception will allow, that the short is single, the long double – I mean in the time they occupy. I can do this only because they are past and gone. Therefore it is not the syllables which I am measuring, but something in my memory which stays fixed there.)

70 *Confessions* 11.27.36: 'Nam et voce atque ore cessante peragimus cogitando carmina et versus et quemque sermonem motionumque dimensiones quaslibet et de spatiis temporum, quantum illud ad illud sit, renuntiamus non aliter, ac si ea sonando diceremus. Voluerit aliquis edere longiusculam vocem et constituerit praemeditando, quam longa futura sit, egit utique iste spatium temporis in silentio memoriaeque commendans coepit edere illam vocem, quae sonat, donec ad propositum terminum perducatur: immo sonuit et sonabit; nam quod eius iam peractum est, utique sonuit, quod autem restat, sonabit atque ita peragitur, dum praesens intentio futurum in praeteritum traicit deminutione futuri crescente praeterito, donec consumptione futuri sit totum praeteritum.' (For without any sound or utterance we mentally recite poems and lines and speeches, and we assess the lengths of their movement and the relative amounts of time they occupy, no differently from the way we would speak if we were actually making sounds. Suppose someone wished to utter a sound lasting a long time, and decided in advance how long that was going to be. He would have planned that space of time in silence. Entrusting that to his memory he would begin to utter the sound which continues until it has reached the intended end. It would be more accurate to say the utterance has sounded and will sound. For the part of it which is completed has sounded, but what remains will sound, and so the action is being accomplished as present attention transfers the future into the past. The future diminishes and the past grows, until the future has completely gone and everything is in the past.)

71 This passage is pointed out by Vance, *Mervelous signals*, 46; and Vecchio, *Le parole come segni*, 112. Translations from the *De vera religione* are taken from *Of True Religion*, trans. L.O. Mink (South Bend: Gateway, 1959). In his *Classical and Christian Ideas of World Harmony* (Baltimore: Johns Hopkins University

Press, 1963), 29, Leo Spitzer points to a passage in Augustine where God is described as the 'modulator' of history and comments, 'In one of his letters (Migne, 33, 527) Augustine speaks of world harmony, of the *universi saeculi pulchritudo*, the *magnum carmen creatoris et moderatoris*, as conceived in terms of time; it is an hymn scanned by God, since God allots the convenient things to the convenient time. No wonder that he expresses the continuous "moderations" or interventions of God by a series of verbs, the "Zeitwörter" par excellence: "[Deus] qui multo magis quam homo novit quid cuique tempori accommodate adhibeatur; quid quando impertiat, addat, auferat, detrahat, augeat, minuatve, immutabilis mutabilium sicut creator, ita moderator, donec universi saeculi pulchritudo, cuius particulae sunt quae suis quibusque temporibus apta sunt, velut *magnum carmen* [variant: *musicum carmen*] cuiusdam ineffabilis·modulatoris excurrat, atque inde transeant in aeternam contemplationem speciei qui Deum rite colunt, etiam cum tempus est fidei"' (*Letters* 138.1.5). (He knew much better than man what it is suitably adapted to each age ... He knows as well what and when to give, to add to, to take away, to withdraw, to increase, or to diminish, until the beauty of the entire world, of which the individual parts are suitable each for its own time, swells, as it were, into a mighty song of some unutterable musician, and from thence the true adorers of God rise to the eternal contemplation of His face, even in the time of faith.) Translations from the *Epistulae* are taken from *Letters* 3, trans. W. Parsons (Washington, DC: Catholic University of America Press, 1953).

72 For a description of the structure of language in the works of the grammarians of late antiquity, see E. Vineis and A. Maierù, 'Medieval Linguistics,' in *History of Linguistics*, vol. 2, *Classical and Medieval Linguistics*, ed. G. Lepschy (London: Longman, 1994), 134–315.

73 *Instututiones gramaticae* 17.2, in *Grammatici Latini*, ed. H. Keil (Leipzig: Teubner, 1855; repr., Hildesheim: Verlag, 1981), 3:108. The consequentiality is also evident in the definition of the single parts. Letters are the minimal part of a composed voice: 'Litera est pars minima vocis compositae, hoc est quae constat compositione literarum, minima autem, quantum ad totam comprehensionem vocis literatae – ad hanc enim etiam productae vocales brevissimae partes inveniuntur – vel quod omnium et brevissimum eorum, quae dividi possunt, id quod dividi non potest. Possumus et sic definire: litera est vox, quae scribi potest individua' (*Institutiones* 1.2.3; *Grammatici Latini* 2.6. Translations are mine). (The letter is the minimal part of the composed voice, which results from the composition of letters. Minimal with respect to the comprehension of the voice made of letters, toward which vowels, the

shortest parts, are produced. Or it is the shortest of the parts that can be divided; that which cannot be divided. We can define it as such: the letter is a voice that can be written individually.)

The syllable is featured by accent and inflection: 'Syllaba est comprehensio literarum consequens sub uno accentu et uno spiritu prolata; abusive tamen etiam singularum vocalium sonos syllabas nominamus. Possum tamen et sic definire syllaba: syllaba est vox literalis, quae sub uno accentu et uno spiritu indistanter profertur' (*Institutiones* 2.1.1; *Grammatici Latini* 2.44). (The syllable is an orderly grouping of letters that is uttered under one accent and one spirit. Thus, it is incorrect to call syllables the sounds of the single vowels. We can define the syllable as such: it is a voice made of letters, which is uttered under one accent and one spirit without interruption.)

The word is the minimal unit of meaning: 'Dictio est pars minima orationis constructae, id est in ordine compositae: pars autem, quantum ad totum intellegendum, id est ad totius sensus intellectum; hoc autem dictum est, ne quis conetur "vires" in duas partes dividere, hoc est in "vi" et "res," vel quaedam huiuscemodi. Non enim ad totum intellegendum haec fit divisio. Differt autem dictio a syllaba, non solum quod syllaba pars est dictionis, sed etiam quod dictio dicendum, hoc est intellegendum, aliquid habet' (*Institutiones* 2.3.14; *Grammatici Latini* 2.53). (The word is the minimal part of constructed speech that is; composed in order. It is part with respect to a full understanding, that is the understanding of the full sense. I say this so that one doesn't attempt to divide 'vires' into two parts, 'vi' and 'res,' or something like that. This division does not account for full understanding. The word is different from the syllable not only because the syllable is a part of the word, but also because the word has something to be said, that is to be understood.)

The speech is the perfection of linguistic construction: 'Oratio est ordinatio dictionum congrua, sententiam perfectam demonstrans' (*Institutiones* 2.3.15; *Grammatici Latini* 2.53). (The speech is the congruous order of words, showing a perfect sentence.) Donatus, who is closer in time, and according to Law, in 'spirit' to Augustine has the same understanding of the construction of speech, although his exposition is more concise than that of Priscian. His *Ars maior* treats in succession voice, letters, syllables, punctuation, and the eight parts of the speech. It is worth noticing that Donatus dwells more at length than Priscian on the metrical aspect of the syllable, with an entire section 'de pedibus' devoted to the metric foot, which constitutes the precise enumeration of syllables and times: 'pes est syllabarum et temporum certa dinumeratio' (*Ars Grammatica* 1.2–4; *Grammatici Latini* 4.369).

74 *De ordine* 2.12.36: 'Progressa deinde ratio animadvertit eosdem oris sonos
quibus loqueremur et quos litteris iam signaverat, alios esse qui moderato
varie hiatu, quasi enodati ac simplices faucibus sine ulla collisione deflu-
erent, alios diverso pressu oris, tenere tamen aliquem sonum, extremos
autem qui nisi adiunctis sibi primis erumpere non valerent. Itaque litteras
hoc ordine quo expositae sunt vocales, semivocales et mutas nominavit.
Deinde syllabas notavit deinde verba in octo genera formasque digesta sunt
omnisque illorum motus, integritas, iunctura, perite subtiliterque distincta
sunt.' (When reason had gone further it noticed that of those oral sounds
which we used is speaking and which it had already designated by letters,
there were some which by a varied modulation of the parted lips flowed clear
and pure from the throat without any friction; that others acquired a certain
kind of sound from the diversified pressure of the lips; and that there were
still other sounds, which could not issue forth unless they were conjoined
with these. Accordingly, it denominated the letters in order of their exposition: vowels, semivowels and mutes. In the next place, it took account of syllables. Then words were grouped into eight classes and forms; and their
entire evolvement, purity and articulation were skillfully and minutely differentiated.)

Grammar, according to Augustine, is also implicated with literature (as
traditionally held) and history. See *De ordine* 2.12.37: 'Poterat iam perfecta
esse grammatica, sed quia ipso nomine profiteri se litteras clamat, unde
etiam latine litteratura dicitur, factum est ut quidquid dignum memoria litteris mandaretur ad eam necessario pertineret. Itaque unum quidem nomen,
sed res infinita, multiplex, curarum plenior quam iucunditatis aut veritatis,
huic disciplinae accessit historia, non tam ipsis historicis quam grammaticis
laboriosa.' (The science of grammar could now have been complete. By
since by its very name it proclaims that it knows letters – indeed on this
account it is called 'Literature' in Latin – it came to pass that whatever was
committed to letters as worth remembering, necessarily pertained to it. And
in this way history – whose name is one but whose subject matter is undefined and many-sided, and which is filled more with cares than with enjoyment or truth, and more burdensome to grammarians than to the historians
themselves – was added to this science.) Translations from the *De ordine* are
taken from *Divine Providence and the Problem of Evil (De ordine)*, trans. R. Russell
(New York: Cosmopolitan, 1942).

75 Vecchio (*Le parole come segni*, 55) points out a passage from the *De quantitate
animae* (32.66–7), in which the relationship between letters and words is discussed in the context of the relationship between soul and body. Body and

soul stand in the same relation as sound and meaning ('sonum esse corpus, significationem autem quasi animam soni'). While the sound of a word can be divided into letters, its meaning can't. The 'soul' of the word abandons the dissected body ('dilaniato corpore discessisse animam'), and causes its death. Thus, Augustine concludes, 'Si ergo satis perspexisti in hac similitudine, quomodo possit dissecto corpore anima non secari; accipe nunc quomodo frusta ipsa corporis, cum anima secta non sit, vivere possint. Iam enim concessisti, et recte, ut opinor, significationem quae quasi anima soni est, dum nomen editur, per seipsam nullo pacto dividi posse, cum ipse sonus, quod velut corpus eius est, possit. Sed in solis nomine ita soni est facta divisio, ut nulla pars eius significationem aliquam retineret. Itaque illas litteras, dilacerato corpore nominis, tamquam exanima membra, id est, significatione carentia, considerabamus.' (If, therefore, this illustration makes it clear enough to you how it is impossible to cut up the body without dividing the soul, understand how the segments of a body can live, although the soul does not suffer any division. For, you have admitted, and correctly, I think, that the meaning – which is like the soul of the sound that is made in uttering a word – cannot possibly be divided, while the sound itself – which is like the body – can be divided. Now, in the noun 'sun' any division of the sound leaves no meaning whatever in the parts. Therefore, after the body of the noun is rent, we would consider the letters simply as members bereft of all life, that is, without meaning.) Translations from the *De quantitate animae* are taken from *The Magnitude of the Soul*, trans. J.J. McMahon (Washington, DC: Catholic University of America Press, 1974). This passage is discussed also by R.E. Buckenmeier, 'St Augustine and the Life of Man's Body in the Early Dialogues,' *Augustinian Studies* 3 (1972): 131–46, esp. 134.

76 *De quantitate animae* 32.67: 'Quamobrem si aliquod nomen invenerimus, quod divisum queat etiam singulis partibus quidpiam significare; concedas oportet, non omnimodam veluti mortem tali praecisione factam esse, cum tibi membra separatim considerata quodlibet significantia et quasi spirantia videbuntur ... Lucifer mihi occurrit; qui profecto inter secundam et tertiam syllabam scissus nonnihil priore parte significat, cum dicimus, Luci, et ideo in hoc plusquam dimidio corpore nominis vivit. Extrema etiam pars habet animam: nam cum ferre aliquid iuberis, hanc audis. Qui enim posses obtemperare, si quis tibi diceret, Fer codicem, si nihil significaret Fer? quod cum additur Luci, Lucifer sonat, et significat stellam; cum autem demitur, nonnihil significat, et ob hoc quasi retinet vitam.

Cum autem locus et tempus sit, quibus omnia quae sentiuntur occupantur, vel potius quae occupant; quod oculis sentimus, per locum; quod auribus, per tempus dividitur. Ut enim vermiculus ille plus loci totus, quam pars eius occupabat; ita maiorem temporis moram tenet, cum Lucifer dicitur, quam si Luci tantummodo diceretur. Quare si hoc significatione vivit in ea diminutione temporis, quae diviso illo sono facta est, cum eadem significatio divisa non sit (non enim ipsa per tempus distendebatur, sed sonus); ita existimandum est, secto vermiculi corpore, quamquam in minore loco pars eo ipso quo pars erat viveret, non omnino animam sectam, nec loco minore minorem esse factam, licet integri animantis membra omnia per maiorem locum porrecta simul possederit. Non enim locum ipsa, sed corpus quod ab eadem agebatur, tenebat: sicut illa significatio non distenta per tempus, omnes tamen nominis litteras suas moras ac tempora possidentes, velut animaverat atque compleverat.' (But, if we find some noun whose parts after division can have some meaning, you must allow that such division did not result in complete death, as it were, because the parts, considered separately, evidently retain some meaning and breath of life, as it were ... Lucifer comes to mind, and, when this word is split between the second and third syllable, the first part has a meaning when we say 'luci.' So, therefore, life exists in more than one half of its body. The part that is left also has a soul, for, when you are told to carry something, that is what you hear. How could you obey if some one were to say to you: 'Carry the book' [fer librum], if 'fer' [carry] has no meaning? Then, when 'Luci' is added, the sound is Lucifer and means a star. But, when that is taken away, it still signifies something and therefore retains life, in a certain sense. But, since everything that the senses perceive is contained in time and place, or rather, the senses perceive what time and space contain, then what we perceive by the eyes is divided by space; what we perceive by the ears is divided by time. For, just as that worm occupied more space as a whole than any part of it, so Lucifer takes a longer amount of time to pronounce than 'Luci.' Wherefore, if this part of the word has meaning and, therefore, life, in a shorter interval of time that was reduced by dividing the sound, not the meaning [for the sound and not the meaning is extended in time], so in the same way we ought to conclude about the worm. Namely, even though a part, just because it is a part, lives in a smaller space after the body has been cut, we should not conclude that the soul has been cut or that it is smaller in space, despite the fact that in the undivided living worm the soul was the equal possession of all the parts and the parts occupied a larger space. For, the soul did not occupy a place, but held the body which was moved by it. Just as the meaning of a word, without being extended in time, gave life, so to speak, and filled out all the letters that take up slight intervals of time [to pronounce].)

77 On Augustine and music, see Spitzer, *Classical and Christian Ideas of World Harmony*, M. Bettetini, ed., *Ordine, Musica, Bellezza* (Milan: Rusconi, 1992); and A. Carrera, 'La traccia dell'eterno: Tempo e musica in Sant'Agostino,' in *Lo spazio materno dell'ispirazione: Agostino, Blanchot, Celan, Zanzotto* (Florence: Cadmo, 2004), 81–124.

78 See *De musica* 2.1.1: 'Atqui scias velim totam illam scientiam, quae grammatica graece, latine autem litteratura nominatur, historiae custodiam profiteri, vel solam, ut subtilior docet ratio; vel maxime, ut etiam pinguia corda concedunt. Itaque verbi gratia cum dixeris, *cano,* vel in versu forte posueris, ita ut vel tu pronuntians producas huius verbi syllabam primam, vel in versu eo loco ponas, ubi esse productam oportebat; reprehendet grammaticus, custos ille videlicet historiae, nihil aliud asserens cur hunc corripi oporteat, nisi quod hi qui ante nos fuerunt, et quorum libri exstant tractanturque a grammaticis, ea correpta, non producta usi fuerint. Quare hic quidquid valet, auctoritas valet. At vero musicae ratio, ad quam dimensio ipsa vocum rationabilis et numerositas pertinet, non curat nisi ut corripiatur vel producatur syllaba, quae illo vel illo loco est secundum rationem mensurarum suarum.' (But first I want you to know that the whole of that science called *grammatica* Greek-wise, but Latin-wise *litteratura*, professes the conservation of historical precedent – either that alone, as reason in its subtler moments teaches, or for the most part, as even stupid minds concede. And so, for example, when you say *cano*, or put it in verse, in such a way as to prolong its first syllable when you pronounce it or in such a place as to make it necessarily long, the grammarian will censure you; he, of course, the guardian of history, giving no other reason why this syllable should be contracted than that those who lived before us and whose books survive and are discussed by grammarians used it as a short syllable, not as a long one. And so, whatever prevails here, prevails as authority. On the contrary, the reason of music, whose province is the rational and numerical measure of sounds, takes care only the syllable in this or that place be contracted or prolonged according to the rationale of its measures.) Translations of the *De musica* are taken from 'On Music,' trans. R.C. Taliaferro, in *Writings of Saint Augustine* (Washington, DC: Catholic University of America Press, 1947), 2:151–379.

79 On this point, see Vecchio, *Le parole come segni,* 112.

80 *De natura boni*, 8: 'Coetera vero quae sunt facta de nihilo, quae utique inferiora sunt quam spiritus rationalis, nec beata possunt esse, nec misera. Sed, quia pro modo et specie sua etiam ipsa bona sunt, nec esse quamvis minora et minima bona, nisi a summo bono Deo potuerunt, sic ordinata sunt, ut cedant infirmiora firmioribus, et invalidiora fortioribus, et impotentiora potentioribus, atque ita coelestibus terrena concordent tamquam praecellentibus subdita. Fit autem decedentibus et succedentibus rebus temporalis

quaedam in suo genere pulchritudo, ut nec ipsa quae moriuntur, vel quod erant esse desinunt, turpent aut turbent modum et speciem et ordinem universae creaturae: sicut sermo bene compositus utique pulcher est, quamvis in eo syllabae atque omnes soni tamquam nascendo et moriendo transcurrant.' (But the rest of things that are made of nothing, which are assuredly inferior to the rational soul, can be neither blessed nor miserable. But because in proportion to their fashion and appearance are things themselves good, nor could there be good things in a less or the least degree except from God, they are so ordered that the more infirm yield to the firmer, the weaker to the stronger, the more impotent to the more powerful; and so earthly things harmonize with celestial, as being subject to the things that are pre-eminent. But to things falling away, and succeeding, a certain temporal beauty in its kind belongs, so that neither those things that die, or cease to be what they were, degrade or disturb the fashion and appearance and order of the universal creation; as a speech well composed is assuredly beautiful, although in it syllables and all sounds rush past as it were in being born and in dying). Translations from the *De natura boni* are taken from 'On the Nature of Good,' New Advent, http://www.newadvent.org/fathers/1407.htm (accessed 12 December 2006).

81 For a survey of Augustine's reflection on beauty, see *Ordine, Musica, Bellezza*, and R. Piccolomini, ed. *La bellezza* (Rome: Città Nuova, 1995).

82 *Confessions* 13.28.43: 'hoc dicunt etiam quaeque pulchra corpora, quia longe multo pulchrius est corpus, quod ex membris pulchris omnibus constat, quam ipsa membra singula, quorum ordinatissimo conventu completur universum, quamvis et illa etiam singillatim pulchra sint.' (This truth is also declared by the beauty of bodies. A body composed of its constituent parts, all of which are beautiful, is far more beautiful as a whole than those parts taken separately; the whole is made of their well-ordered harmony, though individually the constituent parts are also beautiful.)

83 *De ordine* 1.1.2: 'At enim hoc ipsum est plenius quaestionum, quod membra pulicis disposita mire atque distincta sunt, cum interea humana vita innumerabilium perturbationum inconstantia versetur et fluctuet. Sed hoc pacto si quis tam minutum cerneret, ut in vermiculato pavimento nihil ultra unius tessellae modulum acies eius valeret ambire, vituperaret artificem velut ordinationis et compositionis ignarum, eo quod varietatem lapillorum perturbatam putaret, a quo illa emblemata in unius pulchritudinis faciem congruentia simul cerni collustrarique non possent. Nihil enim aliud minus eruditis hominibus accidit, qui universam rerum coaptationem atque concentum imbecilla mente complecti et considerare non valentes, si quid eos offenderit, quia suae cogitationi magnum est, magnam rebus putant inhaerere foeditatem.' (Yet there is a point suggestive of even more questioning:

that the organic parts of the flea are marvelously fitted and framed, while
human life is surrounded and made restless by the inconsistency of countless
disorders. On this line of reasoning, if one were examining the details in an
inlaid pavement, and if his searching eye could grasp no more than the out-
line of one little cube, he might censure the artificer for lacking skill of
arrangement and order. On this account he might think the uniformity of
the little stones disarranged, just because the drawn lines harmonizing into
one integral form of beauty could not be seen and examined all at once.
Something very similar to this is found in the case of uninstructed men who,
on account of their feeble mentality, are unable to grasp and to study the
integral fittingness of things. They think that the whole universe is disarranged if something is displeasing to them, just because that thing is magni-
fied in their perception.)

84 In *De ordine* 2.12–17, Augustine traces the search for order within the ladder
of education starting from the birth of language, and proceeding on to
grammar, dialectics, metrics, music, where the image of numbers appears
more clearly.

85 Question 36 (*de nutrienda caritate*) follows 35 (*quid sit amandum*), another survey on the 'order of love' and begins with the definition of *dilectio*: 'Caritatem
voco qua amantur ea quae non sunt prae ipso amante contemnenda, id est,
quod aeternum est et quod amare ipsum aeternum potest. Deus igitur et animus cum amantur; caritas proprie dicitur, purgatissima et consummata, si
nihil aliud amatur; hanc et dilectionem dici placet.' (Charity denotes that
whereby one loves those things whose worth, in comparison to the lover itself,
must not be thought to be of lesser value, those things being the eternal and
what can love the eternal. Therefore in its consummate and purest sense
charity is used only for the love of God and of the soul by which he is loved
(and this is also appropriately called *dilectio*.)

86 For a list of the recurrences of the image of the weight of love, see Gilson,
Christian Philosophy, 310n29.

87 *De civitate Dei* 11.28: 'Si enim pecora essemus, carnalem vitam et quod secundum sensum eius est amaremus idque esset sufficiens bonum nostrum et
secundum hoc, cum esset nobis bene, nihil aliud quaereremus. Item si
arbores essemus, nihil quidem sentiente motu amare possemus, verumta-
men id quasi appetere videremur, quo feracius essemus uberiusque fructuo-
sae. Si essemus lapides aut fluctus aut ventus aut flamma vel quid huiusmodi,
sine ullo quidem sensu atque vita, non tamen nobis deesset quasi quidam
nostrorum locorum atque ordinis appetitus. Nam velut amores corporum
momenta sunt ponderum, sive deorsum gravitate sive sursum levitate nitan-
tur. Ita enim corpus pondere, sicut animus amore fertur, quocumque fertur.
Quoniam igitur homines sumus ad nostri Creatoris imaginem creati, cuius

est vera aeternitas, aeterna veritas, aeterna et vera caritas, estque ipse aeterna
et vera et cara Trinitas neque confusa neque separata.' (For if we were cattle
we should love the carnal and sensual life and this would be our sufficient
good; and when it was well with us, in respect of it, we should seek nothing
else. Again, if we were trees, we could not, of course, be moved by the senses
to love anything, but we should seem to desire, as it were, that by which we
might become more abundantly and bountifully fruitful. If we were stones or
waves or wind or flames or anything of that kind, we should, indeed, be without both sensation and life, but we should still not lack a kind of desire for
our own proper place and order. For the weight of bodies is, as it were, their
love, whether they are carried downwards by gravity or upwards by their
lightness. For the body is carried by its weight wherever it is carried. Just as
the soul is carried by its love. We, however, are men, created in the image of
our Creator, Whose eternity is true, and Whose truth is eternal, Whose love
is eternal and true, and Who is Himself the eternal, true and beloved Trinity,
in Whom there is neither confusion nor separateness.)

88 Gilson, *Christian Philosophy*, 310n29, 321–2n81; Bochet, *Saint Augustin et le désir
de Dieu*, 323–34. As Bochet explains, Augustine draws the notion of *delectatio*
from Cicero's *Tusculanae*, where it is described as one of the pleasures of the
soul, and modifies it through Plotinus' notion of desire-pleasure. As a consequence of sin, *delectatio* is split between the carnal and the spiritual. Not surprisingly, it is the Word made flesh which readdresses pleasure-desire toward
its spiritual end. Bochet quotes *In Evangelium Ioannis* 26.4: 'Porro si poetae
dicere licuit: 'Trahit sua quemque voluptas', non necessitas, sed voluptas; non
obligatio, sed delectatio, quanto fortius nos dicere debemus trahi hominem
ad Christum, qui delectatur veritate, delectatur beatitudine, delectatur iustitia, delectatur sempiterna vita, quod totum Christum est?' (Moreover, if it was
allowed to a poet to say, 'His own pleasure draws each man,' not need, but
pleasure, not obligation but delight, how much more forcefully ought we to
say that a man is drawn to Christ who delights in truth, delights in happiness,
delights in justice, delights in eternal life – and all this is Christ?)

For the notion of delight, see also P. Brown, *Augustine of Hippo* (Berkeley:
University of California Press, 1967), 153–7.

89 See *De musica* 6.11.30: 'In quibus multa nobis videntur inordinata et pertur-
bata, quia eorum ordini pro nostris meritis assuti sumus, nescientes quid de
nobis divina providentia pulchrum gerat. Quoniam si quis, verbi gratia, in
amplissimarum pulcherrimarumque aedium uno aliquo angulo tamquam
statua collocetur, pulchritudinem illius fabricae sentire non poterit, cuius et
ipse pars erit. Nec universi exercitus ordinem miles in acie valet intueri. Et in
quolibet poemate si quanto spatio syllabae sonant, tanto viverent atque sen-
tirent, nullo modo illa numerositas et contexti operis pulchritudo eis place-

ret, quam totam perspicere atque approbare non possent, cum de ipsis singulis praetereuntibus fabricata esset atque perfecta.' (And so many of these
things seem to us disordered and perturbed, because we have been sewn
into their order according to our merits, not knowing what beautiful things
Divine Providence purposes for us. For, if someone should be put as a statue
in an angle of the most spacious and beautiful building, he could not perceive the beauty of the building he himself is a part of. Nor can the soldier
on the front line of battle get the order of the whole army. And in a poem, if
syllables should live and perceive only so long as they sound, the harmony
and beauty of the connected work would in no way please them. For they
could not see or approve the whole, since it would be fashioned and perfected by the very passing away of these singulars.)

90 *De musica* 6.14.44: 'Laboriosior est huius mundi amor. Quod enim in illo
anima quaerit, constantiam scilicet aeternitatemque, non invenit: quoniam
rerum transitu completur infima pulchritudo, et quod in illa imitatur constantiam, a summo Deo per animam traicitur.' (The love of this world is
more wearisome. For, what the soul seeks in it, consistency and eternity, it
does not find, since the lowest beauty is finished out with the passage of
things, and what there imitates constancy is thrown through the soul by the
highest God.)

91 *In Epistolam Ioannis ad Parthos tractatus decem* 4.6: 'Tota vita christiani boni,
sanctum desiderium est. Quod autem desideras, nondum vides; sed desiderando capax efficeris, ut cum venerit quod videas, impleavis ... sic Deus dif-
ferendo extendit desiderium, desiderando extendit animum, extendendo
facit capacem. Desideremus ergo, fratres, quia implendi sumus ... Haec est
vita nostra, ut desiderando exerceamur. Tantum autem nos exercet sanctum
desiderium, quantum desideria nostra amputaverimus ab amore saeculi. Jam
diximus aliquando, "Exinani quod implendum est."' (The whole life of a
good Christian is a holy longing. But what you long for you do not yet see,
but by longing, you are made capacious so that when what you are to see has
come, you may be filled ... So God, by postponing, stretches the longing, by
longing, stretches the soul, by stretching makes it capacious. Let us long,
therefore, brothers, because we are going to be filled ... This is our life, that
we should be trained by longing. But holy longing trains us to the extent that
we have pruned our longings away from the love of this world. We have
already said at another time: empty out what is to be filled.) Translations are
taken from *Tractates on the First Epistle of John*, trans. J.W. Retting (Washington, DC: Catholic University of America Press, 1995).

92 For the chronological development of the 'significatory concept of the
Incarnation,' see Johnson, '*Verbum* in Early Augustine,' 48–9: 'From 389

onwards he begins to make explicit parallels between words and incarnation, referring to it as a corporeal demonstration, and even comparing Christ's celestial and earthly presence with the sound of a word which is present everywhere but it is received by each person in its entirety.' Johnson quotes here a passage from *De doctrina christiana* 1.13, in which the analogy between Christ and human utterance is expressed with almost the same words as the later formulation of the *De Trinitate*. On this passage see also Jordan, 'Incarnation and Signification,' 187–8.

93 Johnson ('*Verbum* in Early Augustine,' 30n25) notices that 'the distinction between *verbum* and *vox* ... only develops much later in conjunction with the concept of "inner word." The earliest indication of this distinction is found in Sermon 288, dated about 405. Here Augustine calls Jesus the *verbum*, while John is the *vox*, the voice crying in the wilderness.'

94 See the previous discussion of *De magistro* (11.38) and *Confessions* (11.7). The relation between Christ as inner teacher and the interior word is formulated by L. Ferretter in the following terms: 'The teacher is the inner light of truth in which one can see intellectual objects and judge their truth or falsity; the *verbum quod in corde dicimus* is the image of such an object in consciousness. The word is a likeness of Christ in mental life; the inner light is his presence there' ('The Trace of the Trinity,' 262).

95 The homology between the two middle terms of the proportion, if taken into the realms of mathematics would, curiously, allow the interpretation of Augustine's system of language as a hyperbola. The middle terms being the same (x = Christ; then $nx:x = x: x/n$; or, dividing by x, $n:1 = 1:1/n$), the first and the last terms are one the inverse of the other. Representing the three elements of the proportion in Cartesian coordinates (x, y), we get the following plot:

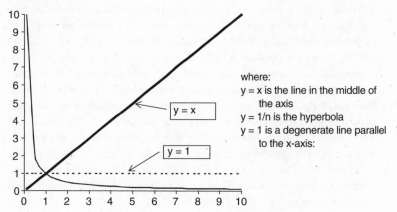

where:
$y = x$ is the line in the middle of the axis
$y = 1/n$ is the hyperbola
$y = 1$ is a degenerate line parallel to the x-axis:

Taking the limit for x going to infinity, the straight line goes to infinity, whereas the hyperbola tends to zero: that is to say that when the Word *in principio* tends to infinite (eternity), the exterior word (sign) tends to zero. Moreover the point where the straight line (Word *in principio*) and the hyperbola (exterior word) intersect is also the point where the line y = 1 (the mathematical representation of the middle term of the above proportion) passes. This line is constant in time and unchangeable. If we go back to our original proportion, 1 = Christ, the hyperbola represents the trajectory of the human being and time, that intersects the line of God/eternity in Christ. In the perspective of eternity, the human semiotic/temporal universe is reduced to zero, and Christ stays constant.

96 *De Trinitate* 15.9.16: 'Proinde, quantum mihi videtur, sicut nomine speculi imaginem voluit intellegi; ita nomine aenigmatis quamvis similitudinem, tamen obscuram et ad perspiciendum difficilem.' (Therefore, it seems to me, as he would have us understand an image by the word 'mirror,' so a likeness by the word 'enigma,' yet a likeness that is obscure and difficult to perceive.)

97 *De Trinitate* 15.14.24: 'Verbum autem nostrum, illud quod non habet sonum neque cogitationem soni, sed eius rei quam videndo intus dicimus, et ideo nullius linguae est; atque inde utcumque simile est in hoc aenigmate illi Verbo Dei; quod etiam Deus est; quoniam sic et hoc de nostra nascitur, quemadmodum et illud de scientia Patris natum est.' (But that word of ours which has neither sound nor thought of sound, is the word of that thing which we inwardly speak by seeing it and, therefore, it belongs to no language; hence, in this enigma there is a likeness, be it what it may, to that Word of God who is also God, since it is also so born from our knowledge as that Word was also born from the knowledge of the Father.)

98 This last quality is particularly interesting because the interior word, within the framework of the analogy, acquires some of the performative qualities of the Word of God. Action, then, is portrayed as 'the creature' of the interior word. See *De Trinitate* 15.11.20: 'Est et haec in ista similitudine verbi nostri similitudo Verbi Dei, quia potest esse verbum nostrum quod non sequatur opus; opus autem esse non potest, nisi praecedat verbum: sicut Verbum Dei potuit esse nulla existente creatura; creatura vero nulla esse posset, nisi per ipsum per quod facta sunt omnia.' (In the likeness of our word, there is also this likeness of the Word of God, that our word can exist and yet no work may follow it; but there can be no work unless the word precedes, just as the Word of God could be, even though no creature existed, but no creature could be, except through that Word through whom all things were made.)

99 *De Trinitate* 15.15.25: 'Sed quid est quod potest esse verbum, et ideo iam dignum est verbi nomine? Quid est, inquam, hoc formabile nondumque formatum, nisi quiddam mentis nostrae, quod hac atque hac volubili quadam motione iactamus, cum a nobis nunc hoc nunc illud, sicut inventum fuerit vel occurrerit cogitatur? Et tunc fit verum verbum, quando illud quod nos dixi volubili motione iactare, ad id quod scimus pervenit, atque inde formatur, eius omnimodam similitudinem capiens; ut quomodo res quaeque scitur, sic etiam cogitetur, idest, sine voce, sine vocis cogitatione, quae profecto alicuius linguae est, sic in corde dicatur.' (What is that which can be a word, and, therefore, is already worthy of the name of a word? What, I say, is this word, formable and not yet formed, except something of our own mind which we cast this way and that by a kind of revolving motion, according as we think now of this and now of that thing, just as they are found, or as they occur to our mind? And it then becomes a true word when that which we cast, as I have said, by a revolving motion, arrives at that which we know, and is formed by it by taking its perfect likeness, so that as any thing is known, so it is also thought, so it is spoken in the heart, that is, without sound, without the thought of sound, such as certainly belongs to some language.)

See also 15.16.25: 'Quapropter ita dicitur illud Dei Verbum, ut Dei cogitatio non dicatur, ne aliquid esse quasi volubile credatur in Deo, quod nunc accipiat, nunc recipiat formam, ut verbum sit, eamque possit amittere, atque informiter quodam modo volutari.' (Thus He is so called 'the Word of God' as not to be called 'the thought of God,' lest it be believed that there is, as it were, something revolving in God that now receives and now recovers a form in order to be a word, and that it can lose this form, and in some manner revolve formlessly.)

100 Insofar as the word of man is concerned, the vision face to face will grant the disappearance of falsity, of the 'revolving motion' in thought, and of the formed vs. unformed distinction (*De Trinitate* 15.16).

101 For the interior word, see Schindler, *Wort und Analogie*; Johnson, 'Verbum in Early Augustine'; Alici, *Il linguaggio come segno e come testimonianza*, 38–73; G. Santi, 'Interiorità e Verbum mentis,' in *Interiorità e Intenzionalità in S. Agostino*, ed. L. Alici (Rome: Augustinianum, 1990), 133–43; and Vecchio, *Le parole come segni*, 57–68. For the notion of interior word in ancient philosophy, see C. Chiesa, 'Le problème du langage intérieur dans la philosophie antique de Platon à Porphire,' *Historie épistémologie langage* 1, no. 2 (1992): 15–30. For the interior word in the Middle Ages, see H. Arens, '*Verbum cordis*: zur Sprachphilosophie des Mittelalters,' *Historiographia Linguistica* 7 (1980): 13–27.

102 See, for instance, *In Evangelium Ioannis* 14.7: 'Nos loquimur verba volantia
et transeuntia: mox ut sonuerit ore tuo verbum tuum, transit; peragit strepi-
tum suum et transit in silentium. Numquid potes sequi sonum tuum, et
tenere ut stet? Cogitatio tamen tua manet, et de ipsa cogitatione manente
dicis multa verba transeuntia.' (We speak fleeting and transient words: as
soon as your word has sounded in your mouth, it passes, it produces its
noise and passes into silence. Can you pursue your sound and hold it fast so
that it may stay? Yet your thought remains, and about that thought which
remains you say many words which pass away.)

The whole *Sermo 288* (*de voce et verbo*) deals with the relationship between
the interior and the exterior word, where *verbum* stands for Jesus this time,
and *vox* for John the Baptist. Augustine also describes the other half of communication: the 'passing voice' gets to the hearer and there, as a sign,
points to another word/thought that stay. The speaker's thought is not
diminished by its passing in time and becoming the hearer's.

103 On the twofold nature of the interior word, see in particular Vecchio, *Le
parole come segni*, 58–63.

104 Translations from the *De catechizandis rudibus* are taken from *The First Catechetical Instructions*, trans. J. Christopher (New York: Newman, 1962).

105 *De catechizandis rudibus* 2.3: 'Totum enim quod intelligo, volo ut qui me
audit intelligat; et sentio me non ita loqui, ut hoc efficiam: maxime quia ille
intellectus quasi rapida coruscatione perfundit animum, illa autem locutio
tarda et longa est, longeque dissimilis, et dum ista volvitur, iam se ille in
secreta sua condidit.' (For I desire my hearer to understand all that I understand; and I feel that I am not speaking in such a manner as to effect that.
This is chiefly because intuition floods the mind, as it were, with a sudden
flash of light, while the expression of it in speech is a slow, drawn out, and
far different process, and while speech is being formed, intellectual apprehension has already hidden itself in its secret recesses.)

106 *De catechizandis rudibus* 2.3: 'Aliter enim Latine ira dicitur, aliter Grece, aliter
atque aliter aliarum diversitate linguarum: non autem Latinus aut Graecus
est vultus irati. Non itaque omnes gentes intellegant, cum quisque dicit: iratus sum, sed Latini tantum; at si affectus excandescentis animi exeat in
faciem vultumque faciat, omnes sentiunt qui intuentur iratum. Sed neque
ita licet educere et quasi exporrigere in sensum audientium per sonum
vocis illa vestigia, quae imprimit intellectus memoriae, sicut apertus et manifestus est vultus: illa enim sunt intus in animo, iste foris in corpore. Quapropter coniiciendum est, quantum distet sonus oris nostrae ab illo ictu
intelligentiae, quando ne ipsi quidem impressioni memoriae similis est.'

(For instance, anger is designated by one word in Latin, by another in Greek, and by others again in various other tongues; but the expression on the face of an angry man is neither Latin nor Greek. Thus it is that not all nations understand when a man says: *Iratus sum*, but Latins only; but if the feeling present in his mind as it kindles to white heat comes out upon his features and gives him a certain look, all who see him understand that he is angry. But again, it is not in our power to bring forth those imprints which intellectual apprehension stamps upon the memory and, as it were, submit them by the sound of our voice to the perception of those listening, in any way parallel to the open and evident expression of the face. For the former are within, in the mind; but the latter is without, in the body. And, therefore, we might infer how much the sound of our voice differs from that instantaneous flash of intellectual apprehension, seeing that it does not resemble even the memory-impression.)

Contrary to what he says in this passage, in *De Trinitate* 15.10.19, Augustine treats sound and gesture in the same way: 'Necesse est enim cum verum loquimur, id est, quod scimus loquimur, ex ipsa scientia quam memoria te-nemus, nascatur verbum quod eiusmodi sit omnino, cuiusmodi est illa scien-tia de qua nascitur. Formata quippe cogitatio ab ea re quam scimus, verbum est quod in corde dicimus: quod nec graecum est, nec latinum, nec lin-guae alicuius alterius; sed cum id opus est in eorum quibus loquimur per-ferre notitiam, aliquod signum quo significetur assumitur. Et plerumque sonus, aliquando etiam nutus, ille auribus, ille oculis exhibetur, ut per signa corporalia etiam corporis sensibus verbum quod mente gerimus innotescat. Nam et innuere quid est, nisi quodam modo visibiliter dicere?' (For when we speak the truth, that is, speak of what we know, then the word which is born from the knowledge itself which we retain in the mem-ory must be altogether of the same kind as that knowledge from which it is born. For the thought formed from that thing which we know is the word which we speak in our heart, and it is neither Greek, nor Latin, nor of any other language, but when we have to bring it to the knowledge of those to whom we are speaking, then some sign is assumed by which it may be made known. And generally this is a sound, but at a time also a nod; the former is shown to the ears, the latter to the eyes, in order that that word which we bear in our mind may also become known by bodily signs to the senses of the body. For even to nod, what else is but to speak, as it were in a visible manner?)

107 See *De Trinitate* 15.11.20: 'Omnium namque sonantium verba linguarum etiam in silentio cogitantur, et carmina percurruntur animo, tacente ore

corporis: nec solum numeri syllabarum, verum etiam modi cantilenarum, cum sint corporales, et ad eum, qui vocatur auditus, sensum corporis perti- nentes, per incorporeas quasdam imagines suas praesto sunt cogitantibus, et tacite cuncta ista volventibus.' (For all words, no matter in what language they may sound, are also thought in silence; and hymns run through our mind, even when the mouth of the body is silent; not only the numbers of the syllables, but also the melodies of the hymns, since they are corporeal and belong to that sense of the body called 'hearing,' are present by their own kind of incorporeal images to those who think of them, and silently turn all of them over in their minds.)

108 *De Trinitate* 15.11.20: 'Sed illud Verbum Dei quaerimus qualitercumque per hanc similitudinem nunc videre, de quo dictum est: *Deus erat Verbum*; de quo dictum est: *Omnia per ipsum facta sunt*; de quo dictum est: *Verbum caro factum est*; de quo dictum est: *Fons sapientiae Verbum Dei in excelsis*. Pervenien- dum est ergo ad illud verbum hominis, ad verbum rationalis animantis, ad verbum non de Deo natae, sed a Deo factae imaginis Dei, quod neque pro- lativum est in sono, neque cogitativum in similitudine soni, quod alicuius linguae esse necesse sit, sed quod omnia quibus significatur signa praecedit, et gignitur de scientia quae manet in animo, quando eadem scientia intus dicitur, sicuti est. Simillima est enim visio cogitationis, visioni scientiae. Nam quando per sonum dicitur, vel per aliquod corporale signum, non dic- itur sicuti est, sed sicut potest videri audirive per corpus. Quando ergo quod in notitia est, hoc est in verbo, tunc est verum verbum, et veritas, qualis exspectatur ab homine, ut quod est in ista, hoc sit et in illo; quod non est in ista, non sit et in illo; hic agnoscitur: *Est, est; Non, non*.' (But by means of this likeness we are endeavoring to see that Word of God, in whatever way we can, of whom it was said: 'The Word was God,' of whom it was said: 'All things were made through him,' of whom it was said: 'The Word was made flesh,' of whom it was said: 'The Word of God on high is the fountain of wis- dom.' We must, therefore, come to that word of man, to the word of a living being endowed with reason, to the word of the image of God, not born of God but made by God: this word cannot be uttered in sound nor thought in the likeness of sound, such as must be done with the word of any language; it precedes all the signs by which it is signified, and is begotten by the knowledge which remains in the mind when this same knowledge is spoken inwardly, just as it is. For the sight of thought is very similar to the sight of knowledge. For, when it is spoken through a sound or through some bodily sign, it is not spoken just as it is, but as it can be seen or heard through the body. When, therefore, that which is in the knowledge is in the word, then

it is a true word, and the truth which is expected from man, so that what is in the knowledge is also in the word, and what is not in the knowledge is not in the word; it is here that we recognize: 'Yes, yes; no, no.')

109 Clear expositions of this key issue in Augustine's philosophy can be found in Gilson, *Christian Philosophy*, esp. 217–24; Bodei, *Ordo amoris*, 163–87; Coleman, *Ancient and Medieval Memories*, 101–11; and in the introduction by A. Trapè and F. Sciacca to *La Trinità* (Rome: Città Nuova, 1998). For the role of the Word within the Trinity and for Augustine's theology in the context of early Christian doctrine, see H. Paissac, *Théologie du verbe: Saint Augustin et saint Thomas* (Paris: Les éditions du Cerf, 1951), 1–100. For the Trinity in connection to language, see Alici, *Il linguaggio come segno e come testimonianza*, 55–63; Daniels, 'The Argument of the *De Trinitate* and Augustine's Theory of Signs; and Ferretter, 'The Trace of the Trinity.'

110 Augustine started working on the *De Trinitate* around 399 (at the same time as the writing of Book 13 of the *Confessions*). The first twelve books were completed within the year 412; this partial version was released without Augustine's consent. The completed (end of Book 12 to Book 15) and revised version was finished by 420–1.

111 The traditional division is today considered overly reductive and is often challenged by scholars, especially in the light of Augustine's own summary of the work at the beginning of Book 15. See Trapè, introduction to *La Trinità*, xv–xvi; and Daniels, 'The Argument of the *De Trinitate*,' 33–7.

112 Gilson, *Christian Philosophy*, 351n21, notices that 'Augustine successively proposed the most diverse traces of the Trinity, and yet none of them excludes the other' and lists some of the most interesting.

113 On the theme of image and likeness, see Gilson, *Christian Philosophy*, 210–14; and R.A. Markus, '*Imago* and *similitudo* in Augustine,' *Revue des études augustiniennes* 7 (1971): 125–43.

114 For a clear exposition of the scriptural names, see Trapè's introduction to *La Trinità*, xxxix–xli.

115 For the second person as the Strength and the Wisdom of God, see Book 6.1–4.

116 See *De Trinitate* 6.5.7: 'Spiritus ergo Sanctus commune aliquid est Patris et Filii, quidquid illud est, aut ipsa communio consubstantialis et coaeterna; quae si amicitia convenienter dici potest, dicatur, sed aptius dicitur caritas.' (The Holy Spirit is, therefore, something common, whatever it is, between the Father and the Son. But this communion itself is consubstantial and co-eternal, and if this communion itself can be appropriately designated as friendship, let it be so called, but it is more aptly called love.)

117 *De Trinitate* 6.10.11: 'Imago enim si perfecte implet illud cuius imago est, ipsa coaequatur ei, non illud imagini suae. In qua imagine speciem nominavit, credo, propter pulchritudinem ubi iam est tanta congruentia et prima aequalitas et prima similitudo nulla in re dissidens et nullo modo inaequalis et nulla ex parte dissimilis, sed ad identidem respondens ei cuius imago est.' (For if any image answers perfectly to that of which it is the image, then it is made equal to it, not the object to its own image. He gave the name form to the Image, I believe, on account of the beauty which arises from this perfect harmony, this primal equality, this primal similarity, where there exists no difference, no disproportion, no dissimilarity, but which corresponds in everything to that of which it is the image.)

118 *De Trinitate* 6.10.11: 'hoc esse est unum omnia tamquam Verbum perfectum, cui non desit aliquid et ars quaedam omnipotentis atque sapientis Dei plena omnium rationum viventium incommutabilium, et omnes unum in ea sicut ipsa unum de uno cum quo unum. Ibi novit omnia Deus quae fecit per ipsam, et ideo cum decedant et succedant tempora, non decedit aliquid vel succedit scientiae Dei. Non enim haec quae creata sunt ideo sciuntur a Deo quia facta sunt, ac non potius ideo facta sunt, vel mutabilia quia immutabiliter ab eo sciuntur.' (The Image is a perfect word to which nothing is wanting; it is as it were the art of the omnipotent and wise God, full of all the living and immutable essences, and all in it are one, as itself is one from one, with whom it is one. Therein God knows all things which he has made through it, and, therefore, although the times come and go, nothing comes and goes in the knowledge of God. For these things which have been created are not known by God because they have been made, rather they have been made, even though changeable, because they are known unchangeably by him.)

119 For the gluing powers of the Holy Spirit, this time between Christ and the soul, see also *De doctrina christiana* 1.34.38: 'Sic enim ait: *Ego sum via et veritas et vita*, hoc est, per me venitur, ad me pervenitur, in me permanetur. Cum enim ad ipsum pervenitur, etiam ad Patrem pervenitur, quia per aequalem ille cui est aequalis agnoscitur; vinciente et tamquam agglutinante nos Spiritu Sancto, quo in summo atque incommutabili bono permanere possimus.' (For Christ says, 'I am the way, the truth, and the life'; that is, 'you come by me, you come to me, you abide in me.' For when you come to him, you come also to the Father, because God, to whom he is equal, is recognized through his equal, and the spirit binds us and as it were cements us together, so that we can abide in the supreme and unchangeable good.)

120 *De Trinitate* 6.10.12: 'Haec igitur omnia quae arte divina facta sunt et unitatem quamdam in se ostendunt et speciem et ordinem. Quidquid enim

horum est et unum aliquid est, sicut sunt naturae corporum ingeniaque
animarum, et aliqua specie formatur, sicut sunt figurae vel qualitates corporum ac doctrinae vel artes animarum, et ordinem aliquem petit aut
tenet, sicut sunt pondera vel collocationes corporum atque amores aut
delectationes animarum. Oportet igitur ut Creatorem *per ea quae facta sunt
intellecta conspicientes* Trinitatem intellegamus, cuius in creatura quomodo
dignum est apparet *vestigium.*' (All these things, therefore, which have been
made by the divine art, manifest a certain unity, form and order in themselves. For each of them is some one thing, as are the natures of the bodies
and the skills of the souls; is shaped according to a determined form, as are
the figures and qualities of bodies and the sciences and arts of souls; and
either seeks for or maintains a certain order as are the weights and arrange-
ments of bodies and the loves and delights of the souls. When in our mind,
therefore, we perceive the Creator through the things which have been
made, we have to recognize Him as the Trinity of which a trace appears, as
is fitting, in the creature.)

121 *De Trinitate* 8.10.14: 'Quid est autem dilectio vel caritas, quam tantopere
Scriptura divina laudat et praedicat, nisi amor boni? Amor autem alicuius
amantis est, et amore aliquid amatur. Ecce tria sunt: amans, et quod amatur,
et amor. Quid est ergo amor, nisi quaedam vita duo aliqua copulans, vel
copulari appetens, amantem scilicet, et quod amatur? Et hoc etiam in extre-
mis carnalibusque amoribus ita est.' (But what is love or charity, which the
Divine Scripture praises and proclaims so highly, if not the love of the
good? Now love is of someone who loves, and something is loved with love.
So then there are three: the lover, the beloved, and the love. What else is
love, therefore, except a kind of life which binds or seeks to bind some two
together, namely, the lover and the beloved? And this is so even in external
and carnal love.)

In 15.6.10, where he sums up the reflections of the preceding books,
Augustine refers to this first trinity as ineffable.

122 The contrast between the outer and the inner trinity is explained through a
comparison between science and wisdom (Book 12). In Book 14, where
Augustine sums up the contrast between science and wisdom, Augustine
explains their working in terms of trinitarian analogy. Science works according to 'signs, knowledge of the learner, will,' and therefore 'memory of the
signs, gaze of the mind, will' (14.8); whereas wisdom according to 'memory,
sight, love,' and therefore 'memory, understanding, will.'

123 *De Trinitate* 9.4.4: 'Sicut autem duo quaedam sunt, mens et amor eius, cum
se amat; ita quaedam duo sunt, mens et notitia, cum se novit. Igitur ipsa
mens et amor et notitia eius tria quaedam sunt et haec tria unum sunt et

cum perfecta sunt, equalia sunt.' (But just as there are two things, the mind
and its love, when it loves itself, so there are two things, the mind and its
knowledge, when it knows itself. Therefore, the mind itself, its love and its
knowledge are a kind of trinity; these three are one, and when they are pre-
fect they are equal.)

124 *De Trinitate* 9.7.12: 'Cum autem ad alios loquimur, verbo intus manenti mi-
nisterium vocis adhibemus, aut alicuius signi corporalis, ut per quandam
commemorationem sensibilem tale aliquid fiat etiam in animo audientis,
quale de loquentis animo non recedit.' (But in conversing with others we
add the service of our voice or of some bodily sign to the word that remains
within, in order to produce in the mind of the listener, by a kind of sensible
remembrance, something similar to that which does not depart from the
mind of the speaker.)

Although Christ is not mentioned in this passage, L. Ferretter notices a
suggestive fact: the word *commemoratio*, here used to describe the passage
from inner to outer word, 'recalls the institution of the Eucharist, "hoc est
corpus meum, quod pro vobis datur; hoc facite in meam commemorationem"' ('The Trace of the Trinity,' 261).

125 *De Trinitate* 9.7–8.13: 'Quod verbum amore concipitur, sive creaturae, sive
Creatoris, id est aut naturae mutabilis, aut incommutabilis veritatis. Ergo
aut cupiditate aut caritate; non quo non sit amanda creatura, sed si ad creatorem refertur ille amor, non iam cupiditas sed caritas erit. Tunc enim est
cupiditas, cum propter se amatur creatura. Tunc non utentem adiuvat, sed
corrumpit fruentem. Cum ergo aut par nobis aut inferior creatura sit, infe-
riore utendum est ad Deum, pari autem fruendo sed in Deo. Sicut enim te
ipso, non in te ipso frui debes, sed in eo qui fecit te; sic etiam illo quem di-
ligis tamquam te ipsum.' (This word is conceived in love, whether it be the
word of the creature or the word of the Creator, that is, of a changeable
nature or of the unchangeable truth. Therefore, it is conceived either by
[lust], or love: not that the creature ought not to be loved, but if that love
for him is referred to the Creator, it will no longer be [lust] but love. For
[lust] is then present when the creature is loved on account of himself.
Then it does not help him who uses it, but corrupts him who enjoys it. Since
the creature, therefore, is either equal or inferior to us, we must use the
inferior for God and enjoy the equal, but in God. For just as you ought to
enjoy yourself, but not in yourself but in Him who made you, so you ought
also to enjoy him whom you love as yourself.)

Here and elsewhere I translate *cupiditas* as 'lust,' as opposed to the translator's 'desire,' in order not to confuse it with the positive aspect of desire.

126 *De Trinitate* 9.9.14: 'Conceptum autem verbum et natum idipsum est, cum voluntas in ipsa notitia conquiescit, quod fit in amore spiritalium. Qui enim, verbi gratia, perfecte novit perfecteque amat iustitiam, iam iustus est, etiamsi nulla exsistat secundum eam forinsecus per membra corporis operandi necessitas. In amore autem carnalium temporaliumque rerum, sicut in ipsis animalium fetibus, alius est conceptus verbi, alius partus. Illic enim quod cupiendo concipitur, adipiscendo nascitur. Quoniam non sufficit avaritiae nosse et amare aurum nisi et habeat.' (The word that has been conceived and born is one and the same when the will rests in the knowledge of itself; this happens in the love of spiritual things. For example, he who knows justice perfectly and loves it perfectly is already just, even though the necessity does not exist for acting outwardly according to it through the members of his body. But in the love of carnal and temporal things, as in the offspring of animals, the conception of the word is one thing and the birth another thing. In such cases, what is conceived by desiring is born by attaining. For it does not suffice for avarice to know and love gold, unless it also possesses it.)

127 The *caritas* vs. *cupiditas* pattern has an interesting outcome in the field of vision, which Augustine chooses as the sense to exemplify the trinity of the outer man, in *De Trinitate* 11. There too the will runs the risk of turning into *cupiditas*, or worse, *libido*. And, interestingly, desire for signs turns itself into a sign (the chameleon, the birthmarks): 'Voluntas autem tantam habet vim copulandi haec duo [species corporis et imago eius], ut et sensum formandum admoveat ei rei quae cernitur, et in ea formatum teneat. Et si tam violenta est, ut possit vocari amor, aut cupiditas, aut libido, etiam ceterum corpus animantis vehementer afficit, et ubi non resistit pigrior duriorque materies, in similem speciem coloremque commutat. Licet enim videre corpusculum chamaeleontis ad colores quos videt facillima conversione variari. Aliorum autem animalium, quia non est ad conversionem facilis . corpulentia, fetus plerumque produnt libidines matrum, quid cum magna delectatione conspexerint ... Sed anima rationalis deformiter vivit, cum secundum trinitatem exterioris hominis vivit; id est, cum ad ea quae forinsecus sensum corporis formant, non laudabilem voluntatem, qua haec ad utile aliquid referat, sed turpem cupiditatem qua his inhaerescat, accomodat' (11.2.5, and 3.6). (The will possesses such power in uniting these two that it moves the senses to be formed to that thing which is seen, and keeps fixed on it when it has been formed. And if it is so violent that it can be called love, or [lust], or passion, it likewise exerts a powerful influence on the rest of the body of this living being. And where a duller and harder mat-

ter does not offer resistance, it changes it into a similar form and color. Note how easily the little body of the chameleon turns very easily into the colors that it sees. In other animals, whose bodily bulk does not lend itself so easily to such changes, the offspring usually show some traces of the passionate desires of their mothers, whatever it was that they gazed upon with great delight ... The rational soul, however, lives disgracefully when it lives according to the trinity of the outer man, that is, when it applies to those things which form the sense of the body from without – not the laudable will by which it refers them to some useful end, but the shameful (lust) by which it has clung to them.)

128 *De Trinitate* 9.12.18: 'quia notitia iam inventum est, quod partum vel repertum dicitur, quod saepe praecedit inquisitio eo fine quietura' (because that has already been found through knowledge which is called born or discovered, and is usually preceded by a search which will come to rest in its knowledge as its goal).

129 *De Trinitate* 9.12.18: 'Nam inquisitio est appetitus inveniendi, quod idem valet si dicas, reperiendi. Quae autem reperiuntur, quasi pariuntur, unde proli similia sunt; ubi nisi in ipsa notitia? Ibi enim quasi expressa formantur. Nam etsi iam erant res quas quaerendo invenimus, notitia tamen ipsa non erat, quam sicut prolem nascentem deputamus. Porro appetitus ille, qui est in quaerendo, procedit a quaerente, et pendet quodam modo, neque requiescit fine quo intenditur nisi id quod queritur inventum quaerenti copuletur. Qui appetitus, id est, inquisitio, quamvis amor esse non videatur, quod id quod notum est, amatur; hoc enim adhuc ut cognoscatur agitur, tamen ex eodem genere quiddam est. Nam voluntas iam dici potest, quia omnis qui quaerit invenire vult. Quod si ardenter atque instanter vult, studere dicitur; quod maxime in assequendis atque adipiscendis quibusque doctrinis dici solet.' (For inquiry is a desire to find, which is the same as saying, to discover. But things that are discovered are, as it were, brought forth. Hence, they are similar to an offspring; but how else are they born, except through knowledge itself? For they are, as it were, uttered there and formed. For even though the things already were, which we find by seeking, yet the knowledge itself did not exist which we regard as an offspring that is born. Further, that desire, which is latent in seeking, proceeds from one who seeks, remains as it were in suspense, and only comes to rest in the goal towards which it is directed, when that which is sought has been found and is united with him who seeks. Although this desire, that is, this seeking does not seem to be love, by which that which is known is loved, for we are still striving to know, yet it is something of the same kind. For it can already be

called 'will,' since everyone who seeks wishes to find; and if what he seeks belongs to the order of knowledge, then everyone who seeks wishes to know. And if he wishes it ardently and earnestly, he is said to study, a term we generally use for those who pursue and acquire any branch of learning.)

130 *De Trinitate* 10.1.2: 'Quid ergo amat, nisi quia novit atque intuetur in rationibus rerum quae sit pulchritudo doctrinae, qua continentur notitiae signorum omnium; et quae sit utilitas in ea peritia, qua inter se humana societas sensa communicat, ne sibi hominum coetus deteriores sint quavis solitudine, si cogitationes suas colloquendo non misceant? Hanc ergo speciem decoram et utilem cernit anima, et novit, et amat; eamque in se perfici studet, quantum potest, quisquis vocum significantium quaecumque ignorat, inquirit. Aliud est enim quod eam in veritatis luce conspicit, aliud quod in sua facultate concupiscit. Conspicit namque in luce veritatis quam magnum et quam bonum sit omnes omnium gentium linguas intellegere ac loqui, nullamque ut alienigenam audire, et a nullo ita audiri. Cuius notitiae decus cogitatione iam cernitur, amaturque res nota; quae ita conspicitur, atque inflammat studia discentium, ut circa eam moveantur, eique inhient in omni opera quam impendunt consequendae tali facultati, ut etiam usu amplectantur quod ratione praenoscunt; atque ita quisque, cui facultati spe propinquat, ei ferventius amore inardescit.' (What does he love then, except that he knows and beholds in the reason of things, what the beauty of learning is, in which the knowledge of all the signs is contained; and what usefulness there is in that skill by which human society mutually communicates its thoughts, so that the assemblies of men may not be worse for them than any solitude, if they were to share their thoughts in conversation. The soul, therefore, perceives, knows and loves this beautiful and useful form, and whoever seeks the meaning of whatever significant words he does not know is endeavoring as much as he can to perfect it in himself. For what he sees in the light of the truth is one thing, and what he desires with his own faculty is another thing. For in the light of the truth he realizes how great and how good it is to understand and to speak all the languages of all the countries, to hear no language as foreign, and to be so heard in every language that no one may detect him as a foreigner. The splendor of such knowledge is already seen in his thoughts, and is loved by him as something known; and it is so seen and so arouses the zeal of learners that they are spurred into activity on account of it. They yearn for it in all the labor which they expend in acquiring this faculty, so that they may also embrace in practice what they already know in theory. And so the closer he comes to this faculty of hope, the more ardently he is inflamed with love.)

131 *De Trinitate* 10.1.2: 'Omnibus enim fere animis rationalibus in promptu est
ad videndum huius peritiae pulchritudo, qua hominum inter se cogitata,
significantium vocum enuntiatione noscuntur; propter hoc notum decus,
et ob hoc amatum quia notum, studiose quaeritur verbum illud ignotum.'
(For the beauty of this knowledge, through which men's thoughts are
mutually made known by the enunciation of significant words is quickly discerned by almost all rational minds; and because he knows the beauty of
this knowledge and loves it because he knows it, he, therefore, eagerly
searches of the unknown word.)

For another fascinating account of the process of learning, see *De Trinitate*
10.5.7: 'tanta vis est amoris, ut ea quae cum amore diu cogitaverit, eisque
curae glutino inhaeserit, attrahat se cum etiam cum ad se cogitandam
quodam modo redit. Et quia illa corpora sunt, quae foris per sensus carnis
adamavit, eorumque diuturna quadam familiaritate implicata est, nec se
cum potest introrsus tamquam in regionem incorporeae naturae ipsa corpora inferre, imagines eorum convolvit et rapit factas in semetipsa de
semetipsa.' (yet the force of love is so great that the mind draws in with itself
those things upon which it has long reflected with love, and to which it has
become attached by its devoted care, even when it returns in some way to
think of itself. And because they are bodies which it has loved outside of itself
through the senses of the body, and with which it has become entangled by a
kind of daily familiarity, it cannot bring them into itself as though into a
country of incorporeal nature, and, therefore, it fastens together their
images, which it has made out of itself, and forces them into itself.)

132 For the image of God in the creature, see *Confessions* 13 and *De Trinitate* 14.
For the process of deformation and reformation of that image by means of
love and desire and through Christ, see Bochet, *Saint Augustin et le désir de
Dieu*, 193–231.

133 See *De Trinitate* 14.4.6: 'Ac per hoc si secundum hoc facta est *ad imaginem
Dei* quod uti ratione atque intellectu ad intellegendum et conspiciendum
Deum potest, profecto ab initio quo esse coepit ista tam magna et mira
natura, sive ita obsoleta sit haec imago, ut pene nulla sit, sive obscura atque
deformis, sive clara et pulchra sit; semper est.' (Therefore if it [the soul]
were made according to the image of God in respect to this, namely, that it
is able to use its reason and intelligence to understand and behold God,
then certainly from the first moment that so great and so marvelous a
nature began to be – whether this image be so effaced as almost to amount
to nothing, or whether it be obscured and disfigured, or whether it be clear
and beautiful – it always exists.)

See also *Confessions* 13.2.3: 'Aut quid te promeruit inchoatio creaturae spiritalis, ut saltem tenebrosa fluitaret similis abysso, tui dissimilis, nisi per idem verbum converteretur ad idem, a quo facta est, atque ab eo illuminata lux fieret, quamvis non aequaliter tamen conformis formae aequali tibi? ... *Bonum autem* illi *est haerere* tibi semper, ne, quod adeptus est conversione, aversione lumen amittat et relabatur in vitam tenebrosae abysso similem.' (What claim upon you had the inchoate spiritual creation even to be merely in a dark fluid state like the ocean abyss? It would have been dissimilar to you unless by your Word it had been converted to the same Word by whom it was made, so that, illuminated by him, it became light and, though not in equal measure, became conformed to a form equal to you ... But 'it is good for it always to cleave to you' lest, by turning away from you and by slipping back into a life like the dark abyss, it lose the light it obtained by turning to you.)

134 *De Trinitate* 14.14.20: 'qua in se imagine Dei tam potens est, ut ei cuius imago est valeat inhaerere. Sic enim ordinata est naturarum ordine, non locorum, ut supra illam non sit nisi ille' [by which image of God itself it (the mind) is so powerful that it is able to cleave to him whose image it is. For it has been so established in the order of natures, not of places, that no one, save He, is above it.].

135 For the role of prayer in Augustine and its connections to the theory of language see Antoni, *La prière chez saint Augustin*.

136 See *Enarrationes in Psalmos* 37.14: 'Et quis agnoscebat unde rugiebat? Subjecit: Et ante te est omne desiderium meum. Non enim ante homines, qui cor videre non possunt: sed ante te est omne desiderium meum. Sit desiderium tuum ante illum; et Pater qui videt in occulto, reddet tibi. Ipsum enim desiderium tuum, oratio tua est: et si continuum desiderium, continua oratio. Non enim frustra dixit Apostolus, Sine intermissione orantes. Numquid sine intermissione genu flectimus, corpus prosternimus, aut manus levamus, ut dicat, Sine intermissione orate? Aut si sic dicimus nos orare, hoc puto sine intermissione non possumus facere. Est alia interior sine intermissione oratio, quae est desiderium. Quidquid aliud agas, si desideras illud sabbatum, non intermittis orare. Si non vis intermittere orare, noli intermittere desiderare. Continuum desiderium tuum, continua vox tua est. Tacebis, si amare destiteris. Qui tacuerunt? De quibus dictum est: Quoniam abundavit iniquitas, refrigescet charitas multorum. Frigus charitatis, silentium cordis est: flagrantia charitatis, clamor cordis est. Si semper manet charitas, semper clamas; si semper clamas, semper desideras; si desideras, requiem recordaris.' (Set your desire on Him, and the Father who sees in

secret will repay you. This very desire is your prayer; and if your desire is continual, your prayer is continual too. It was not for nothing that the Apostle said: *Pray without ceasing.* Can we unceasingly bend our knees, bow down our bodies, or uplift our hands, that he should tell us: *pray without ceasing?* No; if it is thus he bids up pray, I do not think we can do so without ceasing. There is another way of praying, interior and unbroken, and that is the way of desire. Whatever else you are doing, if you long for that sabbath, you are not ceasing to pray. If you do not want to cease praying, do not cease longing. Your unceasing desire is your unceasing prayer. You will lapse into silence if you lose your longing. Who do lapse into silence? Those of whom it has been said: *Because iniquity hath abounded, the charity of many shall grow cold.* The coldness of charity is the heart's silence; its glowing ardor, the heart's outcry. If charity is always present, you are ever crying out; if always crying out, you are ever longing; if longing, you have not forgotten repose.)

Translations are taken from *On the Psalms*, trans. S. Hebgin and F. Corrigan (London: Longmans, Green, 1961).

137 *De Trinitate* 15.28.51: 'Cum ergo pervenerimus ad te, cessabunt *multa* ista quae *dicimus, et non pervenimus*; et manebis unus *omnia in omnibus*: et sine fine dicemus unum laudantes te in unum, et in te facti etiam nos unum.' (But when we shall come to You, these 'many things' which we say and 'fall short' shall cease and You as One shall remain, you who are all in all; and without ceasing we shall say one thing, praising you in the one, we who have also been made one in You.)

2. Modistae: The Syntax of Nature

1 For the twofold implication of the image of the wheel, see John Freccero's remarks on the second last line of the *Divine Comedy* ('sì come rota ch'igualmente è mossa') in 'The Final Image,' in *Dante: The Poetics of Conversion* (Cambridge, MA: Harvard University Press, 1986), 245–57.

2 *Aristoteles Latinus* 1, 9, 192a 12–120: 'Subiecta quidem enim cum forma causa est eorum que fiunt, sicut mater; altera autem pars contrarietatis multotiens imaginabitur ad malefactum ipsius protendenti intellectum neque esse extra omne. Existente enim quodam divino et optimo et appetibili, quod quidem contrarium est ipsi, dicimus, est, aliud autem aptum natum esse appetere et desiderare ipsum secundum ipsius naturam. Quibusdam autem accidit contrarium appetere sui ipsius corruptionem. Et neque ipsa se ipsam possibile est appetere speciem propter id quod non esse indiget, neque contrarium (corruptiva enim sunt ad invicem con-

traria), sed horum est materia, sicut si femina masculi et turpe boni; nisi quod non per se est turpe, sed secundum accidens, neque femina, sed secundum accidens.' (For the one which persists is a joint cause, with the form, of what comes to be – a mother, as it were. But the other part of the contrariety may often seem, if you concentrate your attention on it as an evil agent, not to exist at all. For admitting that there is something divine, good and desirable, we hold that there are two other principles, the one contrary to it, the other such as of its own nature to desire and yearn for it. But the consequence of their view is that the contrary desires its own extinction. Yet the form cannot desire itself, for it is not defective; nor can the contrary desire it, for contraries are mutually destructive. The truth is that what desires the form is matter, as the female desires the male and the ugly the beautiful – only the ugly or the female not in itself but accidentally.)

Translations are taken from *The Complete Works of Aristotle*, vol. 1, ed. J. Barnes (Princeton: Princeton University Press, 1984).

3 See L.G. Kelly, *The Mirror of Grammar: Theology, Philosophy and the Modistae* (Amsterdam: Benjamins, 2002), 57. For desire in the context of medieval hylomorphism, see C. Bynum *The Resurrection of the Body in Western Christianity, 200–1336* (New York: Columbia University Press, 1995), 229–78; and B. Stock, *Myth and Science in the Twelfth Century: A Study of Bernard Silvester* (Princeton: Princeton University Press, 1972), 63–118. For the concept of matter in antiquity and the Middle Ages, see E. McMullin, ed., *The Concept of Matter in Greek and Medieval Philosophy* (Notre Dame: University of Notre Dame Press, 1965).

4 *Physica* 1.3.17: '[materia] potest esse sicut moti a motore, qui habet appetitum, a quo procedens motus est actus mobilis. Et sic materia habet appetitum et hoc modo preordinat sibi finem, in quem directe movetur ... Cum enim materia iam habeat incohationem esse divini in seipsa recipiens actum motoris, desiderat conformari plenius, quantum est possibile, primo, et quia non potest nisi per motum, ideo desiderat transmutari.' (and [matter] can behave as the moved by the mover, which has desire – and the motion proceeding from it is the moving act. And as such matter desires and in this way it organizes itself toward an end, toward which it moves directly ... Since matter already has the disposition of the divine being in itself, when receiving the act of the mover, it desires to conform more fully, as much as it is possible, to it, and since it cannot do it unless by motion, therefore, it desires to transmute.) Translations are mine.

5 *Physica* 1.3.17: 'Secundum quod enim ipsa [forma] est finis motus, sic dicta est esse divinum et optimum et appetibile ... Secundum autem quod quietat

appetitum imperfecti, sic est appetibile quiddam.' (Insofar as the form is the end-term of motion, it is called something divine, good and desirable ... Insofar as it quenches the desire of the imperfect, it is something desirable.)

6 G.L. Bursill-Hall, 'Toward a History of Linguistics in the Middle Ages, 1100–1450,' in *Studies in the History of Linguistics: Traditions and Paradigms*, ed. D. Hymes (Bloomington: Indiana University Press, 1974), 77–92, esp. 79–80.

7 For the critique by their contemporaries and the subsequent decline of the Modistae, see M.A. Covington, *Syntactic Theory in the High Middle Ages: Modistic Models of Sentence Structure* (Cambridge: Cambridge University Press, 1984), 120–6; and A. Maierù, 'Medieval Linguistics,' in *History of Linguistics*, vol. 2, *Classical and Medieval Linguistics*, ed. G. Lepschy (London: Longman, 1994), 303–6.

8 Peirce quotes the *Grammatica speculativa* at length in his lecture on Ockam (1869); Heidegger wrote his dissertation on *Die Kategorien- und Bedeutungslehere des Duns Scotus* (1916); Derrida mentions in passing Thomas of Erfurt in his *On Grammatology*. See J. Zupko, 'Thomas of Erfurt,' The Stanford Encyclopedia of Philosophy (Spring 2003), ed. Edward N. Zalta, http://plato.stanford.edu/archives/spr2003/entries/erfurt/ (accessed 17 December 2006).

9 The work of description and systematization of the Modistae's theory was inaugurated by J. Pinborg with *Die Entwicklung der Sprachtheorie im Mittelalter* (Münster-Copenhagen: Aschendorff-Frost Hansen, 1967). Of the same author see also 'Speculative Grammar,' in *The Cambridge History of Late Medieval Philosophy: From the Rediscovery of Aristotle to the Disintegration of Scolasticism*, ed. N. Kretzmann, A. Kenny, J. Pinborg, and E. Stump (Cambridge: Cambridge University Press, 1982), 253–69. The work of R.W. Hunt has shed light on the modalities of the commentary on Priscian in the Middle Ages and helps reconstruct the early days of speculative grammar. It is now collected in *The History of Grammar in the Middle Ages*, ed. G.L. Bursill-Hall (Amsterdam: Benjamins, 1980). The main references on the Modistae are G.L. Bursill-Hall, *Speculative Grammar of the Middle Ages* (The Hague: Mouton, 1971); I. Rosier, *La grammaire spéculative des Modistes* (Lille: Presses universitaires de Lille, 1983); Covington, *Syntactic Theory in the High Middle Ages*; and C. Marmo, *Semiotica e linguaggio nella scolastica: Parigi, Bologna, Erfurt; La semiotica dei modisti* (Rome: Istituto Storico Italiano per il Medioevo, 1994).

10 For this debate, see W. Keith-Percival, 'Deep and Surface Structure Concepts in Renaissance and Medieval Syntactic Theory,' in *History of Linguistic Thought and Contemporary Linguistics*, ed. H. Parret (Berlin: de Gruyter, 1976), 238–53, and in the same volume, J. Trentman, 'Speculative Grammar

and Transformational Grammar: A Comparison of Philosophical Presuppositions,' 279–301; R. Lambertini, 'Sicut tabernarius vinum significat per circulum: Directions in Contemporary Interpretations of the Modistae,' in *On the Medieval Theory of Signs*, ed. U. Eco and C. Marmo (Amsterdam: Benjamins, 1989), 107–42; P. Benedini, 'La teoria sintattica dei modisti: attualità dei concetti di reggenza e dipendenza,' *Lingua e Stile* 23 (1988): 113–35; and C. Marmo, 'I Modisti e l'ordine delle parole: su alcune difficoltà di una grammatica universale,' *Versus: Quaderni di Studi Semiotici* 61, no. 3 (1992): 47–70.

11 M.D. de Chenu, 'Grammaire et théologie aux XIIe et XIIIe siècle,' *Archives d'histoire doctrinale et littéraire du moyen âge* 10 (1935): 5–28; L.M. de Rijk, *Logica Modernorum: A Contribution to the History of Early Terministic Logic* (Assen: Van Gorcum, 1962); J. Pinborg, *Logik und Semantik im Mittelalter: Ein Überblick* (Stuttgart-Bad Cannstatt: Frommann-Holzboog, 1972); E.J. Ashworth, 'Signification and Modes of Signifying in Thirteenth-Century Logic,' *Medieval Philosophy and Theology* 1 (1991): 39–67; I. Rosier, 'Signes et sacraments: Thomas d'Aquin et la grammaire spéculative,' *Revue des sciences philosophiques et théologiques* 74 (1990): 392–436, and *La parole comme acte: Sur la grammaire et la sémantique au XIIIe siècle* (Paris: Vrin, 1994); L.G. Kelly, 'La *Physique* d'Aristote et la phrase simple dans les ouvrages de grammaire spéculative,' in *La grammaire générale: des modistes aux idéologues*, ed. A. Joly and J. Stefanini (Villeneuve d'Ascq: Publications de l'Université de Lille III, 1977), 107–24, and *The Mirror of Grammar*.

For the attempt to connect the Modistae to Dante, see chapter 3 of the present volume, note 6.

12 For the chronological arrangement of the grammarians, see Pinborg, *Die Entwicklung der Sprachtheorie*, 57–135; Bursill-Hall, *Speculative Grammar*, 32; M.A. Covington, *Syntactic Theory in the High Middle Ages*, 23–4; Rosier, *La grammaire*, 18–22; Marmo, *Semiotica e linguaggio*, 7–12; and Kelly, *The Mirror of Grammar*, 2.

Scholars tend to group the grammarians into three generations. Marmo lists them as follows. First: Martin, Boethius, Matthew of Bologna; second: John, Michel de Marbais, Simon, Gentile da Cingoli; third: Radulphus, Sigier, Thomas. Paris is unquestionably the propulsory centre of Modistic grammar, which also flourishes in Bologna and Erfurt.

The seven authors can be read in the following editions: *Corpus philosophorum danicorum medii aevi*, vol. 2, *Martini de Dacia Opera*, ed. H. Roos (Copenhagen: Gad, 1961); *Corpus philosophorum danicorum medii aevi*, vol. 4, *Boethii Daci Opera*, ed. J. Pinborg and H. Roos (Copenhagen: Gad, 1969); *Corpus philosophorum danicorum medii aevi*, vol. 1, *Iohannis Daci Opera*, ed. A. Otto

(Copenhagen: Gad, 1955); *Corpus philosophorum danicorum medii aevi,* vol. 3, *Simonis Daci Opera,* ed. A. Otto (Copenhagen: Gad, 1963); *Les philosophes belges,* vol. 7, Sigier de Courtrai, *Les oeuvres de Sigier de Courtrai,* ed. G. Wallerand (Louvain: Institut supérieur de philosophie, 1913), and *Studies in the History of Linguistics,* vol. 14, Sigier de Courtrai, *Summa modorum significandi: Sophismata,* ed. J. Pinborg (Amsterdam: Benjamins, 1977); Radulphus Brito, *Quaestiones super Priscianum Minorem,* ed. H. Enders and J. Pinborg (Stuttgart-Bad Cannstatt: Frommann-Holzboog, 1980); Thomas of Erfurt, *Grammatica speculativa,* ed. G.L. Bursill-Hall (London: Longman, 1972). Translations are mine.

Two works are published in the edition of Simon of Dacia: the *Domus gramatice* and the *Quaestiones.* Scholars now maintain that they have to be ascribed to two different authors bearing the same name. The *Domus* is believed to be the work of a pre-modista, sometimes called 'Domifex' to distinguish him from the Simon Modista author of the *Quaestiones.* On this see Pinborg, *Die Entwicklung der Sprachtheorie,* 95–7; Covington, *Syntactic Theory,* 135; and Marmo, *Semiotica e linguaggio,* 6.

13 For the tradition of the commentary on Priscian in the Middle Ages as evidence of the early emergence of speculative grammar, see the studies of R.W. Hunt now collected in *The History of Grammar in the Middle Ages.*

14 The threefold structure of the treatises substitutes the traditional division into *ortographia* (letters and syllables), *prosodia* (accents), *etymologia* (morphology), and *diasyntetica* (syntax). See Bursill-Hall, *Speculative Grammar,* 42–3, 122–3.

15 See C.H. Haskins, *Studies in the History of Mediaeval Science* (Cambridge, MA: Harvard University Press, 1924); J. Le Goff, *Les intellectuelles au moyen âge* (Paris: Seuil, 1957); F. van Steenberghen, *Aristotle in the West* (Louvain: Nauwelaerts, 1970); van Steenberghen, *La philosophie au XIIIe siècle,* 2nd ed. (Louvain: Institut supérieur de philosophie, 1991); and van Steenberghen, *Maître Sigier de Brabant* (Louvain: Publication Universitaires, 1977); R. de Vaux, 'La premiere entrée d'Averroes chez les Latins,' *Revue des sciences philosophiques et théologiques* 22 (1933): 193–245; M. Grabman, *I divieti ecclesiastici di Aristotele sotto Innocenzo III e Gregorio IX* (Rome: Typis Pontificiae Universitatis Gregorianae, 1941); and R. Hissette, *Enquête sur les 219 articles condamnés à Paris le 7 mars 1277* (Louvain: Publications Universitaires, 1977).

16 Sigier and Boethius are often mentioned together in manuscripts relative to the 1277 condemnation. One manuscript containing the 219 condemned propositions carries, for instance, the rubric 'contra Sigierum et Boethium hereticos,' another states that 'principalis assertor istorum articulorum fuit quiddam clericus Boethius appellatus.' See the introduction to *Boethii Daci*

Opera, 31. Although Boethius's work features quite prominently in the 1277 condemnation (see Hissette, *Enquête*, passim), scholars tend to limit his heterodoxy by describing him (or at least some of his work) as moderately Averroistic. See Steenberghen, *La philosophie*, 361–70, and his introduction to the second commentary to Aristotle's *de Anima*, in *Trois commentaires anonymes sur le traité de l'âme d'Aristote*, ed. M. Giele, F. van Steenberghen, and B. Bazán (Louvain: Publications universitaires, 1971), 121–33.

17 See O. Lewry, 'The Oxford Condemnations of 1277 in Grammar and Logic,' in *English Logic and Semantics from the End of the Twelfth Century to the Time of Ockham and Burleigh*, ed. H.A.G. Braakhuis, C.H. Kneepkens, and L.M. de Rijk (Nijmegen: Ingenium, 1981), 235–77. Of the four grammatical propositions condemned, two deal with the congruity of construction ('ego currit, tu currit, currit et curro eque sunt perfecte et congrue orationes. Similiter currens est ego,' and 'Item Socratis legere, Socrati legere sicut Socratem legere,' 254n7), the third with the verb ('Item quod verbum manens verbum potest privari omnibus accidentis,' 257n27), and the fourth with the noun ('Item quod nullum nomen est tertie persone,' 258n32). On the Oxford condemnation, see also I. Rosier, '"O magister ...": Grammaticalité et intelligibilité selon un sophisme du XIIIe siècle,' *Cahiers de l'institut du moyen âge grec et latin* 56 (1988): 1–102, esp. 40–6.

18 Edited by J. Paetow (Berkeley: University of California Press, 1914).

19 Necromancy is said by Henri to come from Toledo and Naples and may stand for the most unorthodox development of Arabic scientific thought in Spain and in the realm of Frederick II.

20 As G. Mazzotta observes in the introduction to his *Dante's Vision and the Circle of Knowledge* (Princeton: Princeton University Press, 1993), 'the Divine Comedy, which begins by resurrecting – literally by recalling – Virgil from his "long silence," both heeds and fulfils the prophecy' (11).

21 On the theoretical primacy of Boethius and for a clear description and interpretation of his discussion of the general problems of language, see G.L. Bursill-Hall, 'Some Notes on the Grammatical Theory of Boethius of Dacia,' in *History of Linguistic Thought and Contemporary Linguistics*, 164–88. Among the other grammarians under consideration, only John dwells more at length on general problems of grammar. See *Summa grammatica*, 47–83.

22 Maierù, 'Medieval Linguistics,' 280.

23 *Modi significandi*, 7: 'quamdiu ipse est in speculatione ipsarum rerum et modorum essendi, qui eis appropriantur, et modorum intelligendi, ipse est philosophus. Cum autem ipsam rem voci copulat faciendo ipsam vocis significatum, et modos essendi modos intelligendi faciendo, et modos intelli-

gendi modos significandi vocis, iam incipit esse grammaticus, – ea enim,
quae ad grammaticam pertinent, ad vocem referuntur.' (insofar as one spec-
ulates on the things themselves, on the modes of being that come from
them, and on the modes of understanding, that one is a philosopher. But
when one joins the thing itself to a voice, making of it the meaning of the
voice, and turning the modes of being into the modes of understanding, and
the modes of understanding into the modes of signifying, one already begins
to be a grammarian: what belongs to grammar refers to the voice.)

24 *Die Entwicklung der Sprachtheorie*, 21–30. See also Covington, *Syntactic Theory*,
19–20. For the history of the classification of sciences in the Middle Ages, see
J.A. Weisheipl, 'Classification of Sciences in Medieval Thought,' *Mediaeval
Studies* 27 (1965): 54–90.

25 Dominicus Gundissalinus, *De divisione philosophiae*, ed. L. Baur (Münster:
Beiträge zur Geschichte der Philosophie des Mittelalters, 1903), 45–6: 'Unde
ad evitanda haec vicia [solecismus et barbarismus] scientia lingue, quae
omnium scienciarum naturaliter prima est, primum in duo diuiditur, scilicet
in scienciam considerandi et obseruandi quid unaqueque dictio significet
apud gentem illam cuius lingua est, et in scientiam observandi regulas
illarum dictionum. Illa est sciencia intelligendi ad quid significandum sin-
gule dictiones sint imposite, ista est sciencia ordinandi singulas dictiones in
oracione ad significandum concepciones anime. Illa naturaliter solo auditu
addiscitur a paruulis, hec doctrina et studio addiscitur ab adultis. Illa solo
usu audiendi, ista regulis magisterii apprehenditur. Illa variatur apud omnes
secundum diuersitatem linguarum, hec pene eadem est apud omnes secundum similitudinem regularum.' (In order to avoid these errors [solecismus
and barbarismus] the science of language, which naturally is the first among
all sciences, is divided into two parts: the science that considers and looks at
the signification of each word among the people who speak that language,
and the science that looks at the rules of those words. The former science
studies the way in which the single words are imposed to signify something,
the latter is the science that orders the single words into speech in order to
signify the concepts of the mind. One is learned by children simply through
listening, the other by adults through learning and study. The former is
apprehended only through hearing, the latter through the rules of schooling. One varies among people, according the diversity of the languages, the
other is basically one for everybody according to the likeness of the rules.)

For the role of Gundissalinus within medieval grammar, see Hunt, *The History of Grammar in the Middle Ages*, 118–31. Gundissalinus seems to diverge
from Alfarabi on the universality of grammar as the science of rules.
Although recognizing that the science of rules can span languages, Alfarabi

held that grammar dealt with a particular language, whereas the common
aspects of languages were the domain of logic. See M. Mahdi, 'Science, Philosophy and Religion in Alfarabi's *Enumeration of the Sciences*,' in *The Cultural
Context of Medieval Learning*, ed. J.E. Murdoch and E.D. Sylla (Dordrecht:
Reidel, 1975), 113–47, esp. 119.

26 *De divisione philosophiae*, 46: 'Quia igitur recte scribendi recteque loquendi
regule in sola arte grammatica inueniuntur, ideo ipsa merito scribendi et
loquendi recte sciencia esse perhibetur.' (Since the rules of writing and
speaking correctly are found only in the grammatical art, it is rightly called
the science of writing and speaking correctly.)

27 For Boethius's classification of sciences and the way it was received in the
Middle Ages, see Weisheipl, 'Classification of Sciences in Medieval Thought.'

28 See Rosier, *La grammaire spéculative*, 38–41; and Kelly, *The Mirror*, 1–10.

29 *Modi significandi*, 17: 'ea, de quibus est grammatica, apprehensibilia sunt ab
intellectu, et etiam habent causas per se, sicut constructio et omnis differen-
tia eius et modi significandi et sic de aliis; propter quod grammatica est scientia.' (the subject matter of grammar is what is apprehensible by the
intellect and has causes in itself, such as construction and all its degrees and
the modes of signifying, etc. Therefore, grammar is a science.)

30 *Modi significandi*, 18: 'grammatica est scientia speculativa, non tamen ipsa est
naturalis nec mathematica nec divina. Et hoc quia ipsa non est essentialis
pars philosophiae, sed est scientia introductoria et valet ad cognitionem sci-
entiarum speculativarum, quae essentiales partes philosophiae sunt. Unde
sciendum quod omnis scientia speculativa, quae est pars essentialis
philosophiae vel naturalis, vel mathematica, vel divina.' (grammar is a speculative science, although it is not natural, mathematical or divine science.
This is why it is not an essential part of philosophy, but it is, instead, an introductory science and it is important in the knowledge of the speculative sciences that are essential parts of philosophy. Therefore, we have to know that
any speculative science which is an essential part of philosophy is either natural, mathematical or divine.)

31 *Modi significandi*, 27: 'abstrahit a sermone graeco et latino divisim, et non
coniunctim. Et iterum grammatica abstrahit a sermone non quantum ad
substantiam sermonis sed quantum ad diversam figurationem vocis, qua differunt diversa idiomata.' ([grammar] abstracts from the Greek and Latin
language separately and not conjointly. Moreover, grammar abstracts from
speech not in terms of substance but in terms of the different figurations of
the voice, through which the various languages differ.)   ·

32 *Modi significandi*, 27: 'grammatica est sermocinalis scientia, qua docetur congrua iunctura dictionum per suos modos significandi in oratione per vocem

expressa, quae quidem iunctura orationum imitatur ordinationem intelligibilium apud intellectum per suos modos intelligendi. Unde omnia, quae grammaticus docet, illa sermonis sunt vel sicut elementa, ut litterae vel syllabae et cetera, vel sicut passiones sermonum et principia illarum passionum. Si quid autem fuerit ante sermonem, hoc non considerat grammaticus in quantum grammaticus, sed secundum quod philosophus.' (grammar is a science of language which teaches the correct joining of expressions through their modes of signifying, as it is expressed through voice in speech. This joining of speech imitates the order of the intelligibles in the intellect through their modes of understanding. Therefore, all things which the grammarian teaches belong to speech, either as elements [letters, syllables etc.] or as passions of speech and the principles of those passions. If something exists before speech, the grammarian doesn't consider it is as a grammarian, but as a philosopher.)

33 *Modi significandi*, 31: 'Sic et grammaticus docet modum exprimendi mentis conceptum intentum per sermonem congruum, et hoc est subiectum in grammatica et eius finale bonum, quod expectatur ex hac scientia, quae grammatica est.' (Thus the grammarian teaches the way of expressing a concept understood by the mind through correct speech. This is the subject of grammar and the final goal, which is expected from this science which is called grammar.)

34 *Modi significandi*, 33–4: 'grammatica est scientia specialis, cuius ratio est, quia ipsa docet aliquod scibile speciale distinctum contra scibilia, quae docent aliae artes et scientiae. Docet enim grammatica modum exprimendi conceptum intentum per sermonem congruum et omnia, quae attribuuntur sibi ... Grammatica tamen est ars communis, quia illa, quae grammatica docet, valent in omni arte et scientia. Regulae enim, quas docet grammaticus, et universaliter omnia, quae ipse docet, non magis attribuuntur uni materiae quam alteri. Propter quod ipsa est ars communis, quamquam sit scientia specialis. Eodem modo dico de logica.' (The reason by which grammar is a special science is that it teaches a knowledge that is different from the knowledge that other sciences and arts teach. Grammar teaches the way of expressing an intellected concept by means of a correct speech, and all the things that are attributed to it ... Grammar is, however, a common art, since what grammar teaches is valid for every art and science. The rules, and in general all things which the grammarian teaches, cannot be attributed more to one subject matter than to another. For this reason it is a common art, although it is a special science. And I say the same about logic.)

35 *Modi significandi*, 55: 'Unde iuxta hoc diligenter considera, quod si dicatur "homo est animal," ibi est congruitas causata ex modis significandi, quos

grammaticus considerat, vel est probabilitas causata ex habitudine locali speciei ad genus – est enim problema de genere – et sic considerat dialecticus, vel est veritas, quam considerat philosophus naturalis. Res enim naturales sunt, quae per terminos istos significantur. Et sic in eadem oratione sunt diversa, quae pertinent ad diversos artifices et circa hoc multa alia considerare potes, quae ad praesens dimittimus causa brevitatis.' (Consider also this. If one says 'homo est animal' there is a congruity caused by the modes of signifying which the grammarian considers; or there is a probability, caused by the local disposition of *species* to *genus* – it is in fact a problem of *genus* – and, as such, the dialectician considers it; or there is a truth involved which the natural philosopher considers. The things, which are signified by these terms, are in fact natural. Thus in the same sentence there are different aspects which pertain to the different masters. This issue can be discussed at greater length, but we shall now skip it for reasons of brevity.)

36 For the relationship between grammar and logic, see de Rijk, *Logica modernorum*, vol. 2, tome 1, 94–125; J. Pinborg, *Logik und Semantik*, and *Medieval Semantics: Selected Studies on Medieval Logic and Grammar*, ed. S. Ebbesen (London: Variorum Reprints, 1984); Rosier, *La grammaire spéculative*, 41–3; Covington, *Syntactic Theory*, 8–12; D. Black, 'Aristotle's "Peri hermeneias" in Medieval Latin and Arabic Philosophy: Logic and the Linguistic Arts,' in *Aristotle and His Medieval Interpreters*, ed. R. Bosley and M. Tweedale (Calgary: University of Calgary Press, 1991), 25–83; and Marmo, *Semiotica e linguaggio*, passim.

37 Covington, *Syntactic Theory*, 11.

38 *Logica modernorum*, vol. 2, tome 1, 116.

39 Rosier, *La grammaire spéculative*, 43.

40 Quoted by C.H. Kneepkens in 'Roger Bacon's Theory of the Double Intellectus: A Note on the Development of the Theory of *Congruitas* and *Perfectio* in the First Half of the Thirteenth Century,' in *The Rise of British Logic: Acts of the Sixth European Symposium on Medieval Logic and Semantics*, ed. O. Lewry (Toronto: Pontifical Institute of Mediaeval Studies, 1985), 115–43, 117; and Kelly, *The Mirror*, 175.

41 See Kneepkens, 'Roger Bacon's Theory of the Double Intellectus.' On the interplay between grammar and semantics, see also I. Rosier, '"O magister ...,"' and 'Un courant méconnu de la grammaire spéculative,' in *History and Historiography of Linguistics: Papers from the Fourth International Conference on the History of the Language Science*, ed. H.J. Niederehe and K. Koerner (Amsterdam: Benjamins, 1990), 179–203. In the latter essay Rosier proves on semantic grounds the existence of an 'anti-modistic' current contemporary to modism.

42 *Grammatica speculativa*, 308: 'Unde patet, quod congruitas sit de consideratione grammatici per se. Sed convenientia vel repugnantia significatorum

specialium a grammatico per se non consideratur, sed magis a logico; ergo
congruitas vel incongruitas in sermone ab his non causatur. Dicendum est
ergo, quod congruitas et incongruitas causantur ex conformitate vel discon-
formitate modorum significandi, quae per se sunt de consideratione grammatici. Tamen proprietas vel improprietas sermonis causatur ex convenientia
vel repugnantia significatorum specialium. Unde haec est congrua et propria, *cappa nigra*; et haec impropria, *cappa categorica*: tamen utraque istarum
est congrua.' (Hence, it is clear that congruity is a matter for consideration by
the grammarian only. But the accord and opposition of special meanings is
not considered by the grammarian per se, but rather by the logician; therefore congruity and incongruity are not caused by them [the special mean-
ings]. We have therefore to say that congruity and incongruity are caused by
the conformity or non-conformity of the modes of signifying, which per se
are the subject matter of the grammarian. However, the property or improp-
erty of the speech is caused by the accord or opposition of special meanings.
Hence, this is a congruous and proper construction, *cappa nigra* and this is
improper, *cappa categorica*. Both, however, are congruous.)

43 *Grammatica speculativa*, 318: 'duplex est perfectio constructionis, scilicet,
secundum sensum, et secundum intellectum. Perfectio secundum sensum
est, cum ambo constructibilia constructionis sunt voce tenus expressa, ut *ego
lego*. Perfectio secundum intellectum est, cum constructibilia secundum
vocem non exprimuntur, sed alterum ab intellectu apprehenditur, ut
dicendo, *lego*.' (The perfection of a construction is twofold, that is, according
to the sense and according to the intellect. Perfection according to the sense
takes place when both the constructibles are expressed into the voice, as in
ego lego. Perfection according to the intellect takes place when the constructibles are not expressed into voice, but one of the two is understood by the
mind, as in *lego*.)

44 Grammar and natural science also interact in the issue of the voice, where
the domains of the two sciences are easily kept apart. The voice as sound is
the domain of the natural philosopher, the voice as sign that of the grammarian. See, for instance, Boethius in *Quaestio* 10: 'grammaticus non considerat vocem quantum ad id, quod ipsa est per suam essentiam, nec causas et
principia sua, nec modum suae generationis, sed sic considerat eam naturalis, cuius est considerare omnes passiones, quae fiunt in corporibus naturalibus per causas naturales. Grammaticus tamen vocem considerat,
secundum quod ipsa est rei signum et modorum significandi subiectum. Si
enim modi significandi sunt in dictione, ergo in voce, quae est pars dictionis.
Unde unum et idem potest esse diversimode de consideratione plurimum

artificum, ut patet.' (the grammarian does not consider the voice with respect to what it is in its essence, nor to its causes and principles, nor to the modality of its generation. In this respect, the voice is considered by the natural philosopher, whose objective is to consider all the passions that happen in natural bodies due to natural causes. The grammarian, instead, considers the voice insofar as it is the sign of a thing and the subject of the modes of signifying. If the modes of signifying are in the *dictio*, then they are in the voice, which is a part of the *dictio*. Therefore it is clear that the same thing can by considered in different ways by various masters.)

For a lengthier discussion of the voice, see John of Dacia, *Summa grammatica*, 83–105.

45 *Modi significandi*, 43: 'Grammaticus habet docere congruam iuncturam dictionum in contextu orationis, per quam possibile est in qualibet scientia exprimere mentis conceptum intentum. Sine quo ergo stat congrua dictionum iunctura in contextu, sine illo tota stat grammatica, nec illud cadit in consideratione grammatici. Sed sine omni re speciali stat congrua dictionum iunctura in contextu. Non enim est oratio magis congrua, cuius constructibilia significant res praedicamentales, quam cuius non.' (The grammarian has to teach the congruous joining of expression in the context of speech, through which it is possible in every science to express a concept intellected by the mind. Therefore what is not necessary to the congruous joining of the expression in context is not necessary to grammar as a whole, and doesn't fall under the consideration of the grammarian. But the congruous joining of the expressions stands without any *res specialis*. The sentence, whose constructibles signify *res predicamentales* is no more congruous than the one whose constructibles are not.)

And see also later: 'Cum enim sine omni re speciali potest haberi completa cognitio litterae, quid ipsa sit, et secundum omnes differentias eius, quae sunt vocales et consonantes, et secundum sua accidentia, quae sunt nomen, figura, potestas, potest etiam haberi sine re speciali perfecta cognitio dictionis in se quantum ad omnes suas partes integrales et subiectivas et quantum ad omnes eius modos constructionis, et orationis, ut manifestum est consideranti, ergo et tota grammatica haberi complete potest sine omni re speciali' (46). (Since it is possible, without any *res specialis* to have a complete knowledge of the letter, both in terms of what it is and with respect to its differentiations, such as vowels and consonants and to its accidents, such as *nomen, figura, potestas*, then it is also possible to have, without any *res specialis*, a perfect knowledge of the *dictio* in itself with respect to all its integral and subjective parts and with respect to all its modes of construction and speech, as it is clear when one considers this. Therefore, it is possible to have a whole and complete grammar without any *res specialis*.)

46 *Grammatica speculativa*, 134: 'Quoniam quidem intelligere et scire contigit in omni scientia ex cognitione principiorum, ut scribitur I *Physicorum, Text Comment* 1, nos ergo, volentes habere scientiae grammaticae notitiam, circa omnium eius principia, cuius modi sunt modi significandi, per se primo oportet insistere.' (Since it is possible in every science to understand and know from the knowledge of principles, as it is written in *Physics* I, *Text Comment* 1; it is necessary that us too, wishing to have knowledge of the science of grammar, dwell at length on all its principles, whose modes are the modes of signifying.)

47 Louis Kelly, 'La *Physique* d'Aristote et la phrase simple dans les ouvrages de grammaire spéculative,' in *La grammaire générale: des modistes aux idéologues*, ed. A. Joly and J. Stefanini (Villeneuve d'Ascq: Publications de l'Université de Lille III, 1977), 107–24, esp. 107–8.

48 For a discussion of the motus model, see Kelly, 'La *Physique* d'Aristote'; Covington, *Syntactic Theory*, 76–82; Rosier, *La grammaire*, 137–8, 145–7; C.H. Kneepkens, 'On Medieval Syntactic Thought with Special Reference to the Notion of Construction,' *Histoire épistémologie langage* 12, no. 2 (1990): 139–76, esp. 154–5; and Marmo, *Semiotica e linguaggio*, 376–86.

For a survey of the reception of Aristotle's *Physics* in the late Middle Ages, see J.A. Weisheipl, 'The Interpretation of Aristotle's *Physics* and the Science of Motion,' in *The Cambridge History of Late Medieval Philosophy*, 521–36.

49 For a more detailed account of the process of language formation, see Bursill-Hall, *Speculative Grammar*, 62–106; and Rosier, *La grammaire*, 45–70.

50 The Modistae often explain the difference between reality, mind, and language, and the difference between the three modes through the use of a spatial image such as 'Socrates in foro, Socrates in choro, Socrates in ecclesia.' See, for instance, John of Dacia (*Summa grammatica*, 234): 'Unde sicut Socrates in foro, Socrates in choro et Socrates in ecclesia est idem secundum essentiam, differens a se ipso accidentaliter, quia penes diversa ubi, eodem modo modus essendi et intelligendi et modus significandi est eadem rei proprietas differens a se ipsa accidentaliter.' (Therefore, as Socrates in the forum, Socrates in the choir, and Socrates in the church are the same according to essence and differ among themselves in terms of accident [since it is in different places] in the same way, the mode of being, the mode of understanding, and the mode of signifying are the same property of the thing, but differing among themselves in terms of accident.)

51 *Dictio* and *pars orationis* are two concurrent but not exclusive definitions of *word*. The Modistae have different definitions for *word* according to the con-

text under which they are considering it. Thomas, for instance, has four: *vox,
signum, dictio,* and *pars orationis* (146). *Dictio* is in turn often divided by some
Modistae into *vox* and *significatum,* sound and meaning, although the grammarian is concerned only with the *vox significativa.* It is a lexical entity,
whereas *pars orationis* is the *dictio* in syntactical action. On the terminology of
vox, dictio, etc., see Bursill-Hall, *Speculative Grammar,* 77–88; Rosier, *La grammaire,* 52–7; and Marmo, *Semiotica e linguaggio,* 112–14.

52 Bursill-Hall (*Speculative Grammar,* 53–4) distinguishes three different understandings of *ratio* in the Modistae, depending on whether it is used in the
metalanguage, in syntax, or in the discussion of noun and verb. As far as
metalanguage is concerned, Bursill-Hall notes that 'ratio suggests the capa-
bility of doing something.' Rosier (*La grammaire,* 47) explains *ratio* in the following terms: 'Nous rendons souvent le terme *ratio* par potentialité: c'est en
effect parce que la propriété de la chose a la potentialité d'exister sous
forme d'essence, donc est dotée d'une *ratio essentiae,* qu'elle peut exister sous
forme d'essence et être un *modus essendi.*'

53 *Grammatica speculativa,* 142: 'modi essendi, et modi intelligendi passivi, et
modi significandi passivi, sunt idem materialiter et realiter, sed differunt formaliter; quia modus essendi est rei proprietas absolute; modus intelligendi
passivus est ipsa proprietas rei, prout ab intellectu apprehensa; modus significandi passivus est eiusdem rei proprietas, prout per vocem consignificatur.
Et sunt eadem materialiter et realiter, quia quod dicit modus essendi absolute, dicit modus intelligendi passivus, prout refertur ad intellectum; et quod
dicit modus intelligendi passivus, dicit modus significandi passivus, prout
refertur ad vocem; ergo sunt eadem materialiter. Sed differunt formaliter;
quod sic patet: quia qui dicit modum essendi, dicit proprietatem rei absolute, sive sub ratione essentiae; sed qui dicit modum intelligendi passivum,
dicit eamdem rei proprietatem, ut materialem, et rationem intelligendi, sive
concipiendi ut formale; sed qui dicit modum significandi passivum, dicit
eamdem rei proprietatem, ut materiale, et dicit rationem consignificandi, ut
formale.' (the modes of being, the passive modes of understanding, and the
passive modes of signifying are the same in terms of matter and in reality, yet
they differ in terms of form. The mode of being is the property of the thing
in absolute terms. The passive mode of understanding is the same property
of the thing, but insofar as it is apprehended by the mind. The passive mode
of signifying is the property of the same thing, but insofar as it is consignified
by the voice. And they are the same thing in terms of matter and in reality
since, whatever the mode of being expresses absolutely, the passive mode of
signifying also expresses inasmuch as it refers to the mind; and whatever the

passive mode of understanding also expresses, the passive mode of signifying expresses inasmuch as it refers to the voice. Therefore, they are the same in terms of matter, but they are different in terms of form. We can explain it as follows: whoever speaks of the mode of being, intends the property of the thing absolutely or under the faculty of essence; but whoever speaks of the passive mode of understanding, intends the same property of the thing, as a material principle and the faculty of understanding [or of conceiving] as a formal principle; and whoever speaks of the passive mode of signifying, intends the same property of the thing as material principle, and intends the faculty of consignifying as formal principle.)

Covington (*Syntactic Theory*, 31, 139n20) convincingly translates *modi significandi passivi* as 'modes of being signified,' but I prefer the more literal 'passive modes of signifying,' which gives more emphasis to the active-passive interplay of the modi.

54 *Grammatica speculativa*, 144: 'modus essendi, et modus intelligendi activus, et modus significandi activus differunt formaliter et materialiter; quia modus essendi dicit proprietatem rei absolute, sive sub ratione existentiae [essentiae], ut dictum est supra; sed modus intelligendi activus dicit proprietatem intellectus, quae est ratio intelligendi, sive concipiendi; modus significandi activus dicit proprietatem vocis, quae est ratio consignificandi: sed alia est proprietas rei extra animam, et alia intellectus, et alia vocis; ita alia est ratio essendi, alia intelligendi, alia consignificandi; ergo modus essendi et modus intelligendi activus et modus significandi activus differunt in utroque.' (the mode of being, the active mode of understanding, and the active mode of signifying are different in terms of matter and in terms of form. The mode of being expresses the property of the thing absolutely, that is, under the faculty of being, as we said above. The active mode of understanding expresses a property of the mind which is the faculty of understanding, or of conceiving. The active mode of signifying expresses a property of the voice which is the faculty of consignifying. But the property of the thing outside the mind is one thing, and the property of intellect another, and the property of the voice is yet another. Thus, one is the faculty of being, the other the faculty of understanding, and another the faculty of consignifying. Therefore the mode of being, the active mode of understanding, and the active mode of signifying are different in both.)

55 *Grammatica speculativa*, 144: 'modus intelligendi activus, et modus intelligendi passivus differunt materialiter, et conveniunt formaliter. Nam modus intelligendi passivus dicit rei proprietatem sub ratione intelligendi passiva; sed modus intelligendi activus dicit proprietatem intellectus, quae est ratio

intelligendi activa: sed eadem est ratio intelligendi per quam intellectus proprietatem rei intelligit active, et per quam rei proprietas intelligitur passive;
ergo proprietates sunt diversae, et ratio eadem; ergo materialiter differunt,
et sunt formaliter idem.' (the active mode of understanding and the passive
mode of understanding differ in terms of matter but agree in terms of form.
The passive mode of understanding, in fact, expresses the property of the
thing by means of the passive faculty of understanding. The active mode of
understanding expresses the property of the intellect, i.e., the active faculty
of understanding. Yet it is the same faculty of understanding by which the
intellect actively understands the property of the thing, and by which the
property of the thing is passively understood: therefore the properties are
different and the faculty is the same; i.e., they differ in terms of matter and
are the same in terms of form.)

In the paragraph that follows (144–6), Thomas proposes the same discourse for *modus significandi activus* and *passivus*.

56 *Grammatica speculativa*, 140–2: 'modi significandi activi sumuntur immediate
a modis intelligendi passivis; quia modi significandi activi non sumuntur a
modis essendi, nisi ut hi modi essendi ab intellectu apprehenduntur: modi
autem essendi, prout ab intellectu apprehensi, dicuntur modi intelligendi
passivi; ergo modi significandi activi sumuntur a modis essendi, mediantibus
modis intelligendi passivis; et ideo immediate modi significandi activi a
modis intelligendi passivis sumuntur.' (the active modes of signifying are
derived directly from the passive modes of understanding because the active
modes of signifying are not derived from the modes of being, unless these
modes of being have been apprehended by the mind. But the modes of
being, inasmuch as they are apprehended by the mind, are called passive
modes of understanding, therefore the active modes of understanding are
derived from the modes of being with the mediation of the passive modes of
understanding and, therefore, the active modes of signifying derive directly
from the passive modes of understanding.)

57 *Grammatica speculativa*, 136: 'Iuxta quod notandum est cum intellectus
vocem ad significandum, et consignificandum imponit, duplicem ei rationem tribuit, scilicet, rationem significandi, quae vocatur significatio, per
quam efficitur signum, vel significans; et sic formaliter est dictio; et rationem
consignificandi, quae vocatur modus significandi activus, per quam vox significans fit consignum, vel consignificans; et sic formaliter est pars orationis;
ita quod pars est pars secundum se per hanc rationem consignificandi, seu
modum significandi activum, tanquam per principium formale; sed est pars
relatam ad aliam per eamdem rationem consignificandi activam, tanquam

per principium efficiens extrinsecum.' (moreover, we have to note that since
the intellect imposes a voice in order to signify and consignify, it attributes a
double faculty to the voice, i.e., the faculty of signifying, which is called signification, through which a sign [or a significant] is produced, and so it is formally a *dictio*; and the faculty of consignifying through which the signifying
voice becomes a con-sign, or a con-significans and so, formally, it becomes a
part of speech. The part, therefore, becomes a part through this faculty of
consignifying [or active mode of signifying] as a formal principle, but the
part is related to another part through the same active faculty of consignifying as an extrinsic efficient principle.)

58 For the Modistae's metalanguage, see Bursill-Hall, *Speculative Grammar*,
    46–113; and Kelly, *The Mirror*, 39–60.

59 See Kelly, *The Mirror*, 27.

60 See Covington, *Syntactic Theory*, 23–4.

61 See the introduction to Thomas of Erfurt's *Grammatica speculativa*, 24.

62 For the philosophical relevance of the triad *esse: intelligere: significare*, see de
    Chenu, 'Grammaire et théologie'; Rosier, *La grammaire*, 66–70, and 'Res
    significata et modus significandi: les implications d'une distinction
    médiévale,' in *Sprachtheorien in Spätantike und Mittelalter*, ed. S. Ebbesen
    (Tubingen: Narr, 1995), 135–68; and Kelly, *The Mirror*, 38–68. For the three
    modes in the works of the grammarians and for the diversification into
    active and passive, see Rosier, *La grammaire*, 62–70; and Marmo, *Semiotica e
    linguaggio*, 143–59. For diverging perspectives on the evolution of the
    notion of the active and passive modes, see Covington, *Syntactic Theory*,
    31–3; and G.C. Alessio, 'Il commento di Gentile da Cingoli a Martino di
    Dacia,' in *L'insegnamento della logica a Bologna*, ed. D. Buzzetti, M. Ferriani,
    and A. Tabarroni (Bologna: Istituto per la Storia dell'Università, 1992),
    3–71, esp. 13–16.

63 *Modi significandi*, 6: 'modi essendi et modi intelligendi et modi significandi
    sunt idem penitus quod patet ex dictis, differunt tamen accidentaliter. Et
    huius probatio est: sicut se habet res extra, intellecta et significata, sic se
    habent modi essendi, modi intelligendi et modi significandi. Sed res extra,
    intellecta et significata sunt una et eadem res. Quare et modi essendi, modi
    intelligendi et modi significandi sunt idem penitus, licet differant per
    accidens, scilicet penes signum et significatum. Et declaratur in simili: sicut
    Socrates nunc in camera, nunc in choro, nunc in foro est unum et idem
    Socrates in numero, licet per accidens non sit idem, quia differt secundum
    diversa ubi, similariter est in istis modis.' (it is clear from what was said that
    the modes of being, the modes of understanding and the modes of signify-
    ing are completely the same thing, although they differ accidentally. And

this is the proof: as the thing exists outside, as intellected, and as signified, so there are modes of being, modes of understanding, and modes of signifying. The thing outside, intellected and signified is one and the same thing. Therefore, the modes of being, the modes of understanding and the modes of signifying are completely the same thing, although they differ in terms of accident, as with the sign and the signified. It is proven by analogy: as Socrates – now in the room, now in the choir and now the forum – is one and the same Socrates, although not the same accidentally, because he differs according to the different place, so it happens with these modes.)

In the paragraph that follows, Martin argues that the relation between the modes shouldn't be understood as the relation between sign and signified, since only the *vox* is the sign of the modes.

64 *Similitudo*, the medieval translation for Aristotle's ὁμοίωμα, is a key term in the process of intellectual knowledge and the counterpart of *proportio* (ἀναλογία) – as the foundation of the all-encompassing medieval notion of analogy. As Kelly remarks, 'Logician and theologians formalised the genesis of the *dictio* in the light of three key concepts the *modistae* exploited but hardly mention, *dicibile, similtudo* and *participatio*' (41).

65 Boethius mentions at times the distinction between active and passive modes of signification (5, 42, 64, 67) but he doesn't seem to connect it to the process of language formation.

66 *Summa grammatica*, 382: 'per modos significandi passive intelligimus modos essendi seu proprietates rei consignificatas per vocem, et per modos significandi active intelligimus rationes consignificandi vocis, quibus refertur vox ad consignificata, et iste rationes consignificandi nichil sunt realiter additum substantie vocis, sed solum entia rationis attributa voci ab intellectu.' (with the modes of signifying passively we understand the modes of being or the properties of the thing as they are consignified through the voice, and with the modes of signifying actively we understand the faculties of consignifying, by which the voice is referred to the consignified things. These faculties of consignifying are actually not something really added to the substance of the voice, but only rational entities attributed to the voice by the intellect.)

In what follows, John claims that the passive, not the active modes of signification are the principles of construction: 'Modi tamen significandi passive sunt principia constructionis, tum quia per illos referuntur constructibilia ad se invicem tum etiam quia aliquid sunt rei preter acceptionem nostram' (383). (However, the modes of signifying passively are the principles of construction, both because through them the constructibles are related and because in our understanding they are something of the thing).

67 See Sigier of Courtrai's *Summa*, 94, and Radulphus Brito's *Quaestiones*, 153. For the role played by commentators in the evolution of the notion of active and passive modes, see Marmo, *Semiotica e linguaggio*, 155–6.

68 For the history of the notion of consignification, see Kelly, *The Mirror*, 31–8.

69 Marmo, *Semiotica e linguaggio*, 62, and Maierù, 'Medieval Linguistics,' 292. See Martin of Dacia, *Modi significandi*, 8: 'modus significandi et significatum speciale sic differunt quia intellectus apprehendens rem extra ut dictum est, copulat sibi vocem et id quod per ipsam repraesentatur est significatum speciale ... et haec est copulatio sive impositio vocis quae ab antiquis dicebatur prima articulatio vocis. Modus autem significandi est proprietas rei consignificatam per vocem.' (the mode of signifying and the special meaning are different is this way: when the intellect takes hold of the thing outside, as explained, joins a voice and what is represented by this voice is the special meaning. This joining is what the ancients called first articulation. The mode of signifying on the contrary is the property of the thing consignified by the voice.)

70 For the etymology of *ars* < *arctare*, found in Cassiodorus, Isidore of Seville, and John of Garland, see R. Dragonetti, 'La conception du langage poétique dans le *De vulgari eloquentia* de Dante,' *Aux frontières du langage poétique (Études sur Dante, Mallarmé, Valéry) Romanica Gandensia* 9 (1971): 9–77, 74.

71 *Modi significandi*, 262–3: 'ante impositionem suam vox erat libera et indifferens ad significandum quemcumque mentis conceptum, cum autem ipsa est impositam ad significandum, ablata est eius indifferentia et est artata ad aliquod determinatum significatum; et haec est articulatio vocis prima. Et quia naturaliter prius est significare quam significare hoc modo vel illo sicut nominaliter vel verbaliter, ideo cum vox in sua impositione artatur ad determinatum significatum, artatur etiam ad determinatum modum significandi; et haec est articulatio vocis secunda sive artatio eius.' (before imposition, the voice was free and could indifferently signify any concept of the mind, but when it is imposed to signification it is taken away from its undifferentiation and forced toward a determinate meaning, and this is the first articulation of the voice. And since to signify naturally comes before to signify in this or the other way, as a noun or as a verb, when the voice in its imposition is forced to a determined signification, it is also forced to a determinate mode of signifying; and this is the second articulation of the voice, or its tightening [*artatio*].)

72 On this point, see also Rosier, *La grammaire*, 66.

73 For the problem of the inexpressible, already present in Aristotle's *De interpretatione*, see Bursill-Hall, *Speculative Grammar*, 133–6; Marmo, *Semiotica e linguaggio*, 144–50.

74 *Modi significandi*, 73: 'nullus modus significandi potest esse alcuius rei sive

res illa habeat esse extra animam sive apud animam, quae non potest habere modus essendi sibi similem.' (there cannot be a mode of signifying anything which cannot have a mode of being similar to it, whether that thing has existence outside the mind or inside the mind).

75 *Summa grammatica*, 201–2: 'Uno modo non ens actu, potentia tamen ens, sicut sunt naturalia, quae de potentia ducuntur ad actum, aut aliqua alia, quorum esse est tantum in potentia, ut materia. Alio modo est non ens, quod nec potentia nec actu est ens, habet tamen aliquam ymaginationem alicuius entis quia ad modum entis alicuius cadentis sub ymaginatione sicut mons eneus vel aureus. Ymaginando enim montem et aurum vel es yamaginabitur mons aureus vel eneus. Similiter est de chimaera, vel yrcoceruo et de aliis figmentis, quorum partes sunt aliquid in natura et propter hoc ymaginationem habent alicuius entis. Tertio modo aliquid est non ens, quod nec actu nec potentia est ens nec entis ymaginationem habet, et tale ens nullo modo cadit in intellectu nec per consequens significari potest per vocem, quia vox est indicativa intellectus.' (First, there is a non-being in act, which is, however, a being in potency, as are things in nature that from potency are led to act, or other things, whose being is only in potency, as matter. Second, there is a non-being, which is a being neither in potency nor in act, but has, however, a certain imagination of some being, as something which falls under imagination, as a bronze or a golden mountain. By imagining a mountain of gold or bronze, a golden or bronze mountain will be imagined. The same happens for the *chimera*, or the *yrcocervus* [goat-stag] and other fictions, whose parts are something in nature and, therefore, have the imagination of some kind of being. In the third way, something is non-being when it is non-being in act and in potency and doesn't have imagination of a being. Such a being doesn't in any way fall under the consideration of the mind and therefore cannot be signified through a voice, and the voice is indicative of the concept.)

76 As de Chenu points out, a grammatical reflection is the first attempt to a rational approach on the process of signification of divine reality and it prepares, and later joins, the negative theology of Dionysius the Areopagite. See 'Grammaire et théologie,' 22–8, especially 26: 'Le langage nous enferme en nous-mêmes; nous ne pouvons transférer à Dieu nos noms et prédicats, sinon par artifice et en métaphore – ou alors par une volatilisation de toute forme dans sa suréminence essentielle, au delà de tout 'mode': la grammaire prépare, et déjà rejoint Denys et ses négation mystiques.' On the name of God, see also Rosier, 'Res significata et modus significandi.'

77 *Summa grammatica*, 205–6: 'deus sive intelligentie apprehenduntur, non quia deus cadat sub motu aut sub ymaginatione nec per se nec per accidens.

Nullo enim modo movetur, sed apprehenditur et cognoscitur per creaturas, que sunt effectus illius, in quibus sua potentia, sua sapientia et sua bonitas relucet. Nam in multitudine creaturarum ostenditur eius potentia, et in ordine et dispositione earum manifestatur sua sapientia, et in perpetuitate aliquarum ostenditur sua bonitas, et inde nominatur bonus, sapiens, et potens sicut omnipotens ... Deus enim non est plene nominabilis uno nomine, sed sunt multa nomina, quibus ipsum aliquo modo nominamus et de ipso loquimur.' (God and the intelligences are understood not because God falls under motion or imagination, neither per se nor accidentally. In no way He moves, but is understood and known through the creatures which are his effect, in which His power, wisdom and goodness shine. His power is shown in the multitude of creatures, His wisdom in the order and disposition of them, His goodness in the perpetuity of some. Hence, we call Him good, wise and powerful, that is: omnipotent ... God is not fully nominable by one name, but there are many names, by which somehow we call Him and talk about Him.)

On language and cognition in John of Dacia, see M. Sirridge, 'The Science of Language and Linguistic Knowledge: John of Denmark and Robert Kilwardby,' in *Sprachtheorien in Spätantike und Mittelalter*, 109–34.

78 *Summa grammatica*, 203–6: 'Item nichil potest per vocem significari, quod non potest per locutionem enarrari. Nam locutio est sermo significativus ex institutione. Sed causa prima non potest locutione enarrari, quia prima causa super omnem enarrationem est et deficiunt lingue in enarratione eius, ut dicitur in libro de causis. Quod exponit idem commentator dicens, quod enarratio non est nisi per locutionem, locutio vero per intelligentiam, intelligentia autem per cogitationem et cogitatio per meditationem, meditatio autem per sensum. Sed constat, quod causa prima non cadit sub sensu. Ergo non potest locutione exprimi ... Cum dicitur, nichil potest per vocem significari, quod non potest per locutionem enarrari, dicendum, quod illa ratio non ostendit, quin deus per vocem significari possit, sed quod non possit plene et perfecte significari, sicut nec ad plenum potest cognosci et hoc potest concedi.' (Also, that which cannot be unfolded in locution, cannot be signified by a voice. Locution is signifying discourse by institution. But the first cause cannot be unfolded in locution, since it is above every narrative and tongues are deficient in telling it, as it is said in the *De causis*. The commentator explains this by saying that narration takes place through locution, locution through understanding, understanding through thinking, thinking through meditation, meditation through senses. Yet, the first cause doesn't fall under the senses. Thus, it cannot be expressed in locution ... When it is said that that which cannot be unfolded through locution cannot be signi-

fied by a voice, we must answer that this argument doesn't explain why God can be signified by a voice, but we can concede that what cannot be fully and perfectly signified cannot be known in full.)

79 *Grammatica speculativa*, 138: 'non oportet, quod semper modus significandi activus dictionis trahatur a proprietate rei illius dictionis, cuius est modus significandi; sed potest accipi a proprietate rei alterius dictionis, et rei illius dictionis tribui, et sufficit quod ipsi non repugnet; et quia substantias separatas non intelligimus, nisi ex istis sensibilibus, ideo sub proprietatibus sensibilium eis nomina imponimus, et nominibus eorum modos significandi activos attribuimus. Unde licet 'in Deo' secundum veritatem non sit proprietas passiva, tamen imaginamur ipsum tanquam patientem a nostris precibus.' (it is not always necessary that the active mode of signifying of a word is taken from the property of the thing of that word, of which it is a mode of signifying. It can be taken from the property of the thing of another word and attributed to the thing of that word: it is sufficient that there is no discordance between the two. Since we don't understand the separate substances, unless by means of sensible things, we impose names on them according to the properties of the sensible things, and we attribute active modes of signifying to their names. Therefore, although *in Deo* is not a passive property in truth, we still imagine Him as made patient by our prayers.)

80 See Radulphus Brito, *Quaestio* 21, 164: '[modi significandi] possunt enim sumi a suo opposito vel simili vel ex modis essendi habituum sive a proprietate alterius rei quae tali rei videtur inesse vel secundum opinionem vel secundum similitudinem vel secundum veritatem.' ([the modes of signifying of a word that doesn't have modes of being] can be derived from the opposite, or the similar, or from the modes of being of the dispositions, or from the property of a different thing which seems to be inherent to this one according to opinion, likeness, or truth.)

81 Marmo, *Semiotica e linguaggio*, 155; *Modi significandi*, 11.

82 For a list and discussion of all the different modes of signifying, see Bursill-Hall, *Speculative Grammar*, 114–285; and Rosier, *La grammaire*, 71–135.

83 Interestingly, in Sigier (144) the two general modes of permanence and becoming enter into the division of the parts of speech between *magis principales* (declinable) and *minus principales* (indeclinable). The indeclinable parts are 'less principal' precisely because their *modi significandi* are derived from less important properties of things. It is also interesting to notice that the most general distinction between substance and accident does not only enter into the description of noun and verb but that it is also applied to the distinction of the indeclinable parts. As Rosier points out (*La grammaire*, 87–9), this latter group is defined by a particular mode, the 'mode of disposition

or of the circumstance of the thing' (*modus dispositionis rei sive circumstantiae rei*), as opposed to the mode of the thing *tout court* (*modus rei*), which identifies the declinables. Within the mode of disposition some parts are ruled by the mode of permanence (e.g., prepositions, since they are related to names in Simon of Dacia), some others by the modes of becoming (e.g., adverbs and interjections, since they are usually related to verbs), and some parts by both (e.g., conjunctions in Simon of Dacia, conjunctions and prepositions in John of Dacia).

84 For the relevance of time as related to the verb in the intersection between the grammatical and the theological discourse, see de Chenu, 'Grammaire et théologie,' 9–22. For the Modistae's theory of the verb, see Bursill-Hall, *Speculative Grammar*, 196–246; Covington, *Syntactic Theory*, 27–8; and L.G. Kelly, 'Time and Verb in Grammatica Speculativa,' in *Matériaux pour une histoire des théories linguistiques*, ed. S. Auroux, M. Glatigny, A. Joly, A. Nicholas, and I. Rosier (Lille: Presses universitaires de Lille, 1984), 173–9.

85 John of Dacia (*Summa grammatica*, 259–64) follows the same argument up to this point and then moves on to show that the noun is more necessary in construction and that it is, therefore, the first part of speech.

86 *Modi significandi*, 96: 'Quanto aliquid magis est necessarium alicui artifici, tanto prius est in consideratione eius et principalius. Verbum autem magis est necessarium grammatico quam nomen, quia loco verbi nihil potest poni; loco autem nominis potest poni pronomen. Ergo verbum est pars orationis prior nomine.' (The more something is necessary to a master, the more it becomes of primary concern. The verb is more necessary to the grammarian than the noun because nothing can be put in its place; while a noun can be replaced by a pronoun. Consequently, the verb is the part of speech that comes before the noun.)

87 *Grammatica speculativa*, 312: 'Finis propinquus est expressio mentis conceptus compositi secundum distantiam.' (The immediate goal [for the completion of the sentence] is the expression of composite concepts of the mind through distance.)

88 For the complex evolution of the notion of *regimen* and the problems related to it, see Bursill-Hall, *Speculative Grammar*, 63–5; Rosier, *La grammaire*, 139–45; Covington, *Syntactic Theory*, 117–19; Kelly, *The Mirror*, 177–83; and Maierù, 'Medieval Linguistics,' 284–7.

89 The passage deserves to be quoted at length: 'Circa tertium est intelligendum quod regimen in entibus grammaticalibus debet sumi ad similitudinem regiminis veri. Nunc secundum quod patet primo Politicorum in qualibet multitudine digniora regunt minus digna; ideo, ut patet ex octavo Physi-

corum et duodecimo Metaphysicae, in genere entium est devenire ad aliquod primum dignissimum et nobilissimum quod omnia entia regit, videlicet causa prima, vel Deus, ut patet ex libro De Causis. Similiter in genere corporum est devenire ad aliquod corpus unum, simplex, dignissimum, quod regit omnia alia corpora quodam ordine divinae Providentiae, videlicet corpus caeleste, ut patet ex libro De Caelo. Et similiter in genere animalium, ad aliquod unum animal dignissimum regens omnia animalia, ut homo; et in Physicis scribitur quod nos sumus finis. Et similiter in eodem homine est devenire ad aliquam partem unam corpoream, quae regit omnia alia membra, videlicet cor; et ideo in medio situatur ut rex in regno, ut patet ex libro De Morte et Vita. Similiter in genere virtutum in homine est devenire ad aliquam unam virtutem quae regit omnes alias videlicet intellectus possibilis, vel, secundum Averroem, intellectus adeptus, ut patet ex intentione Avicennae et Algazelis. Sic ergo patet quod in omni multitudine aliquod unum regimen invenitur. Istud autem, si dirigat illa ad rectum finem, dicitur regimen rectum; si autem non, non dicitur regimen vel non dicitur rectum. Nunc autem ad similitudinem huius sumitur regimen inter partes orationis, ita quod est devenire ad aliquam partem orationis dignissimam respectu talis multitudinis, quia multitudinem et orationem complet, quae proprie regit omnes alias partes et a nulla alia regitur, videlicet verbum' (*Sophismata*, 139).

90 *Grammatica speculativa*, 152–4: 'in rebus invenimus quasdam proprietates comunissimas, sive modos essendi comunissimos, scilicet modum entis, et modum esse. Modus entis est modus habitus et permanentis, rei inhaerens, ex hoc quod habet esse. Modus esse est modus fluxus et successionis, rei inhaerens, ex hoc quod habet fieri. Tunc dico, quod modus significandi activus per modum entis, qui est modus generalissimus nominis, trahitur a modo essendi entis, qui est modus habitus et permanentis. Sed modus significandi activus per modum esse, qui est modus essentialis generalissimus verbi, trahitur a modo essendi ipsius esse, qui est modus fluxus et successionis, ut postea patebit. Ad hanc intentionem *Commentator* IV *Phys. Cap.* 14, dicit quod duo sunt modi principales entium, scilicet modus entis, et modus esse, a quibus sumpserunt grammatici duas partes orationis principales, scilicet nomen et verbum, sub nomine comprehenditur pronomen, sub verbo participium.' (we find in things some very common properties, or very common modes of being, i.e., the *modus entis* and *modus esse*. *Modus entis* is the mode of status and of permanence inherent in the thing insofar as it has essence. *Modus esse* is the mode of flux and succession, inherent in the thing insofar as it has becoming. So I say that the active mode of signifying

through the *modus entis* which is the most general mode of the noun, is derived by the mode of being *entis*, which is the mode of status and permanence. But the active mode of signifying through the mode *esse*, which is the most general mode of the verb, is derived from the mode of being of that very *esse*, which is the mode of flux and succession, as will be later explained. To this purpose the Commentator [IV *Phys. Cap.* 14] says that there are two principal modes of the beings, i.e., *modus entis* and *modus esse*, from which the grammarians derived the two most important parts of speech, i.e., noun and verb. The pronoun is included in the noun and the participle in the verb.)

91 The relationship between permanence and becoming in terms of an opposition is suggested by Thomas at the beginning of his discussion of the essential mode of the verb: 'modus significandi activus per modum esse oritur proprietate rei, quae est proprietas ipsius esse, scilicet proprietas fluxus et successionis, quae opponitur proprietate entis, quae est proprietas habitus et permanentis' (210). (the active mode of signifying through the mode *esse* springs from the property of the thing, which is the property of *esse* itself, i.e., the property of flux and succession, which is opposed to the property of *entis*, which is the property of habitus and permanence.)

92 *Modi significandi*, 100: 'Cum igitur modus essendi per modus habitus repugnat ei, quod significatur per hoc nomen "motus" et "tempus," quia haec numquam sunt in facto esse, sed semper in fieri, unde res, quae significantur per hoc nomen quod est "motus" et per hoc nomen quod est "tempus" non possent significari per nomen, et sic "motus" et "tempus" non essent nomina quod falsum est.' (Therefore, since the modes of being through the mode of stability are discordant with that which is signified by this noun 'motus' and 'tempus' – because these things are never 'being' [*in esse*] in reality, but always becoming [*in fieri*] – as a consequence these things, which are signified by this noun 'motus' and by this noun 'tempus' cannot signify by means of a noun, and, therefore 'motus' and 'tempus' are not nouns, which is false.)

For 'motus' and 'tempus' see also Radulphus, *Quaestio* 21, especially 166. See also Marmo, *Semiotica e linguaggio*, 166.

93 *Grammatica speculativa*, 210: 'et si dicas: esse cuiuslibet rei verbaliter significatur: non tamen omne ens habet esse successivum; nam esse Dei et intelligentiarum non est in fluxu et successione, et tamen dicimus *Deus est*, et *intelligentia est*. Item generatio et corruptio, et illuminatio aëris, non habent esse in successione; et tamen esse illorum verbaliter significatur, ut dicendo: *generatio, et corruptio, et illuminatio aëris sunt, sive fuerunt*.' (and if you say: the being of anything is signified by a verb, but not every thing has a successive

being; since in the being of God and of the Intelligences there is no flux and succession, but yet we say 'God is, the Intelligence is.' In the same way birth and decay and the illumination of the air do not have a being in succession; yet, their being is signified by a verb, as when we say: birth and decay and the illumination of the air are or were.)

For this passage, see Bursill-Hall, *Speculative Grammar*, 209; and Marmo, *Semiotica e linguaggio*, 177–9. See also Radulphus Brito, *Quaestio* 34, 207–13.

It is worth recalling that the verb 'to be' brings into discussion the thorny problem of the so-called *verbum substantivum*, an issue that raised a lot of debate in medieval logic and grammar prior to the Modistae. As de Rijk explains (*Logica modernorum*, vol. 2, pt. 1, 101–8), the problems related to the *verbum substantivum* originate in Priscian's mistranslation of Aristotle's ὑπάρκτικον ῥῆμα and the consequent confusion of the notions of existence and substance, so that the verb 'to be,' instead of denoting existence (as Aristotle suggests) is presented to the Middle Ages as 'signifying substance,' creating a number of logical problems up to the time of Abelard, who is said to have solved the riddle through the 'identity theory' of the copula. For the verbum substantivum, see also Bursill-Hall, *Speculative Grammar*, 198–200; and Kelly, *The Mirror*, 114–15. For the problems rising from the expression *Deus est*, see L. Valente, 'Langage et théologie pendant la seconde moitié du XIIe siècle,' in *Sprachtheorien in Spätantike und Mittelalter*, 33–54, esp. 43–4.

94 Thomas proposes the same argument when he deals with the three tenses of the verb which are portrayed as differences of time: the present tense is, for instance, 'the mode of signifying the thing of the verb as it falls under the difference of the present time' (*Grammatica speculativa*, 238), and the same is stated for the past and the future tenses. And here, once again, the problem of the 'verbalization' of God is raised: 'Et si instetur: *Deus est; Deus intelligit*; tamen esse et intelligere Dei non cadit sub aliquam differentiam temporis; ergo non semper verbum modum et differentiam temporis requirit. Respondetur, quod licet esse et intelligere Dei non cadant sub aliquam differentiam temporis, tamen cadunt sub aliquam differentiam aeternitatis, secundum nostram apprehensionem, ut dictum est superius.' (And if it were argued: 'God is, God understands,' but the being and the understanding of God do not fall under any difference of time and, therefore, the verb doesn't always require the mode and the difference of time. We answer that even though the being and understanding of God doesn't fall under any difference of time, it falls under a difference of eternity, according to our understanding, as we said before.)

95 See also Radulphus's version, where the factorization of eternity into time is abscribed to the *modi intelligendi*: 'Et si dicas quomodo dicitur "deus est," "deus intelligit," cum esse dei non sit in successione temporis, dico quod hoc verbo "sum, es" significat essentiam ut est in successione temporis vel aeternitatis, et licet aeternitas sit tota simul tamen secundum nostrum modum intelligendi intelligimus ibi aliquam successionem et intelligimus ibi parvam vel magnam durationem esse per diversa spatia temporis' (*Quaestiones*, 208). (And if you ask how is it said 'God is, God understands,' even though the being of God is not in the succession of time, I say that the verb 'to be' signifies essence as it is in succession of time or of eternity. And although eternity is a simultaneous whole, we understand, according to our modes of understanding, some kind of succession and a small or large duration through different spaces of time.)

96 *Grammatica speculativa*, 210–12: 'Item illuminatio aeris, licet non sit successiva, prout successio causatur ex resistentia medii, tamen ibi est successio causata ex resistentia terminorum contrariorum, scilicet a quo, et ad quem.' (Also, although the illumination of the sky is not successive, in as far as succession is given by the resistance of the medium, however the succession is caused there by the resistance of opposite terms, i.e., *a quo* and *ad quem*.)

97 *Modi significandi*, 55–6: 'idem conceptus mentis potest esse significatum cuiuslibet partis orationis. Quicquid enim a mente concipi potest, hoc potest per quamlibet partem orationis significari, dummodo modus significandi specificus partium illi non repugnet; et ille mentis conceptus cadens sub modus significandi specifico nominis facit significatum nominis, et cadens sub modus specificum verbi facit significatum verbi, et sic de aliis ut patet dicendo sic "dolor, doleo, dolens, dolenter, et heu," quae omnia idem significant.' (the same concept of the mind can be signified by any part of speech. Whatever can be conceived by the mind can be signified by any part of speech, unless the specific mode of signifying of the parts contradicts it. When that concept of the mind falls under the specific mode of signifying of the noun, it makes a noun, and when it falls under the specific mode of signifying of the verb, it makes the verb and so on. It is clear that when we say 'pain, I suffer, suffering, painfully and ouch,' these all signify the same thing.)

98 *Modi significandi*, 78: 'res ipsa potest significari praeter omnem modum significandi partis orationis, tam generalem quam specialem, tam essentialem quam accidentalem; et huiusmodi possibilitas est tam ex parte rei quam ex parte intellectus. Ex parte rei, quia proprietas, a qua accipitur modus significandi per essentiam a re differt. Ergo potest significari sine modo significandi, qui designat illam proprietatem circa rem significatam. Est etiam

possibilitas ex parte intellectus, quia intellectus rem ipsam et proprietatem eius bene distinguit. Ergo potest significare rem praeter omnem modum significandi exprimentem illam proprietatem.' (the thing itself can signify irrespective of every mode of signifying of the part of speech, whether general or specific, whether essential or accidental. There is the same possibility on the part of the thing and on the part of the intellect. On the part of the thing because the property from which the mode of signifying is achieved differs by essence from the thing itself. Therefore it can signify without a mode of signifying, which designates that particular property about the signified thing. The intellect has the same possibility, since it keeps well discrete the thing itself and the property. Therefore it can signify the thing besides every mode of signifying which expresses that particular property.)

99 *Modi significandi*, 83–4: 'quod si modi intelligendi et modi essendi essent tota et perfecta causa constructionis, quae est in sermone, tunc posset fieri constructio sermonis circumscriptis omnibus modis significandi, quia illa est perfecta causa alicuius effectus, extra quam nihil exigitur ad esse illius effectus. Perfectum enim est, extra quod nihil de his, quae pertinent ad rem illam, ut docetur V Metaphysicae. Licet autem modi essendi et modi intelligendi sint aliqua causa constructionis, quae est in sermone, non tamen sunt causa perfecta. Non enim omnis causa rei est perfecta causa rei, sed solum illa, quae producit rem nullo alio conferente.' (But if the modes of being and the modes of understanding were the complete and perfect cause of the construction which is in speech, then there could be a construction of speech outside all modes of signifying, since the perfect cause of some effect is the one outside of which nothing is required for the existence of that effect, as it is taught in book V of *Metaphysics*. Even though the modes of being and the modes of signifying are some cause of construction, they are not the perfect cause of construction. Not every cause of something is its perfect cause, but only that cause that produces a thing, without anything else coming into it.)

100 On this point see also Martin, *Modi significandi*, 88: 'Est enim quaedam constructio rerum, quaedam conceptuum, quaedam dictionum, et hoc est quod consuevit dici quod constructionum quaedam est realis, quaedam mentalis, quaedam vero rationalis sive sermocinalis.' (There is, in fact, a kind of construction of things, one of concepts and one of words; and this is what used to be said; that, among the constructions, one is real, one is mental and one is rational or linguistic.)

And John, *Summa grammatica*, 248: 'constructio est triplex: quaedam enim est realis, cuius principia sunt modi essendi; alia est mentalis, cuius

principia sunt modi intelligendi; alia est vocalis, cuius principia sunt modi
significandi' (construction is threefold: one is real and its principles are the
modes of being; one is mental, and its principles are the modes of signifying; one is vocal, and its principles are the modes of signifying.)
See also Kneepkens, 'On Medieval Syntactic Thought,' 166.

101 See Boethius, *Modi significandi*, 56: 'tunc complete habetur grammatica,
quando nullus conceptus potest ex re in mente fieri, quin sibi respondeat
aliquis modus exprimendi similis sibi traditus in grammatica.' (Grammar is
complete when no concept of the thing takes place in the mind to which a
similar mode of expression carried by grammar doesn't respond.)

102 For the notion of mental syntax in nominalist grammar, see Kneepkens,
'On Medieval Syntactic Thought,' 168–71.

103 *Modi significandi*, 5: 'Intellectus vero in re ipsa istas proprietates considerans
eam cum talibus proprietatibus intelligit, concipit sive apprehendit, quia
ipse intellectus intelligit rem cointelligendo eius proprietates, et ipsa res sic
intellecta dicitur res intellecta, concepta sive apprehensa, et eius proprietates quae prius dicebantur modi essendi rei extra dicuntur modi intelligendi rei intellectae.'· (The mind, considering these properties in the thing,
understands [or conceives, or apprehends] the thing with such properties,
because the mind understands the thing by co-intellecting its properties,
and the thing thus intellected is called understood, conceived or apprehended. Its properties, which before were called the modes of being of the
thing outside, are now called the modes of understanding of the intellected
thing.)

104 See *Quaestiones* 18–20, 152–62, in particular 155: 'quantum ad id quod est
ibi materiale, idem sunt modi significandi et intelligendi passivi cum modi
essendi, tamen quantum ad esse consignificatum et cointellectum quod est
ibi formale differunt' (the passive modes of understanding and signifying
are the same as the modes of being in terms of matter, but they are different with regard to the formal aspect, i.e., the consignified and cointellected
being) and 158: 'ergo modus significandi et modus intelligendi activi licet
non sint idem, sunt tamen similes, ita quod modus intelligendi activus est
ratio cointelligendi, per quam intellectum refertur ad rei proprietatem, et
istam rationem quam habet aliquis voci attribuit, per quam vox est consignificans respectu proprietatis rei.' (the active modes of signifying and
understanding are not the same, but they are similar, insofar as the active
mode of understanding is a faculty of co-understanding, through which the
intellect is referred to the property of the thing. This faculty is attributed to
the voice and through it the voice is consignificant with respect to the property of the thing.)

105 For the theological significance of the notion of co-intellecting, see Kelly, *The Mirror*, 49.

106 In *Quaestio* 28 ('utrum modi significandi sint in anima') Boethius states that the modes of signifying are already present in the mind, as the efficient cause of language ('in anima sicut in causa efficiente'). Construction, therefore, is not a product of language but of the human being: 'si modi significandi essent perfecta et de se sufficiens causa constructionis, cum sint in dictiones ut in subiecto, dictiones ex se construerentur ad invicem sine anima ordinante. Nunc autem non est ita, sed anima, vel homo per animam ut melius dicatur, ordinat dictiones in contextu secundum modos significandi proportionales in eis inventos' (85–6). (If the modes of signifying were a perfect and self-sufficient cause of construction – since they are in the expression as in a subject – the expressions would construct themselves reciprocally, without the mind ordering them. Instead, the mind – actually the human being through the mind – orders the expressions in context according to proportional modes of signifying.)

Thomas of Erfurt accounts for the presence of the active modes of signifying in the whole process from thing to construction in terms of causes: 'Modus autem significandi activus, cum sit proprietas vocis significativae, materialiter est in voce significativa ut in subiecto; in proprietatem autem rei sicut causatum in causa efficienti radicali et remota; et in intellectum sicut causatum in causa efficienti proxima; et in constructione ut causa efficiens in suo effectu proprio' (*Grammatica speculativa*, 146). (The active mode of signifying, as the property of the signifying voice, is materially in the signifying voice as in the subject, in the property of the thing as the effect in the remote, radical efficient cause; in the intellect as the effect in the immediate efficient cause, and in construction as the efficient cause in its proper effect.)

For Thomas, the intellect actively combines the constructibles into articulated discourse: 'Sed principium efficiens extrinsecum est intellectum, qui constructibilia per modos significandi disposita et praeparata actu unit in constructione et sermone. Constructibilia enim, qualitercumque summe disponantur ad unionem per suos modos significandi, numquam tamen unum constructibile actu se alteri unit; sed hoc fit per intellectum, ut dictum est. Et dicitur intellectus principium extrinsecum, quasi extra constructibilia manens' (*Grammatica speculativa*, 276). (But the efficient extrinsic principle is the intellect, which unites in construction and discourse the constructibles disposed and prepared through the modes of signifying. In fact, although the constructibles are fully prepared for this union through their modes of signifying, it still never happens that a constructible unites itself to another. This happens in the intellect, as was said. The intellect is called the extrinsic principle since it remains, so to speak, outside of the constructibles.)

107 See Martin, *Modi significandi*, 91: 'intellectus potest construere, quamvis non componat ut *homo albus*' (the intellect can construct, but it does not arrange as *homo albus*). For the problem of the order of words within a sentence, see Marmo, 'I Modisti e l'ordine delle parole,' 53–9; and Rosier, 'Transitivité et ordre des mots chez les grammairiens médiévaux,' in *Matériaux pour une histoire des théories linguistiques*, 181–90.

108 On this passage, see also Marmo, *Semiotica e linguaggio*, 132; and Kelly, *The Mirror*, 55–8.

109 *Summa grammatica*, 179: 'Unde intellectus primo apprehendit conceptum, et hunc conceptum sequitur quidam appetitus virtutis intellective, et tunc intellectus iubet organis virtutis sensitive, quod exprimat conceptum, quem intellectus concepit, et tunc exprimitur conceptus, et ita fit vox significativa.' (Hence the intellect first apprehends the concept, and this concept is followed by a desire of the intellective power, and then the intellect commands the organs of the sensitive virtue to express the concept which the intellect conceived, and then the concept is expressed and the signifying voice is created.)

110 *Summa grammatica*, 180: 'habet vox esse in anima ut in causa efficiente, quia vox est percussio aeris ab anima cum ymaginatione significandi, ut dicitur secundo de anima, et tunc vox habet esse in anima per appetitum et ymaginationem. Hee enim due virtutes concurrunt ad formationem vocis, ut dicit philosophus, et hoc tam in brutis quam in hominibus. Sed in brutis vis appetitiva et ymaginativa ut in pluribus sunt indistincte et confuse.' (the voice is in the mind as in the efficient cause, because the voice is a percussion of the air coming from the mind with the imagination of signification, as it is said in the second book *De anima*, and so the voice has existence in the soul through desire and imagination. These two virtues concur to the formation of the voice, as the philosopher says, and this happens both in brutes and humans. But in brutes the power of desire and imagination are mostly indistinct and confused.)

111 *Summa grammatica*, 182: 'Unde iste appetitus non est cuiuslibet virtutis, sed virtutis cognoscitive, quae appetit et iubet virtuti sensitive ut exprimat.' (and this desire doesn't belong to any power, but to the intellective power which desires and commands the sensitive power to express.)

112 Marmo (*Semiotica e linguaggio*, 133–4) quotes another interesting connection between the theories of perception and signification: in the pseudo-

Kilwardby, the relationship between *vox* and signification is compared
with that between the diaphanous (the medium for vision) and the
visibile.

113 As far as the seven authors under consideration are concerned, sections on
syntax are available only for Martin of Dacia's *Modi significandi* (85–118),
Simon of Dacia's *Quaestiones*, which mainly deal with the construction of
nouns and verbs, Radulphus Brito's *Quaestiones*, passim, and Thomas of
Erfurt's *Grammatica speculativa* (272–321). John of Dacia's *Summa grammatica* is abruptly interrupted at the discussion of the noun. The editors (introduction, xx) posit that illness or death hindered the completion of his monumental work. The texts of Boethius and Sigier end with morphology. The
fact that the sections on syntax written by the speculative grammarians did
not always survive in the manuscript tradition might indeed testify to
greater interest in syntax during their times. As Bursill-Hall notes (introduction to Thomas of Erfurt's *Grammatica speculativa*, 95–6) of the forty-five
manuscripts of Thomas's treatise, only six contain the section on syntax,
which might point to the fact that the sections on syntax circulated separately and were consumed more quickly.

   The main references for the study of the Modistae's syntactical theory are
Burshill-Hall, *Speculative Grammar*, 286–326, and his introduction to Thomas's *Grammatica speculativa*, 95–115; Rosier, *La grammaire*, 134–98; Marmo,
Semiotica e linguaggio, 374–416; Covington, *Syntactic Theory*; and Kneepkens,
'On Medieval Syntactic Thought.'

114 *Grammatica speculativa*, 318: 'illud quod habet se per additionem ad alterum
posterius est eo; ideo ex dictis patet, quod congruitas est posterior constructione, et perfectio posterior congruitate. Nam constructio non requirit aliquid aliud nisi absolute constructibilium unionem ex modorum significandi
conformitate causatam, ut dicendo *vir est albus*, ita bene est constructio,
sicut ista, *vir est bonus*; quia utrobique est conformitas modorum significandi. Sed congruitas requirit constructibilium unionem, non quamcumque, sed debitam, ex conformitate modorum significandi illius constructionis tantum ad illam speciem constructionis requisitorum. Perfectio
requirit constructibilium unionem, non quorumcumque, sed solum suppositi cum apposito, ex conformitate omnium modorum significandi causatam, cum sufficientia exprimendi mentis conceptum compositum
secundum distantiam, et generandi perfectum sensum in animo auditoris.
Et sic patet, quod perfectio super congruitatem addit propria principia, et
similiter congruitas super constructionem, et ideo perfectio praesupponit
congruitatem, et congruitas constructionem. Constructio ergo est passio

sermonis prima, congruitas secunda, perfectio tertia et ultima.' (that which takes place as an addition to something else, comes after. Therefore, it is clear that congruity comes after construction and perfection after congruity. For construction doesn't require anything else than the absolute union of the constructibles, caused by the conformity of the modes of signifying. Therefore, 'vir est albus' is a construction as well as 'vir est bonus,' because in both cases there is a conformity of the modes of signifying. Congruity requires not any union of constructibles, but a correct union, according to the conformity of the modes of signifying of that particular construction, as they are required by that type of construction. Perfection requires the union not of any constructible, but of suppositum and appositum, caused by the conformity of all the modes of signification, with all the things necessary to express a composite concept of the mind, according to distance, and to generate a perfect sense in the mind of the hearer. So it is clear that perfection adds its own principles to congruity, and similarly congruity to construction, and, therefore, perfection presupposes congruity and congruity construction. Construction is thus the first passion of the speech, congruity the second and perfection the third and last.)

115 For the terminology *constructio, locutio, oratio*, see Kneepkens, 'On Medieval Syntactic Thought,' 143–7.

116 *Speculative Grammar*, 310, and introduction to Thomas's *Grammatica speculativa*, 105.

117 *Semiotica e linguaggio*, 376; 'I Modisti e l'ordine delle parole,' 49. Marmo also sums up the positions of the other scholars.

118 Kelly, 'La *Physique*'; Rosier, *La grammaire*, 145–50; and Covington, *Syntactic Theory*, 76–82.

119 See also Simon of Dacia's *Quaestiones* 112: 'quia oportet, quod in omni constructione unum constructibile sit dependens et alterum dependentiam terminans, et quia constructibile dependens est in potentia, quia habet se sicut materia, et constructibile terminans est in actu, quia habet se sicut forma ... ergo sic ex eis bene fit unum, scilicet constructio.' (since it is necessary that in every construction one constructible is the dependent and the other the terminant of the dependence, and because the dependent is in potency, like matter, and the terminant is in act, like form ... therefore, from these two one is created, that is construction.) For this passage, see Covington, *Syntactic Theory*, 49; and Kelly, *The Mirror*, 184.

120 On this point see Burshill-Hall, *Speculative Grammar*, 311–12; Rosier, *La grammaire*, 139–45, especially 144; Covington, *Syntactic Theory*, 50; and Marmo, 'I Modisti e l'ordine delle parole,' 51. Benedini ('La teoria sintattica dei modisti,' 120) argues against the connection between *de-*

pendentia and *regimen.* Kelly, instead, persuasively argues for it (*The Mirror,* 183–4).

121 Maria Luisa Ardizzone, *Guido Cavalcanti: The Other Middle Ages* (Toronto: University of Toronto Press, 2002), 71–94.

122 *Quaestiones* 110–11: 'unum extremorum in qualibet constructione se habet ut terminans et per se stans et ut potentiale constructibile, et aliud extremum quod habet se ut dependens est ut formale ... constructibile dependens est magis formale constructibile, quia constructio causatur ex dependentia unius constructibilis ad alterum. Quod ergo magis operatur ad formam orationis quae est unio constructibilium, hoc est constructibile formalius. Sed hoc est dependens.' (One of the extremes in any construction behaves as the terminant, in itself, and as potential constructible, and the other extreme, which behaves as dependent, is formal ... the dependent constructible is more formal because the construction is caused by the dependence of one constructible from the other. Therefore, the element which operates more toward the form of the speech, which is the union of constructibles, is the more formal constructible. And this is the dependent.)

Covington (*Syntactic Theory,* 50) doesn't seem to acknowledge the importance of this move, when he comments upon this passage: 'that no great weight is to be given to the matter-form analogy is shown by the fact that Radulphus Brito gets it the other way around identifying matter with the *terminans* and form with the *dependens.*' Marmo (*Semiotica e linguaggio,* 383–6) interprets Radulphus's switch in light of the theory of relations.

123 Introduction to Thomas of Erfurt's *Grammatica speculativa,* 106.

124 For the interaction of the notions of *exigentia, regimen, dependentia,* see Rosier, *La grammaire,* 139–45; and Kelly, *The Mirror,* 177–83.

125 The etymology provided by Vincentius Heremitus is quoted by Kelly, *The Mirror,* 175. See *Compendium modorum significandi a Vincentio Heremito compositum,* ed. J. Pinborg, *Cahiers de l'institut de moyen âge grec et latin* 1 (1969): 13–17: 'Unde gramatici dicunt, quod 'congruitas' a gruibus traxit originem; grues enim aves sunt talis nature, quod una volant cum alie volant ad eius similitudinem vel convenientiam, et ita dictione ingrediente constructione aliquid iam debet sequi ad eius similitudinem seu convenientiam aliquorum existentium in constructibilibus.' (Hence the grammarians say that congruity originated from the cranes [*grues*]. The cranes are birds of such a nature that they fly together in likeness or agreement with the other. In the same way, when a word enters a construction it must follow something in the likeness and agreement of the others in the constructibles.)

126 See Radulphus's solution, which levers on the notion of *proportio*: 'in composito naturali videmus quod oportet membra componentia aliquod totum

ad invicem esse proportionata, ergo in composito per arte sicut est oratio
grammaticalis oportet constructibilia esse proportionata ad invicem in
modis significandi ... Sed est notandum quod in quibusdam modis significandi requiritur proportio ad hoc quod sit oratio congrua, in quibusdam
aliis similitudo ... Similitudo tamen numquam reperitur sine proportione.
Sed proportio sine similitudine in multis ... Et cum dicitur quod aliqua con-
traria possunt componere aliquod compositum in natura, verum est dummodo sint proportionalia. Unde calidum, siccum, frigidum, humidum ut
sunt proportionalia ad invicem faciunt unum mixtum. Sic etiam debet esse
in modis significandi quod debent esse proportionales ad hoc quod oratio
sit congrua.' (*Quaestiones* 132–4) (in a composite in nature we see that the
components of a whole must be reciprocally proportional and, therefore,
in an artificial composite, as is grammatical speech, the constructibles must
be reciprocally proportional in their modes of signifying ... But we have to
notice that in certain modes of signifying proportion is required to the congruity of the sentence, in others likeness ... Likeness is never found without
proportion, whereas proportion is often without likeness ... And when it is
said that in nature contrary elements can make a composite, this is true as
long as they are proportional. Thus hot, dry, cold, humid compose a mix in
the way they are reciprocally proportional. The same must be for the
modes of signifying which must be proportional for the congruity of the
sentence.)

127 *Speculative Grammar,* 63–4. For *similitudo* and *proportio* in *congruitas,* see also
Covington, *Syntactic Theory,* 62–4; Marmo, *Semiotica e linguaggio,* 408–12, and
'I Modisti e l'ordine delle parole,' 52.
    To exemplify the workings of the two terms, see *Grammatica speculativa,*
310: 'quandoque constructibile dependens habet aliquos modos significandi, non ex proprietatibus suae rei per se, sed ex proprietatibus rei constructibilis terminantis; et tunc inter illos modos exigitur similitudo ... Nam
adiectivum habet tam genus, quam numerum, quam personam ex proprietatibus rei subiectae, ut dictum est supra. Unde ex parte substantivi non
requirit modos proportionabiles, sed similes ... Si autem constructibile
dependens habet aliquos modos significandi ex proprietatibus suae rei per
se, et non ex proprietatibus rei constructibilis terminantis, tunc exigitur in
illis modis significandi proportio et non similitudo. Et quia adjectivum
habet modum adiacentis proprie et de proprietatibus suae rei, ideo per
huiusmodi modum adiacentis requirit in subiecto modum per se stantis,
qui sibi est proportionabilis.' (when a dependent has certain modes of signifying which derive not from the property of its own thing but from the
properties of the thing of the terminant, then *similitudo* is required between

those modes ... The adjective has gender, number and person of the subject thing, as said above. So, it doesn't require in the suppositum proportional modes, but similar ... But if the dependens has certain modes of signifying deriving from the properties of its own thing, and not from the properties of the thing of the terminant, then it demands *proportio*, and not *similitudo* in those modes of signifying. And since the adjective has the mode of adjacency properly and from the properties of its thing, then by the modes of this adjacency it demands in the subject the mode of independence, which is proportional to it.)

128 *Grammatica speculativa*, 314: 'Et quia intellectus super compositionem primam non quiescit, cum sit incompleta, sed de prima procedit ad secundam, ideo constructio non est ad exprimendum primum conceptum compositum, sed ad exprimendum secundum conceptum compositum secundum distantiam finaliter ordinata. Finis autem remotus constructionis est generare perfectum sensum in animo auditoris, ex constructibilium debita unione.' (Since the intellect is not pacified with the first construction, which is incomplete, but moves from the first to the second, the construction is not ordered in terms of finality to express the first composite concept, but to express the second composite concept. The remote goal of the construction is to produce a perfect sense in the mind of the hearer through the correct union of the constructibles.)

129 *Grammatica speculativa*, 314: 'tria requiruntur ad perfectionem sermonis. Primum est suppositum et appositum; quia cum constructio perfecta sit ad exprimendum mentis conceptum compositum secundum distantiam finaliter ordinata, oportet quod, sicut est distantia inter conceptos mentis compositos, sic etiam sit distantia in constructibilium unione. Sed haec distantia solum est inter suppositum et appositum, ex hoc quod solum verbum est appositum, quod per modum distantis se habet. Secundo, requiritur omnium modorum significandi conformitas, prout ad congruitatem requiribatur. Tertio, requiritur ex parte constructionis quod nulla dependentia non sit terminata, quae retrahat ipsam ab eius fine qui est mentis conceptum compositum exprimere, et perfectum sensum in animo auditoris generare.' (there are three requirements for the perfection of speech. First is the presence of a *suppositum* and an *appositum*. Since perfect construction aims at the expression of a composite concept of the mind according to distance, it is necessary that there also be distance in the union of the constructibles – as there is a distance between the composite concepts of the mind. But this distance can exist only between a *suppositum* and an *appositum* because only the verb, which exists under the mode of distance, is an *appositum*. Second, the conformity of all the modes of signifying is required,

as it is required by congruity. Third, on the part of the construction it is required that no dependence be left non-terminated, which could hold it from its final goal, which is to express the concept of the mind and to generate a perfect sense in the mind of the hearer.)

130 *Grammatica speculativa*, 316: 'Tertio modo etiam est perfecta, quia potest facere sibi simile, id est, perfectum sensum in animo auditoris generare. Ex his patet, quod signum perfectionis constructionis est generare perfectum sensum in animo auditoris, ita quod omnis illa constructio erit perfecta, quae perfectum sensum in animo auditoris generabit. Sed haec perfectio sensus in animo auditoris non est punctualis, sed habet gradum perfectionis secundum magis et minus; et secundum hoc constructio dicitur magis et minus perfecta. Nam ea magis perfecta est, quae magis quietat animum auditoris; et quae minus quietat, minus perfecta erit.' (In a third way it is perfect, since it can produce something similar to itself, i.e., generate a perfect sense in the mind of the hearer. From all this it is clear that the sign of perfection is to generate a perfect sense in the mind of the hearer so that the construction that is perfect will generate a perfect sense in the mind of the hearer. But this perfection of the sense in the mind of the hearer is not punctual but has a degree of perfection according to more and less; and according to this, the construction is said [to be] more or less perfect. More perfect is that which further pacifies the mind of the hearer; and the one which least pacifies it will be less perfect.)

3. Dante: The Syntax of Poetry

1 I quote the *Commedia* from the text established by G. Petrocchi, *La Commedia secondo l'antica vulgata* (Milan: Società Dantesca Italiana, 1966–8). Translations are taken from *The Divine Comedy*, trans., commentary C.S. Singleton (Princeton: Princeton University Press, 1975).

2 In Dante, *costrutto* in poetry and *construzione* in the prose clearly mean 'sentence, syntactical construction.' This is shown by the one recurrence in *Purgatorio* (28.147, 'udito avëan l'ultimo costrutto' [they had heard these last words]), and the two in *Paradiso*. In canto 11 (67) 'costrutto' is referred to the name of Dominic, i.e., he who belongs to the Lord ('e perché fosse qual era in costrutto' [that he might in very construing be what he was]). In canto 23 (24) Dante chooses to 'passarmen ... senza costrutto' (pass by undescribed) Beatrice's beauty. In *Inferno*, the structure of the circle of violence is also described in the form of the unfolding of an order (11.30): 'in tre gironi è distinto e costrutto' (it is divided and constructed in three rings). The term recurs also in *Convivio* 2.11.9 and 13.10 and in *Rime* 106.65.

3 For the context of this passage see P. Boyde, 'Creation (*Paradiso* XXIX, 1–
   57),' in *Dante, Phylomythes and Philosopher: Man in the Cosmos* (Cambridge:
   Cambridge University Press, 1981), 235–47. For a complete treatment of the
   issue of order in the *Commedia*, see G. Mazzotta, 'Order and Transgression'
   in *Dante's Vision and the Circle of Knowledge* (Princeton: Princeton University
   Press, 1993), 197–218.

4 I read the *Vita Nova* in the critical edition by G. Gorni (Turin: Einuadi,
   1996), where the *prosimetron* is divided into thirty-one chapters. In previous
   editions of *Vita Nuova*, the hints to language are found in chapters 13 and
   24–5.

5 The most influential and extended discussion of Dante's theory of language
   is contained in the work of Pier Vincenzo Mengaldo, beginning with his critical edition of the work – *De vulgari eloquentia* (Padua: Antenore, 1968),
   which superseded the previous editions by Rajna (1896) and A. Marigo
   (1938) – and developed in *Linguistica e retorica in Dante* (Pisa: Nistri Lischi,
   1978), and his introduction and commentary in *Opere Minori* (Milan: Ricciardi, 1979), 2:3–337. Other key works on Dante's theory of language that constitute the basis of the present discussion are B. Nardi, 'Il linguaggio,' in
   Dante e la cultura medievale (Bari: Laterza, 1949), 173–95; A. Pagliaro, 'I "primissima signa" nella dottrina linguistica di Dante,' in *Nuovi saggi di critica
   sematica* (Messina: D'Anna, 1963), 215–46; G. Vinay, 'Ricerche sul *De vulgari
   eloquentia*,' *Giornale storico della letteratura italiana* 136 (1959): 236–74, 367–88;
   G. Cambon, 'The Drama of Language,' in *Dante's Craft* (Minneapolis: University of Minnesota Press, 1969), 23–45; C. Grayson, '*Nobilior est vulgaris*: latino e volgare nel pensiero di Dante,' in *Cinque saggi su Dante*, 1–31 (Bologna:
   Patron, 1972); R. Dragonetti, 'La conception du langage poétique dans le *De
   vulgari eloquentia* de Dante,' *Aux frontières du langage poétique (Études sur Dante,
   Mallarmé, Valéry) Romanica Gandensia* 9 (1971): 9–77; M. Picone, 'Lingua e
   Poesia,' in *Vita Nuova e tradizione romanza* (Padua: Liviana, 1979), 1–26; M.
   Corti, 'Parigi e Bologna: novità filosofiche e linguistiche' and 'Lingua universale e lingua poetica in Dante,' in *Dante a un nuovo crocevia* (Florence:
   Società Dantesca Italiana, 1981), 9–32, 33–76, and 'Linguaggio poetico e lin-
   gua regulata,' in *Percorsi dell'invenzione* (Turin: Einaudi, 1993), 75–112; I.
   Pagani, *La teoria linguistica di Dante: 'De Vulgari Eloquentia'; discussioni, scelte,
   proposte* (Naples: Liguori, 1982); A.R. Ascoli, '*Neminem ante nos*: Historicity
   and Authority in *de vulgari eloquentia*,' *Annali d'Italianistica* 8 (1990): 186–31;
   G. Cestaro, '*Quanquan Sarnum biberimus ante dentes*: The Primal Scene of
   Suckling in Dante's *De vulgari eloquentia*,' *Dante Studies* 109 (1991): 119–47,
   and *Dante and the Grammar of the Nursing Body* (Notre Dame: University of
   Notre Dame Press, 2002); M. Shapiro, *De vulgari eloquentia: Dante's Book of*

Exile (Lincoln: University of Nebraska Press, 1990); and Z. Barański, '*Sole nuovo, luce nuova': Saggi sul rinnovamento culturale di Dante* (Turin: Scriptorium, 1996), in particular 15–127. Particularly relevant to my argument is the essay 'La linguistica scritturale di Dante,' which I will quote in the English version, Z. Barański, 'Dante's Biblical Linguistics,' *Lectura Dantis* 5 (1989): 105–43.

6 The Dante-Modistae quarrel, mainly revolving around the influence of the Modistae in the *De vulgari eloquentia*, is a long and thorny one and has overshadowed the consideration of the treatise since the publication of Maria Corti's groundbreaking essays in *Dante a un nuovo crocevia* and *Percorsi dell'invenzione*. Although they certainly represent three milestones in Dante criticism, I believe that the debate initiated by these essays is flawed by a methodological problem. Maria Corti and her followers, as well as her opponents, aim at reconstructing Dante's hypothetical library and look for direct evidence of the Modistae's influence on Dante, which turns into a quest for direct quotation, and often results in a misinterpretation of both texts. Such a method of inquiry – which privileges the circulation of books over the circulation of ideas – applies modern categories to the medieval system, and is, therefore, not always apt to describe medieval cultural phenomena. Without entering into detail, my opinion on the Dante-Modistae quarrel is the following: (1) Dante and the Modistae belonged to the same intellectual environment and faced the same problem: the challenge brought to Latin by the vernacular synchronically and by the language of God 'diachronically.' (2) Dante was aware of the Modistae (as the historical/philological criticism proves by highlighting the relevance of speculative grammar in Bologna), but didn't quote them directly in the *De vulgari eloquentia*, because (3) different needs drive the solution of the problem of language in Dante and in the Modistae. A theoretical urgency moves the quest of the philosophers/logicians for universal language, while a practical pressure pushes the poet to operate on the borders of universal grammar (vernacular/Edenic language). Therefore, rather than looking for quotes from the Modistae in the *De vulgari eloquentia* it is more fruitful, I believe, to compare the tenets of their linguistic systems, especially in terms of the significance of syntax in Dante's linguistic reflection and poetic practice. For instance, if I were to look for evidence of the Modistae in Dante, I would rather pick a line such as 'concreato fu ordine e costrutto' (*Paradiso* 29.31), which embodies the notion of the syntax of matter and form as it underlies the Modistae's system.

Interesting chapters in the Dante-Modistae debate are A. Maierù, 'Dante al crocevia?' *Studi Medievali* 3, no. 24 (1983): 735–48; M. Corti, 'Postille a una recensione,' *Studi Medievali* 3, no. 25 (1984): 839–45; A. Maierù, 'Il testo come pretesto,' *Studi Medievali* 3, no. 25 (1984): 847–55; G.C. Alessio, 'La grammatica speculativa e Dante,' *Letture Classensi* 13 (1984): 69–88; F. Lo Piparo, 'Sign and Grammar in Dante: A Non-Modistic Language Theory,' in *The History of Linguistics in Italy*, ed. P. Ramat, H. Niederehe Ramat, and K. Koerner (Amsterdam: Benjamins, 1986), 1–22; A. Fratta, 'Discussioni esegetiche sul primo libro del DVE,' *Medioevo Romanzo* 13 (1988): 39–54; and Shapiro, *De vulgari eloquentia: Dante's Book of Exile.*

7 J. Freccero, *The Poetics of Conversion* (Cambridge, MA: Harvard University Press, 1986), 258–71.

8 Freccero points out that the Christian theory of recapitulation derives from linguistic categories and can be traced back to rhetoric (in Quintilian, for instance, as 'rerum congregatio et repetitio'). With the early Greek fathers of the church, recapitulation becomes 'the essence of the Christian theory of history' (266). 'In the West, with the Donatist Tychonius, it comes to have a more specialized meaning, as one of the seven rules for the interpretation of Scripture. A recapitulation is made when a biblical writer speaks simultaneously of both the type and the anti-type, the promise and the fulfillment. It was in this form that the term was passed on to the Latin West, through the extensive paraphrase made of Tychonius' remarks by Augustine in the *De doctrina christiana*. Like the story of the *Divine Comedy*, Christian history is a forward motion toward an end term which is the beginning: "In the beginning it was the Word ... and the Word was made flesh"' (268–9).

9 The legitimacy of looking for answers in Heaven requires some methodological caution. The poem (and especially *Paradiso*), as a result of the peculiarity of its fiction *sub specie aeternitatis*, allows Dante, and entices the student of the poet, to consider it the place of definite answers. On the other hand, *Convivio* and *De vulgari eloquentia*, because of their abruptly unfinished status, tend to be considered as the general rehearsals for the poem, interrupted under the pressure of the poem itself, and, therefore, they often appear to illuminate the *Commedia* as secondary texts or footnotes. This problem is clearly posited by A.R. Ascoli in '*Neminem ante nos*: Historicity and Authority in *De vulgari eloquentia*.' My strategy for bypassing this is first to subscribe to Dante's teleological construction by establishing a direct question-and-answer confrontation between the earlier works and *Paradiso*. The answers gathered in *Paradiso* will then allow me to raise a subsequent question – that of the 'syntax of poetry' – to answer which I will once again turn to the prose works.

10 A detailed survey of the recurrences of the term *grammar* in the *Convivio* and the *De vulgari eloquentia*, as well as a summary of the scholarly positions on it, can be found in Cestaro, '*Quanquan Sarnum biberimus ante dentes*,' 122–3. On

this theme see also Mengaldo, *Linguistica e retorica in Dante*, 60–76, and *grammatica* in *Enciclopedia Dantesca* (Rome: Istituto dell'Enciclopedia Italiana, 1970–8), 3:259–69; and Grayson, '*Nobilior est vulgaris.*'

11 Dante's *gramatica* is not the universal grammar of the Modistae. In the *De vulgari eloquentia* Dante clearly states that *gramatica* is an a posteriori production, and not an a priori underlying structure of language. In *Convivio* 1.6.7, Dante explains that Latin 'knows' the vernacular in general, but not in the specific, otherwise a perfect knowledge of Latin would lead to a perfect knowledge of the vernacular, a conclusion that Dante strongly rejects, affirming instead that he does not consider *gramatica* a universal structure of language. For *forma locutionis* as universal structure of language, see note 27 of this chapter.

12 Right at the beginning of the *De vulgari eloquentia* Dante stresses the fact that Latin is not the only *gramatica*: 'Est et inde alia locutio secundaria nobis, quam Romani gramaticam vocaverunt. Hanc quidem secundariam, Greci habent et alii, sed non omnes: ad habitum vero huius pauci perveniunt, quia non nisi per spatium temporis et studii assiduitatem regulamur et doctrinamur in illa' (1.1.3). (There also exists another kind of language, at one remove from us, which the Romans called *gramatica*. The Greeks and some – but not all – other people also have this secondary kind of language. Few, however, achieve complete fluency in it, since knowledge of its rules and theory can only be developed through dedication to a lengthy course of study.)

 English translations are taken from *De vulgari eloquentia*, trans. S. Botterill (Cambridge: Cambridge University Press, 1996).

13 Local and temporal challenges are historically the two factors that contribute to the rise of interest in grammar as a discipline in different ages. As H.R. Robins points out in *Ancient and Medieval Grammatical Theory in Europe* (London: Bell, 1951), 6 and throughout, interest in grammar arises either diachronically, when a discrepancy is sensed between the past and the present of a certain language (as was the case for the school of Alexandria with Homer and for Priscian and Donatus with Virgil), or synchronically, through contact with a foreign language. Dante acknowledges both these challenges when he describes the 'invention' of *gramatica*: 'quae quidem gramatica nichil aliud est quam quedam inalterabilis locutionis ydemptitas diversibus temporibus atque locis. Hec, cum de comuni consensu multarum gentium fuerit regulata, nulli singulari arbitrio videtur obnoxia, et per consequens nec variabilis esse potest. Adinvenerunt ergo illam ne, propter variationem sermonis arbitrio singularium fluitantis, vel nullo modo vel saltim imperfecte antiquorum actingeremus autoritates et gesta, sive illorum quos a nobis locorum diversitas facit esse diversos' (1.9.11). (for their *gramatica* is nothing less than

a certain immutable identity of language in different times and places. Its rules having been formulated with the common consent of many people, it can be subject to no individual will; and, as a result, it cannot change. So those who devised this language did so lest, through changes in language dependent on the arbitrary judgment of individuals, we should become either unable, or, at best, only partially able, to enter into contact with the deeds and authoritative writings of the ancients, or of those whose difference of location makes them different from us.)

14 An intriguing issue raised by some scholars is the question of when, in Dante's opinion, Latin was turned into a ruled language; that is, were the Roman *auctores* writing in a natural or grammatical language? On the topic, see Grayson, '*Nobilior est vulgaris*,' 5–7.

15 Discussion of this passage from *Convivio* can also be found in Mengaldo, *grammatica* in *Enciclopedia Dantesca*, 261–2; Grayson, '*Nobilior est vulgaris*,' 7–9; and Cestaro, '*Quanquan Sarnum*,' 122–4.

16 I quote the text of the *Convivio* from the critical edition by F. Brambilla Ageno (Florence: Le Lettere, 1995). Translations are taken from *The Banquet*, trans. R. Lansing (New York: Garland, 1990). For the commentary, see *Convivio* in *Opere minori*, tome 1, pt. 2, ed. C. Vasoli and D. De Robertis (Milan: Ricciardi, 1979).

17 See Grayson, '*Nobilior est vulgaris*,' 7–9; and Mengaldo, *grammatica*, 262. This passage is read as subversive rather than problematic by Cestaro ('*Quanquan Sarnum*,' 123), who comments, 'Far from a supremely rational construct, grammar is beyond reason; hardly an instrument of stability, it is the very *locus* of mutability; no longer the domain of an élite few, grammar here reaches out to embrace the whole of human linguistic experience. It is at once bound (like the lunar body) and limitless (like the innumerable particles that compose it). The poet conjures up an image of Darwinian selection on an infinite linguistic gene pool.'

18 For Dante as Ulysses in *Paradiso* 2, see M. Corti, 'Metafisica della luce come poesia,' in *Percorsi dell'invenzione*, 147–63.

19 B. Nardi, 'La dottrina delle macchie lunari nel secondo canto del *Paradiso*,' and 'Dante e Pietro d'Abano,' in *Saggi di filosofia dantesca* (Florence: La Nuova Italia, 1967), 3–62.

20 *Paradiso* 1.70–1: 'Trasumanar significar *per verba* non si poria, / però l'essemplo basti' (The passing beyond humanity cannot be set forth in words; let the example suffice).

21 A suggestion for my reflection on these lines comes from G. Stabile, 'Navigazione celeste e simbolismo lunare in Par. II,' *Studi medievali* 30, no. 1 (1980): 153–74, in particular 125.

22 G. Mazzotta, 'Sacrifice and Grammar (*Paradiso* 3, 4, 5),' in *Dante's Vision and the Circle of Knowledge*, 34–55.

23 All the scholars mentioned in this section (see note 5) discuss the issue of Adam's language. Lengthier and closer discussions are found in Nardi, 'Il linguaggio,' 241–47; Mengaldo, 'La lingua di Adamo,' in *Enciclopedia Dantesca*, 1:47–8, and *Linguistica e retorica*, 137–9, 222–46; Corti, *Dante ad un nuovo crocevia*, 48–56; and Barański, 'Biblical Linguistics.' See also G. Casagrande, '"I s'appellava in terra il sommo bene" (Par. XXVI. 134),' *Aevum* 50 (1976): 249–73; and D. Castaldo, 'L'etica del primiloquim di Adamo nel *De vulgari eloquentia*,' *Italica* 59 (1982): 3–15.

24 Other omissions listed by Barański ('Biblical Linguistics,' 113) are: God naming day and night and God talking to Adam and Eve after the original sin. Not strictly related to this passage, but equally noticeable is, later, his silence on Pentecost as a corrective measure against Babel. Castaldo ('L'etica del primiloquim di Adamo,' 4) mentions also the omission of Adam talking about Eve after her creation. Dragonetti, who suggestively explains the first exchange between God and Adam in the *De vulgari eloquentia* as a covenant ('La conception du langage,' 17), convincingly explains the omission of the naming of the animals with Dante's preference for a notion of speech as interaction, rather than a monological series of words in isolation (13–14). On this point, I agree with Barański that, although convincing, this 'solution does not explain why Dante should have gone to the potentially dangerous inconvenience of rewriting Genesis.' Additionally, I agree with Barański that 'the reference to Eve as the first speaker is a smoke-screen. It is a pseudo-problem introduced to give a veneer of logical legitimation and the appearance of a valid philosophical *quaestio* to the ensuing discussion' (118).

25 It is very interesting to recall with Mengaldo (*Linguistica e retorica*, 137–9) that on this point the philosophical and exegetical tradition was silent, but the popular tradition seemed to hold the same position as Dante, as shown by the reference to a dialogue with God in texts such as the *Joca Monachorum*, the *Jeu d'Adam*, and the *Mystère du Vieil Testament*.

26 Dante figures God's language as coming from an 'alteration' of the air, like other natural phenomena. Interestingly, God is still responsible for 'distinguishing' the words before yielding them to the air (1.45–6): 'Oritur et hinc ista questio, cum dicimus superius per viam responsionis hominem primum fuisse locutum, si responsio fuit ad Deum: nam, si ad Deum fuit, iam videretur quod Deus locutus extitisset, quod contra superius prelibata videtur insurgere. Ad quod quidem dicimus quod bene potuit respondisse Deo interrogante, nec propter hoc Deus locutus est ipsa quam dicimus locutionem. Quis enim dubitat quicquid est ad Dei nutum esse flexibile, quo qui-

dem facta, quo conservata, quo etiam gubernata sunt omnia? Igitur cum ad
tantas alterationes moveatur aer imperio nature inferioris, que ministra et
factura Dei est, ut tonitrua personet, ignem fulgoret, aquam gemat, spargat
nivem, grandines lancinet, nonne imperio Dei movebitur ad quedam sonare
verba, Ipso distinguente, qui maiora distinxit? Quid ni?' (From this arises a
question: if, as I said above, the first man spoke in the form of an answer, was'
that answer addressed to God? For if it was, it would seem that God had
already spoken – which would appear to raise an objection to the argument
offered above. To this, however, I reply that Adam may well have answered a
question from God: nor, on that account, need God have spoken using what
we would call language. For, who doubts that everything that exists obeys a
sign from God, by whom, indeed, all things are created, preserved, and,
finally, maintained in order? Therefore, if the air can be moved, at the command of the lesser nature which is God's servant and creation, to transformations so profound that thunderbolts crash, lightning flashes, waters rage,
snow falls, and hailstones fly, can it not also, at God's command, so be moved
as to make the sound of words, if He distinguishes them who has made much
greater distinctions? Why not?)

On the 'loquacious air,' see Barański, 'Biblical Linguistics,' 120–1.

27 Although Maria Corti ('Linguaggio poetico e lingua regulata,' 87–95) is very
convincing in demonstrating that *forma locutionis* is an innate capacity for
language – a linguistic structure, the formative principle of language rather
than a fully articulated language, namely Hebrew – her fascinating interpretation still seems to clash with the following peremptory text: 'hac forma
locutionis locutus est Adam; hac forma locutionis locuti sunt omnes posteri
eius usque ad edificationem turris Babel, que 'turris confusionis' interpreta-
tur; hanc formam locutionis hereditati sunt filii Heber, qui ab eo dicti sunt
Hebrei. Hiis solis post confusionem remansit, ut Redemptor noster, qui ex
illis oriturus erat secundum humanitatem, non lingua confusionis sed gratie
frueretur. Fuit ergo hebraicum ydioma illud quod primi loquentis labia fab-
ricarunt' (1.6.5–6). (In this form of language Adam spoke; in this form of
language spoke all his descendants until the building of the Tower of Babel
[which is interpreted as 'tower of confusion']: this is the form of language
inherited by the sons of Heber, who are called Hebrews because of it. To
these alone it remained after the confusion, so that our redeemer, who was
to descend from them [in so far as He was human], should not speak the
language of confusion but that of grace. So the Hebrew language was that
which the lips of the first speaker moulded.)

If *forma locutionis* were the same as the Modistae's universal grammar, a further contradiction would spring forth, since only the Jews – who abstained

from building the tower – were granted possession of not only the 'language of grace' but also of the formative principle of language *tout court*: how could it be a universal principle when restricted only to one nation? how could other peoples 'fabricate' their own language without a structural principle? Therefore, in the passage 'qua quidem forma omnis lingua loquentium uteretur' (1.6.4: and this form of language would have continued to be used by all speakers), which Corti (88) signals as a proof of the distinction between *forma locutionis* and language, I believe that 'lingua' should be intended as the tongue itself and not as language.

28 Nardi, 'Il linguaggio,' 241–7. See also Mengaldo, *Linguistica e retorica*, 243–4. For Edenic language among patristic and scholastic thinkers, see P. Rotta, *La filosofia del linguaggio nella Patristica e nella Scolastica* (Turin: Bocca, 1909).

29 A particularly erudite essay on this topic is Casagrande, '"I s'appellava in terra il sommo bene."'

30 Barański, 'Biblical Linguistics,' 126.

31 For the problem of unity vs. fragmentation in medieval culture, see C. Bynum, *Fragmentation and Redemption: Essays on Gender and the Human Body in Medieval Religion* (New York: Zone Books, 1991).

32 For the context of canto 26, see K. Brownlee, 'Language and Desire in *Paradiso* XXVI,' *Lectura Dantis* 6 (1990): 46–59. For other connections between charity and language, see Corti, 'Dante ad un nuovo crocevia,' 52–6; and Barański, 'Biblical Linguistics,' 139n24.

33 Mengaldo (*Linguistica e retorica*, 239) recalls some answers to the question 'why Adam here?' in terms of Adam being the image of a new Baptism (Getto) or the image of a universal paradigm of fall and redemption.

34 See, for instance, canto 7, 25–34: 'Per non soffrire a la virtù che vole / freno a suo prode, quell'uom che non nacque / dannando sé, dannò tutta sua prole; / onde l'umana specie inferma giacque / giù per secoli molti in grande errore, / fin ch'al Verbo di Dio discender piacque / u' la natura, che dal suo fattore / s'era allungata, unì a sé in persona / con l'atto sol del suo etterno amore' (By not enduring for his own good a curb upon the power that wills, that man who never was born, in damning himself damned all his progeny; wherefore the human race lay sick down there for many centuries in great error, until it pleased the Word of God to descend where He, by the sole act of His eternal love, united with Himself in person that nature which had estranged itself from its Maker); the elaborate figure of the chest in canto 13, 37–41: 'nel petto onde la costa / si trasse per formar la bella guancia / il cui palato a tutto 'l mondo costa, / e in quel che, forato da la lancia, / e prima e poscia tanto sodisfece, / che d'ogne colpa vince la bilancia' (into the breast from which the rib was drawn to form her beautiful

cheek whose palate costs dear to all the world, and into that which, pierced by the lance, made such satisfaction, both after and before, that it turns the scale against all fault); Eve next to Mary in canto 32 (4–6): 'La piaga che Maria richiuse ed unse, / quella ch'è tanto bella da' suoi piedi / è colei che l'aperse e che la punse' (The wound which Mary closed and anointed, that one who is so beautiful at her feet is she who opened it and pierced it).

35 On this point, see Mazzotta, 'Sacrifice and Grammar,' 51: 'In effect, Adam's recitation makes the "proper" of proper name vanish, and he thereby annihilates the myth of an Edenic language in which there is a necessary, natural and stable relation between words and things. It is from the perception of the shattered unity between *res* and *signa* that Dante gets the impulse to establish a poetic order capable of gathering within itself the scattered fragments of language.' On this theme, see also Shapiro, *De vulgari eloquentia: Dante's Book of Exile*, 152, 171, 180, 194.

36 Translations of the *Ars poetica* are taken from *Satires, Epistles and Ars Poetica*, trans. H.R. Fairclough (Cambridge, MA: Harvard University Press, 1970).

37 My reading of the two texts follows a ὕστηρον–πρτόηρον strategy: I will first examine the dynamic Fall-Redemption formulated in the Babel episode and then explore the possible remedy to it in the *Convivio*. I believe this strategy is allowed by the composition so close in time of the two first books (scholars generally agree that the writing of the *De vulgari eloquentia* started after the completion of the first book of the *Convivio*) and is supported by the conceptually tight (although practically contradictory) approach to the problem of language within the two texts, so that they can be described, in A.R. Ascoli's words, as 'the hermaphroditic halves of an original intention that is somehow unable (as yet) to make itself whole' ('*Neminem ante nos*,' 222). See also 194: 'Two general observations can be made about the treatise as a pair. 1) That their concerns, especially with the problem of establishing the authorities of vernacular culture and of Dante himself as its representative, overlap to a very great extent; and 2) that, given their proximity in time and their affinity in agenda, they show a disconcerting propensity for qualifying and even contradicting one another.'

38 For a discussion of the relevance of Babel in the Middle Ages and in Dante's work, see M. Corti, 'Dante e la torre di Babele: una nuova "allegoria in factis,"' in *Il viaggio testuale* (Turin: Einaudi, 1978), 245–56; Barański, 'Biblical Linguistics'; and Ascoli, '*Neminem ante nos*.'

39 *De vulgari eloquentia* 1.8.1: 'Ex precedenter memorata confusione linguarum non leviter opinamur per universa mundi climata climatumque plagas incolendas et angulos tunc primum homines fuisse dispersos.' (The confusion of language recorded above leads me, on no trivial grounds, to the opinion

that it was then that human beings were first scattered throughout the whole
world, into every temperate zone and habitable region, right to its furthest
corners.)

40 *Convivio* 1.5.9–10: 'Onde vedemo nelle cittadi d'Italia, se bene volemo
aguardare, da cinquanta anni in qua molti vocaboli essere spenti e nati e
variati; onde se 'l picciol tempo così transmuta, molto più transmuta lo maggiore. Sì ch'io dico che se coloro che partiro d'esta vita già sono mille anni
tornassero alle loro cittadi, crederebbero la loro cittade essere occupata da
gente strana, per la lingua da[lla] loro discordante. Di questo si parlerà
altrove più compiutamente in uno libello ch'io intendo di fare, Dio conce-
dente, di Volgare Eloquenza.' (Thus in the cities of Italy, if we care to take a
close look, we find that within the last fifty years many words have become
obsolete, been born, and been altered; if a short period of time changes language, much more does a greater period change it. Thus I say that if those
who departed this life a thousand years ago were to return to their cities,
they would believe that they were occupied by foreigners, because the language would be at variance with their own. This will be more fully discussed
elsewhere in a book I intend to write, God willing, on Eloquence in the
Vernacular.)

   De vulgari eloquentia 1.9.7–8, responds directly to *Convivio* 1.5: 'Nec dubitandum reor modo in eo quod diximus 'temporum', sed potius opinamur
tenendum: nam si alia nostra opera perscrutemur, multo magis discrepare
videmur a vetustissimis concivibus nostris quam a coetaneis perlonginquis.
Quapropter audacter testamur quod, si vetustissimi Papienses nunc resur-
gerent, sermone vario vel diverso cum modernis Papiensibus loquerentur.
Nec aliter mirum videatur quod dicimus quam percipere iuvenem exoletum
quem exolescere non videmus: nam que paulatim moventur, minime per-
penduntur a nobis, et quanto longiora tempora variatio rei ad perpendi
requirit, tantum rem illam stabiliorem putamus.' (Nor did I think that this
principle can be doubted even when I apply it, as I just have, to time; rather,
it should be held with conviction. For, if we thoroughly examine other works
of humanity, we can see that we differ much more from ancient inhabitants
of our own city than from our contemporaries who live far off. On this
account, therefore, I make so bold as to declare that if the ancient citizens of
Pavia were to rise from the grave, they would speak a language distinct and
different from that of the Pavians today. Nor should what I have just said
seem more strange than to see a young man grown to maturity when we have
not witnessed his growing.)

41 For the discussion of the widely debated issue of Dante's contradiction on
the topic of the greater/lesser nobility of Latin with respect to the vernacu-

lar, see the updated and balanced account of Z. Barański, 'I trionfi del volgare: Dante e il plurilinguismo,' in '*Sole nuovo, luce nuova*,' 41–78.

42 The vernacular is indeed the very cause of the poet's existence, as the conjunctive force that united his parents in procreation: see *Convivio* 1.13.4:
'Non è secondo ... a una cosa essere più cagioni efficienti, avegna che una sia
massima dell'altre: onde lo fuoco e lo martello sono cagioni efficienti dello
coltello, avegna che massimamente è il fabro. Questo mio volgare fu con-
giungitore delli miei generanti, che con esso parlavano, sì come 'l fuoco è
disponitore del ferro al fabro che fa lo coltello: per che manifesto è lui
essere concorso alla mia generazione, e così essere alcuna cagione del mio
essere.' (It is not impossible, according to the philosopher, as he says in the
second book of the Physics, for a thing to have several efficient causes,
although among them one is principal; thus the fire and the hammer are the
efficient causes of the knife, although the smith is the principal one. This
vernacular of mine was what brought my parents together, for they con-
versed in it, just as it is the fire that prepares the iron for the smith who
makes the knife; and so it is evident that it has contributed to my generation,
and so was one cause of my being.)

The image of the blacksmith, of Aristotelian origins, recurs also in *Convivio* 4.4.12, and, interestingly, also in *Paradiso* 2 (127–9), in the context of
Beatrice's explanation of moon spots: 'lo moto e la vertù d'i santi giri, /
come dal fabbro l'arte del martello, / da' beati motor convien che spiri.'
(The motion and the virtue of the holy spheres, even as the hammer's art by
the smith, must needs be inspired by the blessed movers.)

43 In the *De vulgari eloquentia* Dante strongly condemns the affection to one's
vernacular as follows (1.6.2): 'In hoc, sicut etiam in multis aliis, Petramala
civitas amplissima est, et patria maiori parti filiorum Adam. Nam quicumque
tam obscene rationis est ut locum sue nationis delitiosissimum credat esse
sub sole, hic etiam pre cunctis proprium vulgare licetur, idest maternam
locutionem, et per consequens credit ipsum fuisset illud quod fuit Ade.' (In
this, as in many other matters, Pietramala is a great city indeed, the home of
the greater part of the children of Adam. For whoever is so misguided as to
think that the place of his birth is the most delightful spot under the sun
may also believe that his own language – his mother tongue, that is – is pre-
eminent among all others; and, as a result, he may believe that his language
was also Adam's.)

44 *Convivio* 1.10.12–13: 'però che si vedrà la sua vertù, sì com'è per esso
altissimi e novissimi concetti convenevolemente, sufficientemente e aconcia-
mente, quasi come per esso latino, manifestare; [la quale non si potea bene
manifestare] nelle cose rimate per le accidentali adornezze che quivi sono

connesse, cioè la rima e lo tempo e lo numero regolato: sì come non si può bene manifestare la bellezza d'una donna, quando li adornamenti dell'azzimare e delle vestimenta la fanno più ammirare che essa medesima. Onde chi vuole bene giudicare d'una donna, guardi quella quando solo sua naturale bellezza si sta con lei, da tutto accidentale adornamento discompagnata: sì come sarà questo comento, nel quale si vedrà l'agevolezza delle sue sillabe, le propietadi delle sue costruzioni e le soavi orazioni che di lui si fanno; le quali chi bene aguarderà, vedrà essere piene di dolcissima e d'amabilissima bellezza.' (its virtue will be made evident, namely how it expresses the loftiest and the most unusual conceptions almost as aptly, fully, and gracefully as Latin, something that could not be expressed perfectly in verse, because of the accidental adornments that are tied to it, that is, rhyme and meter, just as the beauty of a woman cannot be perfectly expressed when the adornment of her preparation and apparel do more to make her admired than she does herself. Therefore, if anyone wishes to judge a woman justly, let him look at her when her natural beauty alone attends her, unaccompanied by any accidental adornment; so it will be with this commentary, in which the smoothness of the flow of its syllables, the appropriateness of its constructions, and the sweet discourses that it makes will be seen, which anyone upon careful consideration will find full of the sweetest and most exquisite beauty.)

45 As Dragonetti notices ('La conception,' 54): 'Ainsi, le mot *ligare* employé par Dante ne signifie pas purement et simplement "donner un vêtement métrique à des paroles," mais en resserrer tous les éléments autour du *unum* rythmique, pour les stabiliser en leur propre essence.' Dragonetti connects Dante's use of *ligare* to one of the medieval etymologies for *ars* (< *arctare*, to tighten).

46 On this point, see also Mengaldo, *Linguistica e retorica*, 60–72; Corti, 'Linguaggio poetico e lingua regulata,' 111–12; and G.C. Alessio, 'A Few Remarks on the Vulgare Illustre,' *Dante Studies* 113 (1995): 57–67, esp. 62.

47 The trespassing of Dante's linguistics into poetry is evident as early as chapter 9 of the first book, where, as a proof of the internal homology of the 'ydioma tripharium' Dante mentions the identity of the word *amor* (a word that is identical also in the grammatical Latin) in the 'masters' (i.e., poets) of the three languages (Giraut de Borneil, the king of Navarre, and Guido Guinizelli): 'Trilingues ergo doctores in multis conveniunt, et maxime in hoc vocabulo quod est amor' (1.9.3) (Learned writers in all three vernaculars agree, then, on many words, and especially on the word 'love'). The choice of the word *amor* establishes also a connection to the first seed of Dante's theory of language in *Vita Nova* 6, for which see later.

The switch from linguistics to poetry is already implied in the other first instance of Dante's linguistic agenda, *Vita Nova* 16.4–6, by many viewed as a lukewarm and tentative defence of the vernacular. When justifying his personification of Amor (again!), Dante relies on the authority of the Latin poets and remarks, 'E non è molto numero d'anni passati che apparirono prima questi poete volgari; ché dire per rima in volgare tanto è quanto dire per versi in latino, secondo alcuna proportione ... E lo primo che cominciò a dire sì come poeta volgare si mosse però che volle fare intendere le sue parole a donna, alla quale era malagevole d'intendere li versi latini. E questo è contra coloro che rimano sopra altra matera che amorosa, con ciò sia cosa che cotale modo di parlare fosse al principio trovato per dire d'amore' (16.4–5). (Not many years have passed since these vernacular poets first appeared and I call them 'poets' for to compose verse in the vernacular is more or less the same as composing classical metres in Latin ... The first to begin writing as a vernacular poet was moved to do so by a desire to make his words understandable to ladies who found Latin verse difficult to comprehend. And this is an argument against those who compose in the vernacular on a subject other than love, since such a manner of writing was from the beginning invented for the treating of love).

Translations are taken from *Vita Nuova*, trans. M. Musa (Oxford: Oxford University Press, 1992).

48 A.R. Ascoli, 'The Vowels of Authority,' in *Discourses of Authority in Medieval and Renaissance Literature*, ed. K. Brownlee and W. Stephens (Hanover, NH: University Press of New England, 1989), 23–46. In the essay on the *De vulgari eloquentia* ('*Neminem ante nos*,' 215–16), Ascoli argues that this passage also dialogues silently with the *De vulgari eloquentia* 2.7, by showing the relevance of terms connected to binding (*fasciare, ligare*) in this crucial passage of the treatise on the vernacular, where the figure of the poetic author 'constructing' the *cantio* is established. On this point see also Shapiro (*Dante's Book of Exile*, 171–2): 'It [the second book of *De vulgari eloquentia*] amounts to a grammar of poetry dealing with syntax and with context to the near exclusion of other matters ... *Constructio*, or structure, the heart of composition, is what confers the name of poets ("avientes," 2.i.i) on those who bind their argument together metrically, grammatically, and rhetorically.'

On the theme of grammatical construction in the *De vulgari eloquentia*, see also Dragonetti, 'La conception,' 66–70. On *auieo* and the binding quality of poetry, see, by the same author, 'Le sens du cercle et le poète,' in *Aux frontières du langage poétique*, 79–92.

49 For the role of music in Dante, see A.A. Iannucci, 'Casella's Song and the Tuning of the Soul,' *Thought* 65, (1990): 27–46.

50 Dragonetti ('La conception,' 54) remarks on the intimate association

between music and natural language: 'Dante fait observer dans le *Convivio* qu'un langage harmonisé ne saurait être traduit dans une autre langue sans perdre sa douceur et son harmonie. Cela signifie que pour Dante, l'idée de musique est intimement associée à ce qui fait partie de l'essence même d'une langue maternelle.'

51 The role of this passage within Dante's reflection on language is debated by critics. Bruno Nardi ('Il linguaggio,' 218–25) – who first recognized the source of this definition in the glosses to the *Corpus iuris civilis* (as 'nomina sunt consequentia rebus') – denies that this is the first hint of Dante's theory of language. Pagliaro ('I primissima signa,' 249–56) sees it instead as an important point, and acutely discusses the switch from the 'legal' dative to the 'poetic' genitive; M. Corti (*Dante a un nuovo crocevia*, 70–6) makes it a nodal point in Dante's reflection, and beautifully explains the genitive as stressing 'l'incoercibile influsso delle cose attraverso le parole piuttosto che lo loro asettica corrispondenza' (73); Ascoli ('Vowels,' 26) connects this passage in passing with *Convivio* 4.6.3–5 (the discussion of 'auieo'). Finally in *Lettera, nome, numero: L'ordine delle cose in Dante* (Bologna: Il Mulino, 1990), G. Gorni discusses this passage in the context of the various declensions of name of Beatrice (22–5) and later elegantly relates the uttering of the name of Love in *Vita Nuova* 11 with Adam's primiloquium in the *De vulgari* (64–5).

52 *Vita Nova* 15.4–5: 'Queste donne andaro presso di me così, l'una apresso l'altra, e parve che Amore mi parlasse nel cuore e dicesse: "Quella prima è nominata Primavera solo per questa venuta d'oggi; ché io mossi lo imponitore del nome a chiamarla così Primavera, cioè Prima-verrà lo die che Beatrice si mosterrà dopo la yamginatione del suo fedele. E se anche vòli considerare lo primo nome suo, tanto è quanto dire Primavera, però che lo suo nome Giovanna è da quello Giovanni lo quale procedette la verace luce dicendo: *Ego vox clamantis in deserto: parate viam Domini.*"' (These ladies passed close by me, one behind the other, and it seemed that Love spoke in my heart and said: 'The one in front is called Primavera only because of the way in which she comes today; for I inspired the giver of her name to call her Primavera, meaning "she will come first" on the day that Beatrice shows herself after the dream of the faithful one. And if you will also consider her real name, you will see that it too means *prima verrà*, since the name Joan comes from the name of that John who preceded the True Light, saying: "I am the voice of one crying in the wilderness. Prepare ye the way of the Lord."')

53 *De vulgari eloquentia* 1.3.3: 'Hoc equidem signum est ipsum subiectum nobile de quo loquimur: nam sensuale quid est in quantum sonus est; rationale vero in quantum aliquid significare videtur ad placitum.' (This signal, then,

is the noble foundation that I am discussing; for it is perceptible, in that it is a sound, and yet also rational, in that this sound, according to convention is taken to mean something.)

54 Pagliaro ('Primissima signa,' 245) provides a different, more linguistic explanation for the non-contradiction, claiming that the influence of the thing on the name affects only the sensual part of the sign (the sound).

55 A.A. Iannucci, 'Autoesegesi dantesca: la tecnica dell'episodio parallelo,' in *Forma ed evento nella Divina Commedia* (Rome: Bulzoni, 1984), 85–114. For the theme of auto-exegesis in Dante, see also Z. Barański, 'Dante and Medieval Poetics,' in *Dante: Contemporary Perspectives*, ed. A.A. Iannucci (Toronto: University of Toronto Press, 1997), 3–22.

56 See A. Pagliaro, 'Dialetti e lingue nell'oltretomba,' in *Ulisse: Ricerche semantiche sulla Divina Commedia* (Messina: D'Anna, 1967), 2:433–66; Freccero, 'Dante's Ulysses,' in *The Poetics of Conversion*, 142; T. Barolini, *Dante's Poets: Textuality and Truth in the Divine Comedy* (Princeton: Princeton University Press, 1984), 228–33; and S. Botterill, 'Dante and the Authority of Poetic Language,' in *Dante: Contemporary Perspectives*, 167–80.

57 See, for example, *De vulgari eloquentia* 2.4, where the significance and existence itself of the new vernacular tragic style is formulated and upheld on the blueprint of the ancient classic style. And see Barański, 'I trionfi del volgare,' especially 50–7.

58 *De vulgari eloquentia* 1.15.3: 'Accipiunt enim prefati cives ... a Ferrarentibus vero et Mutinensibus aliqualem garrulitatem que proprie Lombardorum est: hanc ex commixtione advenarum Longobardorum terrigenis credimus remansisse. Et hec est causa quare Ferrarensium, Mutinensium vel Regianorum nullum invenimus poetasse: nam proprie garrulitati assuefacti nullo modo possunt ad volgare aulicum sine quadam acerbitate venire.' (So the above-mentioned people of Bologna take ... from the people of Ferrara and Modena ... a certain abruptness which is more typical of the Lombards [to whom it was left, I believe after the mingling of the original inhabitants of the area with the invading Longobards]. And this is why we find that no one from Ferrara, Modena or Reggio has written poetry; for, being accustomed to their native abruptness, they could not approach the high poetic vernacular without betraying a certain lack of sophistication).

In his commentary to this passage, Mengaldo (121) stresses that *garrulitas* is to be taken as 'asperity,' as the classical/medieval interpretation of *garrulus* as guttural, hoarse (the sound of birds, frogs) suggests. As a consequence of the asperity of the Lombard vernacular, the only eloquent Mantuan poet, Sordello, is said to have turned away from his native language, either by giving himself fully to writing in Provençal, or by 'sweetening' the Mantuan dialect with influences from other vernaculars: 'ut Sordellus de Mantua sua ostendit, Cremone, Brixie atque Verone confini: qui, tantus eloquentie vir existens, non solum in poetando sed quomodocunque loquendo patrium vulgare deseruit' (1.15.2) (as is shown by the case of Sordello of Mantua, on the borders of Cremona, Brescia and Verona: this man of unusual eloquence abandoned the vernacular of his home town not only when writing poetry but on every other occasion). For the interpretation of this passage, see Mengaldo's commentary on page 118. Upon meeting his fellow-citizen Virgil in *Purgatorio*, Sordello interestingly praises him – 'the glory of the Latins' – for showing the greatness of 'their' language, certainly not the Mantuan, but a Latin-Romance poetic κοινή. See *Purgatorio* 7.16–18: 'O gloria di Latin, disse, per cui / mostrò ciò che potea la lingua nostra, / o pregio etterno de lo loco ond'io fui.' ('O glory of the Latins' said he, 'through whom our tongue showed forth its power, O eternal praise of the place whence I sprang.')

59 For the style in lower Hell, see T. Barolini, 'Narrative and Style in Lower Hell,' in *The Undivine Comedy: Detheologizing Dante* (Princeton: Princeton University Press, 1992), 74–98.

60 For the problem of language(s) in the episode of Cacciaguida, see also R. Hollander, 'Babytalk in Dante's *Commedia*,' in *Studies in Dante* (Ravenna: Longo, 1980), 116–29; and C. Honess, 'Expressing the Inexpressible: The Theme of Communication in the Heaven of Mars,' *Lectura Dantis* 14/15 (1994): 42–60. Honess provides also an overview on the critics' positions on the problem of language in the episode.

61 The 'clear and precise' language redeemed by Christ can be compared to Augustine's redeemed signs in the *De doctrina christiana*, here discussed in chapter 1.

62 One can establish also a cross-comparison between the four corners of language in terms of their effect on the reader. We can compare Latin and the inner language of *Paradiso* in that they are both 'in need of translation.' On the other hand, although Dante portrays Cacciaguida as speaking in ancient Florentine, he does not give an example of it in the text. The ancient vernacular and the redeemed interior word 'sound' therefore the same to the reader.

63 *Convivio* 2.13.20–4: 'E lo cielo di Marte si può comparare alla Musica per due propietadi: l'una si è la sua più bella relazione: ché, annumerando li cieli mobili, da qualunque si comincia, o dall'infimo o dal sommo, esso cielo di Marte è lo quinto, esso è lo mezzo di tutti, cioè delli primi, delli secondi, delli terzi e delli quarti. L'altra si è che esso Marte [secondo che dice

Tolomeo nel Quadripartito], disecca e arde le cose, perché lo suo calore è simile a quello del fuoco; e questo è quello per che esso pare affocato di colore, quando più e quando meno, secondo la spessezza e raritade delli vapori che 'l seguono: li quali per loro medesimi molte volte s'accendono, sì come nel primo della Metaura è diterminato ... E queste due propiedadi sono nella Musica: la quale è tutta relativa, sì come si vede nelle parole armonizzate e nelli canti, de' quali tanto più dolce armonia resulta quanto più la relazione è bella: la quale in essa scienza massimamente è bella, perché massimamente in essa s'intende. Ancora: la Musica trae a sé li spiriti umani, che quasi sono principalmente vapori del cuore, sì che quasi cessano da ogni operazione: sì e l'anima intera, quando l'ode, e la virtù di tutti quasi corre allo spirito sensibile che riceve lo suono.' (The heaven of Mars may be compared to music because of two properties: one is its most beautiful relation, for in counting the moving heavens, from whichever we begin, whether from the lowest or the highest, this heaven of Mars is the fifth and the middlemost of them all, that is, of the first, second, third, and fourth pairs. The other, as Ptolemy says in the Quadripartitus, is that Mars dries things out and incinerates them because its heat is like that of fire; and this is why it appears fiery in color, sometimes more and sometimes less, according to the density or rarity of the vapors which accompany it, which often ignite by themselves, as is established in the first book of Meteorics ... And these two properties are found in Music, which consists entirely of relations, as we see in harmonized words and in songs, whose harmony is so much the sweeter the more the relation is beautiful, which relation is the principal beauty in this science, because it is its principal aim. Moreover, Music attracts to itself the human spirits, which are, as it were, principally vapors of the heart, so that they almost completely cease their activity; this happens likewise to the entire soul when it hears music, and the virtue of all of them, as it were, runs to the spirit of sense which receives the sound.)

64 Maps of language with which I at times converge and at times diverge can be found in Cambon, 'The Drama of Language,' passim; Barański, 'Biblical Linguistics,' 109–10, 122–5, and *Dante e i segni: saggi per una storia intellettuale di Dante Alighieri* (Naples: Liguori, 2000), passim; and P. Sollers, 'Dante et la traversée de l'écriture,' in *Écriture et l'expérience des limites* (Paris: Seuil, 1960), 14–47. Interesting remarks on the soundscapes of the three realms can be found in E. Sanguineti, 'Infernal Acoustics: Sacred Song and Earthly Song,' *Lectura Dantis* 6 (1990): 69–79.

65 J. Freccero, 'Infernal Irony: The Gates of Hell,' in *The Poetics of Conversion*, 93–109.

66 On the post-Babelic quality of hell, see Cambon, 'The Drama of Language,' 34; and Barański, 'Biblical Linguistics,' 122.

67 A cursory look to canto 31 – a transitional canto between fraud and treason – establishes the centrality of the episode of Nimrod within the canto of the giants. Opening with the disquieting sound of Nimrod's horn, the canto is dominated by the figure of the tower. It begins with Dante's own confusion, when he thinks he is entering a city enclosed by towers (20–1): 'che me parve veder molte alte torri; / ond'io Maestro, di', che terra è questa?' (I seemed to see many lofty towers, whereon I 'Master, say, what city is this?'), and closes with the image of Garisenda, the tower of Bologna. The word *tower* recurs obsessively in lines 20, 31, 40–3 (with the repetition *torri/torreggiavan*), and 107. Moreover, Nimrod is the only biblical reference included in the number of classical giants (Briareus, Antheus, Ephialtes, Tythus, and Typhon), and he stands aside from the tighter narrative that binds the other giants together, as if to highlight his linguistic loneliness. Finally, the figure of Nimrod crosses the three canticles like a thread. In *Purgatorio* 12, Dante captures Nimrod's amazement in the very happening of the *confusio linguarum* (12.34–6: 'vedea Nembròt a piè del gran lavoro / quasi smarrito e riguardar le genti / che 'n Sennaàr con lui superbe fuoro' [I saw Nimrod at the foot of his great labor, as if bewildered; and there looking on were the people who were proud with him in Shinar]). In *Paradiso* 26, Nimrod is mentioned in Adam's speech. Cambon ('The Drama of Language,' 32) suggestively highlights the 'structural relations between Adam's quoting of the aboriginal holy word in the lost Edenic language, and Nimrod's unintelligible outburst in the *Inferno*.' For the episode of Nimrod, see P. Dronke, 'The Giants in Hell,' in *Dante and Medieval Latin Traditions* (Cambridge: Cambridge University Press, 1986), 32–54; and Barański, 'Biblical Linguistics,' 129–32. Interesting remarks can be found also in Ascoli, '*Neminem ante nos*,' 224–5; and Hollander, 'Babytalk,' 122.

68 *Inferno* 31.67–81: '*Raphèl maì amècche zabì almi* / cominciò a gridar la fiera bocca, / cui non si convenia più dolci salmi. / E 'l duca mio ver lui: Anima sciocca, / tienti col corno, e con quel ti disfoga / quand'ira o altra passïon ti tocca! / Cércati al collo, e troverai la soga / che 'l tien legato, o anima confusa, / e vedi lui che 'l gran petto ti doga. / Poi disse a me: Elli stessi s'accusa; / questi è Nembrotto per lo cui mal coto / pur un linguaggio nel mondo non s'usa. / Lasciànlo stare e non parliamo a vòto; / ché così è a lui ciascun linguaggio / come il suo ad altrui che a nullo è noto.' (*Raphèl maì amècche zabì almi*, the fierce mouth, to which sweeter psalms were not fitting, began to cry. And my leader towards him, 'Stupid soul, keep to your horn and with that vent yourself when rage or other passion takes you. Search at

your neck and you will find the belt that holds it tied, O soul confused: see how it lies across your great chest.' Then he said to me 'He is his own accuser: this is Nimrod, through whose ill thought one sole language is not used in the world. Let us leave him alone and not speak in vain, for every language is to him as his is to others, which is known to no one.')

69 For the various interpretations of the two lines, see the entries in the *Enciclopedia Dantesca*: 'Pape Satan,' 4:281–2, and 'Raphèl maì,' 4:851–3.

70 *Inferno* 32.1–12: 'S'ïo avessi le rime aspre e chiocce, / come si converrebbe al tristo buco / sovra 'l qual pontan tutte l'altre rocce, / io premerei di mio concetto il suco / più pienamente; ma perch'io non l'abbo, / non sanza tema a dicer mi conduco; / ché non è impresa da pigliare a gabbo / discriver fondo a tutto l'universo, / né da lingua che chiami mamma o babbo. / Ma quelle donne aiutino il mio verso / ch'aiutaro Anfïone a chiuder Tebe, / sì che dal fatto il dir non sia diverso.' (If I had harsh and grating rhymes, as would befit the dismal hole on which all the other rocks converge and weigh, I would press out more fully the juice of my conception; but since I do not have them, it is not without fear that I bring myself to speak; for to describe the bottom of the whole universe is not an enterprise to be taken up in sport, not for a tongue that cries mamma and daddy. But may those ladies aid my verse who aided Amphion to wall in Thebes, so that the telling may not be diverse from the fact.)

The reverting to infantile language occurs, as critics punctually notice, also on the occasion of the vision of God (33.106–8): 'Omai sarà più corta mia favella, / pur a quel ch'io ricordo, che d'un fante / che bagni ancor la lingua alla mammella.' (Now will my speech fall more short, even in respect to that which I remember, than that of an infant who still bathes his tongue at the breast.) The adjective *aspro*, here paired with *chioccio* may hint, not only to the Rime Petrose (103) or to *Convivio* 4.2.12, but also, in reverse, to Nimrod's utterance 'cui non si convenia più dolci carmi.' On this final proem of *Inferno*, see A.M. Chiavacci Leonardi, 'Il canto disumano,' *L'Alighieri* 25, no. 1 (1984): 23–36.

71 L. Spitzer, 'Speech and Language in *Inferno* XIII,' in *Representative Essays* (Stanford: Stanford University Press, 1988), 143–71.

72 It is interesting to recall that the canto of the suicides begins with the complete and frightful disappearance of order and of 'the sign,' in the wood 'che da neun sentiero era *segnato*' (13.3) (which was not marked by any path).

73 *Inferno* 27.4–12: 'quand'un'altra, che dietro a lei venìa, / ne fece volger li occhi a la sua cima / per un confuso suon che fuor n'uscia. / Come 'l bue cicilian che mugghiò prima / col pianto di colui, e ciò fu dritto, / che l'avea

temperato con sua lima, / mugghiava con la voce de l'afflitto, / sì che, con
tutto che fosse di rame, / pur el pareva dal dolor trafitto' (when another
that came on behind it made us turn our eyes to its tip, for a confused sound
that came from it. As the Sicilian bull [which bellowed first with the cry of
him – and that was right – who had shaped it with his file] was wont to bellow
with the voice of the victim, so that, though it was of brass, yet it seemed
transfixed with pain).

74 See *De vulgari eloquentia* 1.2.5: 'Inferioribus quoque animalibus, cum solo
nature instinctu ducantur, de locutione non oportuit provideri: nam omnibus eiusdem speciei sunt iidem actus et passiones, et sic possunt per proprios
alienos congnoscere; inter ea vero que diversarum sunt specierum non
solum non necessaria fuit locutio, sed prorsus dampnosa fuisset, cum nullum amicabile commertium fuisset in illis.' (As for the lower animals, since
they are guided only by their natural instinct, it was not necessary for them
to be given the power of speech. For all animals that belong to the same species are identical in respect of action and feeling; and thus they can know
the action and feeling of others by knowing their own. Between creatures of
different species, on the other hand, not only was speech unnecessary, but it
would have been injurious, since there could have been no friendly
exchange between them.)

75 On this, see Barański, 'Biblical Linguistics,' 116–17; and D. Yowell,
'Ugolino's "bestial segno": The *De Vulgari Eloquentia* in Inferno XXXII–
XXXIII,' *Dante Studies* 104 (1986): 121–43.

76 On this point, see the commentary by A.M. Chiavacci Leonardi, *Commedia*
(Milan: Mondadori, 1991–97), 283–6.

77 On the historical dimension of Purgatory, see J. Le Goff, *La naissance du Purgatoire* (Paris: Gallimard, 1981).

78 On this theme, see Barolini, *Dante's Poets*, esp. 85–187.

79 It is interesting to notice in passing that the *incipit* of the secular poems function as the *incipit* of the prayers, in that they evoke the whole text for the
educated reader of the time.

80 As critics have noticed, in this passage the *contrapasso* is given not only by the
content but also by the style of Arnaut's poetry, which Dante reproduces in
the form of *trobar leu* as opposed to the *trobar clus*, of which Arnaut was the
recognized master.

81 P. Pizzorno, 'Matelda's Dance and the Smile of the Poets,' *Dante Studies* 112
(1994): 115–32. On pp. 122–3 Pizzorno shows the textual closeness between
Matelda's dance in *Purgatorio* 28.52–60 and the passages describing the *cantio*
in *De vulgari eloquentia* 2 (3, 8, and 10).

82 Chiavacci Leonardi (*Purgatorio*, 852), points out the references to Cavalcanti,

Rime 46.7 ('cantava come donna innamorata') and *Georgics* 4.382–3 ('nymphasque sorores / centum quae silvas, centum quae flumina servant').

83 For a discussion of some aspects of symbolic apparatus of *Purgatorio*, see P. Armour, *The Door of Purgatory: A Study in Multiple Symbolism in Dante's 'Purgatorio'* (Oxford: Clarendon, 1983).

84 For the significance of dreams in Dante's work, see D. Cervigni, *Dante's Poetry of Dreams* (Florence: Olschki, 1980); T. Barolini, 'Non False Dreams and True Errors,' in *The Undivine Comedy*, 143–65; and Z. Barański, 'Il carattere riflessivo dei tre sogni purgatoriali,' in *Dante e i segni*, 255–79.

85 Z. Barański, 'I segni di Dante,' in *Dante e i segni*, 41–76, in particular 41–65.

86 J. Freccero, 'Manfred's Wound and the Poetics of the *Purgatorio*,' in *The Poetics of Conversion*, 195–208.

87 M. Gragnolati, *Experiencing the Afterlife: Body and Soul in Dante and Medieval Culture* (Notre Dame: University of Notre Dame Press, 2005), 128–9. The text Gragnolati refers to is the following: 'Io dicea fra me stesso pensando: *Ecco* / la gente che perdé Ierusalemme / quando Maria nel figlio diè di becco! / Parean le occhiaie anella sanza gemme: / chi nel viso de li uomini legge *omo* / ben avria quivi conosciuta l'emme' (23.28–33). (I said to myself in thought, 'Behold the people who lost Jerusalem, when Mary struck her beak into her son!' The sockets of their eyes seemed rings without gems: he who reads OMO in the face of man would there surely have recognized the M.)

88 *Paradiso* 9.73–81: 'Dio vede tutto, e tuo veder s'inluia, / diss'io, beato spirto, sì che nulla / voglia di sé a te puot'esser fuia. / Dunque la voce tua, che 'l ciel trastulla / sempre col canto di quei fuochi pii / che di sei ali facen la coculla, / perché non satisface a' miei disii? / Già non attendere'io tua dimanda / s'io m'intuassi come tu t'imii.' ('God sees all, and into Him your vision sinks, blessed spirit' I said 'so that no wish may steal itself from you. Why then does your voice, which ever gladdens Heaven – together with the singing of those devout fires that make themselves a cowl with the six wings – not satisfy my longings? Surely I should not wait for your request, were I in you, even as you are in me.')

89 *Paradiso* 15.55–63: 'Tu credi che a me tuo pensier mei / da quel ch'è primo così come raia / da l'un, se si conosce, il cinque e 'l sei / e però ch'io mi sia e perch'io paia / più gaudïoso a te, non mi domandi, / che alcun altro in questa turba gaia. / Tu credi 'l vero; ché i minori e' grandi / di questa vita miran ne lo speglio / in che, prima che pensi, il pensier pandi.' (You believe that your thought flows to me from Him who is First, even as from the unit, if that be known, ray out the five and the six; and therefore who I am, and why I seem to you more joyous than another in this festive throng, you do not ask

me. You believe the truth, for the lesser and the great of this life gaze into the mirror in which, before you think you display your thought.)

90   For a closer analysis of *Paradiso* 18–20, see Barański, 'I segni della salvezza.'

91   The flawless utterance of the eagle, sounding like the clear and jolly murmur of a river, appears as a specular opposite of the tortured and obstructed utterance of the tongues of fire, which in *Inferno* 26 and 27 doesn't find 'via né forame': 'udir mi parve un mormorar di fiume / che scende chiaro giù di pietra in pietra, / mostrando l'ubertà del suo cacume. / E come suono al collo de la cetra / prende sua forma, e sè com'al pertugio / de la sampogna vento che penètra, / così, rimosso d'apettare indugio, / quel mormorar de l'aguglia salissi / su per lo collo come fosse bugio. / Fecesi voce quivi, e quindi uscissi / per lo suo becco in forma di parole, / quali aspettava il core ond'io le scrissi' (*Paradiso* 20.19–30). (I seemed to hear the murmuring of a river which falls down clear from rock to rock, showing the abundance of its high source. And as the sound takes its form at the neck of the lute, and the wind at the vent of the pipe it fills, so, without keeping me waiting longer, that murmuring of the Eagle rose up through the neck, as if it were hollow. There it became voice, and thence it issued through the beak in the form of words such as the heart whereon I wrote them was awaiting.)

In particular, the two passages are connected by the image of the wind, present also in *Inferno* 13. Whereas in *Inferno* the comparison with the wind highlights the pain and fatigue connected to utterance, here it shows it effortlessness.

92   For the performative quality of the *Paradiso*, see Freccero (*The Poetics of Conversion*, 212): 'paradise and the poem are co-extensive, like the terms of a metaphor and, even within the fiction of the story neither can exist without the other.'

93   For the problem of ineffability in the poem, see M. Colombo, *Dai mistici a Dante: il linguaggio dell'ineffabilità* (Florence: La Nuova Italia, 1987).

94   R. Jakobson, 'Two Aspects of Language and Two Types of Aphasic Disturbances,' in *Fundamentals of Language* (The Hague: Mouton, 1971), 69–96.

95   *Inferno* 25.136–8: 'L'anima ch'era fiera divenuta / suffolando si fugge per la valle / e l'altro dietro a lui parlando sputa.' (The soul that was become a brute flees hissing along the valley; and the other, speaking spits after it.)

96   The adjective returns in 1.6.1 as *disconvenevole disordinazione*; in I, viii, 1 as *disconvenevoli disordinamenti*; and in 1.10.5 as *disconvenevoli disordinazioni.*

97   As shown in the analysis of Cacciaguida's language(s), the heaven of Mars is dense with linguistic events. In this context, it is also worth recalling here that upon entering the heaven of Mars, the pilgrim makes an internal offering to God by means of the Augustinian interior word: 'con tutto 'l core e

con quella favella / ch'è una in tutti, a Dio feci olocausto' (14.88–9: with all my heart and with that speech which is one in all men I made a holocaust to God). The Heavens answer him by showing 'tanto lucore e tanto robbi' (14.94: such a glow and such ruddiness); that is, Dante's interior word meets Heaven's exterior apparatus of signification. The vision of the cross follows, with the body of Christ on it. Moreover, as Barolini shows (*The Undivine Comedy*, 220), the Cristo-rhymes in canto 14 are one of the early instances of poetic aphasia.

98 The movement along an ellipse (the annual movement of the earth around the sun, for instance) revolves around two fixed points (foci), and it is described in the plane as the locus of the point whose sum of the distance from the foci is a constant ($d1 + d2$ = constant).

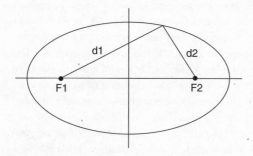

99 Pertile, '"La punta del disio."' In this essay Pertile shows that the words *desiderio* and *desio* do not have the same etymology: the former derives from *desiderare* (to miss), the latter from *desedium* (originally erotic desire). The form *disio* recurs more often than *desiderio*, but 'la scelta paradigmatica non è quindi dettata dal valore etimologico dei termini, ma dalla loro ascendenza letteraria, valore fonico e funzionalità ritmica; non per niente Dante raccomanda nel *De vulg. eloq.* (II vii 5) l'uso di *disio* come forma propria del volgare illustre' (6).

   The system of desire of the last canticle is studied by Pertile in '*Paradiso*: A Drama of Desire,' in *Word and Drama in Dante: Essays on the Divina Commedia*, ed. J.C. Barnes and J. Petrie, 143–80 (Dublin: Irish Academy Press, 1993), and in 'A Desire of Paradise and a Paradise of Desire,' in *Dante: Contemporary Perspectives*, 148–66. By the same author, see also '"L'antica fiamma": metamorfosi del fuoco nella Commedia di Dante,' *Italianist* 11 (1991): 29–60. Some of these essays, together with new insights into the theme of desire in the *Divine Comedy*, are now collected in *La punta del disio: semantica del desiderio nella Commedia* (Fiesole: Cadmo, 2005). For desire in Dante, see

T. Barolini, 'Purgatory as Paradigm: Traveling the New-and-Never-Before-Traveled Path of This Life/Poem,' in *Undivine Comedy*, 99–121; 'Guittone's "Or si parrà," Dante's "Doglia mi reca," and the *Commedia's* Anatomy of Desire,' *Italian Quarterly* 37 (2000): 33–49, and 'Beyond (Courtly) Dualism: Thinking about Gender in Dante's Lyrics,' in *Dante for the New Millennium*, ed. W. Storey and T. Barolini (New York: Fordham University Press, 2003), 65–89. Some of these essays are now collected in T. Bartolini, *Dante and the Origins of Italian Literary Culture* (New York: Fordham University Press, 2006). Yet another perspective on the *Comedy's* system of desire is provided by F. Ferrucci, 'La dialettica del desiderio,' in *Il poema del desiderio: Poetica e passione in Dante* (Milan: Leonardo, 1990), 221–64.

100 The discussion of desire in the third treatise is part of the explanation of the canzone 'Amor che ne la mente mi ragiona' and, therefore, connected to the argument on the significance of human knowledge. In *Convivio* 3.6.7, desire is defined as a drive toward perfection, which is never fulfilled in human life: 'Dove è da sapere che ciascuna cosa massimamente desidera la sua perfezione, e in quella si queta ogni suo desiderio, e per quella ogni cosa è desiderata. E questo è quello desiderio che sempre ne fa parere ogni dilettazione manca: ché nulla dilettazione è sì grande in questa vita che all'anima nostra possa [sì] tòrre la sete, che sempre lo desiderio che detto è non rimagna nel pensiero.' (To confirm this, I add by way of saying And those down here who are in love. Here it should be known that each thing most of all desires its own perfection, and in this it satisfies all of its desires, and for the sake of this each thing is desired. It is this desire that always makes every delight seem defective to us, for no delight in this life is so great as to be able to take away the thirst such that the desire just mentioned does not still remain in our thought.)

Desire is later described as lack, wheras beatitude is perfect (3.15.3): 'Questo piacere in altra cosa di qua giù essere non può, se non nel guardare in questi occhi e in questo riso. E la ragione è questa: che, con ciò sia cosa che ciascuna cosa naturalmente disia la sua perfezione, sanza quella essere non può [l'uomo] contento, che è essere beato; ché quantunque l'altre cose avesse, sanza questa rimarrebbe in lui desiderio: lo quale essere non può colla beatitudine, acciò che la beatitudine sia perfetta cosa, e lo desiderio sia cosa defettiva: ché nullo desidera quello che ha, ma quello che non ha, che è manifesto difetto.' (This joy cannot be found in anything here below except by looking into eyes and upon her smile. The reason for this is that since everything by nature desires its own perfection, without this perfection man could not be happy, that is to say, could not be blessed; for even if he had every other thing, by lacking this perfection desire would

still be present in him, and desire is something that cannot coexist with
blessedness since blessedness is something perfect and desire something
defective; for no one desires what he has but rather what he does not have,
which is an obvious deficiency.)

The partial perfection afforded to human life is knowledge (3.15.4, 5,
and 8): 'con ciò sia cosa che'l naturale desiderio sia [nel]l' uomo di sapere,
e sanza compiere lo desiderio beato essere non possa. A ciò si può chiara-
mente rispondere che lo desiderio naturale in ciascuna cosa è misurato
secondo la possibilitade della cosa desiderante: altrimenti anderebbe in
contrario di se medesimo, che impossibile è' (7, 8) (given that man has a
natural desire to know, without fulfillment of which he cannot be blessed.
To this we may simply reply that the natural desire within all things is pro-
portionate to the capacity within that thing which has desire; otherwise
desire would run counter to itself, which is impossible).

Desire is thus measured against the capacity of the desiring subject who
looks for a partial perfection. Otherwise, one would fall into the paradox of
'desiring to desire' (3.15.9): 'desiderando la sua perfezione, desiderrebbe
la sua imperfezione; imperò che desiderrebbe sé sempre desiderare e non
compiere mai suo desiderio (e in questo errore cade l'avaro maladetto, e
non s'acorge che desidera sé sempre desiderare, andando dietro al numero
impossibile a giugnere.)' (It would run counter to itself because by desiring
its perfection it would desire its imperfection, since it would always desire to
continue desiring and would never fulfill its desire [and it is into this error
that the accursed miser falls, by failing to perceive that he desires to continue desiring by seeking to realize an infinite gain].)

For desire in connection with the Aristotelian theory of perfection, see
also *Convivio* 4.6.8. The dangerous aspect of desire is the risk that it might
obfuscate reason, especially when one gets closer to the desired object. This
time, desire is connected to the Aristotelian theory of passion (3.10.2):
'Dove è da sapere che quanto l'agente più al paziente sé unisce, tanto e più
forte è però la passione, sì come per la sentenza del Filosofo in quello Di
Generazione si può comprendere; onde, quanto la cosa desiderata più
appropinqua al desiderante, tanto lo desiderio è maggiore, e l'anima, più
passionata, più sé unisce alla parte concupiscibile e più abandona la
ragione.' (I make this clear when I say: For my soul was full of fear, so much
so that what I saw in her presence seemed frightening to me. Here we must
know that the more closely the agent is united with the patient the stronger
is the passion, as may be understood from statements made by the Philosopher in his book On Generation; thus the nearer the object desired comes
to him who desires it, the stronger is his desire; and the more the soul is

impassioned, the more closely it is united with the concupiscible appetite, and the more it abandons reason.)

101 For desire in the fourth book of the *Convivio*, see Barolini, 'Purgatory as Paradigm.'

102 *Convivio* 4.12.17: 'Per che vedere si può che l'uno desiderabile sta dinanzi all'altro alli occhi della nostra anima per modo quasi piramidale, che 'l minimo li cuopre prima tutti, ed è quasi punta dell'ultimo desiderabile, che è Dio, quasi base di tutti. Sì che, quanto dalla punta ver la base più si procede, maggiori apariscono li desiderabili; e questa è la ragione per che, acquistando, li desiderii umani si fanno più ampii, l'uno appresso dell'altro.' (Consequently it may be seen that one object of desire stands in front of another before the eyes of our soul very much in the manner of a pyramid, where the smallest object at first covers them all and is, as it were, the apex of the ultimate object of desire, namely God, who is, as it were, the base of all the rest. And so the further we move from the apex toward the base, the greater the objects of desire appear; this is the reason why acquisition causes human desires to become progressively inflated.)

103 Barolini (*Undivine Comedy*, 100) states that 'this passage is virtually a blueprint for the *Commedia*.'

104 *Convivio* 4.12.18–19: 'Veramente così questo cammino si perde per errore come le strade della terra. Ché, sì come d'una cittade a un'altra di necessitade è una ottima e dirittissima via, e un'altra che sempre se ne dilunga (cioè quella che va nell'altra parte), e molte altre, quale meno alungandosi, quale meno appressandosi: così nella vita umana sono diversi cammini, delli quali uno è veracissimo e un altro è fallacissimo, e certi meno fallaci e certi meno veraci. E sì come vedemo che quello che dirittissimo vae alla cittade, e compie lo desiderio e dà posa dopo la fatica, e quello che va in contrario mai nol compie e mai posa dare non può, così nella nostra vita aviene: lo buono camminatore giunge a termine e a posa; lo erroneo mai non l'aggiunge, ma con molta fatica del suo animo sempre colli occhi gulosi si mira innanzi.' (We may, however, lose this path through error, just as we may the roads of the earth. For just as from one city to another there is only one road which is of necessity the best and most direct, and another which leads completely away [namely the one which goes in the opposite direction], and many others, some leading away from it and some moving toward it, so in human life there are different paths, among which only one is the truest way and another the falsest, and some less true and some less false. And just as we see that the path which leads most directly to the city fulfills desire and provides rest when work is finished, while the one which goes in the opposite direction never fulfills it nor provides rest, so it is with

our life. A wise traveler reaches his goal and rests; the wanderer never reaches it, but with great lethargy of mind forever directs his hungry eyes before him.)

For a discussion of the natural appetite of the human soul see also *Convivio* 4.21.13–14.

105 Pertile, '*Paradiso*: A Drama of Desire,' 161. See also 165: 'Poetically too, Dante's doubts have the same retardatory and ambivalent effects as desire, in that each answer, albeit perfect and perfectly satisfying in itself, reveals now uncharted territories that the mind can never hope or presume to possess in advance of a revelation that is persistently deferred.'

106 In the prologue, and therefore not pertaining to *Inferno* properly, we can notice the sporadic recurrence of heavenly desire with Beatrice: 'vegno del loco onde tornar disio' (2.71) (I come from a place to which I long to return): through the immersion into Hell, heavenly desire assumes a nostalgic nuance, which is characteristic of purgatorial desire. In the same canto, desire as the motor of narrative is figured in the pilgrim's answer to Virgil: 'Tu m'hai con desiderio il cor disposto / sì al venire con le parole tue / ch'i' son tornato nel primo proposto.' (2.136–8) (By your words you have made me so eager to come with you that I have returned to my first resolve.)

107 The quality of inevitable loss in this kind of desire is recalled by Virgil himself in *Purgatorio* 3.37–42: 'State contenti, umana gente, al *quia*; / ché, se potuto aveste veder tutto, / mestier non era parturir Maria; / e disïar vedeste sanza frutto / tai che sarebbe lor disio quetato / ch'etternalmente è dato lor per lutto.' (Be content, human race, with the *quia*, for if you had been able to see everything, no need was there for Mary to give birth; and you have seen desiring fruitlessly men such that their desire would have been satisfied which is given them for eternal grief.)

108 The connection with original sin is remarked on by Beatrice at the end of *Purgatorio* (33.61–3): 'Per morder quella, in pena e in disio / cinquemila anni e più l'anima prima / bramò colui che 'l morso in sé punio.' (For tasting of that tree the first soul longed in pain and in desire five thousand years and more for Him who punished on Himself that taste.) As Barolini remarks, 'Sin made the lack in mankind, the desire that is our birthright' (*Undivine Comedy*, 191).

109 For Dante's theory of love, see B. Nardi, 'Filosofia dell'amore nei rimatori italiani del Duecento e in Dante,' in *Dante e la cultura medievale*, 1–92. For the theme of desire in the Purgatorio in connection with the *Convivio*, see Barolini, 'Purgatory as Paradigm.'

110 *Purgatorio* 18.19–27: 'L'animo, ch'è creato ad amar presto, / ad ogne cosa è

mobile che piace, / tosto che dal piacere in atto è desto. / Vostra appren-
siva da esser verace / tragge intenzione, e dentro a voi la spiega, / sì che
l'animo ad essa volger face; / e se, rivolto, inver' di lei si piega, / quel pie-
gare è amor, quell'è natura / che per piacer di novo in voi si lega.' (The
mind, which is created quick to love, is responsive to everything that
pleases, as soon as by pleasure it is roused to action. Your faculty of apprehension draws an image from a real existence and displays it within you, so
that it makes the mind turn to it; and if, thus turned, the mind inclines
toward it, that inclination is love, that inclination is nature that is bound in
you anew by pleasure.)

For the connection between Dante's theory of love in this passage and
the Aristotelian theory of knowledge, see Mazzotta, *Dante's Vision*, 120.

111 Commentators are divided on the interpretation of the last 'fin che,' which
can be read as 'until,' implying that desire ceases when the beloved object
makes the soul rejoice, or 'as long as,' implying that desire continues to
burn throughout. See Pertile, *'Paradiso*: A Drama of Desire,' 176n33.

112 *Purgatorio* 18.36–39: 'però che forse appar la sua matera / sempre esser
buona, ma non ciascun segno / è buono, ancor che buona sia la cera.' (perhaps its matter appears always to be good: but never every imprint is good,
although the wax be good.)

113 *Purgatorio* 18.70–4: 'Onde, poniam che di necessitate / surga ogne amor
che dentro a voi s'accende, / di ritenerlo è in voi la podestate. / La nobile
virtù Beatrice intende / per lo libero arbitrio.' (Wherefore, suppose that
every love which is kindled in you arises of necessity, the power to arrest it is
in you. This noble virtue Beatrice understands as free will.)

114 As Barolini notices in 'Purgatory as Paradigm,' the crux of the Siren who,
contrary to tradition, leads Ulysses astray (*Purgatorio* 19.22–3: 'Io volsi Ulisse
del suo cammin vago / al canto mio') represents a purgatorial memento of
Ulysses' misuse of the order of love: his desire for knowledge, indeed an
'ardore,' overcomes the rightful variations of familial love and hinders his
return, transforming desire's lack into a loss. See *Inferno* 26.94–8: 'né dol-
cezza di figlio, né la pieta / del vecchio padre, né 'l debito amore / lo qual
dovea Penelopè far lieta / vincer potero dentro me l'ardore / ch'i' ebbi a
divenir del mondo esperto.' (neither fondness for my son, nor reverence for
my aged father, nor the due love which would have made Penelope glad
could conquer in me the longing that I had to gain experience of the
world.)

115 The expression 'torcere in suso' is employed in canto 15 (49–54), within
the description of envy: 'Perché s'appuntano i vostri disiri / dove per
compagnia parte si scema, / invidia move il mantaco a' sospiri. / Ma se

l'amor de la spera supprema / torcesse in suso il disiderio vostro, / non vi
sarebbe al petto quella tema.' (Because your desires are centered there
where the portion is lessened by partnership, envy moves the bellows to
your sighs. But if the love of the highest sphere turned upward your desire,
that fear would not be at your heart.)

116 For the interpretation of these lines, see Chiavacci Leonardi, *Purgatorio*,
624. For the reading of *talento* as 'desire' (as opposed to the traditional
reading of *voglia* as 'absolute will' and *talento* as 'relative will') see G.
Padoan, 'Il canto XXI del Purgatorio,' *Nuove letture dantesche* 4 (1970): 327–
54, esp. 342–4. On this passage, see also K. Foster, 'Dante's Idea of Purgatory, with Special Reference to Purgatorio XXI, 58–66,' in *Dies Illa: Death in
the Middle Ages; Proceedings of the 1983 Manchester Colloquium*, ed. J.H.M. Taylor (Liverpool: Cairns, 1984), 97–105. For the double thrust of joy and pain
in purgatorial sufferance, see M. Gragnolati and C. Holzhey, 'Dolore come
gioia: Trasformarsi nel *Purgatorio* di Dante,' *Psiche* 2 (2003): 111–26.

117 The image of the traveller's desire in Dante and its relation with both the
medieval practice of pilgrimage and mystical writings has been studied by
M. Picone, '*Peregrinus Amoris*: La metafora finale,' in *Vita Nuova e tradizione
romanza*, 129–92; and Pertile, '*Paradiso*: A Drama of Desire.'

118 *Paradiso* 24.130–2 'Io credo in uno Dio / solo ed etterno, che tutto 'l ciel
move / non moto, con amore e con disio.' (I believe in one God, sole and
eternal, who, unmoved, moves all the heavens with love and with desire.)

119 *Paradiso* 1.76–8: 'Quando la rota che tu sempiterni / desiderato, a sé mi
fece atteso / con l'armonia che temperi e discerni' (When the revolution
which Thou, by being desired, makest eternal turned my attention unto
itself by the harmony which Thou dost temper and distinguish).

120 *Paradiso* 3.70–86: 'Frate, la nostra volontà quïeta / virtù di carità, che fa
volerne / sol quel ch'avemo, e d'altro non ci asseta. / Se disïassimo esser
più superne, / foran discordi li nostri disiri / dal voler di colui che qui ne
cerne ... Anzi è formale ad esto beato *esse* / tenersi dentro a la divina
voglia, / perch'una fansi nostre voglie stesse; / sì che, come noi sem di
soglia in soglia / per questo regno, a tutto il regno piace / com'a lo re ch'n
suo voler ne 'nvoglia / E 'n sua volontade è nostra pace.' (Brother, the
power of love quiets our will and makes us wish only for that which we have
and gives us no other thirst. Did we desire to be more aloft, our longings
would be discordant with His will who assigns us here ... Nay, it is the
essence of this blessed existence to keep itself within the divine will,
whereby our wills themselves are made one; so that our being thus from
threshold to threshold throughout this realm is a joy to all the realm as to
the King who draws our wills to what He wills; and in His will is our peace.)

121 Pertile, '*Paradiso*: A Drama of Desire,' 154–5.
122 Bynum, *The Resurrection of the Body*, 339, passim.
123 For the role of Dante's last guide, see S. Botterill, *Dante and the Mystical Tradition: Bernard of Clairvaux in the 'Commedia'* (Cambridge: Cambridge University Press, 1994).
124 The word *finii* does not mean in this context the end of desire, but its ripeness and fullness. As Singleton (*Paradiso*, 2:569) remarks, 'The meaning of the verb in this verse is much debated, but one aspect of that meaning seems beyond discussion: "finii" cannot be here in a normal signification of "bringing to an end." Indeed, the context requires that the meaning be the exact opposite, i.e., "I brought the ardor of my desire to the highest intensity." Bernard is urging the wayfarer on precisely in this sense, and the importance of the wayfarer's cooperation in the final act is thus stressed and continues to be stressed.'

　　Chiavacci Leonardi (*Paradiso*, 913–14) points out the similarity with *Convivio* 3.10.2 – 'quanto la cosa desiderata più appropinqua al desiderante, tanto lo desiderio è maggiore' – and with Aquinas's *Summa contra Gentiles* 3.50 – 'Quanto aliquid est finis propinquior, tanto maiori desiderio tendit ad finem.'
125 In the three canticles the movements of desire and will trace three different directions, which, interestingly, correspond to the direction of the structural notion of desire in each canticle. In *Inferno* 5, upon Dante's request of an exchange of words with Paolo and Francesca, desire and will trace a parallel, linear direction, where *chiamate* implies a forward attraction, while *portate* a push from the back (82–4): 'Quali colombe dal desio chiamate / con l'ali alzate e ferme al dolce nido, / vegnon per l'aere dal voler portate.' (As doves called by desire, with wings raised and steady, come through the air, borne by their will to their sweet nest.) In *Purgatorio* 21 (61–6), within Stazio's explanation of how the purged soul passes to heaven, *voglia* and *talento* describe, as previously discussed, a spiral movement, which strikes a balance between the will to rise to Heaven and the desire to be purged. In the final vision, the movement of desire and will is circular.

　　In this context, it is also worth noticing that there is an instance in the *Paradiso* where language too is described as a movement of desire and will, in canto 15 (67–9): 'la voce tua, sicura, balda e lieta / suoni la volontà, suoni il disio / a che la mia risposta è già decreta' (let your voice confident and bold and glad, sound forth the will, sound forth the desire, whereto my answer is already decreed). Through the termination of desire in the final image, language also enjoys a suspended, quiet, circular moment, which coincides with the full stop of the poem. It is then interesting to recall here

the interplay of desire and will in the production of language as described
by Augustine in *De Trinitate* (see chap. 1). Desire and will act in Augustine as
the two drives for the formation of the interior word. The rightful word, the
one born *in caritate*, is the word in which desire doesn't exceed will, and vice
versa. The sinful word, the one born *in cupiditate*, shows an imbalance
between the two forces. Applying Augustine's reflections to the *Divine Comedy*, we can argue that only the perfectly even movement of the final image
grants a perfect balance between the two drives, and therefore it can coincide with 'syntactic' silence.

126 Barolini, 'The Sacred Poem Is Forced to Jump: Closure and the Poetics of
Enjambment,' in *The Undivine Comedy*, 218–56. In the same volume, see also
'Problems in Paradise: The Mimesis of Time and the Paradox of Più e
Meno' (166–93). On *disagguaglianza*, see also Pertile, '*Paradiso*: A Drama of
Desire,' 152–3.

127 *Paradiso* 28.1–3: 'Già si godeva solo del suo verbo / quello specchio beato, e
io gustava / lo mio, temprando col dolce l'acerbo.' (Already that blessed
mirror was enjoying only his own thoughts, and I was tasting mine, temper-
ing the bitter with the sweet.) Notice that in this passage Cacciaguida's
speech belongs to the Augustinian order of *frui* ('godeva'), whereas Dante
still 'tastes' his ('gustava'). It is also worth noticing that the episode, which
closes here with an 'individual' silence, opens instead with a choral silence
of the heaven of Mars. The first silence is, once again, a production of heavenly love, which allows communication between Dante and his ancestor
(15.1–6): 'Benigna volontade in che si liqua / sempre l'amor che dritta-
mente spira, / come cupidità fa ne l'iniqua, / silenzio puose a quella dolce
lira, / e fece quïetar le sante corde, / che la destra del cielo allenta e tira.'
(Gracious will, wherein right-breathing love always resolves itself, as cupidity does into grudging will, imposed silence on that sweet lyre and quieted
the holy strings which the right hand of Heaven slackens and draw tight.)
The two silences indeed mark the significance of the episode, a true 'sentence' in *Paradiso*.

128 For the body in Dante's *Commedia*, see Bynum, *The Resurrection of the Body in
Western Christianity*, 291–305; R. Jacoff, '"Our Bodies, Ourselves": The Body
in the *Commedia*,' in *Sparks and Seeds: Medieval Literature and Its Afterlife:
Essays in Honor of John Freccero*, ed. D. Stewart and A. Cornish (Brepols: Turnhout, 2000), 118–37; and Gragnolati, *Experiencing the Afterlife*. For connections between language and the body, see Cestaro, *Dante and the Grammar of
the Nursing Body*.

129 *De vulgari eloquentia* 1.3.1: 'Nec per spiritualem speculationem, ut angelum,
alterum alterum introire contigit, cum grossitie atque opacitate mortalis

corporis humanus spiritus sit obtectus.' (Nor it is given to us to enter into each other's minds by means of spiritual reflection as the angels do, because the human spirit is so weighed down by the heaviness and density of the mortal body.)

130 In Dante's usage *intero* suggests, both literally and figuratively, the idea of something complete in its parts as opposed to broken up into pieces. See *intero* in *Enciclopedia Dantesca*, 3:484.

131 For the complexity of Dante's usage of the Aristotelian-Thomistic notion of perfection, see A. Niccoli, *perfetto*, and A. Maierù, *perfezione*, in *Enciclopedia Dantesca*, 4:412–17. The simplest definition of the Aristotelian notion of perfection can be found in *Convivio* 4.16.7: 'Questa perfezione intende lo Filosofo nel settimo della Fisica quando dice: 'Ciascuna [cosa] è massimamente perfetta quando tocca e aggiugne la sua vertude propia, e allora è massimamente secondo sua natura; onde allora lo circulo si può dicere perfetto quando veramente è circulo.' (It is this perfection that the Philosopher refers to in the seventh book of the Physics when he says, 'Each thing is most completely perfect when it reaches and attains its own proper virtue, and it is then most completely perfect according to its nature. Hence a circle can then be called perfect when it is truly a circle.') Perfection in nature as described in this passage is modelled in turn on that of the heavens, of the Divine Virtues, and, finally, of God, perfect because 'pure act,' and the source of every perfection.

132 For a discussion of Solomon's speech in the contex of the *Comedy*'s eschatological panorama, see M. Gragnolati, 'From Plurality to (Near) Unicity of Forms: Embryology in Purgatorio 25,' in *Dante for the New Millennium*, 192–210.

133 See A.M. Chiavacci Leonardi, 'Il canto XXX del Paradiso,' in *Paragone* 26, no. 308 (1975): 3–34, especially 14–15. By the same author see also '"Le bianche stole": Il tema della risurrezione nel *Paradiso*,' in *Dante e la Bibbia*, ed. G. Barblan (Florence: Olschki, 1988), 249–71.

134 See C. Singleton, 'The Irreducible Vision,' in *Illuminated Manuscripts of the Divine Comedy*, ed. P. Brieger, M. Meiss, and C. Singleton (Princeton: Princeton University Press, 1969) 1:1–29, especially 22–6.

135 For the controversial interpretation of line 139, see G. Nencioni, 'Ma perché 'l tempo fugge che t'assonna (Par. XXXII 139),' in 'Note dantesche' *Studi Danteschi* 40 (1963): 50–6.

136 For the connection between the bound volume, the scattering of the Sibyl's leaves, and the Augustinian notion of temporal/sequential vs. eternal/simultaneous order, see J. Ahern, 'Binding the Book: Hermeneutics and Manuscript Production in *Paradiso* XXXIII,' *PMLA* 97, no. 5 (1982): 800–9.

137 In canto 14 we also witness another interesting negotiation between the
sign and the body, here the body of Christ. After Solomon's speech on resurrection, the vision of Christ on the cross dissolves signs into unintelligible
meaning, so that only the key words of resurrection, *resurgi* and *vinci*, reach
the pilgrim's understanding. I have already discussed this passage as an
example of aphasia in *Paradiso*. Here it is also worth noticing that the rhyme
between the verb *vinci* (125), celebrating Christ's victory over death, and
the word for 'bindings' (*vinci*, 129) is suggestive of a new form of syntax, a
syntax of the body, that the pilgrim experiences for the first time.

Epilogue

1 Interestingly, *language, desire,* and *poetry* are terms that often recur in the
theological definition of the postmodern god, which appears as a connective, articulative locus of desire. Contemporary theology, more and more
threatened by secularism, looks for justifications into language and desire –
indeed reclaims the spaces of language and desire as made meaningful only
by transcendence. Useful guides to explore the discourse of contemporary
theology on the themes of language and desire are G. Ward, ed., *The Postmodern God: A Theological Reader* (Oxford: Blackwell, 1997); J. Milbank, *The
Word Made Strange: Theology, Language, Culture* (Oxford: Blackwell, 1997); F.
Kerr, *Immortal Longings: Versions of Transcending Humanity* (Notre Dame:
University of Notre Dame Press, 1997); J. Milbank, C. Pickstock, and G.
Ward, eds., *Radical Orthodoxy: A New Theology* (London: Routledge, 1999);
and O. Davies and D. Turner, eds., *Silence and the Word: Negative Theology and
Incarnation* (Cambridge: Cambridge University Press, 2002).
2 F. Nietzsche, *Twilight of the Idols,* trans. R.J. Hollingdale (London: Penguin,
1990), 48. Excellent surveys of the problem of language in the twentieth century are G.C. Lepschy, *La linguistica strutturale* (Turin: Einaudi, 1990) and
Lepschy, *La linguistica del Novecento* (Bologna: Il Mulino, 1992). An extremely
helpful survey of philosophy and linguistics with focus on syntax is G. Graffi,
200 Years of Syntax: A Critical Survey (Amsterdam: Benjamins, 2002).
3 See in particular G. Ward, '"In the Daylight Forever?" Language and
Silence,' in *Silence and the Word,* 159–84, in particular 172–3. Several essays
in this volume mention the abovementioned comparison.
4 L. Wittgenstein, *Tractatus Logico-Philosophicus,* trans. D.F. Pears and B.F.
McGuinnes (New York: Routledge, 1961), 3, 5.
5 G.E.M. Anscombe, *An Introduction to Wittgenstein's Tractatus* (London:
Hutchinson, 1959), 29. See *Tractatus* 2.03: 'In a state of affairs objects fit
into one another like the links of a chain.'

6 Wittgenstein, *Tractatus* 3.26: 'A name cannot be dissected any further by means of a definition: it is a primitive sign.'

7 *Tractatus*, 4.002: 'Man possesses the ability to construct languages capable of expressing every sense, without having any idea how each word has meaning or what its meaning is – just as people speak without knowing how the individual sounds are produced.

Everyday language is a part of the human organism and no less complicated than it.

It is not humanly possible to gather immediately from it what the logic of language is.

Language disguises thought. So much so, that from the outward form of clothing it is impossible to infer the form of the thought beneath it, because the outward form of the clothing is not designed to reveal the form of the body, but for entirely different purposes.

The tacit conventions on which the understanding of everyday language depends are enormously complicated.'

8 Perhaps the best snapshot of Wittgenstein criticism of the *Tractatus* is contained in paragraph 97 of the *Philosophical Investigations*: 'Thought is surrounded by a halo. – Its essence, logic, presents an order, in fact the a priori order of the world, that is, the order of *possibilities*, which must be common to both world and thought. But this order, it seems, must be *utterly simple*. It is *prior* to all experience, must run through all experience; no empirical cloudiness or uncertainty can be allowed to affect it – it must rather be of the purest crystal. But this crystal does not appear as an abstraction; but as something concrete, indeed, as the most concrete, as it were the hardest thing that there is (*Tractatus Logico-Philosophicus* No. 5.5563).

We are under the illusion that what is peculiar, profound, essential in our investigation, resides in its trying to grasp the incomparable essence of language. That is, in the order existing between the concepts of proposition, word, proof, truth, experience and so on. This order is a *super*-order between – so to speak – *super*-concepts. Whereas, of course, if the words "language," "experience," "world," have a use, it must be as humble a one as that of the words "table," "lamp," "door."' *Philosophical Investigations*, trans. G.E.M. Anscombe (Oxford: Blackwell, 1953), 44.

9 A clear exposition of the theme of philosophical grammar is found in N. Garver, 'Philosophy as Grammar,' in *The Cambridge Companion to Wittgenstein*, ed. H. Sluga and D.G. Stern (Cambridge: Cambridge University Press, 1996), 139–70. For a theological perspective on Wittgenstein's theory of language and notion of grammar, see F. Kerr, *Theology after Wittgenstein* (Oxford: Blackwell, 1986); and C. Cunningham, 'Wittgenstein after Theology,' in *Rad-*

ical Orthodoxy, 64–90. Cunningham (69) quotes an interesting rewriting and disowning of the image of the ladder that ends the *Tractatus* from *Culture and Value.* 'I might say: if the place I want to get to could only be reached by way of a ladder, I would give up trying to get there. For the place I really have to go to is a place I must already be at now. Anything that I might reach by climbing a ladder does not interest me.'

10 Circulating between language and the world, the quest for the logical form has a long and varied history throughout the century (the term resurfaces, for instance, in generative grammar as one of the components of language). On this theme, see G. Graffi, 'The Language of Logical Form,' in *Incommensurability and Translation: Kuhnian Perspectives on Scientific Communication and Theory Change,* ed. R. Rossini Favretti, G. Sandri, and R. Scazzieri (Cheltenham: Elgar, 1999), 443–53. The closest approximation between syntax in a grammatical sense, logic, and the form of the world is contained in R. Carnap's *The Logical Syntax of Language* (1934). In the introduction Carnap states that 'logic will become a part of syntax, provided that the latter is conceived in a sufficiently wide sense and formulated with exactitude. The difference between syntactical rules in the narrower sense and the logical rules of deduction is only the difference between formation rules and transformation rules.' *The Logical Syntax of Language,* trans. A. Smeaton (London: Kegan Paul Trench Trubner, 1937), 2. As a result of the imperfect structure of natural language, Carnap's inquiry takes place within symbolic languages taken as a model of the former.

11 F. de Saussure, *Cours de linguistique générale,* ed. C. Bally and A. Sechehaye (Paris: Payot, 1916). On Saussure, see K. Korner, *Ferdinand de Saussure: Origin and Development of His Linguistic Thought in Western Studies of Language* (Braunschwieg: Vieweg, 1973); and Lepschy, *La linguistica strutturale,* 42–53, and *La linguistica del Novecento,* 39–57. An extremely valuable introduction and commentary are contained in the Italian edition, *Corso di linguistica generale,* ed. T. de Mauro (Bari: Laterza, 1968). English translations are taken from *Course in General Linguistics,* trans. W. Baskin (New York: McGraw Hill, 1966). Page numbers refer to the French edition of the *Cours.* For connections between Saussure and the later Wittgenstein on the theme of language games, see R. Harris, *Language, Saussure and Wittgenstein: How to Play Games with Words* (London: Routledge, 1988).

12 Lepschy, *Linguistica del Novecento,* 46.

13 The peremptory conclusion of the *Cours,* which sanctions *langue* as the subject matter of linguistics was, however, an addition of the editors. On this point, see De Mauro, *Corso di linguistica generale,* 455–6n305.

14 For a discussion of linguistic identity, see *Cours,* 150–4.

15 *Cours*, 157: 'Language can also be compared with a sheet of paper: thought is the front and the sound the back; one cannot cut the front without cutting the back at the same time; likewise in language, one can neither divide sound from thought nor thought from sound; the division could be accomplished only abstractedly, and the result would be either pure psychology or pure phonology.'

16 *Cours*, 166: 'A linguistic system is a series of differences of sound combined with a series of differences of ideas; but the pairing of a certain number of acoustical signs with as many cuts made from the mass of thought engenders a system of values; and this system serves as the effective link between the phonic and psychological elements within each sign.' Saussure discusses the notion of linguistic value on pp. 160–6. Both in conceptual (in terms of signification) and in material (phonic) terms, linguistic value is given not by the word or sound itself but by its surroundings.

17 See *Cours*, 97–102; Lepschy, *Linguistica del Novecento*, 44–8. For the 'radicality' of this aspect, see De Mauro, *Corso di linguistica generale*, 412–13n136.

18 *Cours*, 103: 'The signifier, being auditory is unfolded solely in time from which it gets the following characteristics: (a) it represents a span, and (b) the span is measurable in a single dimension; it is a line. While Principle II is obvious, apparently linguists have always neglected to state it, doubtless because they found it too simple; nevertheless, it is fundamental, and its consequences are incalculable. Its importance equals that of Principle I; the whole mechanism of language depends upon it. In contrast to visual signifiers (nautical signals, etc) which can offer simultaneous groupings in several dimensions, auditory signifiers have at their command only the dimension of time. Their elements are presented in succession; they form a chain. This feature becomes readily apparent when they are represented in writing and the spatial line of graphic marks is substituted for succession in time.'

   For the controversial issue of whether Saussure is picturing the linearity of the minimal units of the signifier (and of whether the minimal units of the signifier are the phonemes, as later structural linguistics held), see De Mauro, *Corso di linguistica generale*, 401–3n111 and 419–20n145.

19 *Cours*, 170–1: 'In discourse, on the one hand, words acquire relations based on the linear nature of language because they are chained together. This rules out the possibility of pronouncing two elements simultaneously. The elements are arranged in sequence on the chain of speaking. Combinations supported by linearity are syntagms. The syntagm is always composed of two or more consecutive units ... Outside discourse, on the other hand, words acquire relations of a different kind. Those that have something in common are associated in the memory, resulting in groups marked by diverse rela-

tions ... The syntagmatic relation is *in praesentia*. It is based on two or more terms that occur in an effective series. Against this, the associative relation unites terms *in absentia* in a potential mnemonic series.'

20 *Cours*, 179: 'Our memory holds in reserve all the more or less complex types of syntagms, regardless of their class or length, and we bring in the associative groups to fix our choice when the time for using them arrives.'

21 While the associative aspect belongs fully to *langue*, the syntagmatic is suspended between *langue* and *parole*. 'But we must realize that in the syntagm there is no clear-cut boundary between the language fact, which is a sign if collective usage, and the fact that belongs to speaking and depends on individual freedom. In a great number of instances it is hard to class a combination of unities because both forces have combined in producing it, and they have combined in indeterminable proportion' (*Cours*, 173). Saussure's position on whether the syntagmatic associations (and especially syntax) belong to *langue* or *parole* is truly open and undecided. An open question is posited on p. 148, in evident opposition to the logical tendency to reason in terms of propositions: 'A rather widely held theory makes sentences the concrete units of language: we speak only in sentences and consequently single out words. But to what extent does the sentence belong to language?' In the following discussion (172–3), the sentence is presented as a matter of *parole*, but not every syntagm is (examples of syntagms belonging to *langue* are the ready-made phrases and syntagms built on a regular pattern). While subsequent structural linguistics took the sentence to be a part of *parole*, De Mauro (*Corso di linguistica generale*, 445–7n251) argues convincingly that Saussure's thought on the topic was much more undecided. On this point, see also Graffi, *200 Years*, 169–70.

22 As it is well known, the term *structural linguistics* can be used in two ways. In a narrow sense it identifies only one school, American structuralism, originating from Bloomfield. In a wider sense, it embraces most of twentieth-century linguistics – the Prague and Copenhagen schools, American structuralism, formalist linguistics, all the way to generative grammar. For the justification of the more comprehensive understanding of the term and for an overview of these phases, see Lepschy, *La linguistica strutturale*.

23 See Lepschy, *La linguistica del Novecento*, 59.

24 N. Chomsky, *Aspects of the Theory of Syntax* (Cambridge, MA: MIT Press, 1965), 4.

25 For the Cartesian roots of universal grammar, see N. Chomsky, *Cartesian Linguistics* (New York: Harper & Row, 1966).

26 N. Chomsky, 'Reflections on Language,' in *On Language* (New York: New Press, 1998), 29.

27 See N. Chomsky, 'Language and Responsibility,' in *On Language*, 171.

28 Chomsky, 'Language and Responsibility,' 183.
29 Graffi, *200 Years of Syntax*, 427.
30 Chomsky, 'Language and Responsibility,' 52: 'It is possible that the theory of face perception resembles a generative grammar. Just as in language, if you suppose that there are base structures and transformed structures, then one might imagine a model which would generate the possible human faces, and the transformations which would tell you what each face would look like from all angles. To be sure, the formal theories would be very different from those of language.'
    See also 'Reflections on Language,' 8: 'He [Gregory] suggests further that there may be a "grammar of vision," rather like the grammar of human language and possibly related to the latter in the evolution of the species. Employing this grammar of vision – largely innate – higher animals are able to "read from retinal images even hidden features of objects and predict their immediate future states," thus "to classify objects according to an internal grammar, to read reality from their eyes."'
    On cognitive issues related to language, see also N. Chomsky, *Language and Mind* (New York: New Press, 1968), and *Language and Thought* (Wakefield, RI: Moyer Bell, 1993).
31 See N. Chomsky, *The Minimalist Program* (Cambridge, MA: MIT Press, 1995), 1–10. For a description of these phases, see Graffi, *200 Years of Syntax*, 330–68, 425–85.
32 See N. Chomsky, *Syntactic Structures* (The Hague: Mouton, 1957), 14–17.
33 The thesis for the autonomy of syntax is one of the strongest and most controversial aspects of Chomksy's theory. See *Language and Responsibility*, 138–9: 'one cannot "pick up" a disembodied meaning that floats about in the air and then construct a form which expresses it. It isn't easy to make much sense of any of this. It seems to me that the elements of syntax are not established on a semantic basis, and that the mechanisms of syntax, once they have been constructed, function independently of the other components of the grammar, which are interpretive components ... I think, in fact, that the thesis of the autonomy of syntax, in the form proposed in the fifties and since then is probably correct. However, I have always explicitly denied and rejected a totally different position which has often been attributed to me: namely, that the study of meaning and reference and of the use of the language should be excluded from the field of linguistics.'
34 Chomsky, 'Reflections on Language,' 133.
35 Chomsky, *Aspects of the Theory of Syntax*, 136.
36 See *Aspects*, 135–6: 'Thus the syntactic component consists of a base that generates deep structures and a transformational part that maps them into sur-

face structures. The deep structure of a sentence is submitted to the semantic component for semantic interpretation, and its surface structure enters the phonological component and enters the phonological interpretations. The final aspect of a grammar, then, is to relate a semantic interpretation to a phonetic representation – that is, to state how a sentence is interpreted. This relation is mediated by the syntactic component of the grammar, which constitutes its sole "creative" part.'

37 Lepschy, *Linguistica strutturale*, 179.

38 On the tautology of theology, see K. Burke, *The Rhetoric of Religion* (Boston: Beacon, 1961).

39 Lepschy, *Linguistica del Novecento*, 94.

40 G. Lakoff and M. Johnson, *Philosophy in the Flesh: The Embodied Mind and Its Challenge to Western Thought* (New York: Basic Books, 1999).

41 Ibid., 3. For a discussion of the three tenets, see 3–118.

42 Ibid., 4. Examples of primary metaphors in everyday thought and language are, for instance, 'Affection is Warmth,' 'Happy is Up,' 'Knowing is Seeing' (45–59). Primary metaphors form complex metaphors, as atoms can be built up into molecules. An example of a complex metaphor is 'A Purposeful Life is a Journey' (60–3). An example of metaphor employed in philosophy is Plato's 'the Essences are Ideas' (367–9).

43 Other 'non-essential' aspects of language include 'pragmatics, discourse, linguistic processing, the neural instantiation of language, cultural linguistic differences, and animal communication' (*Philosophy in the Flesh*, 478).

44 The main tenets of cognitive linguistics are discussed on 496–508. A convenient summary can be read on p. 506, of which the following are the most salient points: 'First, it [language capacity] is seen fundamentally as a neural capacity, the capacity to neurally link parts of the brain concerned with concepts and cognitive functions (attention, memory, information flow) with other parts concerned with expression ... Second, the structure of language is inherently embodied ... Third, syntactic categories are induced by conceptual categories ... Fourth, grammatical constructions are parings of complex conceptual categories and cognitive functions with their mean of expression. Fifth, the language capacity is the total capacity to express concepts and cognitive functions ... Sixth, grammatical universals are universals concerning the pairing of form and content; they are not universals of form alone.'

45 *Philosophy in the Flesh*, 512: 'Given that our language never just fits the world, that it always incorporates an embodied understanding, it becomes the job of the philosophy of language to characterize that embodied understanding accurately, and to point out its consequences. Under such a reconceptualization, the philosophy of language, using cognitive linguistics, becomes appli-

cable to every human endeavor. Its job is to reveal the cognitive unconscious in an empirically responsible way and to show why such revelations matter. It is a job of urgent and extraordinary importance in many areas of life – in morality, politics, economics, education, interpersonal relations, religion, and throughout our culture.'

46 J. Kristeva's most influential essays on language are now collected in the volume *Desire in Language: A Semiotic Approach to Literature and Art* (New York: Columbia University Press, 1980). Σημειωτική: *Recherches pour une sémanalyse* (Paris: Seuil, 1969), and *La révolution du langage poétique* (Paris: Seuil, 1974), are worth keeping in mind in their entirety.

47 For Lacan's vision of language as constructing the subject by constricting the multiplicity of its desires, see later in this chapter.

48 Kristeva, *Desire in Language*, 133.

49 See 'The Ethics of Linguistics' in *Desire in Language*, 23–35, in particular, 24–5: 'It follows that formulating the problem of linguistic ethics means, above all, compelling linguistics to change its subject of study. The speech practice that should be its object is one in which signified structure (sign, syntax signification) is defined within boundaries that can be shifted by the advent of a semiotic rhythm that no system of linguistic communication has yet been able to assimilate. It would deflect linguistics toward a consideration of language as articulation of a heterogeneous process, with the speaking subject leaving its imprint on the dialectic between the articulation and its process. In short, this would establish *poetic language* as the object of linguistics' attention in its pursuit of truth in language. This does not necessarily mean, as is often said today, that poetic language is subject to *more* constraints than 'ordinary language.' It means that we must analyze those elements of the complex operation I shall call poetic language (in which the dialectics of the subject is inscribed) that are screened out by ordinary language – a practice *for which any particular language is at the margin*. The term poetry has meaning only insofar as it makes this kind of study acceptable to various educational and cultural institutions. But the stakes it entails are totally different; what is implied is that language, and thus sociability are defined by boundaries admitting of upheaval, dissolution and transformation.'

50 Kristeva, *Desire in Language*, 124–47.

51 See also Kristeva, 'Place Names,' in *Desire in Language*, 271–94.

52 Kristeva, *Desire in Language*, 136: 'Language as symbolic function constitutes itself at the cost of repressing instinctual drive and continuous relation to the mother. On the contrary, the unsettled and questionable subject of poetic language (for whom the word is never uniquely a sign) maintains itself at the cost of reactivating this repressed instinctual, maternal element.

If it is true that the prohibition of incest constitutes, at the same time, language as communicative code and women as exchange objects in order for a society to be established, *poetic language* would be for its questionable subject-in-process *the equivalent of incest*: it is within the economy of signification itself that the questionable subject-in-process appropriates to itself this archaic, instinctual and maternal territory; thus it simultaneously prevents the word from becoming mere sign and the mother from becoming an object like any other – forbidden.'

53 For a hint to poetry in the Chomskian theory, see *Language and Thought*, 93–4. For the project of a 'generative poetics,' see M. Halle and S.J. Keyser, *English Stress: Its Form, Its Growth, and Its Role in Verse* (New York: Harper & Row, 1971).

54 The Modistae had *cappa categorica* (as a congruous but improper construction) vs. *cappa nigra* (a congruous and proper construction). L. Tesnière has 'Le silence vertébral indispose la voie licite,' a sentence composed by the words that follow in the dictionary the words that compose 'Le signal vert indique la voie libre.' See L. Tesnière, *Éléments de syntaxe stucturale* (Paris: Klincksieck, 1959), 42. 'Le silence vertebral' shows a curious affinity to 'green ideas' when subjected to a syntagmatic analysis. When broken up into its components, 'Silence vert-ebral' associatively recalls 'green ideas,' and looks almost like an anagram of the linguistic trade.

For a response to Chomsky, see M.A.K. Halliday, 'Categories of the Theory of Grammar,' *Word* 17 (1961): 241–92, esp. 275.

55 In J. Hollander, *Night Mirror* (New York: Atheneum, 1971), 42. A cursory Web search on 'colorless green ideas' revealed other poetic applications and, curiously, a frequent use of this sentence in advertisements (for example, for a writing workshop for student papers and for a dictionary).

56 A. Rimbaud, 'Voyelles,' in *Oeuvres* (Paris: Garnier, 1960), 110: 'U, cycles, vibrements divins des mers virides, / paix de pâtis semés d'animaux, paix des rides / que l'alchimie imprime aux grands fronts studieux'; and A. Marvell, 'The Garden,' in *The Poems of Andrew Marvell* (London: Pearson, 2003), 157–8: 'the mind, that ocean where each kind / does straight its own resemblance find; / yet it creates, transcending these, far other worlds, and other seas; / annihilating all that's made / to a green thought in a green shade.'

57 M. Heidegger, *On the Way to Language*, trans. P.D. Hertz (New York: Harper and Row, 1971), 69.

58 T.S. Eliot, 'The Social Function of Poetry,' in *On Poetry and Poets* (London: Faber, 1957), 20. Eliot's statement is framed within the consideration of the relevance of national languages for the poet. At the end of the essay, however, Eliot extends his considerations on the power of language to poetic lan-

guage itself: 'But I have found sometimes that a piece of poetry, which I could not translate, containing many words unfamiliar to me, and sentences which I could not construe, conveyed something immediate and vivid, which was unique, different from anything in English – something which I could not put into words and yet felt that I understood' (24).

59 For Nietzsche's theory of language, see C. Crawford, *The Beginnings of Nietzsche's Theory of Language* (Berlin: De Gruyter, 1988); for Nietzsche's use of language, see M. Haar, 'Nietzsche and Metaphysical Language,' in *The New Nietzsche: Contemporary Styles of Interpretation*, David B. Allison, ed. (New York: Dell, 1977), 5–36, and J. Derrida, *Éperons: Les Styles de Nietzsche* (Paris: Flammarion, 1978).

60 The line recurs at least fifteen times in *On the Way to Language*. A fascinating reading of Heiddeger's language/poetry can be found in G. Vattimo, 'Heidegger e la poesia come tramonto del linguaggio,' in *Al di là del soggetto*, 4th ed. (Milan: Feltrinelli, 1991), 75–96. See also G.L. Bruns, *Heidegger's Estrangements: Language, Truth and Poetry in the Later Writings* (New Haven: Yale University Press, 1989).

61 On Saussure's anagrams, see J. Starobinski, *Les mots sous les mots: Les anagrammes de Ferdinand de Saussure* (Paris: Gallimard, 1971); and J. Kristeva, 'Pour une sémiologie des paragrammes,' in Σημειωτικὴ, 113–46.

62 R. Jakobson and L. Waugh, *The Sound Shape of Language* (Brighton: Harvester, 1979), 221.

63 See R. Jakobson, *Collected Writings*, vol. 3, *Poetry of Grammar and Grammar of Poetry* (The Hague: Mouton, 1981), in particular the essays 'Linguistics and Poetics' (18–51), and 'Poetry of Grammar and Grammar of Poetry' (87–97).

64 Jakobson, 'Linguistics and Poetics,' 42.

65 Jakobson, 'Poetry of Grammar and Grammar of Poetry,' 92.

66 'Two Aspects of Language and Two Types of Aphasic Disturbances,' in *Fundamentals of Language*, 69–96. For this essay, see also chapter 3.

67 Jakobson, 'Poetry of Grammar and Grammar of Poetry,' 92 and 95. According to Jakobson, grammar works in poetry as geometry in painting (97).

68 P. de Man, *Resistance to Theory* (Minneapolis: University of Minnesota Press, 1986).

69 J. Butler, *Subjects of Desire: Hegelian Reflections in Twentieth-Century France* (New York: Columbia University Press, 1999).

70 Butler, *Subjects of Desire* (7): 'Hegel claims that "self consciousness in general is Desire" (¶ 167), by which he means that desire signifies the *reflexivity* of consciousness, the necessity that it become other to itself in order to know itself. As desire, consciousness is outside itself; and as outside itself is *self consciousness*.'

71 Interestingly, Hegel's style is compared to a line of poetry: 'Like a line of poetry that stops us and forces us to consider that the *way* in which it is said is essential to *what* it is saying, Hegel's sentences rhetorically call attention to themselves' (18).

72 The theme of language and desire is all-pervasive in Lacan's work. It can be best explored through the following texts. From *Écrits* (Paris: Seuil, 1966): 'Le stade du miroir comme formateur de la fonction du Je,' 93–100; 'Fonction et champ de la parole et du langage en psychanalyse,' 237–322; 'L'instance de la lettre dans l'inconscient ou la raison depuis Freud,' 493–530; 'La direction de la cure et les principes de son pouvoir,' 585–646; 'Remarque sur le rapport de Daniel Lagache: "Psychanalyse et structure de la personnalité,"' 647–84; 'La signification du phallus,' 685–96; 'Propos directifs pour un Congrès sur la sexualité féminine,' 725–36; 'Subversion du sujet et dialectique du désir dans l'inconscient freudien,' 793–828; 'Du "Trieb" de Freud et du désir du psychanalyste,' 851–4; and 'La science et la vérité,' 855–77. From *Le Séminaire III: Les Psychoses* (Paris: Seuil, 1981); *VI: Le Désir et ses interprétations, Ornicar?* 24–27 (1981–3); *XI: Les Quatre concepts fondamentaux de la psychanalyse* (Paris: Seuil, 1973); *XX: Encore* (Paris: Seuil, 1975).

An invaluable guide through Lacan's reflection on language and desire is M. Bowie, *Lacan* (Cambridge, MA: Harvard University Press, 1991). See also J. Muller and W. Richardson, *Lacan and Language: A Reader's Guide to the Écrits* (New York: International Universities Press, 1982); J. Mitchell and J. Rose, *Feminine Sexuality: Lacan and the 'École Freudienne'* (New York: Norton, 1982); J. Gallop, *Reading Lacan* (Ithaca: Cornell University Press, 1985); E. Ragland-Sullivan and M. Bracher, eds., *Lacan and the Subject of Language* (New York: Routledge, 1991); Butler, *Subjects of Desire*, 186–204; and S. Žižek, *The Sublime Object of Ideology* (London: Verso, 1989), esp. 87–129. Since Lacan's thought is recognizably incarnated in his style, I prefer quoting him in French. Translations are taken from *Écrits: A Selection*, trans. B. Fink (New York: Norton, 2002); *The Seminar of Jacques Lacan*, Book III, *The Psychoses*, ed. J.A. Miller, trans. R. Grigg (New York: Routledge, 1993), and *The Seminar of Jacques Lacan*, Book XX, *Encore*, ed. J.A. Miller, trans. B. Fink (New York: Norton, 1998).

73 *Écrits*, 629: 'il [le désir] est discours, discours dont Freud a commencé d'énoncer comme telle la grammaire.' (it is a discourse – a discourse whose grammar Freud began to enunciate as such.)

See also on 621, Lacan's transcription of 'the dream of the smoked salmon': 'Qu'on compte le nombre de renvois qui s'exercent ici pour porter le désir à une puissance géométriquement croissante. Un seul indice ne suffirait pas à en caractériser le degré. Car il faudrait distinguer deux dimensions à ces renvois: un désir de désir, autrement dit un désir signifié par un désir (le désir chez l'hystérique d'avoir un désir insatisfait, est signifié par son désir de caviar: le désir de caviar est son signifiant) s'inscrit dans le registre différent d'un désir substitué à un désir (dans le rêve, le désir de saumon fumé propre à l'amie est substitué au désir de caviar de la patiente, ce qui constitue la substitution d'un signifiant à un signifiant).' (One should try and count the number of referrals made here to bring desire to a geometrically higher power. A single index would not suffice to characterize the exponent. For it would be necessary to distinguish two dimensions in these deferrals: a desire for desire, in other words, a desire signified by desire [the hysteric's desire to have an unsatisfied desire is signified by her desire for caviar: the desire for caviar is its signifier], is inscribed in the different register of a desire substituted for a desire [in the dream, the desire for smoked salmon, characteristic of the patient's female friend, is substituted for the patient's own desire for caviar, which constitutes the substitution of a signifier for a signifier].)

74 *Séminaire XI*, 141: the nodal point between unconscious and sexuality, 'le désir se situe dans la dépendance de la demande – laquelle, de s'articuler en signifiants, laisse un reste métonymique qui court sous elle, élément qui n'est pas indéterminé, qui est une condition à la fois absolue et insaisissable, élément nécessairement en impasse, insatisfait, impossible, méconnu, élément qui s'appelle le désir.'

75 *Écrits*, 691: 'la puissance de la pure perte surgit du résidu d'une oblitération. A l'inconditionné de la demande, le désir substitue la condition "absolue": cette condition dénoue en effet ce que la preuve d'amour a de rebelle à la satisfaction d'un besoin. C'est ainsi que le désir n'est ni l'appétit de la satisfaction, ni la demande d'amour, mais la différence qui résulte de la soustraction du premier à la seconde, le phénomène même de leur refente (*Spaltung*).' (The power of pure loss emerges from the residue of an obliteration. For the unconditionality of demand, desire substitutes the 'absolute' condition: the condition in fact dissolves the element in the proof of love that rebels against the satisfaction of need. This is why desire is neither the appetite for satisfaction nor the demand for love, but the difference that results from the subtraction of the first from the second, the very phenomenon of their splitting [*Spaltung*].)

76 *Écrits*, 97: 'le *stade du miroir* est un drame dont la poussée interne se précipite de l'insuffisance à l'anticipation – et qui pour le sujet, pris au leurre de l'identification spatiale, machines le fantasmes qui se succèdent d'une image morcelée du corps à une forme que nous appellerons orthopédique de sa

totalité, – et à l'armure enfin assumée d'une identité aliénante, qui va marquer de sa structure rigide tout son développement mental.' (the mirror stage is a drama whose internal pressure pushes precipitously from insufficiency to anticipation – and, for the subject caught up in the lure of special identification, turns out fantasies that proceed from a fragmented image of the body to what I will call an 'orthopedic' form of its totality – and to the finally donned armor of an alienating identity that will mark his entire mental development with its rigid structure.)

And 94: 'Mais le point important est que cette forme situe l'instance du *moi*, dès avant sa détermination sociale, dans une ligne de fiction, à jamais irréductible pour le seul individu – ou plutôt, qui ne rejoindra qu'asymptotiquement le devenir du sujet.' (But the important point is that this form situates the agency known as the ego prior to its social determination, in a fictional direction that will forever remain irreducible for any single individual or, rather, that will only asymptotically approach the subject becoming.)

77 *Écrits*, 98: 'C'est ce moment qui décisivement fait basculer tout le savoir humain dans la médiatisation par le désir de l'autre, constitue ses objets dans une équivalence abstraite par la concurrence d'autrui, et fait du *je* cet appareil pour lequel toute poussée des instincts sera un danger.' (It is the moment that decisively tips the whole of human knowledge into being mediated by the other's desire, constitutes its objects in an abstract equivalence due to competition from other people, and turns the I into an apparatus to which every instinctual pressure constitutes a danger.)

78 *Écrits*, 279: 'Servitude et grandeur où s'anéantirait le vivant, si le désir ne préservait sa part dans les interférences et les battements que font converger sur lui les cycles du langage, quand la confusion de langues s'en mêle et que les ordres se contrarient dans les déchirements de l'œuvre universelle' (Servitude and grandeur in which the living being would be annihilated, if desire did not preserve his part in the interferences and pulsations that the cycles of language cause to converge on him, when the confusion of tongues intervenes and the orders thwart each other in the tearing asunder of the universal undertaking).

79 *Écrits*, 322: 'L'expérience psychanalytique a retrouvé dans l'homme l'impératif du verbe comme la loi qui l'a formé à son image. Elle manie la fonction poétique du langage pour donner à son désir sa médiation symbolique. Qu'elle vous fasse comprendre enfin que c'est dans le don de la parole que réside toute réalité de ses effets; car c'est par la voie de ce don que toute réalité est venue à l'homme et par son acte continué qu'il la maintient.' (Psychoanalytic experience has rediscovered in man the imperative of the Word as the law that has shaped him in its image. It exploits the poetic function of

language to give his desire its symbolic mediation. May this experience finally enable you to understand that the whole reality of its effects lies in the gift of speech; for it is through this gift that all reality has come to man and through its ongoing action that he sustains reality.) On this passage, see Bowie, *Lacan*, 85–6.

80 *Écrits*, 502: 'Mais ce n'est pas parce que les entreprises de la grammaire et du lexique s'épuisent à une certaine limite, qu'il faut penser que la signification règne au-delà sans partage. Ce serait une erreur. Car le signifiant de sa nature anticipe toujours sur le sens en déployant en quelque sorte au devant de lui sa dimension.' (But it is not because grammatical and lexical approaches are exhausted at a certain point that we must think that signification rules unreservedly beyond it. That would be a mistake. For the signifier, by its very nature, always anticipates meaning by deploying its dimension in some sense before it.)

81 Lacan here refers to 'Le point de capiton' in his seminar on psychoses: 'Autour de ce signifiant [le mot *crainte*], tout s'irradie et tout s'organise, à la façon de ces petites lignes de force formées à la surface d'une trame par le point de capiton. C'est le point de convergence qui permet de situer rétroactivement et prospectivement tout ce qui se passe dans ce discours' (The quilting point is the word *fear*, with all this trans-significant connotation. Everything radiates out from and is organized around this signifier, similar to this little lines of force that an upholstery button forms on the surface of material. It's the point of convergence that enables everything that happens in this discourse to be situated retroactively and prospectively) (*Séminaire III*, 303–4). For the *point de capiton*, see Žižek, *The Sublime Object of Ideology*, 87–100.

82 *Écrits*, 503: 'Mais il suffit d'écouter la poésie, ce qui sans doute était le cas de F. de Saussure, pour que s'y fasse entendre une polyphonie et que tout discours s'avère s'aligner sur les plusieurs portées d'une partition.' (But it suffices to listen to poetry, which Saussure was certainly in the habit of doing, for a polyphony to be heard and for it to become clear that all discourse is aligned along the several staves of a musical score.)

83 The metaphoric structure is represented by $f(S'/S)\, S \cong S\,(+)\,s$, and explained as follows: 'la structure métaphorique, indiquant que c'est dans la substitution du signifiant au signifiant que se produit un effet de signification qui est de poésie ou de création, autrement dit d'avènement de la signification en question. Le signe + placé entre () manifestant ici le franchissement de la barre – et la valeur constituante de ce franchissement pour l'émergence de la signification. Ce franchissement exprime la condi-

tion de passage du signifiant dans le signifié' (*Écrits*, 515). (metaphoric structure, indicating that it is in the substitution of signifier for signifier that a signification effect is produced that is poetic or creative, in other words that brings the signification in question into existence. The + sign in () manifests here the crossing of the bar, –, and the constitutive value of this crossing for the emergence of signification. This crossing expresses the condition for the passage of the signifier into the signified.)

84 The structure of metonymy is figured by f (S...S') S $\cong$ S (–) s, and explained as follows: 'la structure métonymique, indiquant que c'est la connexion du signifiant au signifiant, qui permet l'élision par quoi le signifiant installe le manque de l'être dans la relation d'objet, en se servant de la valeur de renvoi de la signification pour l'investir du désir visant ce manque qu'il supporte. Le signe – placé dans () manifestant ici le maintien de la barre – , qui dans l'algorithme premier marque l'irréductibilité où se constitue dans les rapports du signifiant au signifié, la résistance de la signification' (*Écrits*, 515). (metonymic structure, indicating that it is the signifier-to-signifier connection that allows for the elision by which the signifier instates lack of being in the object-relation, using signification's referral value to invest it with the desire aiming at the lack that it supports. The - sign placed in () manifests here the maintenance of the bar – which, in the first algorithm, denotes the irreducible nature of the resistance of signification as constituted in the relations between signifier and signified.)

For metonymy and metaphor, see also Gallop, *Reading Lacan*, 114–32. In 'The "Mechanics" of Fluids,' in *This Sex Which Is Not One*, trans. C. Porter and C. Burke (Ithaca, NY: Cornell University Press, 1985), 106–88, L. Irigaray criticizes psychoanalysis for privileging the solidity of metaphor over the fluidity of metonymy, and she notices, '*The object of desire itself*, and for psychoanalysts, *would be the transformation of fluid to solid?*' (113).

85 *Séminaire III*, 248: 'Sans la structure signifiante, c'est-à-dire sans l'articulation prédicative, sans la distance maintenue entre le sujet et ses attributs, on ne pourrait qualifier la gerbe d'avare et de haineuse. C'est parce qu'il y a une syntaxe, un ordre primordial de signifiant, que le sujet est maintenu séparé, comme différent de ses qualités. Il est tout à fait exclu qu'un animal fasse une métaphore, encore que nous n'ayons aucune raison de penser qu'il n'ait pas lui aussi l'intuition de ce qui est généreux et peut lui accorder facilement et en abondance ce qu'il désire. Mais dans la mesure où il n'a pas l'articulation, le discursif – qui n'est pas simplement signification, avec ce qu'elle comporte d'attrait ou de répulsion, mais alignement de signifiant –, la métaphore est impensable dans la psychologie animale de l'attraction, de

l'appétit, et du désir.' (Without the signifying structure, that is, without predicative articulation, without the distance maintained between the subject and its attributes, the sheaf cannot be qualified as miserly or spiteful. It's because there is a syntax, a primordial order of the signifier, that the subject is maintained as separate, as different from its qualities. It's completely out of the question that an animal could create a metaphor, even so we have no reason to think that it doesn't also have an intuition if what is generous and what can easily and abundantly grant it what it desires. But insofar as it doesn't posses the articulation, the discursive – which is not just meaning, is all that this entails about attraction and repulsion, but alignment of signifiers – metaphor is unthinkable within the animal psychology of attraction, appetite and desire.)

The contextualization of metaphor is discussed in linguistics by E. Benveniste. See P. Ricoeur, *La Métaphore vive* (Paris: Seuil, 1975), esp. 87–128.

86 *Écrits*, 518: 'le S et le *s* de l'algorithme saussurien ne sont pas dans le même plan, et l'homme se leurrait à se croire placé dans leur commun axe qui n'est nulle part.' (the S and the s of the Saussurian algorithm are not in the same plane, and man was deluding himself in believing he was situated in their common axis, which is nowhere.)

87 For a later, stronger rewriting of this thought, see *Écrits*, 848: 'le signifiant comme tel, a, en barrant le sujet par première intention, fait entrer en lui le sens de la mort. (La lettre tue, mais nous l'apprenons de la lettre elle-même). C'est ce par quoi toute pulsion est virtuellement pulsion de mort.'

88 *Écrits*, 629: 'Le désir se produit dans l'au-delà de la demande, de ce qu'en articulant la vie du sujet à ses conditions, elle y émonde le besoin, mais aussi il se creuse dans son en-deçà, en ce que, demande inconditionnelle de la présence et de l'absence, elle évoque la manque a être sous le trois figures du rien qui fait le fond de la demande d'amour, de la haine qui va à nier l'être de l'autre et de l'indicible de ce qui s'ignore dans sa requête. Dans cette aporie incarnée dont on peut dire en image qu'elle emprunte son âme lourde aux rejetons vivaces de la tendance blessée, et son corps subtil à la mort actualisée dans la séquence signifiante, le désir s'affirme comme condition absolue. Moins encore que le rien qui passe dans la ronde des significations qui agitent les hommes, il est le sillage inscrit de la course, et comme la marque du fer du signifiant à l'épaule di sujet qui parle. Il est moins passion pure du signifié que pure action du signifiant, qui s'arrête, au moment où le vivant devenu signe, la rend insignifiante.' (Desire is produced in the beyond of demand, because in linking the subject's life to its conditions, demand prunes it of its need. But desire is also excavated in the [area] shy of

demand in that, as an unconditional demand for presence and absence, demand evokes the want-to-be in the three figures of the nothing that constitutes the ground for the demand for love, for the hatred that goes so far as to negate the other's being, and for the unspeakableness of what is not known in its request. In this aporia incarnate – of which one might metaphorically say that demand borrows its heavy soul from the hardy offshoots of the wounded tendency, and its subtle body from death as it is actualized in the signifying sequence – desire asserts itself as an absolute condition. Less still than the nothing that circulates in the rounds of significations to stir men up, desire is the wake left behind by its trajectory and like the signifier's brand on the speaking subject's shoulder. It is not so much a pure passion of the signified as a pure action of the signifier, which stops at the moment when the living being, having become a sign, renders this action meaningless.)

89 *Écrits*, 634: 'Ceci veut dire que c'est d'une parole qui lèverait le marque que le sujet reçoit de son propos, que seulement pourrait être reçue l'absolution qui le rendrait à son désir. Mais le désir n'est rien d'autre que l'impossibilité de cette parole.' (This means that it is only from a kind of speech that would remove the mark the subject receives from what he says that he might obtain the absolution that would return him to his desire. But desire is nothing but the impossibility of such speech.)

90 *Écrits*, 813–14: 'Opacité dont nous allons dire par quel biais elle fait en quelque sorte la substance du désir. Le désir s'ébauche dans la marge où la demande se déchire du besoin ... Marge qui, pour linéaire qu'elle soit, laisse apparaître son vertige.' (I will now explain in what way this opacity in some sense constitutes the substance of desire. Desire begins to take shape in the margin in which demand rips away from need ... A margin which, as linear as it may be, allows its vertiginous character to appear.)

91 See Bowie, *Lacan*, 131, 141–2: 'Desire, born of the impossible confluence of need and demand, is genderless in the same way. But the agent that is called upon to tie the two views together, to give the subject "his" desire by signifying it for him, is the male genital, transcendentalized. No other volunteer has stepped forward.'

92 *Écrits*, 692: 'Le phallus est le signifiant privilégié de cette marque où la part du logos se conjoint à l'avènement du désir. On peut dire que ce signifiant est choisi comme le plus saillant de ce qu'on peut attraper dans le réel de la copulation sexuelle, comme aussi le plus symbolique au sens littéral (typographique) de ce terme, puisqu'il y équivaut à la copule (logique).' (The phallus is the privileged signifier of this mark in which the role of

Logos is wedded to the advent of desire. One could say that this signifier is chosen as the most salient of what can be grasped in sexual intercourse as real, as well as the most symbolic, in the literal [typographical] sense of the term, since it is equivalent in intercourse to the [logical] copula.)

93 As Bowie remarks (*Lacan*, 13), 'The "name of the father," when first introduced in the early fifties, was an emblem of human speech and desire as lawbound: the father's name was that which had to be invoked in order to maintain the incest taboo and which sent forbidden desires on other circuitous journeys through language. But by the mid-sixties the notion had become far prouder: it was now the "Name-of-the-Father," an imperious metaphysical force that could no longer be described in terms of family, society and sexual conduct and that was not so much an observable feature of speech as the origin and ubiquitous condition of human language.' See also pages 108–9 and *Écrits*, 577: 'C'est le défaut du Nom-du-Père à cette place qui, par le trou qu'il ouvre dans le signifié amorce la cascade des remaniements du signifiant d'où procède le désastre croissant de l'imaginaire, jusqu'à ce que le niveau soit atteint où signifiant et signifié se stabilisent dans la métaphore délirante.' (It is the lack of the Name-of-the-Father in that place in which, by the hole that it opens up in the signified, sets off a cascade of reworkings of the signifier from which the growing disaster of the imaginary proceeds, until the level is reached at which signifier and signified stabilize in a delusional metaphor.)

94 *Séminaire XX*, 71: 'et pourquoi ne pas interpréter une face de l'Autre, la face Dieu, comme supportée par la jouissance feminine?' (And why not interpret one face of the Other, the God face, as based on feminine jouissance?)

95 The reformulation of the Cartesian *cogito* is 'prophetically' recorded by Lacan in *Seminar* XI, 141: '*Desidero*, c'est le *cogito* freudien.'

96 See L. Irigaray in *Parler n'est jamais neutre* (Paris: Miniut, 1985). For the relation between grammatical construction and gender construction, see J. Butler, *Bodies That Matter* (London: Routledge, 1993), 4–12.

97 See, for instance, J. Butler's critique of Kristeva's semiotic and symbolic dispositions and of the notion of poetic language in *Gender Trouble: Feminism and the Subversion of Identity* (London: Routledge, 1990), 79–91. According to Butler, Kristeva's notion of the semiotic is built within – and subordinated to – the symbolic: rather than challenging it, then, it indeed safeguards the paternal-symbolic culture, protecting it from the intrusion of the pre-cultural semiotic. Thus, 'for Kristeva, poetry and maternity represent privileged practices within paternally sanctioned culture which permit a nonpsychotic experience of that heterogeneity and dependency characteristic of the maternal terrain' (85).

98 Irigaray, *This Sex Which Is Not One*, 29–30: 'Thus, what they desire is precisely nothing, and at the same time every-thing. Always something more and something else besides that *one* – sexual organ, for example – that you give them, attribute to them. Their desire is often interpreted, and feared, as a sort of insatiable hunger, a voracity that will swallow you whole. Whereas it really involves a different economy more than anything else, one that upsets the linearity of a project, undermines the goal-object of desire, diffuses the polarization toward a single pleasure, disconcerts fidelity to a single discourse.'

99 Ibid., 132: 'might we not say that it is because it has produced and continues to "hold" syntax that the masculine maintains mastery over discourse? Within this syntax, in this order of discourse, woman, even though she is hidden, most often hidden as woman and absent in the capacity of subject, manages to make "sense" – sensation? – manages to create "content." This syntax of discourse, of discursive logic – more generally, too, the syntax of social organization, "political" syntax – isn't this syntax always (how could it be otherwise? At least so long as there is no desire for the other) a means of masculine self-affection, or reproduction, or self-generation or self-presentation – himself as the self-same, as the only standard of sameness?'

100 'I ask of writing what I ask of desire: that it have no relation to the logic which puts desire on the side of possession, of acquisition, or even of that consumption-consummation which, when pushed to its limits with such exultation, links (false) consciousness with death. I do not believe that writing – insofar as it is a production of desire – or the desire which can do anything, cannot be defined, nor that it is to be defined in accordance with death's borders.' H. Cixous, *The Hélène Cixous Reader*, ed. S. Sellers (London: Routledge, 1994), 27.

101 This desire is defined mainly as the opposite of the deadly 'symbolic' desire: 'I have always loved desire. Certainly not the desire which believes itself to be determined according to a lack which it raises up and upon which it depends, so much so that it cannot get over it. That desire, conniving with the forces of death, whose company it keeps, and which it fears, is confused with its limits. It is afraid of itself; it fears being satisfied. It has to use ruses to maintain itself, at a distance from actualization: because it does not venture as far as the real, it has scarcely any chance of changing it. It desires itself more than it desire its objects; it is very familiar, this desire to desire, which so often passes for desire itself, when it is only desire's remorse and prudence ... It preserves itself, surrounding itself with prohibitions, threatening itself with, and living off, danger enveloped in lures and veiled with absences. It is very familiar, it is responsible for making the law and autho-

rizing the laying down of the social order it pretends to abhor. It is upon its weaknesses that power counts, upon its detours that reformism is constituted, upon its petrifying fear of castration that the Church is built' (ibid., 29–30).

102 See in particular Wittig's essays 'The Point of View,' 'The Trojan Horse,' and 'The Mark of Gender,' collected in *The Straight Mind and Other Essays* (Boston: Beacon, 1992).

103 J. Butler, *Gender Troubles* (London: Routledge, 1990), and see also her book *Bodies That Matter.*

104 Butler, *Gender Troubles,* 70–1: 'Transsexuals often claim a radical discontinuity between sexual pleasures and bodily parts. Very often what is wanted in terms of pleasure requires an imaginary participation in body parts, either appendages or orifices, that one might not actually posses, or, similarly, pleasure might require imagining an exaggerated or diminished set of parts. The imaginary status of desire, of course, is not restricted to the transsexual identity; the phantasmatic nature of desire reveals the body not as its ground or cause, but as its *occasion* and its *object.* The strategy of desire is in part the transfiguration of the desiring body itself. Indeed, in order to desire at all it might be necessary to believe in an altered bodily ego which, within the gendered rules of the imaginary, might fit the requirements of a body capable of desire. This imaginary condition of desire always exceeds the physical body through or on which it works.'

105 Ibid., 136: 'That the gendered body is performative suggests that it has no ontological status apart from the various acts which constitute its reality,' and 138: 'The notion of gender parody defended here does not assume that there is an original which such parodic gestures imitate. Indeed, the parody is *of* the very notion of an original.'

106 M. Foucault, *History of Sexuality* (Paris: Gallimard 1976–84), trans. R. Hurley (New York: Vintage, 1978–86).

107 Ibid., 1:82–3: 'However, it seems to me that this analytics can be constituted only if it frees itself completely from a certain representation of power that I would term – it will be seen later why – "juridico-discursive." It is this conception that governs both the thematics of repression and the theory of the law as constitutive of desire. In other words, what distinguishes the analysis made in terms of the repression of instincts from that made in terms of the law of desire is clearly the way in which they conceive of the nature and dynamics of the drive, not the way in which they conceive of power. They both rely on a common representation of power which, depending on the use made of it and the position it is accorded with respect to desire, leads the two contrary results: either to the promise of a "liberation," if power is

seen as having only an external hold on desire, or, if it is constitutive of itself, to the affirmation: you are always-already trapped.'

108 Ibid., 1:92–3: 'It seems to me that power must be understood in the first instance as the multiplicity of force relations immanent in the sphere in which they operate and which constitute their own organization; as the process which, through ceaseless struggles and confrontations, transforms, strengthens, or reverses them; as the support which these force relations find in one another, thus forming a chain or a system, or, on the contrary, the disjunctions and contradictions which isolate them from one another; and lastly, as the strategies in which they take effect, whose general design or institutional crystallization is embodied in the state apparatus, in the formulation of the law, in the various social hegemonies.'

109 I have slightly altered the translation to be closer to the French original.

110 *History of Sexuality*, 2:5: 'this does not mean that I proposed to write a history of the successive conceptions of desire, of concupiscence, or of libido, but rather to analyze the practices by which individuals were led to focus their attention on themselves, to decipher, to recognize, and acknowledge themselves as subjects of desire, bringing into play between themselves and themselves a certain relationship that allows them to discover, in desire, the truth of their being, be it natural or fallen. In short, with this genealogy the idea was to investigate how individuals were led to practice, on themselves and on others, a hermeneutics of desire, a hermeneutics of which their sexual behavior was doubtless the occasion, but certainly not the exclusive domain.'

111 For desire vs. pleasure in Foucault, see G. Deleuze, 'Desire and Pleasure,' in *Foucault and His Interlocutors*, ed. A.I. Davison (Chicago: University of Chicago Press, 1997), 183–92, esp. 189–90.

112 For desire and Marxism, see F. Jameson, *Postmodernism or the Cultural Logic of Late Capitalism* (Durham: Duke University Press, 1991), 202–3. For jouissance and ideology see Žižek, *The Sublime Object of Ideology*, 79–84.

113 G. Deleuze and F. Guattari, *Anti-Oedipus: Capitalism and Schizophrenia*, trans. R. Hurley, M. Seem, and H. Lane (London: Athlone, 1984).

114 For the identity of desiring and social production, see ibid., 10, 299–322, in particular 299–300: 'Just as Ricardo founds political and social economy by discovering the quantitative labor as the principle of every representable value, Freud founds desiring-economy by discovering the quantitative libido as the principle of every representation of the objects and aims of desire ... Freud is thus the first to disengage desire itself, as Ricardo disengages labor itself, and thereby the sphere of production that effectively eclipses representation.'

115 Ibid., 1: 'It is at work everywhere, functioning smoothly at times, at other times in fits and starts. It breathes, it heats, it eats. It shits and fucks. What a mistake to have ever said *the* id. Everywhere *it* is machines – real ones, not figurative ones: machines driving other machines, machines being driven by other machines, with all the necessary couplings and connections.' As the authors warn on p. 41: 'the desiring machine is not a metaphor.'

116 Ibid., 41. The example is that of the feeding baby: 'Let us consider, for example, the milk that the baby throws up when it burps; it is at one and the same time the restitution of something that has been levied from the associative flux; the reproduction of the process of detachment from the signifying chain; and a residuum that constitutes the subject's share of the whole.'

117 Ibid., 31: 'Desiring-machines, on the contrary, continually break down as they run, and in fact run only when they are not functioning properly: the product is always an offshoot of production, implanting itself upon it like a graft, and at the same time the parts of the machines are the fuel that makes it run.'

118 Ibid., 10: 'Capital is indeed the body without organs of the capitalist, or rather of the capitalist being. But as such, it is not only the fluid and petri-fied substance of money, for it will give to the sterility of money the form whereby money produces money. It produces surplus value, just as the body without organs reproduces itself, puts forth shoots, and branches out to the farthest corners of the universe.'

119 Ibid., 26: 'Desire does not lack anything; it does not lack its object. It is, rather, the *subject* that is missing in desire, or desire that lacks a fixed sub-ject; there is no fixed subject unless there is repression. Desire and its object are one and the same thing: the machine, as a machine of a machine. Desire is a machine, and the object of desire is another machine connected to it.'

120 Ibid., 111–12: 'From the moment that lack is reintroduced into desire, all of desiring production is crushed, reduced to being no more than the produc-tion of fantasy; but the sign does not produce fantasies, it is a production of the real and a position of desire within reality. From the moment desire is welded again to the law – we needn't point out what is known since time began: that there is no desire without law – the eternal operation of eternal repression recommences ... but the sign of desire is never a sign of the law, it is a sign of strength ... From the moment desire is made to depend on the signifier, it is put back under the yoke of despotism whose effect is castra-tion, there where one recognizes the stroke of the signifier itself; but the sign of desire is never signifying, it exists in the thousand of productive

break-flows that never allow themselves to be signified within the unary stroke of castration. It is always a point-sign of many dimensions, polyvocity as the basis for a punctual semiology.'

121 Ibid., 134: 'As if the great voices, which were capable of performing a break-through in grammar and syntax and making all language a desire, were not speaking from the depths of psychosis.'

122 Schizophrenia is, for the authors, not only a psychosis, but a vital and universal principle. See *Anti-Oedipus*, 5: 'Schizophrenia is like love: there is no specifically schizophrenic phenomenon or entity; schizophrenia is the universe of productive and reproductive desiring-machines, universal primary production as the "essential reality of man and nature."'

123 Schizoanalysis consists of two actions: the *pars destruens* is quite violent ('destroy, destroy!' 311): 'defamiliarizing, de-oedipalizing, decastrating; undoing theater, dream, and fantasy; decoding, deterritorializing – a terrible curettage, a malevolent activity' (381). The positive part is twofold: first, to discover and to learn about 'the nature, the formation, or the functioning' (322) of the machines and second, to uncover the revolutionary potential hidden in them, by distinguishing, and avoiding the collusion between 'the unconscious libidinal investment of group or desire, and the preconscious investment of class or interest' (343).

124 R. Girard, *Deceit, Desire and the Novel* (Paris: Grasset, 1961), trans. Y. Freccero (Baltimore: Johns Hopkins University Press, 1984). See also his *Things Hidden since the Foundation of the World* (London: Athlone, 1987). On the theme of triangular desire as interpreted by contemporary theology, see R. Williams, 'The Deflections of Desire: Negative Theology in Trinitarian Disclosure,' in *Silence and the Word*, 115–35. For a different perspective on the workings of desire in literature, see L. Bersani, *A Future for Astyanax: Character and Desire in Literature* (Boston: Little, Brown, 1976).

125 An example of external mediation is Quixote as the mediator of Sancho's desires (9). The mother refusing a kiss to the little boy in Proust plays 'the double role characteristic of internal mediation: she is both the instigator of desire and a relentless guardian forbidding its fulfillment' (35).

126 Girard, *Deceit, Desire and the Novel*, 10: 'The impulse toward the object is ultimately an impulse toward the mediator; in internal mediation this impulse is checked by the mediator himself, since he desires, or perhaps possesses, the object ... Far from declaring himself a faithful vassal, he [the subject] thinks only of repudiating the bonds of mediation. But these bonds are stronger than ever, for the mediator's apparent hostility does not diminish his prestige but instead augments it ... The subject is torn between two opposite feelings toward his model – the most submissive reverence and the

most intense malice. This is the passion we call hatred.'

127 Ibid., 55: 'to grasp this metaphysical meaning we must look beyond the individual cases and see the totality. All the heroes surrender their most fundamental individual prerogative, that of choosing their own desire; we cannot attribute this unanimous abandonment to the always different qualities of the heroes.' And 58: 'Just as the three-dimensional perspective directs all the lines of a picture toward a vanishing point beyond or in front of the canvas, Christianity directs existence toward a vanishing point, either toward God or toward the Other ... Denial of God does not eliminate transcendence, but diverts it from *au-delà* to the *en-deçà*. The imitation of Christ becomes the imitation of one's neighbor. The surge of pride breaks against the humanity of the mediator, and the result of this conflict is hatred.'

128 Ibid., 61–2: 'there is nothing less "materialistic" than triangular desire. The passion that drives men to seize or gain more possession is not materialistic; it is the triumph of the mediator, the god with the human face ... The problem of divinity no longer occurs at this low level. The need for transcendency is "satisfied" by mediation.'

129 Interestingly, in the novelistic space – which both linguistics (Jakobson) and psychoanalysts (Lacan) describe as metonymic – Girard identifies metaphor as that which reveals the metaphysical quality of desire. See *Deceit, Desire and the Novel*, 77: 'The metaphor, therefore, should reveal the metaphysical quality of desire. And this is precisely what it does. In Proust's masterpiece the sacred is not only merely another metaphoric domain: it is present whenever the author deals with the relationship between the subject and his mediator.' See also 79.

130 Girard explains the relationship between mediator and object as the one between relic and saint (83): the closer the relic/object is to the saint/mediator the more valuable it is.

131 Girard argues (164–8) that the very abstractness of desire leads the novelistic hero on a pattern of askesis (that can be represented also as boredom or indifference). Indeed, 'askesis for the sake of desire is a universal requirement for the novel of internal mediation.' The best example of a metaphysical novelist is Dostoevsky: at the conclusion of his *Brothers Karamazov*, Girard reads the coincidence of the religious and the novelistic. Rarely, however, does desire find a balance in the novel. In the contemporary novel, the excess of desire is turned, according to Girard, into a 'non-desire,' which is equally virulent (272–3).

132 *Deceit, Desire and the Novel*, 94–5: 'Thus the most diverse forms of triangular desire are organized into a universal structure. There is no aspect of desire,

in any novelist, which cannot be linked with other aspects of his own novel and with all other novels. Desire thus appears as a dynamic structure extending from one end of novelistic literature to the other. This structure can be compared to an object falling in space, whose shape is always changing because of the increasing speed given to it by the fall. Novelists, situated at different levels, describe this object as it appears to them. Usually they have only a suspicion of the various changes it has undergone and will yet undergo.'

133 For similar remarks in a different context, see Butler, *Bodies that Matter*, 10.

134 See I. Prigogine and I. Stengers, *Order Out of Chaos: Man's New Dialogue with Nature* (New York: Bantam, 1984).

Selected Bibliography

Augustine

Texts

Patrologia Latina. Volumes 32–45. Edited by J.P. Migne. Paris: Migne, 1844–64.

Translations

On Christian Teaching. Translated by R.H. Green. Oxford: Oxford University Press, 1997.
The City of God. Translated by R.W. Dyson. Cambridge: Cambridge University Press, 1998.
Confessions. Translated by H. Chadwick. Oxford: Oxford University Press, 1991.
De dialectica. Edited by J. Pinborg. Translated by B.D. Jackson. Dordrecht: Synthese Historical Library 16, 1975.
Divine Providence and the Problem of Evil (De ordine). Translated by R. Russell. New York: Cosmopolitan, 1942.
Eighty-three Different Questions. Translated by D.L. Mosher. Washington, DC: Catholic University of America Press, 1982.
The First Catechetical Instructions. Translated by J. Christopher. New York: Newman, 1962.
On Genesis. Translated by R.J. Teske. Washington, DC: Catholic University of America Press, 1991.
Letters. Translated by W. Parsons. Washington, DC: Catholic University of America Press, 1953.
The Literal Meaning of Genesis. Translated by J.H. Taylor. New York: Newman, 1982.

The Magnitude of the Soul. Translated by J.J. McMahon. Washington, DC: Catholic University of America Press, 1974.

'On Music.' Translated by R.C. Taliaferro. In *Writings of Saint Augustine*, 2:151–379. Washington, DC: Catholic University of America Press, 1947.

On the Nature of Good. New Advent. http://www.newadvent.org/fathers/1407.htm.

On the Psalms. Translated by S. Hebgin and F. Corrigan. London: Longmans, Green, 1961.

The Teacher. Translated by P. King. Indianapolis: Hackett, 1955.

Tractates on the First Epistle of John. Translated by J.W. Retting. Washington, DC: Catholic University of America Press, 1995.

Tractates on the Gospel of John. Translated by J.W. Rettig. Washington, DC: Catholic University of America Press, 1988–93.

The Trinity. 1961. Translated by S. McKenna. Revised and reprinted in *On the Trinity: Books 8–15*, edited by G.B. Matthews. Cambridge: Cambridge University Press, 2002.

Of True Religion. Translated by L.O. Mink. South Bend, IN: Gateway, 1959.

Studies

Alici, L. *Il linguaggio come segno e come testimonianza: Una rilettura di Agostino*. Rome: Studium, 1976.

Ando, C. 'Augustine on Language.' *Revue des études augustiniennes* 40 (1994): 45–78.

– 'Signs, Idols and the Incarnation in Augustinian Metaphysics.' *Representations* 73 (2001): 24–53.

Antoni, G. *La prière chez Saint Augustin: d'une philosophie du langage à la théologie du verbe*. Paris: Vrin, 1997.

Appleyard, J.A. 'How Does a Sacrament "Cause by Signifying"?' *Science et esprit* 23 (1971): 167–200.

Arendt, H. *Love and Saint Augustine*. Edited by J.V. Scott and J.C. Stark. Chicago: University of Chicago Press, 1996.

Arens, H. '*Verbum cordis*: zur Sprachphilosophie des Mittelalters.' *Historiographia Linguistica* 7 (1980): 13–27.

Austin, J.L. *How to Do Things with Words*. Cambridge, MA: Harvard University Press, 1975.

Babcock, W. '*Caritas* and Signification in *De doctrina christiana* 1–3.' In '*Doctrina christiana*': *A Classic of Western Culture*, edited by D.W.H. Arnold and P. Bright, 145–63. Notre Dame: University of Notre Dame Press, 1995.

Baratin, M. 'Origines stoïciennes de la théorie augustinienne du signe.' *Revue des études latines* 59 (1981): 260–8.

Baratin, M., and F. Desbordes. 'Sémiologie et métalinguistique chez saint Augustin.' *Langages* 65 (1982): 75–89.

Bellissima, G. 'Sant'Agostino grammatico.' *Augustinus Magister* 1 (1954): 35–42.

Bettetini, M., ed. *Ordine Musica Bellezza*. Milan: Rusconi, 1992.

Bochet, I. *Saint Augustin et le désir de Dieu*. Paris: Études augustiniennes, 1982.

Bodei, R. *Ordo amoris: Conflitti terreni e felicità celeste*. Bologna: Mulino, 1991.

Brown, P. *Augustine of Hippo*. Berkeley: University of California Press, 1967.

Buckenmeier, R.E. 'St Augustine and the Life of Man's Body in the Early Dialogues.' *Augustinian Studies* 3 (1972): 131–46.

Burnaby, J. *Amor Dei: A Study of the Religion of St Augustine*. London: Hodder & Stoughton, 1938.

Canning, R. 'The Unity of Love for God and Neighbor.' *Augustiniana* 37 (1987): 38–121.

Carrera, A. 'La traccia dell'eterno: Tempo e musica in Sant'Agostino.' In *Lo spazio materno dell'ispirazione: Agostino, Blanchot, Celan, Zanzotto*, 81–124. Florence: Cadmo, 2004.

Chiesa, C. 'Le problème du langage intérieur dans la philosophie antique de Platon à Porphire.' *Historie épistémologie langage* 14, no. 2 (1992): 15–30.

Coleman, J. *Ancient and Medieval Memories*. Cambridge: Cambridge University Press, 1992.

Colish, M. 'St Augustine: The Expression of the Word.' In *The Mirror of Language*, 8–81. New Haven: Yale University Press, 1958.

Daniels, D. 'The Argument of the *De Trinitate* and Augustine's Theory of Signs.' *Augustinian Studies* 7 (1977): 33–54.

Dawson, D. 'Sign Theory, Allegorical Reading and the Motions of the Soul in *De doctrina christiana*.' In *'De doctrina christiana': A Classic of Western Culture*, edited by D.W.H. Arnold and P. Bright, 123–41. Notre Dame: University of Notre Dame Press, 1995.

Derrida, J. 'Signature, Event, Context.' In *Margins of Philosophy*, translated by A. Bass, 308–30. Chicago: University of Chicago Press, 1982.

– *Limited Inc*. Evanston: Northwestern University Press, 1988.

Dideberg, D. *Saint Augustin et la première Épître de saint Jean: Une théologie de l'agapè*. Paris: Beauchesne, 1975.

– '*Caritas*: Prolégomènes à une étude de la théologie augustinienne de la charité.' In *Signum Pietatis: Festgabe für Cornelius Mayer*, ed. A. Zumkeller, 369–81. Wurzburg: Augustinus-Verlag, 1989.

du Roy, O. 'L'experiénce de l'amour et l'intelligence de la foi trinitaire selon Saint Augustin.' *Recherches augustiniennes* 2 (1963): 415–55.

Duchrow, U. '*Signum* und *Superbia* beim jungen Augustin (386–390).' *Recherches augustiniennes* 7 (1961): 369–72.

Eco, U. *Semiotics and the Philosophy of Language*. London: Macmillan, 1984.

Féret, H.M. 'Sacramentum: Res dans la langue théologique de saint Augustin.' Revue des sciences philosophiques et théologiques 30 (1940): 218–43.

Ferguson, M.W. 'Saint Augustine's Region of Unlikeness: The Crossing of Exile and Language.' Georgia Review 29 (1975): 842–64.

Fernandez, Ramos F. 'Los signos en los Tractatus in Ioannem.' Augustinus 33 (1988): 57–76.

Ferretter, L. 'The Trace of the Trinity: Christ and Difference in Saint Augustine's Theory of Language.' Literature and Theology 12 (1998): 256–67.

Fyler, J. 'St Augustine, Genesis and the Origin of Language.' In St Augustine and His Influence in the Middle Ages, edited by E. King and J. Schaefer, 69–78. Sewanee, TN: Press of the University of the South, 1988.

Gilson, E. Christian Philosophy of Saint Augustine. New York: Random House, 1960.

Grammatici Latini. Edited by H. Keil. Leipzig, 1855. Reprint Hildesheim: Verlag, 1981.

Henningfeld, J. 'Verbum-Signum: La définition du language chez saint Augustin et Nicholas de Cues.' Archives de philosophie 54 (1991): 255–68.

Holte, R. Béatitude et Sagesse: St Augustin et le problème de la fin de l'homme dans la philosophie ancienne. Paris: Études augustiniennes, 1962.

Jackson, B.D. 'The Theory of Signs in St Augustine's De doctrina christiana.' Revue des études augustiniennes 15 (1969): 9–49.

Johnson, D.W. 'Verbum in Early Augustine.' Recherches augustiniennes 8 (1972): 3–53.

Jordan, M.D. 'Words and Word: Incarnation and Signification in Augustine's De doctrina christiana.' Augustinian Studies 11 (1980): 177–96.

Jordan, R. 'Time and Contingency in St Augustine.' In Augustine: A Collection of Critical Essays, edited by R.A. Markus, 255–79. New York: Doubleday, 1972.

Kannengiesser, C. 'The Interrupted De doctrina christiana.' In 'De doctrina christiana': A Classic of Western Culture, edited by D.W.H. Arnold and P. Bright, 3–13. Notre Dame: University of Notre Dame Press, 1995.

Law, V. 'St Augustine's De grammatica: Lost or Found?' Recherches augustiniennes 19 (1984): 155–83.

Markus, R.A. 'Saint Augustine on Signs.' Phronesis 2 (1957): 60–83.

– 'Imago and similitudo in Augustine.' Revue des études augustiniennes 7 (1971): 125–43.

– 'Signs, Communication and Communities in Augustine's De doctrina christiana.' In 'De doctrina Christiana': A Classic of Western Culture, edited by D.W.H. Arnold and P. Bright, 97–108. Notre Dame, IN: University of Notre Dame Press, 1995.

Marrou, H.-I. Saint Augustin et la fin de la culture antique. 4th ed. Paris: Boccard, 1958.

– 'Le dogme de la résurrection des corps et la théologie des valeurs humaines selon l'enseignement de saint Augustin.' *Revue des études augustiniennes* 12 (1966): 111–36.

Miles, M.R. *Augustine on the Body.* Missoula, MT: American Academy of Religion Dissertation Series, 1979.

Nicolosi, S. 'La filosofia dell'amore in Sant'Agostino: Dalla comunicazione alla comunità.' *Orpheus* 4 (1983): 42–66.

Norris, J.M. 'Augustine and Sign in *Tractatus in Iohannis Euangelium*.' In *Augustine: Biblical Exegete*, edited by F. Van Fleteren and J.C. Schnaubelt, 215–31. New York: Lang, 2001.

Nygren, A. *Agape and Eros.* Translated by S. Watson. London: SPCK, 1938.

O'Connor, W. 'The Uti/Frui Distinction in Augustine's Ethics.' *Augustinian Studies* 14 (1983): 45–62.

O'Daly, G. *Augustine's Philosophy of Mind.* Berkeley: University of California Press, 1987.

O'Donovan, O. *The Problem of Self Love in St Augustine.* New Haven: Yale University Press, 1980.

– '*Usus* and *fruitio* in Augustine, *De doctrina christiana* 1.' *Journal of Theological Studies* n.s. 33 (1982): 361–97.

Paissac, H. *Théologie du verbe: Saint Augustin et saint Thomas.* Paris: Les éditions du Cerf, 1951.

Pepin, J. 'Le problème de la communication des consciences chez Plotin et saint Augustin.' *Revue de métaphysique et morale* 55 (1950): 128–48.

– *Saint Augustin et la dialectique.* Villanova, PA: Villanova University Press, 1976.

Piccolomini, R., ed. *La bellezza.* Rome: Città Nuova, 1995.

Polk, D.W. 'Temporal Impermanence and the Disparity of Time and Eternity.' *Augustinian Studies* 22 (1991): 63–82.

Pulsiano, P. 'Language Theory and Narrative Patterning in *De Civitate Dei*, Books XV–XVIII.' In *The City of God: A Collection of Critical Essays*, edited by D.F. Donnelly, 241–52. New York: Lang, 1995.

Ricoeur, P. 'The Aporias of the Experiences of Time: Book 11 of Augustine's *Confessions*.' In *Time and Narrative*, 1:5–30. Chicago: University of Chicago Press, 1984.

Riffaterre, M. *The Semiotics of Poetry.* Bloomington: Indiana University Press, 1978.

Rist, J.M. 'Will, Love and Right Action.' In *Augustine: Ancient Thought Baptized*, 148–202. Cambridge: Cambridge University Press, 1994.

Santi, G. 'Interiorità e Verbum mentis.' In *Interiorità e Intenzionalità in S. Agostino*, edited by L. Alici, 133–43. Rome: Augustinianum, 1990.

Schindler, A. *Wort und Analogie in Augustins Trinitätslehre.* Tubingen: Mohr, 1965.

Simone, R. 'Semiologia Agostiniana.' *La Cultura* 7 (1969): 88–117.

Sorabji, R. *Time, Creation and the Continuum: Theories in Antiquity and the Early Middle Ages.* Ithaca: Cornell University Press, 1983.

Spitzer, L. *Classical and Christian Ideas of World Harmony.* Baltimore: Johns Hopkins University Press, 1963.

Stock, B. *Augustine the Reader: Meditation, Self-Knowledge and the Ethics of Interpretation.* Cambridge, MA: Harvard University Press, 1996.

Todorov, T. *Theories of the Symbol.* Translated by C. Porter. Ithaca: Cornell University Press, 1982.

Trapè, A., and F. Sciacca, eds. *La Trinità.* Rome: Città Nuova, 1998.

van Bavel, J. *Recherches sur la christologie de saint Augustin.* Fribourg: Éditions universitaires, 1954.

– 'The Double Face of Love in Augustine.' *Louvain Studies* 12 (1987): 116–30.

Vance, E. 'Augustine's Confessions and the Grammar of Selfhood.' *Genre* 6 (1973): 1–28.

– 'St Augustine: Language as Temporality.' In *Mervelous Signals: Poetics and Sign Theory in the Middle Ages,* 34–50. Lincoln: University of Nebraska Press, 1986.

Vecchio, S. *Le parole come segni: Introduzione alla linguistica agostiniana.* Palermo: Novecento, 1994.

Williams, R. 'Language, Reality and Desire in Augustine's *De doctrina.*' *Journal of Literature and Theology* 3 (1989): 138–58.

Modistae

Texts

Boethii Daci Opera. Edited by J. Pinborg and H. Roos. Vol. 4 of *Corpus philosophorum danicorum medii aevii.* Copenhagen: Gad, 1969.

Iohannis Daci Opera. Edited by A. Otto. Vol. 1 of *Corpus philosophorum danicorum medii aevii.* Copenhagen: Gad, 1955.

Martini de Dacia Opera. Edited by H. Roos. Vol. 2 of *Corpus philosophorum danicorum medii aevii.* Copenhagen: Gad, 1961.

Radulphus Brito. *Quaestiones super Priscianum Minorem.* Edited by H. Enders and J. Pinborg. Stuttgart-Bad Cannstatt: Frommann-Holzboog, 1980.

Sigier de Courtrai. *Les oeuvres de Sigier de Courtrai.* Edited by G. Wallerand. Vol. 7 of *Les philosophes belges.* Louvain: Institut supérieur de philosophie, 1913.

– *Summa modorum significandi: Sophismata.* Edited by J. Pinborg. Vol. 14 of *Studies in the History of Linguistics.* Amsterdam: Benjamins, 1977.

Simonis Daci Opera. Edited by A. Otto. Vol. 3 of *Corpus philosophorum danicorum medii aevii.* Copenhagen: Gad, 1963.

Thomas of Erfurt. *Grammatica speculativa.* Edited by G.L. Bursill-Hall. London: Longman, 1972.

Studies

Alessio, G.C. 'Il commento di Gentile da Cingoli a Martino di Dacia.' In *L'insegnamento della logica a Bologna*, edited by D. Buzzetti, M. Ferriani, and A. Tabarroni, 3–71. Bologna: Istituto per la Storia dell'Università, 1992.

Ardizzone, M.L. *Guido Cavalcanti: The Other Middle Ages*. Toronto: University of Toronto Press, 2002.

Aristoteles Latinus. Edited by L. Minio-Paluello. Brussels: Desclée de Brouwer, 1951–.

Ashworth, E.J. 'Signification and Modes of Signifying in Thirteenth-Century Logic.' *Medieval Philosophy and Theology* 1 (1991): 39–67.

Benedini, P. 'La teoria sintattica dei modisti: attualità dei concetti di reggenza e dipendenza.' *Lingua e Stile* 23 (1988): 113–35.

Black, D. 'Aristotle's "Peri hermeneias" in Medieval Latin and Arabic Philosophy: Logic and the Linguistic Arts.' In *Aristotle and His Medieval Interpreters*, edited by R. Bosley and M. Tweedale, 25–83. Calgary: University of Calgary Press, 1991.

Bursill-Hall, G.L. *Speculative Grammar of the Middle Ages*. The Hague: Mouton, 1971.

– 'Toward a History of Linguistics in the Middle Ages: 1100–1450.' In *Studies in the History of Linguistics: Traditions and Paradigms*, edited by D. Hymes, 77–92. Bloomington: Indiana University Press, 1974.

– 'Some Notes on the Grammatical Theory of Boethius of Dacia.' In *History of Linguistic Thought and Contemporary Linguistics*, edited by H. Parret, 164–88. Berlin: de Gruyter, 1976.

Chenu, M.-D. 'Grammaire et théologie aux XIIe et XIIIe siècle.' *Archives d'histoire doctrinale et littéraire du moyen âge* 10 (1935): 5–28.

Complete Works of Aristotle. Vol. 1, edited by J. Barnes. Princeton: Princeton University Press, 1984.

Covington, M.A. *Syntactic Theory in the High Middle Ages: Modistic Models of Sentence Structure*. Cambridge: Cambridge University Press, 1984.

de Rijk, L.M. *Logica modernorum: A Contribution to the History of Early Terministic Logic*. Assen: Van Gorcum, 1962.

de Vaux, R. 'La premiere entrée d'Averroes chez les Latins.' *Revue des sciences philosophiques et théologiques* 22 (1933): 193–245.

Dominicus Gundissalinus. *De divisione philosophiae*. Edited by L. Baur. Münster: Beiträge zur Geschichte der Philosophie des Mittelalters, 1903.

Giele M., F. van Steenberghen, and B. Bazán, eds. *Trois commentaires anonymes sur le traité de l'âme d'Aristote*. Louvain: Publications universitaires, 1971.

Grabman, M. *I divieti ecclesiastici di Aristotele sotto Innocenzo III e Gregorio IX*. Rome: Typis Pontificiae Universitatis Gregorianae, 1941.

Haskins, C.H. *Studies in the History of Mediaeval Science.* Cambridge, MA: Harvard University Press, 1924.

Henri d'Andeli. *La bataille des sept ars.* Edited by J. Paetow. Berkeley: University of California Press, 1914.

Hissette, R. *Enquête sur les 219 articles condamnés à Paris le 7 mars 1277.* Louvain: Publications universitaires, 1977.

Hunt, R.W. *The History of Grammar in the Middle Ages.* Edited by G.L. Bursill-Hall. Amsterdam: Benjamins, 1980.

Keith-Percival, W. 'Deep and Surface Structure Concepts in Renaissance and Medieval Syntactic Theory.' In *History of Linguistic Thought and Contemporary Linguistics,* edited by H. Parret, 238–53. Berlin: de Gruyter, 1976.

Kelly, L.G. 'La *Physique* d'Aristote et la phrase simple dans les ouvrages de grammaire spéculative.' In *La grammaire générale: des modistes aux idéologues,* edited by A. Joly and J. Stefanini, 107–24. Villeneuve d'Ascq: Publications de l'université de Lille III, 1977.

– 'Time and Verb in Grammatica Speculativa.' In *Matériaux pour une histoire des théories linguistiques,* edited by S. Auroux, M. Glatigny, A. Joly, A. Nicholas, and I. Rosier, 173–9. Lille: Presses universitaires de Lille, 1984.

– *The Mirror of Grammar: Theology, Philosophy and the Modistae.* Amsterdam: Benjamins, 2002.

Kneepkens, C.H. 'Magister Guido's View on Government: On Twelfth-Century Linguistic Thought.' *Vivarium* 16 (1978): 108–41.

– 'Roger Bacon's Theory of the Double Intellectus: A Note on the Development of the Theory of *Congruitas* and *Perfectio* in the First Half of the Thirteenth Century.' In *The Rise of British Logic: Acts of the Sixth European Symposium on Medieval Logic and Semantics,* edited by O. Lewry, 115–43. Toronto: Pontifical Institute of Mediaeval Studies, 1985.

– 'On Medieval Syntactic Thought with Special Reference to the Notion of Construction.' *Histoire épistémologie langage* 12, no. 2 (1990): 139–76.

Lambertini, R. 'Sicut tabernarius vinum significat per circulum: Directions in Contemporary Interpretations of the Modistae.' In *On the Medieval Theory of Signs,* edited by U. Eco and C. Marmo, 107–42. Amsterdam: Benjamins, 1989.

Le Goff, J. *Les intellectuelles au moyen âge.* Paris: Seuil, 1957.

Lewry, O. 'The Oxford Condemnations of 1277 in Grammar and Logic.' In *English Logic and Semantics from the End of the Twelfth Century to the Time of Ockham and Burleigh,* edited by H.A.G. Braakhuis, C.H. Kneepkens, and L.M. de Rijk, 235–77. Nijmegen: Ingenium, 1981.

Mahdi, M. 'Science, Philosophy and Religion in Alfarabi's *Enumeration of the Sciences.*' In *The Cultural Context of Medieval Learning,* edited by J.E. Murdoch and E.D. Sylla, 113–47. Dordrecht: Reidel, 1975.

Marmo, C. 'I Modisti e l'ordine delle parole: su alcune difficoltà di una grammatica universale.' *Versus: Quaderni di Studi Semiotici* 61, no. 3 (1992): 47–70.

– *Semiotica e linguaggio nella scolastica: Parigi, Bologna, Erfurt; La semiotica dei modisti.* Rome: Istituto Storico Italiano per il Medioevo, 1994.

McMullin, E., ed. *The Concept of Matter in Greek and Medieval Philosophy.* Notre Dame: University of Notre Dame Press, 1965.

Pinborg J., ed. *Die Entwicklung der Sprachtheorie im Mittelalter.* Münster: Aschendorff-Frost Hansen, 1967.

– *Compendium modorum significandi a Vincentio Heremito compositum: Cahiers de l'institut de moyen âge grec et latin* 1 (1969): 13–17.

– *Logik und Semantik im Mittelalter: Ein Überblick.* Stuttgart: Frommann-Holzboog, 1972.

– 'Speculative Grammar.' In *The Cambridge History of Late Medieval Philosophy: From the Rediscovery of Aristotle to the Disintegration of Scolasticism,* edited by N. Kretzmann, A. Kenny, J. Pinborg, and E. Stump, 253–69. Cambridge: Cambridge University Press, 1982.

– *Medieval Semantics: Selected Studies on Medieval Logic and Grammar.* Edited by S. Ebbesen. London: Variorum Reprints, 1984.

Rosier, I. *La grammaire spéculative des Modistes.* Lille: Presses universitaires de Lille, 1983.

– 'Transitivité et ordre des mots chez les grammairiens médiévaux.' In *Matériaux pour une histoire des théories linguistiques,* edited by S. Auroux, M. Glatigny, A. Joly, A. Nicholas, and I. Rosier, 181–90. Lille: Presses universitaires de Lille, 1984.

– '"O magister ..." Grammaticalité et intelligibilité selon un sophisme du XIIIe siècle.' *Cahiers de l'institut du moyen âge grec et latin* 56 (1988): 1–102.

– 'Un courant méconnu de la grammaire spéculative.' In *History and Historiography of Linguistics: Papers from the Fourth International Conference on the History of the Language Science,* edited by H.J. Niederehe and K. Koerner, 179–203. Amsterdam: Benjamins, 1990.

– 'Signes et sacraments: Thomas d'Aquin et la grammaire spéculative.' *Revue des sciences philosophiques et théologiques* 74 (1990): 392–436.

– *La parole comme acte: Sur la grammaire et la sémantique au XIIIe siècle.* Paris: Vrin, 1994.

– 'Res significata et modus significandi: les implications d'une distinction médiévale.' In *Sprachtheorien in Spätantike und Mittelalter,* edited by S. Ebbesen, 135–68. Tubingen: Narr, 1995.

Sirridge, M. 'The Science of Language and Linguistic Knowledge: John of Denmark and Robert Kilwardby.' In *Sprachtheorien in Spätantike und Mittelalter,* edited by S. Ebbesen, 109–34. Tubingen: Narr, 1995.

Stock, B. *Myth and Science in the Twelfth Century: A Study of Bernard Silvester.* Princeton: Princeton University Press, 1972.

Trentman, J. 'Speculative Grammar and Transformational Grammar: A Comparison of Philosophical Presuppositions.' In *History of Linguistic Thought and Contemporary Linguistics,* edited by H. Parret, 279–301. Berlin: de Gruyter, 1976.

Valente, L. 'Langage et théologie pendant la seconde moitié du XIIe siècle.' In *Sprachtheorien in Spätantike und Mittelalter,* edited by S. Ebbesen, 33–54. Tubingen: Narr, 1995.

van Steenberghen, F. *Aristotle in the West.* Louvain: Nauwelaerts, 1970.

– *Maître Sigier de Brabant.* Louvain: Publications universitaires, 1977.

– *La philosophie au XIIIe siècle.* 2nd ed. Louvain: Institut supérieur de philosophie, 1991.

Weisheipl, J.A. 'Classification of Sciences in Medieval Thought.' *Mediaeval Studies* 27 (1965): 54–90.

– 'The Interpretation of Aristotle's *Physics* and the Science of Motion.' In *The Cambridge History of Late Medieval Philosophy: From the Rediscovery of Aristotle to the Disintegration of Scolasticism,* edited by N. Kretzmann, A. Kenny, J. Pinborg, and E. Stump, 521–36. Cambridge: Cambridge University Press, 1982.

Dante

Texts

La Commedia secondo l'antica vulgata. Edited by G. Petrocchi. Milan: Società Dantesca Italian, 1966–8.

Convivio. Edited by F. Brambilla Ageno. Florence: Le Lettere, 1995.

Rime. Edited by G. Contini. Turin: Einaudi, 1995.

Vita Nova. Edited by G. Gorni. Turin: Einuadi, 1996.

De vulgari eloquentia. Edited by P.V. Mengaldo. Padua: Antenore, 1968.

Translations and Additional Commentaries

The Banquet. Translated by R. Lansing. New York: Garland, 1990.

Commedia. Commentary by A.M. Chiavacci Leonardi. 3 vols. Milan: Mondadori, 1991–7.

Convivio. In *Opere minori.* Tome 1, part 2. Edited by C. Vasoli and D. De Robertis. Milan: Ricciardi, 1979.

De vulgari eloquentia. In *Opere Minori.* Vol. 2. Edited by P.V. Mengaldo, 3–337. Milan: Ricciardi, 1979.

De vulgari eloquentia. Translated by S. Botterill. Cambridge: Cambridge University Press, 1996.

The Divine Comedy. Translated with a commentary by C.S. Singleton. Princeton: Princeton University Press, 1975.

Enciclopedia Dantesca. Rome: Istituto dell'Enciclopedia Italiana, 1970–8.

Vita Nuova. Translated by M. Musa. Oxford: Oxford University Press, 1992.

Studies

Ahern, J. 'Binding the Book: Hermeneutics and Manuscript Production in *Paradiso* XXXIII.' *PMLA* 97, no. 5 (1982): 800–9.

Alessio, G.C. 'La grammatica speculativa e Dante.' *Letture Classensi* 13 (1984): 69–88.

– 'A Few Remarks on the Vulgare Illustre.' *Dante Studies* 113 (1995): 57–67.

Armour, P. *The Door of Purgatory: A Study in Multiple Symbolism in Dante's 'Purgatorio.'* Oxford: Clarendon, 1983.

Ascoli, A.R. 'The Vowels of Authority.' In *Discourses of Authority in Medieval and Renaissance Literature.* Edited by K. Brownlee and W. Stephens, 23–46. Hanover: University Press of New England, 1989.

– '*Neminem ante nos*: Historicity and Authority in *de vulgari eloquentia*.' *Annali d'Italianistica* 8 (1990): 186–231.

Barański, Z. 'Dante's Biblical Linguistics.' *Lectura Dantis* 5 (1989): 105–43.

– '*Sole nuovo, luce nuova*': *Saggi sul rinnovamento culturale di Dante.* Turin: Scriptorium, 1996.

– 'Dante and Medieval Poetics.' In *Dante: Contemporary Perspectives,* edited by A.A. Iannucci, 3–22. Toronto: University of Toronto Press, 1997.

– *Dante e i segni: saggi per una storia intellettuale di Dante Alighieri.* Naples: Liguori, 2000.

Barolini, T. *Dante's Poets: Textuality and Truth in the Divine Comedy.* Princeton, NJ: Princeton University Press, 1984.

– *The Undivine Comedy: Detheologizing Dante.* Princeton, NJ: Princeton University Press, 1992.

– *Dante and the Origins of Italian Literary Culture.* New York: Fordham University Press: 2006.

Botterill, S. 'Dante and the Authority of Poetic Language.' In *Dante and the Mystical Tradition: Bernard of Clairvaux in the 'Commedia.'* Cambridge: Cambridge University Press, 1994.

– *Dante: Contemporary Perspectives,* edited by A.A. Iannucci, 167–80. Toronto: University of Toronto Press, 1997.

Boyde, P. 'Creation (*Paradiso* XXIX, 1–57).' In *Dante, Phylomythes and Philoso-*

pher: Man in the Cosmos, 235–47. Cambridge: Cambridge University Press, 1981.

Brownlee, K. 'Language and Desire in *Paradiso* XXVI.' *Lectura Dantis* 6 (1990): 46–59.

Bynum, C. *Fragmentation and Redemption: Essays on Gender and the Human Body in Medieval Religion.* New York: Zone Books, 1991.

Cambon, G. *Dante's Craft.* Minneapolis: University of Minnesota Press, 1969.

Casagrande, G. '"I s'appellava in terra il sommo bene" (Par. XXVI. 134).' *Aevum* 50 (1976): 249–73.

Castaldo, D. 'L'etica del primiloquim di Adamo nel *De vulgari eloquentia*.' *Italica* 59 (1982): 3–15.

Cervigni, D. *Dante's Poetry of Dreams.* Florence: Olschki, 1980.

Cestaro, G. '*Quanquan Sarnum biberimus ante dentes*: The Primal Scene of Suckling in Dante's *De vulgari eloquentia*.' *Dante Studies* 109 (1991): 119–47.

– *Dante and the Grammar of the Nursing Body.* Notre Dame: University of Notre Dame Press, 2002.

Chiavacci Leonardi, A.M. 'Il canto XXX del Paradiso.' *Paragone* 26, no. 308 (1975): 3–34.

– 'Il canto disumano.' *L'Alighieri* 25, no. 1 (1984): 23–36.

– '"Le bianche stole": Il tema della risurrezione nel *Paradiso*.' In *Dante e la Bibbia*, edited by G. Barblan, 249–71. Florence: Olschki, 1988.

Colombo, M. *Dai mistici a Dante: il linguaggio dell'ineffabilità.* Florence: La Nuova Italia, 1987.

Corti, M. 'Dante e la torre di Babele: una nuova "allegoria in factis."' In *Il viaggio testuale*, 245–56. Turin: Einaudi, 1978.

– *Dante a un nuovo crocevia.* Florence: Società Dantesca Italiana, 1981.

– 'Postille a una recensione.' *Studi Medievali* 3, no. 25 (1984): 839–45.

– 'Linguaggio poetico e lingua regulata.' In *Percorsi dell'invenzione*, 75–112. Turin: Einaudi, 1993.

Dragonetti, R. 'La conception du langage poétique dans le *De vulgari eloquentia* de Dante.' *Aux frontières du langage poétique (Études sur Dante, Mallarmé, Valéry) Romanica Gandensia* 9 (1971): 9–77.

Dronke, P. 'The Giants in Hell.' In *Dante and Medieval Latin Traditions*, 32–54. Cambridge: Cambridge University Press, 1986.

Ferrucci, F. 'La dialettica del desiderio.' In *Il poema del desiderio: Poetica e passione in Dante*, 221–64. Milan: Leonardo, 1990.

Foster, K. 'Dante's Idea of Purgatory, with Special Reference to Purgatorio XXI, 58–66.' In *Dies Illa: Death in the Middle Ages; Proceedings of the 1983 Manchester Colloquium*, edited by J.H.M. Taylor, 97–105. Liverpool: Cairns, 1984.

Fratta, A. 'Discussioni esegetiche sul primo libro del DVE.' *Medioevo Romanzo* 13 (1988): 39–54.

Freccero, J. *Dante: The Poetics of Conversion*. Edited by R. Jacoff. Cambridge, MA: Harvard University Press, 1986.

Gorni, G. *Lettera, nome, numero: L'ordine delle cose in Dante*. Bologna: Il Mulino, 1990.

Gragnolati, M. 'From Plurality to (Near) Unicity of Forms: Embryology in Purgatorio 25.' In *Dante for the New Millennium*, edited by T. Barolini and W. Storey, 192–210. New York: Fordham University Press, 2003.

– *Experiencing the Afterlife: Body and Soul in Dante and Medieval Culture*. Notre Dame: University of Notre Dame Press, 2005.

Gragnolati, M., and C. Holzhey. 'Dolore come gioia: Trasformarsi nel *Purgatorio* di Dante.' *Psiche* 2 (2003): 111–26.

Grayson, C. '*Nobilior est vulgaris*: latino e volgare nel pensiero di Dante.' In *Cinque saggi su Dante*. Bologna: Patron, 1972.

Hollander, R. 'Babytalk in Dante's *Commedia*.' In *Studies in Dante*, 116–29. Ravenna: Longo, 1980.

Honess, C. 'Expressing the Inexpressible: The Theme of Communication in the Heaven of Mars.' *Lectura Dantis* 14/15 (1994): 42–60.

Horace. *Ars poetica*. In *Satires, Epistles and Ars Poetica*, translated by H.R. Fairclough, 450–89. Loeb Classical Library. Cambridge, MA: Harvard University Press, 1970.

Iannucci, A.A. *Forma ed evento nella Divina Commedia*. Rome: Bulzoni, 1984.

– 'Casella's Song and the Tuning of the Soul.' *Thought* 65 (1990): 27–46.

– ed. *Dante: Contemporary Perspectives*. Toronto: University of Toronto Press, 1997.

– Jacoff, R. '"Our Bodies, Ourselves": The Body in the *Commedia*.' In *Sparks and Seeds: Medieval Literature and Its Afterlife; Essays in Honor of John Freccero*, edited by D. Stewart and A. Cornish, 118–37. Brepols: Turnhout, 2000.

Jakobson, R. 'Two Aspects of Language and Two Types of Aphasic Disturbances.' In *Fundamentals of Language*, 69–96. The Hague: Mouton, 1971.

Le Goff, J. *La naissance du Purgatoire*. Paris: Gallimard, 1981.

Lo Piparo, F. 'Sign and Grammar in Dante: A Non-Modistic Language Theory.' In *The History of Linguistics in Italy*, edited by P. Ramat, H. Niederehe, and K. Koerner, 1–22. Amsterdam: Benjamins, 1986.

Maierù, A. 'Dante al crocevia?' *Studi Medievali* 3, no. 24 (1983): 735–48.

– 'Il testo come pretesto.' *Studi Medievali* 3, no. 25 (1984): 847–55.

Mazzotta, G. *Dante's Vision and the Circle of Knowledge*. Princeton: Princeton University Press, 1993.

Mengaldo, P.V. *Linguistica e retorica in Dante*. Pisa: Nistri Lischi, 1978.

Nardi, B. *Dante e la cultura medievale*. Bari: Laterza, 1949.

– *Saggi di filosofia dantesca*. Florence: La Nuova Italia, 1967.

Nencioni, G. 'Ma perché 'l tempo fugge che t'assonna (Par. XXXII 139).' *Studi Danteschi* 40 (1963): 50–6.

Padoan, G. 'Il canto XXI del Purgatorio.' *Nuove letture dantesche* 4 (1970): 327–54.

Pagani, I. *La teoria linguistica di Dante: 'De Vulgari Eloquentia'; discussioni, scelte, proposte.* Naples: Liguori, 1982.

Pagliaro, A. 'Dialetti e lingue nell'oltretomba.' In *Ulisse: Ricerche semantiche sulla Divina Commedia,* 2:433–66. Messina: D'Anna, 1967.

– 'I "primissima signa" nella dottrina linguistica di Dante.' In *Nuovi saggi di critica sematica,* 215–46. Messina: D'Anna, 1963.

Pertile, L. '"La punta del disio": storia di una metafora dantesca.' *Lectura Dantis* 7 (1990): 3–28.

– '"L'antica fiamma": metamorfosi del fuoco nella Commedia di Dante.' *Italianist* 11 (1991): 29–60.

– '*Paradiso*: A Drama of Desire.' In *Word and Drama in Dante: Essays on the Divina Commedia,* edited by J.C. Barnes and J. Petrie, 143–80. Dublin: Irish Academy, 1993.

– 'A Desire of Paradise and a Paradise of Desire.' In *Dante: Contemporary Perspectives,* edited by A.A. Iannucci, 148–66. Toronto: University of Toronto Press, 1997.

– *La punta del disio: semantica del desiderio nella Commedia.* Fiesole: Cadmo, 2005.

Picone, M. *Vita Nuova e tradizione romanza.* Padua: Liviana, 1979.

Pizzorno, P. 'Matelda's Dance and the Smile of the Poets.' *Dante Studies* 112 (1994): 115–32.

Rotta, P. *La filosofia del linguaggio nella Patristica e nella Scolastica.* Turin: Bocca, 1909.

Sanguineti, E. 'Infernal Acoustics: Sacred Song and Earthly Song.' *Lectura Dantis* 6 (1990): 69–79.

Shapiro, M. *De vulgari eloquentia: Dante's Book of Exile.* Lincoln: University of Nebraska Press, 1990.

Singleton, C. 'The Irreducible Vision.' in *Illuminated Manuscripts of the Divine Comedy,* edited by P. Brieger, M. Meiss, and C. Singleton, 1:1–29. Princeton: Princeton University Press, 1969.

Sollers, P. 'Dante et la traversée de l'écriture.' In *Écriture et l'expérience des limites,* 14–47. Paris: Seuil, 1960.

Spitzer, L. 'Speech and Language in *Inferno* XIII.' In *Representative Essays,* 143–71. Stanford: Stanford University Press, 1988.

Stabile, G. 'Navigazione celeste e simbolismo lunare in Par. II.' *Studi medievali* 30, no. 1 (1980): 153–74.

Vinay, G. 'Ricerche sul *De vulgari eloquentia.*' *Giornale storico della letteratura italiana* 136 (1959): 236–74, 367–88.

Yowell, D. 'Ugolino's "bestial segno": The *De Vulgari Eloquentia* in Inferno XXXII–XXXIII.' *Dante Studies* 104 (1986): 121–43.

Introduction and Epilogue

Anscombe, G.E.M. *An Introduction to Wittgenstein's Tractatus.* London: Hutchinson, 1959.

Bersani, L. *A Future for Astyanax: Character and Desire in Literature.* Boston: Little, Brown, 1976.

Bloch, R.H. *Etymologies and Genealogies: A Literary Anthropology of the French Middle Ages.* Chicago: University of Chicago Press, 1983.

Bowie, M. *Lacan.* Cambridge, MA: Harvard University Press, 1991.

Bruns, G.L. *Heidegger's Estrangements: Language, Truth and Poetry in the Later Writings.* New Haven: Yale University Press, 1989.

Burke, K. *The Rhetoric of Religion.* Boston: Beacon, 1961.

Butler, J. *Gender Trouble: Feminism and the Subversion of Identity.* London: Routledge, 1990.

– *Bodies That Matter.* London: Routledge, 1993.

– *Subjects of Desire: Hegelian Reflections in Twentieth-Century France.* New York: Columbia University Press, 1999.

Bynum, C. *The Resurrection of the Body in Western Christianity, 200–1336.* New York: Columbia University Press, 1995.

Carnap, R. *The Logical Syntax of Language.* Translated by A. Smeaton. London: Kegan Paul Trench Trubner, 1937.

Cerquiglini, B. *La Parole médiévale: discours, syntaxe, texte.* Paris: Minuit, 1981.

Chomsky, N. *Syntactic Structures.* The Hague: Mouton, 1957.

– *Aspects of the Theory of Syntax.* Cambridge, MA: MIT Press, 1965.

– *Cartesian Linguistics.* New York: Harper & Row, 1966.

– *Language and Mind.* New York: New Press, 1968.

– *Language and Thought.* Wakefield: Moyer and Bell, 1993.

– *The Minimalist Program.* Cambridge, MA: MIT Press, 1995.

– *On Language.* New York: New Press, 1998.

Cicero, *Tusculan Disputations.* Translated by J.E. King. Loeb Classical Library. Cambridge, MA: Harvard University Press, 1927.

Cixous, H. *The Hélène Cixous Reader,* ed. S. Sellers. London: Routledge, 1994.

Crawford, C. *The Beginnings of Nietzsche's Theory of Language.* Berlin: De Gruyter, 1988.

Cunningham, C. 'Wittgenstein after Theology.' In *Radical Orthodoxy,* edited by J. Milbank, C. Pickstock, and G. Ward, 64–90. London: Routledge, 1999.

Curtius, E.R. *European Literature and the Latin Middle Ages.* New York: Harper & Row, 1963.

Davies O., and D. Turner, eds. *Silence and the Word: Negative Theology and Incarnation.* Cambridge: Cambridge University Press, 2002.

de Man, P. *Resistance to Theory.* Minneapolis: University of Minnesota Press, 1986.

Deleuze, G., and F. Guattari. *Anti-Oedipus, Capitalism and Schizophrenia.* Translated by R. Hurley, M. Seem, and H. Lane. London: Athlone, 1984.

Deleuze, G. 'Desire and Pleasure.' In *Foucault and His Interlocutors,* edited by A.I. Davison, 183–92. Chicago: University of Chicago Press, 1997.

Derrida, J. *Éperons: Les Styles de Nietzsche.* Paris: Flammarion, 1978.

Dumoulié, C. *Le désir.* Paris: Colin, 1999.

Eliot, T.S. *On Poetry and Poets.* London: Faber, 1957.

Firth, J.R. 'The Semantics of Linguistic Science.' *Lingua* 1 (1949): 393–404.

Foucault, M. *History of Sexuality.* Translated by R. Hurley. New York: Vintage, 1978–86.

Gallop, J. *Reading Lacan.* Ithaca: Cornell University Press, 1985.

Gardiner, F.C. *The Pilgrimage of Desire: A Study of Theme and Genre in Medieval Literature.* Leiden: Brill, 1971.

Garver, N. 'Philosophy as Grammar.' In *The Cambridge Companion to Wittgenstein,* edited by H. Sluga and D.G. Stern, 139–70. Cambridge: Cambridge University Press, 1996.

Gellrich, J.M. *The Idea of the Book in the Middle Ages: Language Theory, Mythology and Fiction.* Ithaca: Cornell University Press, 1985.

Girard, R. *Desire, Deceit and the Novel.* Translated by Y. Freccero. Baltimore: Johns Hopkins University Press, 1984.

– *Things Hidden since the Foundation of the World.* London: Athlone, 1987.

Graffi, G. 'The Language of Logical Form.' In *Incommensurability and Translation: Kuhnian Perspectives on Scientific Communication and Theory Change,* edited by R. Rossini Favretti, G. Sandri, and R. Scazzieri, 443–53. Cheltenham: Elgar, 1999.

– *200 Years of Syntax: A Critical Survey.* Amsterdam: Benjamins, 2002.

Haar, M. 'Nietzsche and Metaphysical Language.' In *The New Nietzsche: Contemporary Styles of Interpretation,* edited by David B. Allison, 5–36. New York: Dell, 1977.

Halle, M., and S.J. Keyser. *English Stress: Its Form, Its Growth, and Its Role in Verse.* New York: Harper & Row, 1971.

Halliday, M.A.K. 'Categories of the Theory of Grammar.' *Word* 17 (1961): 241–92.

Harris, R. *Language, Saussure and Wittgenstein: How to Play Games with Words.* London: Routledge, 1988.

Heidegger, M. *On the Way to Language.* Translated by P.D. Hertz. New York: Harper and Row, 1971.

Hemmeche, C., and J. Hoffmeyer. 'From Language to Nature: The Semiotic Metaphor in Biology.' *Semiotica* 84 (1991): 1–42.

Hollander, J. *Night Mirror.* New York: Atheneum, 1971.

Irigaray, L. *Parler n'est jamais neutre*. Paris: Minuit, 1985.
– *This Sex Which Is Not One*. Translated by C. Porter and C. Burke. Ithaca: Cornell University Press, 1985.
Jakobson, R. *Main Trends in the Science and Language*. London: Allen & Unwin, 1973.
– *Poetry of Grammar and Grammar of Poetry*. Vol. 3 of *Collected Writings*. The Hague: Mouton, 1981.
Jakobson, R., and L. Waugh. *The Sound Shape of Language*. Brighton: Harvester, 1979.
Jameson, F. *Postmodernism or the Cultural Logic of Late Capitalism*. Durham: Duke University Press, 1991.
Kay, L. *Who Wrote the Book of Life? A History of the Genetic Code*. Stanford: Stanford University Press, 2000.
Kerr, F. *Theology after Wittgenstein*. Oxford: Blackwell, 1986.
– *Immortal Longings: Versions of Transcending Humanity*. Notre Dame: University of Notre Dame Press, 1997.
Korner, K. *Ferdinand de Saussure: Origin and Development of His Linguistic Thought in Western Studies of Language*. Braunschweig: Vieweg, 1973.
Kristeva, J. Σημειωτική *Recherches pour une sémanalyse*. Paris: Seuil, 1969.
– *La révolution du langage poétique*. Paris: Seuil, 1974.
– *Desire in Language: A Semiotic Approach to Literature and Art*. New York: Columbia University Press, 1980.
– *Tales of Love*. Translated by L.S. Roudiez. New York: Columbia University Press, 1987.
Lacan, J. *Écrits*. Paris: Seuil, 1966.
– *Le Séminaire XI: Les Quatre concepts fondamentaux de la psychanalyse*. Paris: Seuil, 1973.
– *Le Séminaire XX: Encore*. Paris: Seuil, 1975.
– *Le Séminaire III: Les Psychoses*. Paris: Seuil, 1981.
– *Le Séminaire VI: Le Désir et ses interprétations*. *Ornicar?* 24–27 (1981–83).
– *The Seminar of Jacques Lacan*. Book III, *The Psychoses*. Edited by J.A. Miller. Translated by R. Grigg. New York: Routledge, 1993.
– *The Seminar of Jacques Lacan*. Book XX, *Encore*. Edited by J.A. Miller. Translated by B. Fink. New York: Norton, 1998.
– *Écrits: A Selection*. Translated by B. Fink. New York: Norton, 2002.
Lakoff, G., and M. Johnson. *Philosophy in the Flesh: The Embodied Mind and Its Challenge to Western Thought*. New York: Basic Books, 1999.
Law, V. 'Linguistics in the Earlier Middle Ages: The Insular and Carolingian Grammarians.' *Transactions of the Philological Society* 83 (1985): 171–93.
– *Grammar and Grammarians in the Early Middle Ages*. London: Longman, 1997.

374   Bibliography

– *History of Linguistic Thought in the Early Middle Ages.* Amsterdam: Benjamins, 1993.

Leclerq, J. *The Love of Learning and the Desire for God.* New York: Fordham University Press, 1974.

– *Monks and Love in Twelfth-Century France.* Oxford: Oxford University Press, 1979.

Lepschy, G.C. *La linguistica strutturale.* Turin: Einaudi, 1990.

– *La linguistica del Novecento.* Bologna: Il Mulino, 1992.

Marvell, A. 'The Garden,' in *The Poems of Andrew Marvell.* London: Pearson, 2003.

Milbank, J. *The Word Made Strange: Theology, Language, Culture.* Oxford: Blackwell, 1997.

Milbank, J., C. Pickstock, and G. Ward, eds. *Radical Orthodoxy: A New Theology.* London: Routledge, 1999.

Mitchell, J., and J. Rose. *Feminine Sexuality: Lacan and the 'École Freudienne.'* New York: Norton, 1982.

Muller, J., and W. Richardson. *Lacan and Language: A Reader's Guide to the Écrits.* New York: International Universities Press, 1982.

Nietzsche, F. *Twilight of the Idols.* Translated by R.J. Hollingdale. London: Penguin, 1990.

Prigogine, I., and I. Stengers. *Order out of Chaos: Man's New Dialogue with Nature.* New York: Bantam, 1984.

Ragland-Sullivan, E., and M. Bracher, eds. *Lacan and the Subject of Language.* New York: Routledge, 1991.

Ricoeur, P. *La Métaphore vive.* Paris: Seuil, 1975.

Rimbaud, A. 'Voyelles.' In *Oeuvres.* Paris: Garnier, 1960.

Robins, R.H. *Ancient and Medieval Grammatical Theory in Europe.* London: Bell, 1951.

– *A Short History of Linguistics.* 3rd ed. London: Longman, 1990.

de Saussure, F. *Cours de linguistique générale.* 2nd ed. Edited by C. Bally and A. Sechehaye. Paris: Payot, 1916.

– *Corso di linguistica generale.* Edited by T. de Mauro. Bari: Laterza, 1968.

– *Course in General Linguistics.* Translated by W. Baskin. New York: McGraw Hill, 1966.

Starobinski, J. *Les mots sous les mots: Les anagrammes de Ferdinand de Saussure.* Paris: Gallimard, 1971.

Tesnière, L. *Éléments de syntaxe stucturale.* Paris: Klincksieck, 1959.

Turner, D. *Eros and Allegory: Medieval Exegesis of the Song of Songs.* Kalamazoo, MI: Cistercian Publications, 1995.

Vattimo, G. *Al di là del soggetto.* 4th ed. Milan: Feltrinelli, 1991.

Vineis, E., and A. Maierù. 'Medieval Linguistics.' In *Classical and Medieval Linguistics*. Vol. 2 of *History of Linguistics*, edited by G. Lepschy, 134–315. London: Longman, 1994.

Ward, G., ed. *The Postmodern God: A Theological Reader*. Oxford: Blackwell, 1997.

Williams, R. 'The Deflections of Desire: Negative Theology in Trinitarian Disclosure.' In *Silence and the Word: Negative Theology and Incarnation*, edited by O. Davies and D. Turner, 115–35. Cambridge: Cambridge University Press, 2002.

Wittgenstein, L. *Philosophical Investigations*. Translated by G.E.M. Anscombe. Oxford: Blackwell, 1953.

– *Tractatus Logico-Philosophicus*. Translated by D.F. Pears and B.F. McGuinnes. New York: Routledge, 1961.

Wittig, M. *The Straight Mind and Other Essays*. Boston: Beacon, 1992.

Ziolkowsky, J. *Alain of Lille's Grammar of Sex: The Meaning of Grammar to a Twelfth-Century Intellectual*. Cambridge: Medieval Academy of America, 1985.

Žižek, S. *The Sublime Object of Ideology*. London: Verso, 1989.

Index

Abelard, 14, 81, 91, 97, 286–7n93
Albertus Magnus, 80, 118
Alfarabi, 88, 268–9n25
Andreas Cappellanus, 14
Anscombe, G.E.M., 177
Aristotle, 6, 8, 14, 17, 78–80, 84–5, 86, 88, 90–1, 94, 97, 102–4, 107, 111, 113–16, 118–20, 279n64, 280n73, 286–7n93, 309n42, 322–4n100, 325–6n110, 330n131
Arnaut, Daniel, 150
Ascoli, A.R., 139
Augustine (works); *Confessiones*, 23, 37–40, 42–8, 50, 52, 54, 57, 232–3n58; *De catechizandis rudibus*, 23, 63–5, 75; *De civitate Dei*, 55, 224n27; *De dialectica*, 27, 219n17; *De doctrina christiana*, 15, 23, 25, 27–36, 41, 45, 54, 73, 166, 301n8, 314n61; *De Genesi ad litteram liber imperfectus*, 228–9n45; *De Genesi ad litteram libri XII*, 222–4n26, 228–30n45; *De Genesi contra Manicheos*, 29, 38, 228–9n45; *De magistro*, 15, 23, 27–8, 32, 36, 40–1, 73; *De musica*, 23, 52, 56, 219n17; *De ordine*, 23, 51, 54, 244n84; *De Trinitate*, 4, 16, 23, 26, 42, 59–63,

66–76, 253nn110, 111, 328–9n125; *Enarrationes in Psalmos*, 37; *In Epistolam Ioannis ad Parthos tractatus X*, 57, 75; *In Evangelium Ioannis*, 13, 33, 40–3
Averroes, 84, 101, 105, 115
Averroism, 84

Babel, tower of, 8, 17, 30, 123, 132–5, 138, 146, 180, 213n15, 222–4n26, 224n27, 228–9n45, 304n24, 307nn37, 38, 316n66
Bacon, R., 92
Barańsky, Z., 130, 132, 152
Barolini, T., 168
Beatrice, 126–7, 140, 154, 167–9, 312n51, 325n106
Benedict, Saint, 170–1
Berengar of Tours, 81
Bernard of Chartres, 9
Bernard of Clairvaux, 13–14, 172
Bochet, I., 57
Bodei, R., 44
Boethius of Dacia, 81, 83–4, 86–90, 92, 97, 99–101, 103–6, 108–10, 265–6n12, 266–7n16, 267n21, 279n65, 293n113